THOUGHTS
ON THE
HOLOCAUST

GEORGE FEHER

Feher Publishing
Copyright © 2017 by George Feher

Feher, George.
Thoughts on the Holocaust
by George Feher.
ISBN: 978-0-9906578-9-7

1. History. 2. Holocaust. 3. World War II.
4. Genocide. 5. Jewish Culture.
I. Title.

Library of Congress Control Number: 2017914632

Author's email: gfeher@ucsd.edu

Printed in the United States of America

CONTENTS

PREFACE

At the end of my Shoah interview in 1998[1] I was asked whether I had any message for my children and grandchildren about the lessons learned from the Holocaust.[2] It was the one question of a long interview that I felt I failed to answer adequately. The root-problem was that I did not have the answer to the cardinal question of how such monstrous evil could have been perpetrated by a nation that had been considered civilized. Thus, the answers to the secondary questions—i.e., could it happen again?; could it happen in the United States?; how can we avoid a repetition?—were also beyond reach. I thought a lot about this in between then and now and read many books on the subject, but I have to admit that I have failed to come up with clear and definitive answers. All I was able to accomplish was to suggest some of the many causes and circumstances that are likely to lead to violence, and ultimately genocide.

I recently read that the top prize of the 2007 Frankfurt Book Fair went to the Israeli historian of the Holocaust, Saul Friedländer, who was praised for "creating a space for incomprehensibility—the only possible reaction to such an unfathomable crime." Although it is sort of a consolation that even professional historians are unable to comprehend the Holocaust, to simply relegate it to an incomprehensible evil discourages the quest for understanding it, which is necessary to avoid a repetition. I therefore, decided to write down the results of my quest and ruminations, incomplete and unsatisfactory as they are.

Whereas the WHY? of the Holocaust remains enigmatic, we know the HOW: the sequence of events, the details of what occurred, i.e., when and where the Holocaust was perpetrated. I want to review here the facts as we know them and describe the sequence of events leading to the Holocaust. They include the post-World War I period during which Hitler rose to power, the pre-war 1933–1939 period, and the progression of World War II that made the Holocaust possible. The majority of the Jews murdered by Nazi Germans—95% of them—came from territories outside Germany. Without the conquest of these territories, the Nazis could not have laid hands on their victims.

I then focus on the history and fate of the Jews in Slovakia, my country of birth. This is followed by sections dealing with some unique aspects of the Holocaust compared to other genocides, and the reaction of the outside world to the mass murders. Special tribute is paid to five people, examples of a group, the Righteous Among the Nations who, through their heroic actions, saved the lives of many Jews.

In the final section, the most speculative and important one, the raison d'être of this treatise, I attempt to understand and to discuss how such a monstrous event, the Holocaust, could have happened and what we should do to avoid a repetition.

I lay no claim that my treatment of the topics is original, and shall draw freely on the work of others. You may ask: Why should I write about it if I have nothing new to add to the subject about which so much has already been written? The short answer is: I feel the need to do it, to organize my thoughts by putting them on paper and to express my personal take on the events, in the hope that this will help me exorcize the demons that have haunted me throughout most of my life.

In conclusion, I want to thank my wife, Elsa, for encouraging me to write these thoughts down and for being such a perceptive and responsive sounding board. I thank my secretary Amie Diza for the many literature searches and for typing my manuscript. And I thank our friend Frankie Frey for the detailed editing work she has done with my wife in readying the document for publication.

---

[1] These interviews of Holocaust survivors were undertaken by the Shoah Foundation, an enterprise conceived and funded by Steven Spielberg. About 50,000 interviews were conducted that are stored in the University of Southern California Institute for Visual History.

[2] By Holocaust we mean the genocide of the Jewish people. In Hebrew it is called *Shoah* (for a more detailed discussion, see page 179).

1. SEQUENCE OF EVENTS LEADING TO THE HOLOCAUST

Hatred of Jews was the center of Nazi ideology. It is therefore appropriate to start with a brief history of anti-Semitism.

Anti-Semitism throughout the ages

Hatred and persecution are a normal part of the human experience. Taking a dislike, mild or intense, to people who are different in one way or another, in ethnicity, race, color, creed, eating habits—no matter what—is part of the normal human condition. We find it all over the world and throughout recorded history. If we go back 3,000 years to the Semitic homeland in what we now call the Middle East, we find a small group of people, the Jews or Hebrews or Israelites. They were attacked, denounced, and persecuted by the rest of the population, but not more so than other ethnicities, e.g., Syrians, Egyptians, Greek, Persians, etc. To talk about anti-Semitism during that period seems, therefore, inappropriate. It was just the "us" versus "them" syndrome that prevailed throughout history.

There was, however, one distinction between the rest of the world, which practiced polytheism, and the Jews, with their monotheistic religion. Polytheism was tolerant, each group worshipping its own gods, offering no objections to the worship practices of other groups. Only the Jews insisted that theirs was the only god and there was no other. This could have led to a special hatred toward Jews, but it did not, at least not until the advent of the Roman Empire. The tendency was to ridicule rather than hate the Jews for their faceless, formless god in the clouds, and for such barbarous customs as circumcision, dietary prohibitions, and, most absurdly, for introducing the Sabbath, which made them waste one seventh of their lives.

The Romans were the first to worry that Jewish refusal to worship their pagan gods would jeopardize the security of their state. This unease, coupled with political conflicts, resulted in open persecution of the Jews. In 70 A.D. the Romans destroyed the Jewish temple in Jerusalem, the focal point of Jewish life. Sixty years later, after the defeat of the Bar Kochba uprising, the Romans dispersed the Jews of Palestine, scattering them far from the region that had been their home.

Real anti-Semitism started with the advent of Christianity. Although Christianity was an offshoot of Judaism with which it shared many common values, the early Christians were intensely anti-Semitic, more so than anti-paganistic. This seemingly counter-intuitive phenomenon of hating groups that are similar more than dissimilar, occurs throughout history (e.g., the communists' greater hate of revisionists and social democrats than of capitalists). It exaggerates the gap between "us" and "them," thereby protecting the identity, integrity and purity of the group. To put this hatred on an ideological basis, the Christians put the exclusive blame for the crucification of Jesus on the Jews, although it was specifically a Roman form of punishment. The exculpation of the Romans in the crucifixion was also a strategically shrewd move by the Christians to gain favor with the Roman authorities. The strategy worked: in 400 years, Christianity went from being a persecuted branch of Judaism to becoming the dominant religion of the Roman Empire, with devastating effect on popular attitudes toward the Jews. Thus, for many centuries, hatred and persecution of Jews—the **first phase of anti-Semitism**—was grounded in **religion**.

With the advent of the Enlightenment in the 17th and 18th centuries, European societies became more secular, religious prejudices were discarded and conceived of as bigoted and old fashioned. In the **19th century**, **Napoleon** repealed the restrictions on Jews in Europe and ushered in the era of emancipation. Although the situation of Jews in Western Europe improved, informal limitations often remained. The obvious reason was that anti-Semitism could not be eliminated by decree; it remained strong and virulent as if it were an immutable attitude of the population. New reasons for hating Jews were needed. They were found by transforming the religious basis for hatred to racial, social, economic, and political prejudices.

It is of interest to examine the **racial basis for anti-Semitism,** as it played a key role in Hitler's "Final Solution." Its origin can be traced to 15th century Spain where a large number of Jews were forcibly converted to Christianity. But some doubts arose among the enforcers about the sincerity of the converts. These doubts were well-grounded, as many of the New Christians secretly practiced Judaism. These pseudo-converts were called Marranos. Thus, the practice arose of examining the **racial origin** of the New Christians. Only people who could prove Christian descent for a specified number of generations were accepted as genuine Christians. Purity of blood (*limpieza de la sangre*) was required to hold certain positions and offices. The same ideas were codified in the Nüremberg Laws of Nazi Germany 500 years later. Thus, the racial form of anti-Semitism began in Spain and was systematized in Germany in the 19th century, where the term anti-Semitism was invented and adopted.

The terms Semitic and Aryan were coined by philologists to designate groups of related languages. But the terms were soon transformed from their original linguistic meaning to a racial meaning, and became the basis of a new and different bigotry. The advocates of the idea claimed that their hostility was based on observed and documented racial "otherness" and inferiority of Jews. Parodoxically, the population endowed the "inferior" Jewish people with demonic powers and the intent to take over the world. This is exemplified by the infamous forgery "Protocols of the Elders of Zion,"[3] which, although debunked as a forgery by all competent and respectable scholars and institutions, are believed by many, to this day, to be true.

Let me now pass from generalities to the specific fate of the Jews throughout the centuries. The Middle Ages, from the 9th to the 16th century, were difficult times for Jews in Europe. Violent attacks against Jews, known as pogroms, were common occurrences. They invariably followed disasters. For example, the outbreak of the bubonic plague in **1348** sparked brutal pogroms, as Christians blamed Jews for causing the epidemic. Mobilized by such accusations, Christian mobs—sometimes spontaneously, sometimes urged by state and church leaders—attacked Jewish houses and communities, plundering, destroying, and killing. This scapegoating of Jews by the Christian population became a recurrent theme throughout history, culminating in Hitler's accusations of the Jews for Germany's loss of World War I and the subsequent economic plight of Germany.

---

[3] The "Protocols of the Elders of Zion" is a vitriolic, anti-Semitic fabrication first published in Russia around 1900. The Protocols claim to be the minutes of an international committee of prominent Jewish leaders who hatched a secret plan to overthrow and conquer the Christian world. The protocols were introduced into Western Europe by Russian emigrés and translated into many languages. The Protocols were brought to the United States in the 1920s, and published with Henry Ford's support in the Dearborn Independent in 1921. Philip Graves, an English journalist, demonstrated that the Protocols were clumsily plagiarized from a satire on Napoleon III written in 1865. Although this utterly destroyed the credibility of the Protocols, they remained in circulation, played a major role in Nazi propaganda, and are believed by many to this day.

In addition to sporadic waves of violence, Jews faced harassment and restrictions of various kinds. Sometimes, Jews were required to wear identifying badges. In many places, Jews were forced to live in certain areas, so-called ghettos. Elsewhere, state authorities drove Jews out of their territories altogether. In **1492**, for example, **King Ferdinand** and **Queen Isabella** of Spain expelled all Jews from the Iberian Peninsula except those who agreed to convert to Christianity. Throughout the Middle Ages, Jews everywhere in Europe faced limitations on the occupations in which they could engage, as well as the kind of properties they could hold. They could not own land and could only engage in commerce and moneylending. These activities often led to friction (e.g., when the debtors could not repay their debts), which exacerbated the tensions in the relationship of the Jews with the Christian population. Moreover, Jews were slandered with charges of abominable practices, such as the use of the blood of Christian children for ritual purposes. These allegations, described in detail in the "Protocols of the Elders of Zion," [3] survived until the modern era.

The Protestant Reformation did not improve the lot of European Jews. At first, its leader, the German monk **Martin Luther**, hoped that his break with Rome would inspire mass conversion of Jews to Christianity. When this did not happen, Luther turned against the Jews. In **1542,** he wrote a pamphlet called "Against the Jews and Their Lies." That tract, with its vicious characterization of Jews as parasites, and its calls to "set their synagogues and schools on fire," was later widely quoted in Hitler's Germany.

Between the late 19th century and World War II, Jews—who, by and large, were liberals advocating democracy, internationalism, and pacifism—were attacked both from the left (by revolutionary socialists and communists), and from the right (by fascists in Italy and Germany). It seems that the justification for anti-Semitism always finds a cause.

And what about anti-Semitism in recent times, following the fall of Nazi Germany in 1945? After the atrocities committed by the Germans were revealed, racial hostility was discredited, leaving again a void, which would justify the continuation of anti-Semitism. This third and modern phase might be called, for lack of a better word, **political and ideological Judeophobia**. For over half a century, the memory of the Nazi crimes, and the complicity, acquiescence, and indifference of so many, have imbued the Western World with guilt feelings. Now Israel, with its problems and largely unpopular policies, affords an opportunity to relinquish the uncomfortable posture of guilt, and adopt a more comfortable position: criticizing Israel. True, the occupation of the West Bank, though it grew out of a war Israel did not want, has been a moral and political disaster for Israel (and a nightmare for the Palestinians). This is an issue that needs to be resolved. But the haughty moral superiority of the anti-Israel attacks by the West are a public expression of an anti-Semitism that is taboo in the post-Holocaust world. Judeophobia has found a new and acceptable form, cloaked in an anti-Israel political stance.

There is a special feature of anti-Semitism that needs to be mentioned: Jews are judged by a standard that is different from that applied to others. For example, compare the world reaction to the massacre of the Palestinians by Lebanese-Christian militiamen in Sabra and Shatila in 1982, where some 800 people were killed, with the reaction to the massacre earlier that year in Hama, Syria, where Assad killed 10,000 people. In the latter, not a dog barked. In both cases Arabs killed Arabs, but in Sabra and Shatila the Israeli military presence in Lebanon at the time made it possible to blame the Jews. Another case in point is the accusation that the Jewish lobby in Washington, DC, engages in activities that are disloyal to the United States. In contrast, other lobbies (e.g., the Irish, Greek, Armenian) aren't accused of disloyalty, not even of divided loyalty. Many other examples could be cited that point to the dual standards applied to the Jews and the rest of the world.

Looking back some 2,000 years, one cannot avoid the feeling that there is an innate, deep-seated hatred of the Jews, and that the justifications given over the centuries (i.e., religion, racism, ideology) are mere pretexts, but not the real driving force. If this is the case, what is the underlying cause of anti-Semitism? I have no simple answer to that important question. It is probably a combination of factors: fear of the unknown, envy of success of the Jews in business and the professional world, fear of their dominance, or the irrational insecurity of most people who need a scapegoat.

So far I have focused mainly on anti-Semitism in Western Europe. Let me now say a few words about the status of the Jews in **Eastern Europe** and the **Islamic world**.

After the expulsion of the Jews from Spain in 1492, a large number of them migrated to northern Europe, and from there settled in the **eastern countries of Europe,** e.g., in present-day Poland, Russia, Ukraine, and the other states that later became part of the Soviet Union. At the beginning, the Jews were welcomed by the rulers who believed that the new immigrants would improve their countries' economies by stimulating trade and commerce. But it did not take long for anti-Semitism to emerge. It culminated in **1648** with the horrendous **pogrom** led by the Cossack **Chmielnicki** in the Ukraine, in which 100,000 Jews were massacred. Later, different czars in Russia made anti-Semitism a national policy, and, in the 18th century, **Catherine II expelled Jews into the Pale of Settlement**, where they eked out a miserable living, and where they were exposed to constant harassment and periodic pogroms. The reforms introduced by Napoleon (emancipation) did not reach Eastern Europe.

After the **Russian revolution in 1917**, in which a disproportionate number of Jews participated, the communist constitution **prohibited discrimination** against Jews. Although the law forbade anti-Semitic practices, **hatred against the Jews continued** to flourish.[4] Jews had difficulties entering universities, a disproportionate number of Jews under Stalin were arrested, sent to the Gulag, or executed. A major purge of Jews was averted in the nick of time by Stalin's death in 1953. After the fall of the Soviet Union in 1991, the Church regained its legitimacy, and further fueled anti-Semitism in the Russian people.

A few recent events highlight the present sentiments in Eastern Europe. In Kiev and Odessa, people marched on January 1, 2011, to mark the birthday of Ukrainian hero Stephan Bandera, who, as head of the Organization of Ukrainian Nationals, collaborated with the Nazis and actively participated in the mass murder of Jews following the German occupation of the Ukraine in 1941. In Zagreb and Split, Croatia, memorial masses were conducted on December 28, 2010, to honor Ante Pavelić, head of the brutal regime installed by the Germans, which bears responsibility for the mass murder of 100,000 Serbs and 30,000 Jews during World War II. In Estonia, on December 27, 2011, the defense ministry submitted a bill to Parliament that would recognize Estonians who served as freedom fighters in the German 20th SS Waffen division (Armed Protective Squadron). Members of the SS Waffen division had been actively involved in the killing of Jews and Gypsies in World War II.

---

[4] An incident in Moscow illustrates the situation. In 1972, at an international conference, I tried to explore the question of anti-Semitism in the Soviet Union with a Russian scientist. He claimed there was no anti-Semitism, as the Russian constitution forbids discrimination. I gave him examples, like the difficulties Jews have to get accepted to universities. He was adamant and we made no headway in the discussion. I finally suggested starting from scratch by defining anti-Semitism. He defined it without hesitation: "An anti-Semite is a person who hates Jews more than necessary." No wonder we had difficulties communicating.

Former Lithuanian Foreign Minister Vygaudas Usackas, currently head of the EU delegation to Russia, praised (in an op-ed article in the Wall Street Journal) the German occupation of Lithuania in 1941–1945 as "a few years respite from the communists."

In the **Muslim world** Jews were considerably better off than in the Christian world. Christianity was recognized as a rival world religion, competing with Islam for the domination of humanity. Jews were not suspected of competing for domination and were tolerated. The Ottoman sultans even encouraged Jewish refugees from Spain, Italy, Portugal, and elsewhere to settle in their country and help develop trade and industry, much as had happened in Eastern Europe at the beginning of the Jewish immigration. Although Jews were not considered equal, the general attitude toward them was of a useful, revenue-producing asset—a tolerated minority.

The main negative quality attributed to the Jews in Arab folklore was that they were cowardly and unmilitary—very contemptible qualities in a martial society. This may help us understand the bewilderment, shock, and shame at the Israeli victories in 1948 (and after), when five Arab armies were defeated by half a million Jews with very little weaponry. As a consequence, the perception of the Jews and the attitude toward them changed drastically.

The wounded feelings of the Arabs found solace in the western form of anti-Semitism —the cosmic, satanic version of Jew hatred. Western anti-Semitic writings were translated into Arabic; and blood libel cases against the Jews, which had been explicitly rejected in the 15th and 16th centuries by the Ottoman sultans, resurfaced in the Muslim world. Even before the Israeli victories on the battlefield, anti-Jewish feelings were fueled and ideologically justified by the strong relationship that developed between the Third Reich and the Arab world. The Grand Mufti of Jerusalem established residence in Berlin, and after the fall of France in 1940, Vichy-controlled Syria became an intelligence and propaganda base in the heart of the Arab Middle East. In Iraq, a pro-Nazi regime, headed by Rashid Ali was established in the spring of 1941. The soldiers and civilians of Ali's regime launched murderous attacks on the ancient Jewish community in Baghdad. They were followed by similar attacks in other Arab cities in the Middle East and Northern Africa. Fortunately, Rashid Ali was soon overthrown by the British, and he joined his friend, the Grand Mufti, in Berlin.

The impact of the Nazi propaganda on the Arabs was immense, and increased in importance after the 1948 events, when the humiliated Arabs drew comfort from the doctrine of the Jews as a cosmic evil. The European themes of anti-Semitism—the blood libel, the Protocols of the Elders of Zion, the international Jewish conspiracy—have become standard fare in the Arab world, in the classroom, the public, and the media. And like the Nazi propaganda machine, Muslim leaders spout lies and preposterous accusations against the Jews. After the attack on the World Trade Center in New York in 2001, Sheik Muhammad Gemeaha, the imam of the Islamic Cultural Center of New York, proclaimed: "Only the Jews were capable of destroying the World Trade Center;" in Kuwait there were reports that New York rabbis told their followers to take their money out of the stock market before September 11, 2001; in Egypt, the Mossad was blamed for the attack; and the president of Iran, Ahmedinejad, publicly declared that Israel should be wiped off the face of the earth. The weapons of mass destruction did not vanish with the demise of the Soviet Union, and they pose a greater threat in the hands of Muslim countries in this century than in the last. The existential problem of Israel is real.

1918–1933. The Weimar Republic; the rise to power of the Nazi Party

The Weimar Republic

In the wake of the military defeat in **1918**, Germany introduced a new form of government: a republic based on a democratic constitution. It was called the **Weimar Republic**, named after the town in which the constitution was drafted. Jews played an active role in the government and in rebuilding the broken nation. Two of them rose to special prominence: **Hugo Preuss**, Minister of the Interior of the new government, prepared the draft of the Weimar Constitution; and **Walther Rathenau** served as Minister of Reconstruction, and later as Foreign Minister.

It is commonly assumed that the Weimar Republic was a failed experiment in German democracy, a mere prelude to Nazism. This is not quite correct. First we have to note that the Weimar Republic lasted two years longer (**1918–1933**) than the Nazi regime (**1933–1945**), which, Hitler promised, would be a "Thousand Year Reich." On social issues it was very progressive: it was the first major European power that gave women the vote. It returned Germany to international respectability with the country's incorporation into the **League of Nations in 1926**. Its economy, in spite of the **hyperinflation of 1923**, was one of the strongest in continental Europe. This was aided by the fact that very little of the fighting in World War I had taken place on German soil—in contrast to its neighbors, whose industries had been destroyed.

The national security of the Weimar Republic was also strong. The **Hapsburg Empire**, once Germany's rival, had disintegrated, spawning relatively weak countries surrounding Germany (Austria, Hungary, Czechoslovakia, and Poland). Furthermore, another past rival, the formidable **Russian Empire**, was now gone, and no longer a threat to Germany. So why, in view of these positive developments, did the Weimar Republic fall and give way to a brutal dictatorship? It is generally believed that the confluence of several factors provided the fertile ground for this to happen.

To a large extent it was the shame of defeat and the widespread refusal to accept the defeat. In the fall of **1918**, Germany's military leaders (**Generals Paul von Hindenburg** and **Erich Ludendorff**) realized that Germany did not have the resources to fight on, and insisted on negotiating a peace treaty, which turned out to be devastatingly humiliating for Germany. To save their reputation, they began to spin the following account of events: It was not the military that was responsible for losing the war, but the civilians—the revolutionary home-front that did not support the war, and, in effect, had stabbed the fighting men in the back, and betrayed them to the enemy.

The myth of the "stab-in-the-back" spread quickly. It provided the Germans with a comforting and face-saving explanation of their defeat. The fact that the war ended with no foreign troops on German soil added credence to the myth. In the eyes of many Germans, the new democratic government of the Weimar Republic symbolized the civilian weaklings who had betrayed Germany's fighting heroes. This perception undercut the authority of the Weimar Republic and prepared the way for its fall.

An additional factor that contributed to the fall of the Weimar Republic was that it had **not purged the judiciary and civil service**, so that the same people who served the Kaiser before World War I kept their positions. Many of them considered democracy to be a weak, ineffective, and non-German type of government.' As a result, right-wing extremists, caught in plots to overthrow the government, received only light penalties. So, although there were laws that might have curbed the growth of Nazism, they were simply not enforced. Hitler's early career is a case in point. In **1923** he was charged and convicted for high treason, but served only nine months in prison.

Children that were raised by authoritarian fathers before World War I had become young men who experienced a vacuum upon the return of their defeated, powerless fathers from the war. They fell easy prey to an alternate authority, the Nazi Party, which promised hope and leadership.

The rampant anti-Semitism, which existed in Germany for many years before the rise of Nazism, provided the background for many Germans to willingly accept the Nazi platform with its emphasis on Jew-hatred and the elimination of Jewish influence.

The world depression, following the **1929 stock market crash** in the United States, hit Germany hard and caused a severe economic and political crisis (to be discussed in more detail later). It provided the final impetus for the demise of the Weimar Republic.

The rise to power of the Nazi Party

In the turmoil after World War I, when many people blamed the Jews for Germany's humiliating defeat, a particularly rabid anti-Semitism was promulgated by a new, tiny, political party, the **National Socialistic Workers Party** (*Nationalsozialistische Deutsche Arbeiterpartei*) (**NSDAP**), that become known as the **Nazi Party**.[6] On **February 25, 1920**, the party published in Munich a 25-point program. At the time, the party had only 60 members! Hitler was number seven in the party's hierarchy, but was a member of a three-man team that drafted the programme.

The essence of the programme was to create a "Great German Nation" where members had to be of pure German, Aryan,[7] blood. Another point demanded that all Jews who had come to Germany after 1914 should be forced to leave. On **August 13, 1920**, Hitler spoke for two hours in a Munich beer cellar on the theme "Why we are against the Jews," in which he advocated "the removal of the Jews from the midst of our people."

On **August 1, 1921**, Hitler set up a group known as the **Sturmabteilung (SA)** (Storm Section), intended to defend the Nazi Party meetings from attacks, and to take the offensive whenever the situation called for it. They soon became known as **Brownshirts**, after the color of their uniform. At that stage, the party membership had risen to 3,000. Hatred of the Jews permeated all of Hitler's speeches, and was echoed by the actions of his followers. Jews were attacked in the streets and were blamed for every facet of Germany's problems.

---

[5] It is instructive to consider the mindset of the German intellectuals at the onset of World War I. In 1915, 352 of Germany's most distinguished professors signed a Declaration of Intellectuals proclaiming that it would be just for Germany to acquire Belgium, part of France, the Ukraine, and other territories. In contrast, a pacifist Manifesto to Europeans was signed by only four people, Einstein among them. Clearly, Germans saw themselves as superior to other nations. In light of these attitudes it is not surprising that the promise of glory and world dominance by the Nazi party found fertile ground.

[6] The symbol of the Nazi movement was the swastika (Hackenkreuz in German) 卐. To me it conjures up cruel images of two twisted gallows, or of a torture wheel on which limbs were broken.

[7] The word Aryan was a linguistic term, originally referring to the Indo-European group of languages. But at the end of the 19th century it was given racial connotations to denote superiority over the Semitic race. For Hitler, Aryan was synonymous with "pure," while Semitic was synonymous with "Jew" and "impure." That Arabs, his allies, are also Semites, Hitler conveniently managed to shove under the rug.

8

On **June 24, 1922**, Foreign Minister Rathenau was assassinated, and Hitler publicly expressed his pleasure. He was sentenced to four weeks in prison, but immediately after his release proclaimed: "Jews stand against us as our deadly foe." In **1923**, **Julius Streicher** launched "**Der Stürmer**," a newspaper devoted to the portrayal of the Jews as an evil and dangerous force.

On **November 9, 1923**, Hitler tried and failed to seize power in the so-called **Beer Hall Putsch** in Munich, proclaiming a National Republic. He was arrested, tried, convicted of high treason, and sentenced to five years in prison. He served only nine months, after which he was released. During his imprisonment, Hitler wrote a lengthy account of his life and thoughts entitled "**Mein Kampf**" (My Struggle). Every page contained references to Jews and their evil influence. There were, Hitler argued, two evils that threaten the existence of the German people: Judaism and Marxism, the latter being a Jewish machination, a Jewish trap. He was obsessed with the importance of maintaining the purity of the Aryan race by not adulterating it with inferior, Jewish, blood. In "Mein Kampf," Hitler clearly outlined his mission: to expose and destroy the threat posed by a worldwide Jewish conspiracy.

There was little reason for anyone to pay attention, in the summer of **1925**, to such hate-mongering dribble by a tiny party. The Weimar Republic was successful in establishing a democratic parliamentary regime, the reparation payments to the Allies were lessening from year to year, the hyperinflation of 1923 had passed and the economy was improving. There was also progress on the political front. On **October 16, 1925**, three months after the publication of "Mein Kampf," Germany, as an equal partner with Britain, France, Belgium and Italy, signed the **Locarno Agreement**, guaranteeing the frontiers of Western Europe.

In **December 1926**, Hitler published the second volume of "Mein Kampf." Once again, anti-Jewish venom permeated its pages. He wrote: "If at the beginning of the war 12 or 15,000 of the Jews, who had been corrupting the nation, had been forced to submit to poison gas, just as thousands of German soldiers had to face in the battle field, the lives of a million decent men, of value to Germany, would have been saved." Ominous foreboding of things to come! But nobody paid any attention.

In **1926**, the Party membership stood at 17,000, among them the black-uniformed **Schutzstaffel** (Protective Squad), or **SS**, set up to provide the Nazi leadership with personal protection. On **July 4, 1926**, a youth movement, the **Hitler Youth**, was inaugurated for young Nazis. In **1927** the Nazi membership rose to 40,000.

In **May 1928**, the **NSDAP** (Nazi Party) participated in the German national election and secured 12 (out of 491) seats in the Reichstag (the Parliament). It was an electoral breakthrough for the NSDAP; it became for the first time a force in the Reichstag. It should be noted that this evidence of growing national popularity preceded the Great Depression. It was not simply economic hardship, as is often claimed, that made some Germans support the NSDAP. The European democracies still showed no concern about these, apparently minor, developments.

Suddenly, in **1929**, events began to favor Hitler and his followers. Inflation began to rise again, unemployment rose to an unprecedented level of 3 million by the end of 1929. The growth of the Communist Party triggered a reaction on the right. Extremism threatened the democratic ideals of the Weimar Republic. As the economic distress grew, the Nazis denounced Jewish "wealth" and "conspiracy." On **January 1, 1930**, the Storm troops killed eight Jews in Berlin; these were the first Jewish victims of the Nazi era.

By the **early 1930s**, the rising economical difficulties brought Germany into a political crisis. **Chancellor Brüning** was unable to get the backing of the Reichstag, and he convinced the German president, the old war hero **Paul von Hindenburg, to govern by decree** according to article 48 of the constitution. This effectively spelled the **end of democracy**.

On **September 14, 1930**, elections were held for the Reichstag. To everybody's surprise in Germany and abroad, the number of Nazi seats rose 18%, from 17 to 107. It was a stunning victory for Hitler. Overnight, the Nazi Party went from being the smallest to the second-largest party in Germany.

Hitler becomes Chancellor

In the election for president in **June 1932**, the incumbent president Field Marshal Hindenburg received 53%, Hitler 36%, and the communist Thälmann 10% of the vote. In the **July 1932** elections for the Reichstag, the **Nazi Party** won 37% of the votes and became the **largest party**. In a later election on **November 6, 1932**, it lost some seats, but remained the largest party in the Reichstag. Although their number of seats was less than the combined number of the socialists and communists, Hitler's opponents on the left lacked sufficient unity or sense of danger to unite and fight off the threat of Nazism.

Following a protracted political crisis, former **Chancellor Franz von Papen** convinced Hindenburg to name Hitler as Chancellor. Von Papen reckoned that he himself would become Vice Chancellor, and, with others, he would be able to control the Nazi upstart—a serious miscalculation. On **January 30, 1933**, **Hitler**, at age 43, was **appointed Chancellor** by Hindenburg.

Thus, Hitler was not swept to power by a stampede of German voters, nor did he seize power by an illegal coup d'etat. Power was handed to him. It was an outcome of difficult times, political maneuvering, luck, and miscalculation on the part of many people that catapulted Hitler to power.

A brief biographical sketch of Hitler and members of his inner circle

Before describing Hitler's reign and the atrocities that he and his regime committed, it might be instructive to describe the individuals involved. Besides Hitler, "The Führer," three admiring and loyal followers, who formed his inner circle, played crucial roles in the Nazi Party and later in the Nazi government. They were: **Hermann Göring, Joseph Goebbels, and Heinrich Himmler**.

Adolph Hitler

Hitler (1889–1945) was born in Austria to a middle-class family. He was a mediocre student, although in "Mein Kampf" he claimed that he led his class in geography and history. At age 16 he dropped out of school, and spent the next two and a half years in Linz, idling and dreaming. In **1907**, he relocated to Vienna where he planned to study art. However, he failed to be admitted to art school. In Vienna he became particularly interested in Pan-Germanism and ultra-nationalistic causes. He was a great admirer of **Karl Lüger**, the anti-Semitic mayor of Vienna. In **1913** Hitler went to Munich, and in **1914** he volunteered for the German army, reaching the rank of corporal. His anti-Semitic feelings strengthened after Germany's defeat in 1918, and he joined those who blamed the Jews for the defeat. (This claim was completely unfounded; German and Austro-Hungarian Jews had fought and died loyally along with fellow citizens of their country.)

In **1919**, Hitler got involved in a political organization called the NSDAP, later known as the Nazi Party. Hitler's political activities were described in a previous section and I would like to focus here on his ideas and ideology.

Hitler's core ideas can be summed up in the phrase "**race and space**." Hitler was obsessed with the idea of maintaining the purity of blood of the Germans, the "**Aryan master race**," and the need to expand their living space, which he called "**Lebensraum**" (living space). The expansion that he envisaged was in the east: the territories of Poland and the Soviet Union, which were occupied by an "inferior race," the Slavs. However, the Jews were his mortal enemy, the race that threatened to infiltrate, weaken, and destroy German strength. He had a fanatical hatred of anything Jewish.

Hitler's anti-Semitism incorporated all the aspects of the anti-Semitism of the past. It had religious and metaphysical dimensions: He spoke of Jews as evil enemies of virtues and honor. It was political: The Jewish conspiracy extended in every direction; he described communism, capitalism, democracy, liberalism, pacifism, internationalism, and anarchism, as evil worldviews invented by Jews for Jewish interests. There were cultural elements: He considered jazz and modern abstract art to be degenerate and "Jewish." And there were the familiar social and economic resentments: He shared the stereotypes of Jews as greedy, cheating bankers, lecherous males and seductive females who defiled Aryan blood. This multidimensionality of Hitler's anti-Semitism gave it a mass appeal. Many Germans could find in it something they shared, even if they did not buy the whole package.

Hitler and his followers had a religious fervor, a fanatical conviction that attacks on Jews were necessary to save the world for Aryan Germany. He perceived his mission as a crusade to redeem the world by eliminating the Jews.

Hitler believed that power had to be focused to be effective; the focal point, of course, was himself. The Nazi focus on Hitler as leader gave the entire system a dynamic in which Hitler did not need to issue specific orders. It was enough to let his wishes be known in general terms, and his underlings would push to fulfill them in the hope of winning Hitler's favor, and advancing their careers.

Adolph Hitler was not a brilliant, original thinker. There was really nothing new about his ideas. They were a mix of 19th century racial theories, post-World War I resentments, anti-Semitism, anti-modernism, and sexism. What was new and different was his single-mindedness, the fanaticism and intensity with which he held his views, and his ability to captivate large audiences.

Hitler was a master orator. He began his speeches in low, hesitating tones, gradually raising the pitch and volume of his voice, culminating in a climactic explosion of frenzied indignation. He skillfully played on the emotions of people by raising the level of excitement higher and higher until his audience became a wide-eyed screaming mass that surrendered to his will and looked upon him with religious adoration.[8] No doubt, Hitler's talent as an orator contributed in no small measure to his rise to power and popularity.

The content of Hitler's speeches also resonated with many people. He offered the Germans what they needed most: encouragement and hope. He promised something to everyone: work to the unemployed, prosperity to businessmen, expansion of the army and

---

[8] To this day, I get goose pimples and a queasy feeling in the pit of my stomach when I hear excerpts of a Hitler speech and see the ecstatic crowd chanting "Ein Volk, ein Reich, ein Führer" (one nation, one empire, one leader).

restoration of German glory. He promised to stomp out corruption and to bring order from chaos. He offered a feeling of unity to all and a chance to belong. And sprinkled throughout his speeches were his fanatical tirades against the Jews and the Bolshevik-Jewish conspiracy.

I regret having to conclude this section with an enigma (or should I say anti-climax?) None of the details of Hitler's life provide a clue to explain the strength of his obsessions, or his ability to realize his ambitions. The magnitude of the crimes he initiated remains oddly out of proportion to the banality of his person and his life.

The inner circle

Hermann Göring (1883–1946) was a hero of World War I. He joined the Nazi Party in **1922**, became **commander** in charge of the **German Air Force (Luftwaffe)** and after **1933**, president of the Reichstag. He established the **Gestapo**, the feared political police force. He was an ambitious schemer, a flamboyant, vain individual who relished luxury and excess. When convicted to death at the Nüremberg trials, he committed suicide in his prison cell.

Joseph Goebbels (1897–1945) was an intellectual with a Ph.D. in literature. He joined the Party in **1924**. In **1928**, Hitler made him head of party propaganda and after **1933**, **Minister of Propaganda**. He excelled in stirring up hatred and orchestrated gigantic extravaganzas (e.g., impressive parades and celebrations, and the 1936 Olympic Games in Berlin). He stayed with Hitler to the end. When Hitler committed suicide, Goebbels and his wife did so too, after poisoning their six children.

Heinrich Himmler (1900–1945) was neither flashy like Göring, nor educated like Goebbels. He joined the party in **1926,** and in **1929** became the **leader of the SS** when the 280-man organization was little more than Hitler's bodyguard. His power constantly increased, and by 1942 the SS had 250,000 members and Himmler became, next to Hitler, the most powerful and feared man in the Third Reich. As head of the SS and later chief of all German security forces, he implemented terror and mass murder in all territories dominated by Germany. He was the **"architect of the Holocaust."** He committed suicide in May of 1945, after the fall of Germany.

As a footnote to the description of these men, it is ironic how little they conformed to Hitler's model of a typical Aryan as a tall, strong, handsome, blond man: Göring was an overweight, fat man, Goebbels was short (5ft.5in.) and had a clubfoot, Himmler was a homely man, and Hitler himself was neither blond nor handsome.

1933–1939. The period before World War II

During the first half (1933–39) of the twelve-year period of the Nazi regime in Germany, Hitler consolidated his power, **flouted the Treaty of Versailles** with impunity, rearmed Germany in preparation for war, expanded German territory by **annexing Austria and the Sudetenland of Czechoslovakia,** and, above all, pursued and gradually escalated the persecution of the Jews with fanatical determination. In the following sections I describe these events as they unfolded[9]:

---

[9] These events are well documented and described in many books. The three I used extensively are: Martin Gilbert, "The Holocaust," Henry Holt & Co., 1985; Doris L. Bergen, "War and Genocide," Rowman & Littlefield Publishers, Inc., 2003; Saul Friedländer, "Nazi Germany and the Jews," vol. 1, HarperCollins Publishers, 1997.

The burning of the Reichstag: a pretext to abolish democracy and perpetrate atrocities

Hitler moved rapidly to establish his dictatorship. On **February 5, 1933**, only a week after becoming Chancellor, an emergency bill was passed expropriating all Communist Party buildings and printing presses. Hitler soon found a convenient pretext to implement further anti-communist measures. On **February 27, 1933**, fire broke out in the Reichstag building, and Hitler immediately blamed the communists for having done it. (It actually was done by a non-political, deranged Dutchman, **Marinus van der Lubbe**.) Hitler ordered massive reprisals against the communists. He had thousands arrested and tortured; hundreds were shot. On **March 9, 1933**, the first concentration camp at **Dachau**, near Munich, was established. It housed, at the beginning, 5,000 prisoners, most of them communists. With these actions, Hitler had crippled communist power in Germany.

The Reichstag fire gave Hitler the pretext to dismantle what was left of German democracy. On **March 23, 1933**, Hitler convinced the Reichstag to pass a law that enabled him to proclaim any measure without approval of the Reichstag, and without the need to have the president declare a state of emergency. This act made the Reichstag essentially defunct. Its own members had voted it out of existence. By the end of the **summer of 1933**, Hitler used his authority to outlaw all political parties except the NSDAP—the Nazi Party. As was Hitler's style, he had established his dictatorship through means that were, at least in the narrow sense of the word, legal.

In addition to communists, other groups that Hitler considered "asocial elements" were attacked during the first year. They included **homosexuals, Jehovah Witnesses, Gypsies**[10] **(Roma), Afro-Germans,** the **physically handicapped,** the **mentally handicapped, and the Jews.** In "Mein Kampf" he wrote that "he would deal with" the **Jews.**

A boycott of Jewish shops was decreed on **March 27, 1933**. A rally in New York's Madison Square Garden threatened to counter-boycott all German goods. The Nazis relented and called off the boycott.

On **April 7, 1933**, all civil servants who were not of Aryan origin were dismissed. Expulsion of Jews from Universities was rapid and total. The Nobel Prize-winning chemist Fritz Haber was deprived of his professorship. Ironically, it was due to his discoveries that Germany was able to carry on fighting in World War I for four years. Albert Einstein was forced into exile.

On **May 10, 1933**, in front of the Berlin Opera House, thousands of books by Jews and anti-Nazi authors were burned, a spectacle to be repeated in the coming years. The German poet **Heinrich Heine's** prescient writings of 100 years ago come to mind: "They that start by burning books will end by burning men."[11] For the most part, the German public was indifferent, or, worse, cheered and participated in these Nazi offenses. By the end of **July 1933**, 26,000 Germans, many of them Jews, had been taken to concentration camps.

---

[10] It is ironic and absurd that Nazi ideology considered Gypsies impure and unworthy to live. Gypsies were, in fact, more "Aryan" than the Nordic Germans. Gypsies originated in India, home of the original Aryan tribe whose name was appropriated by the European racists for their own purposes.

[11] From Heine's play "Almansor" (1821). In another of Heine's famous passages one can discern the prediction of a catastrophe, which could be interpreted as being the Holocaust: "Thought precedes action as lightning precedes thunder. German thunder comes rolling somewhat slowly, but ... its crash ... will be unlike anything before in the history of the world. ... At that uproar the eagles of the air will drop dead, and lions in farthest Africa will draw in their tails and slink away. ... A play will be performed in Germany which will make the French Revolution look like an innocent idyll."

On the domestic front, Hitler worked hard to gain the admiration and loyalty of the German people. He introduced a massive and very successful public works program to create badly needed jobs. This accelerated the process of economic recovery, and enhanced his prestige and power. The Nazis also set up an agency called Strength Through Joy to organize workers' leisure activities and plan holiday trips. For many Germans, such group activities provided an exciting sense of belonging.

Hitler and his Minister of Propaganda, Goebbels, realized the importance of pageantry as a show of might and intimidation. They organized endless torchlight parades with columns of men marching in unison, singing songs with vicious and terrifying lyrics, like "Jewish blood spurting from German knives." This projected an image of unanimity, invincibility, and determination designed to intimidate any potential opponent of the regime. These spectacles had a mesmerizing and frightening effect on onlookers, as I can vouch from my personal experience.

In general, Germans who were not opposed to the policies of the Third Reich (which encompassed the majority of the population), and who were not victims of persecution (as were the Jews and Roma), lived comfortable and satisfying lives until World War II.

Hitler's foreign policy moves during the first year

Hitler was a master at making his aims look safely conventional, while his intentions were dangerously radical. His first major foreign policy success came in **July 1933**. Hitler signed an agreement with the Pope called **Concordat with the Vatican**. In exchange for recognition of his regime's legitimacy, Hitler promised to protect the rights of the Catholic Church in Germany. For Hitler, the Concordat turned out to be a very effective way to buy support from the Catholics, who represented 40% of the German population.

Other important political decisions during the first year of Hitler's regime included Germany's **withdrawal from the League of Nations** in **October 1933,** and the signing of a **non-aggression pact with Poland** in **January 1934**. However, the most important decision Hitler made was to begin to rearm. Since this violated the prohibition of the Treaty of Versailles, it was done, at the beginning at least, in utmost secrecy.

The Night of the Long Knives

An important event, which showed Hitler's brutality, took place in **June 1934**. It was known as the **Röhm Putsch** or the Night of the Long Knives. **Ernst Röhm**, now head of the 2.5 million Stormtroopers of the SA, had been Hitler's associate since the 1920s and had played an important role in helping Hitler attain power. Now that he was Chancellor, Hitler no longer needed the SA for protection and started to view them as thugs who disrupted public order. Furthermore, Himmler, head of the SS, had grown more powerful, and viewed the SA as a rival organization that he wanted to eliminate. Hitler sided with Himmler, and on **June 30, 1934** gave the order to strike against the SA. In a bloody rampage, SS men killed Röhm and 80 high-ranking Stormtroopers. Hitler used the purge to kill many other people he found problematic. The total number of people killed is unknown; the estimates vary between several hundred and several thousand.

Hitler dressed the bloodbath in the guise of morality. Ernst Röhm was openly homosexual. The killings were described by the press as a cleansing of the Party, a necessary measure against decadence and perversion. Officially, Hitler's cabinet declared the purge legal, and President Hindenburg sent a cable to Hitler, congratulating him for restoring order.

14

Hitler did not dismantle the SA but he clipped its wings and made it subordinate to the SS. Himmler was now in charge of the SA, SS, and the political police known as the Gestapo.

The Röhm Putsch shows Hitler's mode of action in the crassest way. He regarded murder as a legitimate means for attaining his goals: He used murder to eliminate past associates whom he no longer needed; to kill his enemies whom he perceived a threat to his power; and to eliminate innocent, apolitical people—to "cleanse the Aryan race."

The death of President Hindenburg; Hitler proclaims himself Supreme Commander

In **August 1934,** President Hindenburg died. Hitler took this opportunity to unite the office of the president and the chancellor into one person—his own. According to the German constitution, still officially in force, the president was the Supreme Commander of the armed forces. Consequently, members of the military had to swear allegiance to Hitler. To the anti-Nazi Germans, the death of Hindenburg and the taking over of his position by Hitler meant the end of any hope that Hitler and Nazism could be stopped.

The Nüremberg Laws; the plight of the Jews intensifies

Hitler was eager to legalize Nazi measures as a way of gaining respectability and acceptance. The key pieces of legislation concerning attacks on Jews were the Nüremberg Laws, passed on **September 15** and **November 15, 1935.** The first part dealt with the Protection of German Blood and Honor. It forbade marriage and sexual relations between Jews and Aryan Germans. The second part was the Reich Citizenship Law, which defined who was to be considered a Jew. The law stipulated that people with at least one Jewish grandparent were Jews. Since the Nüremberg Laws were based on racial and not religious grounds, conversions were not recognized. Germans defined as "Jews" lost all rights associated with German citizenship.

The Nüremberg Laws elevated random discrimination into a system. The laws proved to be a crucial step toward the destruction of German Jews. All kinds of attacks were now sanctioned, even mandated, by law. Moreover, once Jews were defined, it was much easier to identify, rob, deport, and eventually kill them.

An insidious aspect of the Nazi regime was the encouragement of people to report on one another. This resulted in a spate of denunciations that flooded the offices of the Gestapo. It even happened that children denounced their parents for having criticized the Nazi regime. It also resulted in revenge denunciations of one's enemies.

The denunciations bring to mind a story by **Stefan Zweig** that made a strong impression on me when I read it many years ago. Two families, one Jewish and one Aryan, had been close friends for many years. With the advent of Nazism, the Aryan family members joined the Nazi Party and became great admirers of Hitler, and one day they denounced their Jewish friends to the Gestapo. The Jewish family members were arrested and sent to a concentration camp where they perished, except for one of the sons who was able to save himself and emigrate to the US. He vowed to take revenge on the Nazi family. He started to write them letters using suspicious code words and alluding to their anti-Nazi conversations and plottings of the past—all made up, of course. The family in Germany responded by pleading with him to stop writing these letters that were routinely opened by censors. They were interrogated by the Gestapo, and were getting into deep trouble with the authorities. But the son in the US continued to write letters with more and more incriminating remarks until one of his letters returned, marked "Address Unknown." He had accomplished his goal.

Preparations for war; Hitler's occupation of the Rhineland and his involvement in Spain

In **1935,** Hitler's government introduced mandatory conscription into the armed forces and revealed Germany's military machine to the world. The rearmament blatantly violated the terms of the Treaty of Versailles, but neither the British nor the French were in the mood to engage in a new conflict with Germany, and the United States adopted an isolationist policy. At this stage, Hitler's expansionist policies could easily have been stopped. The world was to pay dearly for this inaction.

Encouraged by the lack of response to Germany's violation of the Treaty of Versailles, Hitler took his biggest foreign policy gamble yet. On **March 7, 1936**, he announced that Germany would **reoccupy the Rhineland**, which after World War I was declared a demilitarized zone policed by France. As anticipated by Hitler, France did not fight but retreated. The gamble paid off. There was tremendous euphoria in Germany and Hitler's prestige got an enormous boost. Hitler's success in occupying territories without firing a shot was to be repeated in Austria and the Czech lands, in 1938 and 1939 respectively. (See below, and pages 17–18)

Since **1936**, German forces had been involved in the **Spanish Civil War** on the side of General Francisco Franco. It gave Germany a chance to test its new weapons and hone its capabilities in warfare. It also provided an opportunity to fight the communists of the Soviet Union, who backed the Spanish Republic.

In the winter of 1937–1938, Hitler further consolidated his power by replacing the old elite who brought him to power with a younger, more aggressive cadre of loyal supporters. He relieved 14 senior generals, and replaced the head of the army, **Werner von Fritsch,** with **Walter von Brauchitsch**. Hitler also replaced the conservative Foreign Minister **Constantin von Neurath** with the more aggressive loyal Nazi **Joachim von Ribbentrop**. Preparations for the war were now well underway.

The Anschluss: German annexation of Austria

Hitler had repeatedly announced to the world that he was responsible for German-speaking people wherever they were. On **March 12, 1938**, Hitler translated his avowed responsibility into action. He ordered his army to cross the border into Austria and annex the country to the German Reich. The reaction of the Austrian people was enthusiastic and the German army was greeted by cheering crowds. I remember the event well. We were living in Bratislava, Slovakia, only 30 miles from Vienna, and were shocked and fearful that the German army would enter Slovakia.

The 180,000 Jews of Austria, most of them living in Vienna, became part of the German hegemony overnight. Whereas the isolation and abuse of the Jews in Germany had been gradual, the attacks and torments of Jews in Austria were sudden and immediate. And the Austrian Nazis turned out to be even more vicious than their German counterparts. They took great pleasure, often with the participation of the civilian population, in cruel and humiliating acts. For instance, they forced prominent Jews, including the **70-year-old Rabbi of Vienna, Dr. Taglich**, to clean the pavements with toothbrushes. They also made Jews eat grass in the Prater, the Viennese Amusement Park. As they ate, Stormtroopers trampled on their hands. During the first few weeks after the Anschluss, many Jews suffered heart attacks, and 500 committed suicide.

Getting ahead of our story and fast-forwarding to the situation after World War II: The Austrians were, and still are, slow and hesitant to admit their guilt for their behavior during the Nazi regime. Most of them hypocritically claim that they were invaded by Hitler's army against their will. But their true character is revealed by the prevailing present-day anti-Semitism,[12] and the fact that in 1986 they elected the **ex-Nazi Kurt Waldheim** as their president.

Appeasement at Munich; the annexation of the Sudetenland

Hitler, emboldened by the lack of resistance to his occupation of Austria, demanded now that the German-speaking region of Czechoslovakia, the Sudetenland, be ceded to Germany. His demands were backed by threats of military force. On **September 29, 1938,** at Munich, the British **Prime Minister, Neville Chamberlain,** and the French and Italian leaders bowed to Hitler's demands. The Sudetenland would become part of Greater Germany on **October 10, 1938**—a disastrous appeasement that I discuss in more detail elsewhere.[13] (See page 47.)

Kristallnacht: The Night of Broken Glass

On **October 28, 1938**, three weeks after annexing the Sudetenland, Hitler struck again, expelling 18,000 Jews to Poland who, although living in Germany since 1918, had been born in Polish territory. One of them was Zyndel Grynszpan, who wrote to his son Hirsch (who was a student in Paris at the time) about the brutality of the German action. Young Hirsch, enraged by what he read, went to the German Embassy in Paris on **November 6, 1938,** and shot the first German official who received him, **Ernst vom Rath**.[14] Hitler, Goebbels and his cohorts were quick to denounce the deed as part of a Jewish-inspired world conspiracy against Germany. An unprecedented wave of violence broke over the German Jews, which became known as **Kristallnacht (The Night of Broken Glass)**.

Bonfires were lit in every neighborhood where Jews lived, and prayer books, Torah scrolls, and books by Jewish authors were burned. A hundred Jews were killed; 30,000 (10% of the Jewish population) were arrested and sent to concentration camps. Tens of thousands of Jewish shops were destroyed, and 200 synagogues were set on fire. But it wasn't only the Stormtroopers who perpetrated these cruel acts. The civilian population, who started out as passive bystanders, enthusiastically joined the pillages with cries of "Down with the Jews!" To add insult to injury, German Jewry was fined a billion marks (the equivalent of 500,000 dollars) for damages done.

The British ambassador in Berlin, **Sir George Orgilvie-Forbes**, reported to the Foreign Office in London on these acts of medieval barbarism, and warned that "this is not a national but a world problem which, if neglected, will have terrible repercussions." In New

---

[12] Jokes often hit the nail on the head in describing prevailing situations. Here is a typical one: A Jewish woman goes to an Austrian travel agency in New York and says: "I would like to spend my summer holiday in Vienna, but I am afraid there is still anti-Semitism there"; to which the agent replies: "Anti-Semitism, Madam? Not during the tourist season!"

[13] G. Feher: "Reminiscences and Ruminations," October 2009, pages 35–37.

[14] It is a tragic irony that, as vom Rath walked toward his death, he was being investigated by the Gestapo because of his opposition to the treatment of the Jews.

York, on **November 23, 1938**, a mass demonstration protested against the acts of violence. Two days later, a similar protest was organized in Chicago. But the Germans no longer cared about world opinion.

Germany occupies Bohemia and Moravia; Slovakia declares independence

At Munich, Hitler had promised to respect the sovereignty of truncated Czechoslovakia, but only a few months later, on **March 15, 1939**, Hitler reneged on his promise and German forces occupied the Bohemian and Moravian provinces, and made them a German protectorate. Slovakia declared independence on **March 14, 1939,** and became a puppet state of Germany. The 54,000 Jews living in Prague, of whom 25,000 were refugees from Germany, joined now the ranks of persecuted German Jews.

Hitler's foreign policy approach: a lesson to be learned

How did Hitler accomplish his expansionary successes without firing a shot? First and foremost, he took a calculated gamble by assuming, correctly as it turned out, that there would be no effective resistance to his actions. His approach was: push forward hard and see if anybody is pushing back. If not, keep pushing. But nobody was pushing back, and once the world powers caved in, starting with the 1936 occupation of the Rhineland, a domino effect set in and success bred further success. "Why intervene in the occupation of Bohemia and Moravia when we did not do so in the ceding of the Sudetenland and annexation of Austria?"

On the diplomatic front, Hitler's approach was to talk peace while planning for war, and to make promises and pacts that served him well for the moment but that he had no intentions of keeping. For example, the Concordat with the Vatican, a non-aggression pact with Poland, an Anglo-German Naval Agreement to limit the German fleet to a certain percentage of the British navy, and the Munich Agreement in which he promised to honor the sovereignty of Czechoslovakia. But the most startling of all was the Soviet-German Non-Aggression Pact to be discussed later. In retrospect, it is amazing how gullible the leaders of the free world were. They believed what they wanted to believe.

I hope that the world has learned a lesson from its past mistakes. Appeasement does not work. Reluctance to make a firm stand ultimately results in disaster and bloody confrontation. At present I am particularly worried about Iran and its Supreme Leader Ayatallah Ali Khamenei, a "Middle East Hitler" whose proclaimed goal is to wipe Israel off the surface of the Earth. And with a nuclear weapon he could try to do just that. Hitler, at the beginning, was not taken seriously and was labeled a crazy, inconsequential maverick. Let us not repeat that mistake with Iran!

Anti-Jewish actions in other European countries

In several states outside the borders of Germany, anti-Jewish outbreaks, fanned by German propaganda, started to take place in 1936. These states, especially those of Eastern Europe, took Germany as an example to allow their anti-Jewish prejudices to flourish.

In **Poland,** on **March 9, 1936**, a pogrom took place in Przybyt, a town near Warsaw. The peasants entered Jewish houses, smashing windows and furniture. Several Jews were tortured to death. In **August 1936**, the Polish Minister of Commerce ordered all shops to display the name of the owner. This made the fact that the owner was Jewish obvious to every Pole, and provided instant incitement for the anti-Semites. On **May 13, 1937**, Polish anti-Semites attacked the Jews of Brest-Litovsk under the slogan "We owe our troubles to the Jews."

In **Romania**, in the city of **Timisoara**, in **1936**, members of the Iron Guard attacked the audience of a Jewish theater; a bomb was thrown and several Jews were killed. Elsewhere in Romania, including Bucharest, the capital, anti-Jewish riots took place. On **January 21, 1938**, the Romanian government abrogated the minority rights of the Jews.

In **Hungary**, the government passed its **First Law** on **May 29, 1938**, restricting to 20% the number of Jews allowed to hold jobs in commerce, industry, the liberal professions, and the administration. On **May 3, 1939**, the Hungarian government issued a **Second Jewish Law** forbidding any Hungarian Jew from becoming a judge, lawyer, schoolteacher, or a member of parliament.

In **Slovakia**, after its proclamation of autonomy on **October 6, 1938**, severe anti-Jewish actions were taken. They are discussed in detail on pages 76–90.

The anti-Jewish activities outside of Germany, although viewed as severe at the time, were a mere prelude to the mass killings to take place as these countries came under the grip of Nazi Germany's power.

Jewish emigration from Germany; difficulties from within and from the outside

Jews had lived in Germany for over a thousand years. They had formed one of Europe's most assimilated and cultured communities. The contributions of German Jews to medicine, literature, science, music, and industry, as well as their sacrifices on the battlefields of World War I, had been a source of great pride to them. Many of them felt more German than Jewish, and, despite the prevailing anti-Semitism, they felt deeply rooted and at home in Germany. These sentiments posed a strong emotional barrier to leaving Germany as the situation went from bad to worse. In addition, their unrealistic belief—at the beginning at least—was that Hitler's regime would not last long. Furthermore, by emigrating they would lose most of their property, which they would have had to leave behind. But the biggest obstacle was the restriction on immigration by the foreign governments, in particular by the most desirable countries to emigrate to, i.e., the United States, Canada, and Britain. In spite of these difficulties, internal and external, about half of the Jewish population left Germany during the **1933–1939** period. In this section I shall describe the Jewish exodus from Germany during the pre-war period.

The aim of the Nazis was to eliminate Jewish influence from every facet of German life. In the first years of their ascendancy to power, the Nazis had no objections to Jewish emigration. In fact they encouraged it. During 1933, about 5,000 German Jews immigrated to Palestine, and 30,000 Jews left for other countries. There was a strong Arab reaction to the growth of immigration to Palestine. At the end of **October 1933**, **Arab riots** broke out in **Nablus, Jaffa,** and **Jerusalem.** The British suppressed the riots, but were forced to re-examine their immigration laws, and, in due course, restrict Jewish entry into the Jewish National Home that had been proclaimed in the **Balfour Declaration in 1917**. But in **1934**, the British still let 7,000 Jews enter Palestine. At the end of 1934, two years after Hitler came to power, 50,000 Jews, about 10% of the Jewish population, had left Germany. This level of emigration continued throughout 1935, during which another 25,000 Jews left Germany.

On **April 15, 1936, renewed Arab riots** broke out in Palestine, in response to the immigration of 12,000 Polish Jews following the pogrom in Przytyk. Twenty-one Jews were killed during the riots. These events had a disturbing impact on the emigration from Germany. Many German Jewish parents were now hesitant to send their children to

Palestine. As a consequence of these events, as well as new restrictions on immigration by the authorities of the British mandate, only 3,600 Jews reached Palestine in 1937.

In the **autumn of 1937**, one individual had a small success in saving some Jews. **David Glick**, a Pittsburgh lawyer, negotiated as representative of the **American Jewish Joint Distribution** Committee (the Joint) with the Gestapo, and arranged the release of 120 Jews being held at Dachau. The Gestapo agreed to release them on the condition that the released Jews emigrate immediately to a country outside Europe. Glick negotiated with the British Consul in Munich to issue Palestine visas on the condition that 5,000 pounds be paid to assist the settlement of the refugees in Palestine. Glick's experiment was later repeated on a larger scale. Three thousand German Jews were sent with a similar payment to Bolivia, financed by **Don Mauricio Hochschild**, a Jewish tin-mine millionaire in Peru.

After the Anschluss and Kristallnacht in 1938, the pressure on Jews in Germany and Austria intensified. Jews in larger numbers than ever applied for visas to countries in the free world. This new wave of potential refugees roused worldwide fears of an endless flow of the dispossessed. One by one, the countries now imposed new restrictive rules and regulations on immigration.

On **July 6, 1938**, an international conference convened at **Evian**, a resort town on the shores of Lake Geneva, to discuss the problem of the reception of refugees. About 150,000 Jews (out of a total of approximately 700,000) from Germany and Austria had found refuge: 55,000 in the United States, 40,000 in Palestine, 15,000 in France, 14,000 in Switzerland, 8,000 in Brazil, 2,000 in Belgium, and several thousands in Bolivia, Sweden, Denmark, and Norway.

Many delegates at Evian were not sympathetic to the Jewish plight. The Australian delegate, **T.W. White,** told the conference that "As we have no racial problem, we are not desirous to import one." The British Mandate in Palestine and the United States tightened their rules of admission. Four South American countries, Argentina, Chile, Uruguay, and Mexico, adopted laws severely restricting the number of Jews who were allowed to enter (in the case of Mexico, to 100 a year). The lack of effective positive actions at Evian to alleviate the plight of the Jews, represents a great moral failure of the free world. For this, it has to share in the guilt for the mass murders of the Holocaust. (For a more detailed account of the Evian Conference see pages 101–107.)

The negative attitude, often outright anti-Semitic, of the European government officials in Europe is exemplified by a personal comment made by the British Prime Minister **Neville Chamberlain** on **July 30, 1939**: "No doubt, Jews are not lovable people; I don't care about them myself. But that is not sufficient to explain the pogroms." His remark reminds me of the anti-Semitic definition of an anti-Semite: "A person who hates Jews more than necessary."

The hardening response of the European powers towards Jewish refugees was typified on **August 13, 1938**, when the Cabinet in Finland, in a secret meeting, decided not to honor the unauthorized entry visas issued to Austrian Jews by the Finish ambassador in Vienna. On **August 17, 1938**, when 53 Austrian Jews reached Helsinki by sea, they were not allowed to disembark, and the boat was ordered to return to Germany. On the way back to Germany, three of the refugees committed suicide by throwing themselves overboard.

The following year, a similar episode, on a larger scale and more publicized by the international press, took place on **May 13, 1939**, when the steamer, the **St. Louis**, left Hamburg for Havana, Cuba, with about 1,000 Jewish refugees aboard. They had been granted Cuban visas, but while the ship was at sea, the Cuban government changed its mind and the passengers were not allowed to disembark in Havana. The United States also refused to let the St. Louis dock on its shore, and the ship was forced to return to Germany. At the last minute, before the ship arrived in Germany, the refugees were admitted to Britain, France, Belgium and Holland. Only a small fraction of them survived the later German occupation (for a more detailed description see pages 107–110). One of them is my friend and colleague, Fred Reif, who managed later to immigrate with his mother and sister to the United States.

In contrast to these two sad episodes, I want to describe a positive one, involving a British official, **Captain Frank Foley**, head of the British Passport Control Office in Berlin, whose humanitarian instincts overcame bureaucratic regulations. In **1939**, there were no visa requirements for refugees to immigrate to Shanghai. Several thousand German Jews availed themselves of this opportunity, and took a boat from Germany to Shanghai. The Foreign Office in London hesitated to approve this action. Nevertheless, Captain Foley supported it, saying: "It might be considered humane on our part not to interfere officially to prevent the Jews from choosing their own graveyards. They would rather die as free men in Shanghai than as slaves in Dachau." Actually, the refugees in Shanghai survived, albeit under difficult conditions, and after the war most of them emigrated to other countries.

To sum up the emigration of Jews from Germany during the 1933–1939 period: about 250,000, half of the German Jews, managed to leave Germany. The number of Jews killed in Germany during that period is estimated to be several hundred, a number that pales in comparison to the 6 million Jews killed during the next six years.

The Soviet-German Non-Aggression Pact

On **August 23, 1939**, an event took place that shook the world. Nazi Germany signed a non-aggression pact with the Soviet Union. After six years of Nazi persecution of communists, and intensive anti-Soviet propaganda, this was an unexpected turn of events. It was particularly shocking to us, members of the leftist Zionist movement, Hashomer Hatzair, in Bratislava, who looked to the Soviet Union for political guidance. "How could the Soviets sign up with the devil?" was the topic of many heated discussions among us, disillusioned members of the Shomer Hatzair. At the time, nobody, of course, knew of the secret clause in the agreement that ceded half of Poland—that Germany anticipated capturing—to the Soviet Union.

The Non-Aggression Pact meant that if Germany were to attack Poland, Russia would not interfere. This fact made a German attack on Poland much more likely. It was an ominous prospect, not only for the 3.25 million Jews of Poland, but also for the whole world.

1939–1940. War against Poland; experiments in brutality[15]

The German conquest of Poland

On **September 1, 1939**, German forces invaded Poland. German planners tried to disguise this act of aggression as a defensive measure. They dressed 150 concentration camp inmates in Polish uniforms and used them to stage a mock attack on a German radio station near the border. The corpses of the inmates in Polish uniforms were used as "proof" of Polish belligerence and justification for the attack on Poland.

---

[15] The war years 1939–1945 are described in the books referenced on page 12, as well as by William L. Shirer, "The Rise and Fall of the Third Reich," Simon & Schuster, 1959; and Saul Friedländer, "The Years of Extermination," HarperCollins Publishers, 2007.

Against the superior German army the Poles had no chance. The Germans attacked with an army of 1.5 million men in motorized vehicles, directed and coordinated through a maze of sophisticated electronic communication networks. It was a monstrous juggernaut such as the world had never seen. Although the Poles fought valiantly, especially some cavalry units, horses against tanks faced hopeless odds. The Polish army was vanquished in a week in what came to be known as **Blitzkrieg**—a war at lightning speed. In the assaults, 70,000 Poles were killed, and 1 million were taken prisoner. The Polish leadership fled to London to establish a government in exile.

On **September 3, 1939**, two days after the German invasion of Poland, Britain and France declared war on Germany. But the two powers remained militarily inactive, and provided no effective help to the Poles. The Germans called the Allied involvement a **Sitzkrieg**, an immobile "war of sitting," in contrast to their rapid Blitzkrieg. It was yet another cowardly inaction of the two great European powers, and a failure to honor a pre-war agreement to defend Poland in case it was attacked.

The part of Poland occupied by the Germans was divided into two. The western areas, known as the **Incorporated Territories**, were annexed to the German Reich. The remaining part of the Polish territory was called the **General Government** and was administered like a colony by Governor **General Hans Frank**. It was to become the site of Nazi brutality, where the majority of mass killing of Jews after 1941 would take place.

For the German Nazi activists, the defeat of Poland meant a new career opportunity. Each Nazi tried to distinguish himself from the others by being more effective—that is, more brutal—in the treatment of the Jews and the Polish local population.

On **September 7, 1939**, **Reinhard Heydrich**, head of the German Reich Security Office, issued an order to his men to destroy the leadership of Poland, and expel all Jews from the Incorporated Territories. His orders were: "Nobility, clergy, intellectuals, prominent Poles, and Jews must be killed." The goal of his bosses, Hitler and Himmler, was to reduce the Poles to a people of slaves. They shut down Polish newspapers, and used forced labor and public hanging to make examples of Poles who defied them.

The war in 1939 brought a massive expansion of the network of concentration camps in the newly acquired territories—places such as **Majdanek**, near Lublin, or **Plaschaw**, near Krakow, which are depicted in Spielberg's movie, Schindler's List. In these camps most measures applied to Polish Gentiles and Jews alike, although the Germans often showed additional improvised brutality toward their new Jewish subjects, of which there were many. Whereas in Germany in 1933 Jews made up less than 1% of the population, in Poland they represented 10%.

Nazi racial policy had two sides: attack on people deemed undesirable, and advancement of Aryan Germans, which included relocating ethnic Germans into the Incorporated Territories. By 1940, the ethnic Germans that had signed up for resettlement and needed homes numbered 200,000. That year the Germans forced 300,000 Poles to leave the Incorporated Territories for the General Government, and tens of thousands of Polish Jews were squeezed into ghettos in the cities.

The Nazi goal was to deport as many Poles and Jews as possible from the Incorporated Territories to the General Government. But by 1941, the situation became so chaotic and overcrowded that Governor Frank announced that he could not take in any more people. An alternate solution had to be found—the seeds of the "**Final Solution**," i.e., annihilation, were sown.

Dangling promises of Jewish property in front of Gentile Poles gave Poles a stake in attacks on Jews, and encouraged them to betray Jews to the Germans.

Polish clergymen begged the Pope to take action, but **Pope Pius XII** remained silent. A staunch opponent of Communism, he may have thought that Nazi Germany—even given its excesses—was preferable to Soviet domination. His silence in the fall of 1939, when the victims of German aggression were priests of his own church, made it hard for him to speak out later in the face of crimes against the Jews.

Occasionally, members of the German army protested against the brutalities. A case in point is **General Johannes Blaskowitz**, commander of a military region in occupied Poland. He wrote a long memorandum directly to Hitler warning against the demoralizing effect on the army and the reaction abroad to the brutalities and atrocities committed by Germans. Blaskowitz's memo had no effect on the behavior of the Germans, but it is interesting that he was neither punished nor demoted but simply transferred out of Poland. It indicates that opposition could have been effective if it had occurred on a massive scale. Unfortunately this was not the case, and over time such protests ceased in the face of Germany's dramatic military triumphs.

Ghettoization of Jews was a stopgap measure that German authorities developed in late 1939 and 1940. It was considered as a sort of holding pattern until subsequent steps could be taken. But what were those steps to be? In 1939 and 1940 some Nazi officials were talking about a Jewish reservation in the West, near Lublin. Others proposed another scheme, the **Madagascar Plan**, to ship all European Jews to an island off the coast of Africa. During this phase of uncertainty as to the fate of the Jews, between 1939 and 1941, over half a million Polish Jews died in ghettos. Many died of starvation or of diseases brought on by overcrowding and terribly unsanitary conditions; many were shot or beaten to death. The ghettos were not yet a formal program of annihilation, but they proved deadly enough for hundreds of thousands of Polish Jews.

The Jewish Councils in the ghettos

There are two topics relating to the Holocaust that are controversial, sensitive and emotionally charged. One deals with the role of the Jewish leaderships—the Jewish Councils (Judenraete)—of the ghettos, and the other with Jewish resistance (or lack of it) to the mass murders (to be discussed later on pages 40–41). I believe one reason for the acrimonious discussions on these topics is the tendency to generalize. But the behavior of the Judenraete spans a large spectrum, and one's attitude towards it depends on whether one focuses on the positive or negative aspects. At any rate, I shall follow the advice of Rabbi Hillel, who, over 2,000 years ago, wrote: "Judge not thy neighbor until thou art in his place." Instead of passing judgment, I shall try to describe the situation that prevailed, and give examples of how different Judenraete dealt with the problems. The Jewish Councils were set up by the Germans to administer aspects of daily life in the ghetto. It was yet another fiendish stratagem of the Nazis. It lightened their own responsibility, and often caused suffering and friction within the Jewish community.

The Jewish Councils were criticized, in particular by the Jewish author **Hannah Arendt**, for complicity or even collaboration with the German authorities. But the Jewish Councils found themselves in an extremely difficult situation; they had no autonomy or real power, and were subservient to German goals and priorities. In cases when members of the councils refused to cooperate, German officials dismissed them, or had them shot and then replaced with more compliant men.

The Jewish Councils were caught between two conflicting sets of demands. Above them loomed German orders to make lists of people and their property, and to hand them over on demand. Below them were the desperate needs of the Jewish communities for food, clothing, and medical resources to survive. It was impossible to reconcile these two sets of goals, which were essentially the destruction of the Jews on one hand, and their survival on the other hand. In most cases the councils did the best they could. They attempted to reason and plead on behalf of the Jews, and tried to maintain productivity: to make the ghettos valuable to the war efforts so that Germans would want to keep Jews alive.

Critics of the Jewish Councils claim that they should have warned the people about their ultimate fate. But could the Councils be blamed for not realizing in 1939 or 1940 what even top Nazis did not grasp until sometime in mid-1941, i.e., that the Nazi goal was the annihilation of every Jew in Europe?

Let me now describe the specific actions taken by Jewish Councils in different ghettos. The ghetto of **Minsk**, located in the capital of Bielorussia, was the fourth largest ghetto in Eastern Europe, housing about 80,000 Jews. As head of the Judenrat, the Germans appointed **Eliahu Mishkin**, a former member of the city councils. From the beginning, this Judenrat became the center of resistance against the Nazis. It collaborated fully with the underground, which was commanded by Jewish communists. Eventually, the Minsk ghetto and the Judenrat were eliminated, but not before they successfully smuggled out of the ghetto 10,000 people, many of whom survived the war as partisan fighters.

The spirit of the leaders of the Minsk ghetto is perhaps best illustrated by the following incident. When Mishkin was murdered, he was succeeded by **Moshe Yaffe,** who carried out his predecessor's policies of resistance to the Nazis. On **July 28, 1942**, 25,000 Jews were assembled in the square of the ghetto, and the Nazis ordered Yaffe to calm them down in preparation for their deportation to the killing centers. Instead, Yaffe told them to escape and hide. He was shot on the spot.

In contrast to the praiseworthy behavior of the Judenrat in Minsk, is the despicable behavior of **Mordechai Chaim Rumkowski**, head of the Judenrat in the **Lodz** ghetto. By the middle of 1942, Rumkowski undoubtedly knew that the Jews that were transported out of the ghetto were being murdered, but he did not share this information with the Jews of the ghetto lest it cause unrest and opposition to the deportations. When the Germans demanded that all children be delivered to them, powerful opposition arose in the ghetto. Despite this, Rumkowski, in concert with his Jewish ghetto police and the Germans, succeeded in kidnapping the children and sending them to their death.

By **July 1944**, the Lodz ghetto, with about 70,000 Jews, was the only one left in Poland. The reason for its existence was that its workshops supplied important products for the German war effort. Rumkowski was still at the head of the Judenrat and reigned powerfully and ruthlessly over the Jewish inmates. He even had money and stamps printed bearing his image.

In **August 1944**, with the Russians only about 70 miles from Lodz, the liquidation of the ghetto began. With all his power and pomp, Rumkowski ended up in a transport from Lodz to a killing center. Rumor had it that he was killed during the transport by his fellow Jews.

Between the extreme behaviors of the two Judenraete described above, fall the behaviors of the Judenraete in the many other ghettos. They are described in detail by M. Gilbert (see page 12, footnote 9) and I shall mention only a few of the larger ghettos. In **Kovno**, the capital of Lithuania, the head of the Judenrat was the physician **Johanan Elkes**.

He helped people leave the ghetto, and clandestinely supported the underground activities. Elkes negotiated with the Nazis openly and honorably; he never groveled, and knew how to press his point although his powers were clearly limited. On the other hand, the **Vilna** ghetto in Lithuania was headed by **Yakob Gens,** who cooperated with the Nazis more willingly, and actively assisted in the German murder actions. In the **Warsaw** ghetto, the chairman of the Jewish council, **Adam Czerniakow**, could not cope with the German demands, his conscience, and being a tool of the Germans and a witness to the suffering of his people. On **July 23, 1942**, he committed suicide.

Although the spectrum of behavior of the Judenraete varied widely, the final fate of all ghettos was the same—total liquidation and annihilation. Nevertheless, how they behaved before they were murdered is, I believe, an important moral issue.

The situation in Poland; relations between Jews and the Gentile-Polish population

Poland occupies a particular place in the history of the Holocaust. Half of the Jews murdered during the Nazi era were Polish, and most of the actual killing occurred in concentration camps built in territories taken from Poland. Of course, there were also significant sites of slaughter elsewhere; for example, the killing fields in Transnistria, Romania, and the shooting pits in Lithuania and the Ukraine.

Polish Gentiles in the early decades of the 20th century were strongly anti-Semitic, more so even than their German neighbors. During the 1939 German and Russian occupation of Poland, many Polish Gentiles were killed alongside Polish Jews. One may think that the shared hardship would have drawn the two peoples together, but the opposite happened. The division of Poland between Germany and the Soviets exacerbated Polish anti-Semitism. There were several reasons for this.

Many Poles, especially the wealthy, staunch nationalists and devout Catholics, considered Soviet rule the worst tragedy that could befall them. Many Polish Gentiles considered the German occupation preferable over the Russian occupation, and fled in the fall of 1939 to the parts of Poland under German control. The Polish Jews, in contrast to their Gentile neighbors, regarded Soviet rule as a lesser evil than Nazi domination, and fled to the east. The Polish Gentiles resented the fact that the Jews cast their lot with the Soviets and considered it a betrayal. Furthermore, Polish anti-Semitism was fueled by envy of the perceived Jewish wealth. Now the German aggression provided them with a chance to grab Jewish property. Thus, Polish Gentiles, unlike their Italian, Danish, or Bulgarian counterparts, did not obstruct Nazi plans to expropriate Jewish property and eventually annihilate the Jews. They became willing collaborators, and, in some cases, even initiators of atrocities.

A case in point was the massacre of Jews in the Polish town of **Jedwabne, in July 1941**. Half the residents of the town, the Polish Gentiles, murdered the other half—more than 1,500 Jews. It was the Poles, not the Germans, that initiated the slaughter.

Nevertheless, there were exceptions to the general anti-Semitic behavior of the Poles. Many accounts show Poles who risked their lives to save Jews. As a matter of fact, of all the countries of Europe, Poland has the largest number of Gentiles recognized by Yad Vashem for heroism towards Jews. An important example of Polish rescue efforts is the organization known as **Zegata**. It provided aid, food, and medication to Jews all over Poland. Its work is credited with saving the lives of 40–50,000 Jews.

1940–1941. Exporting war and terror

The previous section described the first year of the war as a period of Nazi experiments in conquest, persecution and mass killings. During the period described in this section, most of Europe was brought under Nazi control. Horrendous as the atrocities were during the 1939–1940 period, the territorial expansion of Nazi Germany during the 1940–1941 period extended their projects of racial purification, brutality, and murder.

The conquest of the north and west of Europe

Hitler's plan was to conquer Western Europe first, and then move against the Soviet Union in the east, where, in the eyes of the Germans, the racially inferior Slavs would be easily conquered by members of the master race. But before attacking the two strongest western nations, France and Britain, Hitler attacked the weaker nations in the north and west.

In **April 1940**, German forces entered **Denmark,** and that small nation surrendered without a struggle. The Germans then moved on to **Norway**, where they had to fight their way in, but by **June 1940**, they had defeated the Norwegians too. These conquests were of strategic importance for the Germans, who needed to secure the supply route of Swedish iron. They also wanted to secure Scandinavian naval bases from which to attack the British with submarines.

In **May 1940**, just a month after the offensive against Denmark and Norway, German forces invaded and conquered the neutral nations of the **Netherlands**, **Belgium**, and **Luxembourg**. Here, too, victory was swift. On **May 14, 1940**, the Luftwaffe introduced a new kind of warfare: They bombed the city of Rotterdam, killing many civilians, in an attempt to terrorize the Dutch into surrender. Within a few years, the Germans would reap what they had sown, when their own cities were destroyed from the air.

German conquest of France

In **May 1940**, German troops entered **France** through Belgium from two directions, the north and also the south. The French had concentrated their forces in the north and were unprepared for a German attack through the forest of Ardennes in southern Belgium. By **May 20**, the Germans broke through to the coast of the English Channel, thereby cutting the Anglo-French troops in two.

The Anglo-French army concentrated its forces in the French seaport of **Dunkirk,** which the German army approached and encircled. The German army could have wiped out the Allied forces at Dunkirk, but, in spite of the German generals pleading to attack, Hitler refused to give the order. This was one of the grave mistakes Hitler made during the war. As a consequence, the Allies managed to evacuate some 340,000 of their soldiers and save their army.

On **June 14, 1940**, German troops marched triumphantly into Paris. Unlike the Dutch, Norwegian, and Czechoslovak governments, the French government did not go into exile. Instead, they signed an Armistice Agreement under which France was divided into two parts: a zone occupied by Germany, and an unoccupied southern zone known as **Vichy France**. The head of the Vichy state was **Marshal Henri Pétain** (1856–1951), a hero of World War I, an old man by 1940. His Prime Minister was **Pierre Laval** (1883–1945). These two men would become symbols of French collaboration with Nazi Germany. Some of the French, however, refused to accept defeat. Among those was **General Charles de Gaulle** (1890–1970), who escaped to London and became the leader of the free French forces.

The fall of France was a catastrophe not only for French Jews but also for Jews from other parts of Europe who had taken refuge in France. They now came into the hands of the Germans and their new French partners. Among them was a young boy, Saul Friedländer, born in Prague in 1933, mentioned in the introduction of this chapter. Saul's parents perished in a concentration camp but he survived, emigrated to Israel, and became one of the leading authorities on the Holocaust.

The Battle of Britain

With the fall of France, **Britain** remained the only Western European country to be able to fight Germany. It became the last refuge for people fleeing Nazi Germany.

After the conquest of France, Hitler proceeded with plans for landing in Britain. It had the code name Operation Sea Lion. Its first goal was to destroy the Royal Air Force (RAF) and control the skies, considered by Hitler a prerequisite for a successful invasion of Britain. In **August 1940,** the Luftwaffe began attacks on British air and naval installations. For the next two months hundreds of planes fought in the skies over Britain. The Germans, however, could not gain the mastery they expected. On **September 15, 1940**, the RAF shot down 60 aircraft, and two days later, Hitler postponed the invasion "until further notice." It was Germany's first military failure of the war. Hitler's intention was to return to the battle of Britain after conquering the Soviet Union. (For more details see pages 54–55.)

The war during the months of **August** and **September 1940** became known as the **Battle of Britain**. It was a very hard time for the British population. The German bombings took a heavy toll on civilian life and property, but British morale remained firm. This was in no small part due to **Winston Churchill,** who succeeded the "appeaser," Prime Minister Neville Chamberlain. Churchill's rousing words helped strengthen and inspire British determination and morale. Here are a couple of examples from his speeches:

"The Battle of Britain is about to begin. Upon this battle depends the survival of Christian civilization. If we fail, then all we have known and cared for will sink into the abyss of a new Dark Age."

".... We shall fight on the beaches, we shall fight on the landing grounds, we shall fight in the fields and in the streets, we shall fight in the hills; we shall never surrender ..."

One can't help but wonder how world events would have evolved had Churchill been Prime Minister in 1938 during the Munich crisis.

The positions and allegiances of the other nations in Europe

No nation in Europe remained untouched by the war. Even the countries that remained neutral, most notably Switzerland, Sweden, Spain, Portugal, and Turkey played different roles during the war. Some profited considerably from the war. **Swiss banks** grew rich on stolen gold sent there by German authorities, and from deposits from German Jews who perished in the Holocaust. **Sweden** profited from massive deliveries of iron ore to Germany. **Spain, Portugal**, and **Turkey** provided escape routes for victims of German persecution. (In **April 1941,** I escaped from Slovakia to Palestine via Turkey.) **Switzerland**, which could have saved a large number of Jews, turned many refugees away.

In **1940,** Germany entered into the **Three-Power Pact** with Italy and Japan, and in **1941, Hungary, Slovakia, Bulgaria,** and **Croatia** joined the pact. All of these nations hoped to expand their territories with German and Italian help.

Soviet assault on Finland and the Baltic states

Stalin used the protective cover of German conquests in Europe to pick up spoils of his own. In **November 1939**, the Soviets invaded **Finland** in the hope of overwhelming the 3.5 million Finns in rapid Blitzkrieg style. But the Finns mounted a heroic resistance and held out until **March 1940**, when they were forced to sign a peace treaty and cede territory to the Soviet Union.

The difficulty that the mighty Soviet army had in subduing the small Finnish army undoubtedly boosted German confidence and resolve to attack the Soviet Union. I believe that the Finns deserve a lot of credit for the German miscalculation of Soviet might that ultimately led to Germany's defeat.

Germany attacks Yugoslavia and Greece

Before attacking the Soviet Union, Hitler and his generals considered it necessary to control the Balkan states to secure their southeastern flank and safeguard access to Romanian oil. This meant the conquest of **Yugoslavia** and **Greece**, as Romania, Bulgaria, and Hungary were already allied with Germany.

Yugoslavia's government had also been friendly to Germany until **March 26, 1941,** when a popular uprising by the army installed an anti-German government. Hitler took it as a personal affront that this Balkan country should dare to defy him. His megalomania, that fatal disease of all conquerors, took hold, and he vowed to punish them ruthlessly.

On **April 6, 1941,** the Luftwaffe launched an air raid on Belgrade followed by an invasion of Yugoslavia. The Yugoslav army was surrounded, and it capitulated on **April 17, 1941.**[16] On Hitler's orders, the capital, Belgrade, was largely destroyed. However, this did not end the German fight in Yugoslavia. There was a tough partisan resistance under the leadership of Tito (Josip Broz, 1892–1980) that Germany had to deal with for the remainder of the war.

In Yugoslavia the German forces stooped to new depths of brutality, surpassing even their behavior in Poland. For every German killed by Yugoslav partisans, the German authorities ordered 100 of the local population shot. The Germans took their first victims from among the local Jewish and Gypsy population, but they also shot many Serbs, Greeks, and Bosnian Muslims. It is noteworthy that these atrocities were committed by the Wehrmacht (the regular soldiers in the German army) and not just by special SS units, as in Poland.

Greece had already been a target of aggression in 1940 by Hitler's Italian ally, Mussolini. But the Italian offensive bogged down until the Germans took over in the spring of 1941. In **April** and **May 1941,** German forces overran Greece. Here too the Germans brutally assaulted civilians in so-called "special actions," wiping out entire villages. It was in Greece that **Kurt Waldheim**, who later became president of Austria (1986–1992), was active as an SA officer in a German army unit that committed atrocities during World War II.

---

[16] When we passed through Romania in April 1941 on our way to Palestine, we saw a massive deployment of German troops.

George Feher

The Yugoslav and Greek campaigns forced Hitler to delay the assault on Russia by several weeks. This, as will be described later (see pages 57–58), had disastrous effects on the German army, which became bogged down during the severe Russian winter. The delay of the German offensive was probably the most catastrophic single decision in Hitler's career.

German assault on the Soviet Union

Hitler had always planned a war with the **Soviet Union**; it was only a question of when. He made his intentions clear already in "Mein Kampf." The Lebensraum he sought could only be found in the East. But what about the Hitler-Stalin non-aggression pact of 1939? Like all of Hitler's diplomatic agreements, it was made to be broken. It seems highly unlikely that by mid-1941 Hitler or his generals gave it a thought.

On **June 22, 1941,** German troops invaded the Soviet Union. The invasion was given the code name **Barbarossa**. The German assault on the Soviet Union was not a war of army against army: It was a war whose goal was total destruction of the Soviet Union, seizure of its land, and enslavement or killing of its people. The German army, flushed with successes in the West, had become accustomed to brutalities and killings and was no longer likely to protest the atrocities as it had done in 1939. An estimated **27 million Soviet citizens** were killed, the majority of them civilians.

Hitler and his generals expected the campaign against the Soviet Union to be quick and easy. They thought Slavs were stupid and incompetent, and believed the communist Soviet Union to be in the grip of Jews, whom they considered cowardly. These attitudes caused Hitler and his staff to make serious miscalculations.

The German invasion did not turn out as planned. The Soviets were better equipped and fought harder than the Germans had predicted. The German army was overextended and, anticipating a quick victory, was not prepared for the Russian winter. As mentioned before, the German army paid dearly for the delay in attacking the Soviet Union.

The annihilation of the Soviet population in the wake of the German invasion of the Soviet Union

From the beginning of the war with the Soviet Union, the German leadership (Hitler, Himmler, and Heydrich) made it clear that no mercy was to be shown to the local population, whether Jews, communists, or Russian prisoners of war. Hitler issued the infamous **Kommisarbefehl** (commissar's order) ordering that all political commissars attached to the Red Army are to be shot. It resembled Hitler's instructions of **August 1939** to annihilate the Polish leadership. The Nazis proceeded to implement their idea of "race and space" with unprecedented ruthlessness and brutality.

The most glaring sign of Germany's brutal style of warfare in **1941** was the use of special murder squads, called **Einsatzgruppen** (action groups). They included about 1,000 men each. Their instructions from Heydrich were to kill Jews and prominent communists. Many local people, Ukrainians, Latvians, and Bielorussians collaborated with the Einsatzguppen in their grisly work.

The mode of action of the Einsatzguppen was to round up the Jews in a given area and order them to dig large pits, which would be their own graves. At gunpoint they made the victims undress and stand at the edge of the pit. Then they shot them, and the victims fell directly into the pit.

The biggest slaughter carried out by the Einsatzgruppen was the massacre at **Babi Yar**, a ravine on the outskirts of the Ukrainian city of Kiev. In just two days in **September 1941**, German mobile killing units shot 30,000 Jews. Over the next months, the number of people killed at Babi Yar reached 100,000.

After the Babi Yar massacre, nine elderly Jews returned to Kiev and sat by the old synagogue. Nobody dared to approach or leave food or water for them, as this could mean immediate execution. One after another the Jews died until only two remained. A passerby went to the German sentry and suggested shooting the two old Jews instead of letting them starve to death. The guard thought for a moment and then shot them.

After the war the Soviets put up a monument to the victims of Babi Yar. The plaque dedicates the memorial to the 100,000 Soviet citizens killed there. Nowhere does it mention that most of those murdered were Jews.

The number of people killed by the mobile units is estimated at 2 million. Of these there were 1.3 million Jews, 250,000 Gypsies; the rest were mostly Russians. Such an enormous number of killings could not have been carried out without the cooperation of the soldiers of the Wehrmacht. The official justification offered to them was that it was a necessary part of the German struggle against partisans and enemies of the Reich. Perhaps these explanations helped men live with themselves. Conformity, no doubt, contributed to the willingness to kill. Everybody was doing it, so people were hesitant to stand out by refusing to kill. It should be pointed out, however, that the few who refused to participate in the killings were not punished and were transferred to other duties. Defense attorneys of Germans accused of war crimes committed during World War II have looked hard for a case of a German punished for refusing to kill. Such a case would support the claim that their clients were forced to kill. But no one ever found an example of a German punished for refusing to kill. This supports Goldhagen's contention that ordinary Germans were Hitler's willing executioners.[17]

By the end of 1941, the intent of the Nazi regime was made explicit and public. On **November 16, 1941**, Goebbels published an article, "The Jews are Guilty," which was disseminated all over Germany. It provided one of the clearest communications to the German people that Jews were going to be exterminated.

On **November 28, 1941**, Hitler met with the **Grand Mufti of Jerusalem** and promised that no Jews would be allowed to emigrate to Palestine, and declared that his objective in the Middle East after the war will be the annihilation of Jews living now under British protection in Arab lands.

1942–1943. The peak years of killing

With each successive year of war, human suffering tends to increase. This certainly was true for World War II. By the end of 1942, the Germans were heading into their fourth year of war. Their victories helped to make their bereavement and hardship tolerable. However, for the people they conquered, German occupation practices produced an ever-escalating reign of terror and demoralization. The more Hitler's empire extended its reach, the more its forces sought to destroy those it deemed enemies—above all, the Jews. For this reason, 1942 and 1943, the years when German power in Europe reached its height, were

---

[17] D.J. Goldhagen, "Hitler's Willing Executioners," Alfred A. Knopf Inc., 1996.

also the peak years of killing. At the beginning of 1942, 75% of the six million Jews that would be murdered were still alive. A year later, that number had dropped to 25%.

The Wannsee Conference: The blueprint for the "Final Solution" is officially ratified

By the end of 1941, the German leadership concluded that mass shootings were not the most efficient way to carry out their so-called "Final Solution." Led by SS **General Reinhard Heydrich**, Chief of the Security Police, top German officials met on **January 20, 1942**, in Wannsee, a suburb of Berlin, to discuss, coordinate, and streamline the annihilation of the Jews.

The 15 participants included high officials from the Foreign Office, representatives of the SS, Einsatzgruppen, Nazi Party headquarters, Justice Ministry, and Hans Frank, head of the General Government of Poland. The meeting was chaired by Heydrich. His deputy, **Eichmann**, wrote the final report in which it was made clear that all the Jews of Europe were to be annihilated.

At the conference, the method of killing was discussed. Killing centers with gas chambers emerged as the method of choice. At the same time, the previous methods of killing by shooting, starvation, overwork, abuse, and disease were to continue. The leadership of the annihilation of the Jews, the "Final Solution," was assigned to the SS. Its hierarchical order of leadership was Himmler, Heydrich, and Eichmann.

At the Wannsee Conference, the genocide[18] received an official stamp of approval with a blueprint for how to proceed. The unanimity of the various agencies and leaders of the Reich should be noted. Hitler did not cross the line to genocide alone.

The main killing centers: Chelmno, Belzec, Sobibor, Treblinka, Majdanek, Auschwitz-Birkenau

Chelmno was a small village 40 miles from Lodz, in the part of Poland annexed to the Reich (see map). Jews were brought by train to Chelmno where they were addressed by an SS man. He told them that they were to be sent to Germany, but first had to take a shower. They were handed a towel and soap and about 90 people were forced into a specially equipped van, with pipes from the diesel exhaust leading into the back of the van. The van drove slowly for a few miles into a forest while the people inside were asphyxiated. At the forest, the door was opened and the people dumped out. Guards shot anybody that was still alive. The Germans kept a few Jews around to bury the bodies. They were known as the **Sonderkommando** (special unit). Members of the Sonderkommando did not last very long. After a few weeks they were shot and replaced by new people.

From **December 1941** to the **end of 1942**, 140,000 Jews and 5,000 Gypsies were murdered in the gas vans. In late 1942, this killing center was closed as more efficient ones emerged.

Belzec, located near Lublin, was built on the initiative of the local district SS leader **Globočnik**. It is noteworthy that the genocide measures occurred initially without an explicit order from the top.[19] Of course, Hitler's rhetoric provided the justification for their actions, assuring the perpetrators that murder was appropriate.

---

[18] The word "genocide" is derived from the Greek *genos* (tribe, race), and the Latin *cide* (killing, as in homicide).

[19] Eastern Galicia offers a similar picture of regional initiative. On **October 12, 1941**, the local SS leader **Fritz Katzmann** embarked on a huge killing program of Jews without having received orders from the High Command. Tens of thousands of Jews were murdered during that action.

Belzec began operation in **March 1942**. It had a fixed installation for gassing that used diesel fuel. By the time the camp was closed in the spring of 1943, some 600,000 Jews had been murdered there.

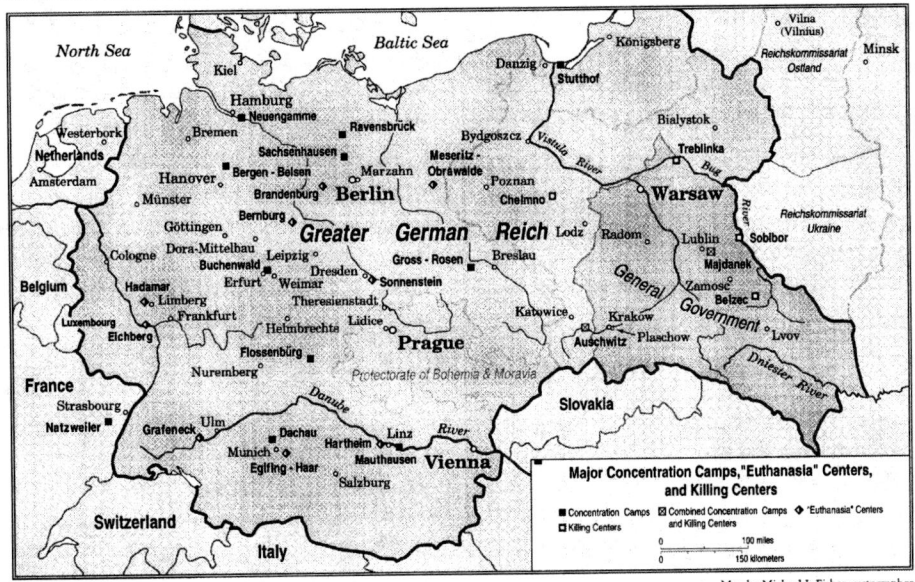

Map of the major concentration camps.

Map by Michael J. Fisher, cartographer

An account of the gassing at Belzec comes from an unusual source: an SS man named **Kurt Gershen**. Gershen had some training in sanitation and medical matters, and received the post of chief disinfection officer at Belzec. Horrified by what he saw, he tried to get the word out about the German mass murder of Jews. He told the story to a Swedish diplomat, and went to the papal nuncio in Berlin to pass the news to the pope. But there was little response from them. They probably could not grasp what must have seemed to them the ravings of a madman. At the end of the war, Gershen was captured by the French and charged with war crimes. He died in prison.

Sobibor was constructed solely for killing. Its first commandant was the Austrian **Franz Stangl**. It operated between **April 1942** and **October 1943**. During that period, 250,000 Jews, mostly from eastern Poland but also from other European countries, were killed.

In **October 1943** there was an uprising at Sobibor by its inmates who staged a mass escape. Most were recaptured, but a few survived the war.

Treblinka, located 80 miles from Warsaw, was also built solely as a killing center. It had a fake railway station: a façade to create a semblance of normalcy so that people would not suspect they were about to be killed. Treblinka began operations in **July 1942,** and became the grave of a staggering number of Jews, 300,000 of them from Warsaw and the rest from all over central Poland, Germany, Austria, Czechoslovakia, and Greece. In all, close to a million Jews were murdered at Treblinka. In **August 1943**, Jewish workers at Treblinka revolted, after which German authorities shut the camp down.

Majdanek, a mile from the city of Lublin, combined a labor camp with a killing center. Originally built for Soviet POWs in July 1940, it was expanded in 1942 with the addition of gas chambers. Gassing, for the most part, was reserved for Jews. The SS men in

Majdanek were known as sadists, who enjoyed killing children in front of their mothers. In just one day, **November 3, 1943**, guards at Majdanek mowed down 17,000 prisoners with machine guns, and forced the few left alive to bury the dead. In all, 125,000 Jews and 75,000 Gentiles were killed in the camp.

Auschwitz-Birkenau was the last camp established as a killing center, but it functioned the longest in that capacity, and became the most notorious of them. It was this camp that the West learned about in **July 1942** through the German industrialist Schulte. (See page 167.)

Auschwitz, like Belzec and Majdanek, started as a labor camp. In the **summer of 1941**, Himmler decided to transform it into a killing center and put **Rudolf Hoess** in charge of the task. The killing center became known as Auschwitz II, or Birkenau. In **September 1941**, they started experimenting with Zyklon B by gassing 900 Soviet POWs. By **March 1942**, Auschwitz-Birkenau became the destination of Jews rounded up for killing from Slovakia, France, and all over Europe.

The killing procedure at Auschwitz-Birkenau was similar to that elsewhere. German officials met the Jews at the ramp as they came off the train. There, the selection conducted by **Dr. Josef Mengele**, an SS doctor, took place. By a wave of hand, Mengele and his associates sorted those deemed useful for work from those fit only for killing. The people fit for work were rented out by the SS as slave laborers to nearby industrial plants, like the Buna Rubberworks of the IG Farben chemicals company. The employers did not worry about treating the slave laborers humanely and keeping them alive; there were always more where they came from.

The killing centers marked the culmination of the killing process. They were not separate from the Nazi German War for race and space, but were an integral part of it. In all, an estimated 3 million Jews were murdered in the six killing centers described above.

Other types of camps

Besides the killing centers, there were hundreds of concentration camps; the main ones are shown on the map. The most notorious of them were: **Bergen-Belsen, Buchenwald, Theresienstadt, Flossenbürg, Matthausen,** and **Ravensbrück** (for women). In these camps the inmates were not gassed, but died in great number due to starvation, beatings, back-braking labor, and diseases.

Some concentration camps and killing centers were combined with labor camps, in which those that were able to work had a better chance to survive. There were also pure labor camps, where most of the inmates were non-Jews from conquered nations. German authorities used them for work connected with the war effort. One example was **Dora-Mittelbau** near Göttingen where, in underground facilities, slave laborers built V-2 rockets. The Germans viewed slave labor as a renewable resource; their lives had no value. Death tolls in the camps were astronomical.

The structure and life in the camps

All concentration camps and killing centers shared a common theme: utter brutality and the dehumanization of the inmates. The top positions in the camps were taken by SS men, many of whom took pleasure in torture and killing. Prime examples are the notoriously sadistic Austrian **Amos Goetz**, commander of the **Plaschaw** labor camp, immortalized in the film "Schindler's List," and the SS guard at **Birkenau, Josef Schillinger**, whose favorite pastime was choking Jews to death while they were eating their meager meals. Lowlier guards commonly came from the population of the conquered countries, often providing an opportunity for one nationality to dominate over another. For example, the German-hired Ukrainians guarded Poles, and Croatians guarded Serbs, Gypsies, and Jews. Generally, women guards were overseeing women prisoners. Some of them, like some of the men guards, were notorious for their cruelty. Most infamous were **Irma Griese**, a guard at Auschwitz, and **Ilse Koch**, known as the "Bitch of Buchenwald," who had a fondness for lampshades made of tattooed human skin.

The inhumanity of the guards is illustrated by the following story:

An SS guard had one glass eye that was so perfectly made that it was indistinguishable from the real one. One day the guard challenged a group of inmates to tell him which was the real eye and which was the glass one. If the volunteer guessed right, he would get extra food rations; if he was wrong he would be shot. One person volunteered and without hesitation correctly pointed out the glass eye. The surprised guard asked what characteristic made him pick out the glass eye. "It is the one that shows a little humanity," answered the inmate.

The above story is probably apocryphal. Here is a real one:

Among the inmates in a camp was a father with his three sons. One of the sons succeeded in escaping. As punishment, the SS guard ordered the father to pick one of his two remaining sons and hang him. The father pleaded with the guard that he be shot instead. But the guard did not relent and threatened to shoot the father, his two sons, and 10 other inmates if he did not obey. The father had no choice. He closed his eyes, blindly picked one of his sons and put the noose around his neck. The next morning they found the father dead in the outhouse. He had hanged himself.

One of the most pernicious practices of the German authorities was to appoint prisoners, known as **kapos**, to oversee their fellow prisoners: Jews policing Jews. The Germans encouraged kapos in their brutality by rewarding them for it. This further demoralized and undermined the solidarity among the prisoners.

To reinforce divisions among prisoners, the Germans introduced a system of colored badges to identify various groups and establish a competitive and hierarchical structure within the camps. Highest in the hierarchy were the criminals; they wore a green triangle. Then came the communists, who wore red; Jehovah's Witnesses wore purple; homosexuals, pink; Gypsies, black; and Jews, yellow. Jews had the lowest status, and were taunted, not only by the guards, but also by the members of the other groups.

At Yad Vashem in Jerusalem one can see videos of stories told by Holocaust survivors. I spent an afternoon in 2005 listening to them—a terrible, heart-wrenching experience. Here is an example, a story showing how one man lost his humanity:

Jakob is an 85-year-old survivor of Auschwitz, where he and his father were inmates in 1944. Jakob's father was close to death from starvation. He kept, like many prisoners, a piece of bread under his pillow. Jakob knew that his father's end was near and the piece of bread would not save him. But he could not deprive his father of the piece of bread, for it would signal to his father his imminent death. One night, just before his father died, somebody stole the bread. The son understood then and there that to survive the camp, morality, dignity, and humanity had to be abandoned, and he decided henceforth to act accordingly. A situation soon arose where he could act on his resolution. One evening, Jakob found that his cap was missing. All inmates had to wear their caps during roll call; to not do so most likely meant he would be shot. In spite of knowing this, during the night Jakob stole a cap from another inmate. The following morning during roll call, the SS guard shouted: "You stinking Jew-pig in the last row, where is your cap?!" No answer. The guard went to the back row. A shot rang out. Jakob didn't turn around; he did not want to see the person he had killed. Jakob broke down at the end of the video. It was the first time in 60+ years that he had told the story that had haunted him all his life.

Primo Levi, the Italian writer who survived Auschwitz wrote: "To be human means more than to eat and breathe. It means having an identity, relationships with others, ties to a past and future, and a sense of decency and dignity." The camp took all that away. Physical abuses heaped on the prisoners, starvation and beating, together with the many humiliations and indignities they suffered, eroded their sense of humanity. In the camp, prisoners lost their names and became numbers. Emaciated, sick, shorn and forced to wear rags, they looked nothing like their former selves. Brutality and deprivation turned them against each other. Pain and despair made them forget the values they had once lived by. Very few managed to remain human under such inhuman circumstances—it was this destruction of people's humanity that was the most terrible crime of the Holocaust.

The Nazis were, of course, fully aware of the importance of destroying the humanity and identity of their victims, which made them passive and resigned, unwilling to revolt, and march compliantly to the gas chambers. This point is vividly illustrated by the following story: A famous dancer was recognized by the Nazi officer who directed incoming inmates in Auschwitz to the gas chambers. The SS officer asked the dancer to perform for them. The dancer complied with his request and started to dance, slowly bringing her performance to an ecstasy she hadn't experienced for a long time. At the end of the dance she approached the officer, pulled his gun from its holder and shot him dead. By becoming a dancer again, she had regained her identity and capacity to revolt.

I have written this section during the weeks preceding Passover, which celebrates the exodus of the Jews from Egypt. Throughout our history we recite on Passover night: "In every generation, a person must regard himself as though he came out of Egypt." Perhaps it might be more appropriate to say today: "In every generation, a person must regard himself as though he had survived the Holocaust."

Secrecy, denial, disbelief, self-interest; what was known, when, and by whom?

German authorities tried to keep the operation of the killing centers secret. But the killing operations were too big and they involved too many people to be kept secret. News of the atrocities leaked to the outside world. However, most of the time they surfaced as rumors and because of their monstrosity were, at the beginning at least, mostly disbelieved and ignored by the general population and future victims.

Jews had problems grasping the reality of genocide. The word wasn't even in use until after World War II. A case in point is the disbelief encountered by two young men, who escaped from Chelmno in the spring of 1942 and told about the gassing of Jews. The two escapees arrived at the small town of **Protrkow** in the Incorporated Territories, and told their stories. The leaders of the Jewish community met and decided that the excesses described by the two young men must be a local aberration. Who could imagine mass gassing as part of a systematic, government program to annihilate Jews? Such a thing had never happened before. Nazi planners exploited that inability to believe the worst.

George Klein,[20] the Nobel Prize-winning Jewish-Hungarian medical researcher at the Karolinska Institute in Stockholm, wrote about his experiences as a Jewish teenager in Hungary during the war. In **May 1944,** he worked in the offices of the Jewish Council in

---

[20] George Klein, "Pietà," pages 128–130, MIT Press, 1992.

Budapest and was privy to the **Auschwitz Report** prepared by **Rudolf Vrba**[21] and **Alfred Wetzler**, two Slovak inmates of Auschwitz who managed to escape on **April 7, 1944** (see page 88). The report outlined in detail the horrors and certain death that awaited the Hungarian Jews. Klein warned a dozen people, family and friends, but not one of them believed him, and they all boarded the trains that took them to their deaths. It shows the tremendous gap that exists between information and knowledge, and between knowing and believing. Klein hid and survived. His description of meeting his "savior" Vrba 50 years later is a gripping story.

The Allied governments knew much more about the German atrocities than they let on. Because of self-interest, they kept this information from the public until **December 1942**. Already in 1941, British codebreakers were reading dispatches describing murders of Jews and other civilians by Einsatzgruppen. In the summer and **autumn of 1942**, two detailed personal accounts of German mass killing were passed on to the Allies.

The German industrialist **Eduard Schulte** had met with Himmler in **July 1942**, and heard from him the plans for Auschwitz and the annihilation of the Jews. He was shocked, and immediately traveled to Switzerland and passed on this ominous information to the Swiss and Allied governments (see pages 167–169 for a detailed account). It was only half a year later, in mid-December, that the Allies made this information public.

The other, independent, information came from a member of the Polish underground, **Jan Karski**. In the **autumn of 1942**, Karski was charged with a mission. He was to carry a report to the Polish government in exile that described the situation in German-occupied Poland. Before Karski left Poland, the Jewish leaders wanted him to see what was happening to their people. They smuggled him, disguised as a guard, into the Jewish ghetto in Warsaw and the killing center in Belzec. Karski was devastated by what he saw. At Belzec he broke down and had to be taken out, vomiting.

Karski delivered his report and spoke personally with Churchill and President Roosevelt. But all of Karski's perseverance did not get the results he so desperately wanted. He could get no effective help for the Jews from any nation, government, or the church.

What prevented the Allies from broadcasting their knowledge about the slaughter of European Jews when it became known to them? Foremost, there was a war to be won, and the leaders of Britain and the United States focused on that goal, and didn't want to be distracted by other issues ("sideshows" as they called them). Disbelief was another important reason; many people could not fully grasp the unprecedented nature of the mass murders, and those who could were preoccupied with winning the war. I shall return to the inaction of the Allies in later sections (see Chapter 3).

Resistance to the Nazi regime

Resistance to the Nazi regime took on many forms, from individual dissents to protests by groups. Some were peaceful, others were militant. Some occurred in Germany, others in the occupied countries, and some were staged by the main victims—the Jews. But sadly, the level of resistance was small compared to the compliance, silence, and inaction of most.

---

[21] Vrba was a classmate of mine in the Slovak gymnasium in Bratislava (1935–1939). His name at that time was Walter Rosenberg.

Particularly deplorable was the lack of opposition to the Nazi atrocities by the **Roman Catholic Church**. Perhaps we shouldn't be surprised considering the behavior of the Church in the past. It is ironic how many deaths were committed throughout the centuries by the followers of Jesus, who preached the gospel of love. During the Holocaust the Church committed the evil of inaction by being mostly silent. And that includes the Pope, Pius XII. Moreover, their inaction during the Nazi regime was followed by a pro-Nazi action after Germany's defeat: The Vatican helped many Nazi war criminals evade justice by facilitating their escape abroad, many of them to South America and to the Middle East.

Among **individual dissenters** we must count the thousands of people who risked their lives to save Jews. The actions of a selected few are described in detail in the section on the Righteous Among the Nations (pages 166–177). Their actions spoke louder than any verbal dissent.

The story of one person who belatedly realized that "virtue is not simply refraining from sin; it requires action," is that of **Pastor Martin Niemöller** (1892–1984). Niemöller was a Navy officer who, during World War I, became one of Germany's most successful submarine commanders. After the war he decided to study theology, and was ordained as a Lutheran pastor in 1924. Early on he became a staunch supporter of Hitler and the Nazi Party, and remained so after Hitler's rise to power. He did, however, oppose Hitler's religious policies. He was particularly concerned by Hitler's order that converted Jews should not be considered Christians.

In the autumn of 1934, Niemöller joined other Protestant churchmen, like **Karl Barth, Dietrich Bonhoeffer,** and **Hermann Maas,** to form the **Conference Church** that opposed the Nazification of German Protestant churches. Niemöller, however, remained a member of the Nazi party, in contrast, for example, to Maas, who unequivocally opposed every form of anti-Semitism and persecution, and who was later accorded the title Righteous Among the Nations by Yad Vashem in Jerusalem. Ironically, Maas has been mostly forgotten while Niemöller, in his rather limited opposition to Hitler, is remembered as a symbol of resistance.

Niemöller openly spoke out against the arrest of members of his Church. In 1937, he was himself arrested, and spent from 1937 until the end of the war in the concentration camps of Sachsenhausen and later Dachau.

After the war, Niemöller expressed regrets that he had not done enough to help the victims of the Nazi regime. He was instrumental in drafting the **Stuttgart Confession of Guilt**, in which the German Protestant churches formally accepted their complicity in allowing the suffering caused by Hitler's reign.

Niemöller wrote the following memorable lines in 1945:

"First they came for the communists, and I didn't speak up, because I wasn't a communist.

Then they came for the Jews, and I didn't speak up, because I wasn't a Jew.

Then they came for the socialists, and I didn't speak up, because I wasn't a socialist.

Then they came for the trade unionists, and I didn't speak up because I wasn't a trade unionist.

Then they came for the Catholics, and I didn't speak up, because I wasn't a Catholic.

Then they came for me, and by that time there was no one left to speak up for me."

We would do well to heed Niemöller's words and to remember that the evil of inaction facilitates the evil of action.

It is often claimed, in defense of inaction, that any opposition to the all-powerful Nazi regime was futile and suicidal. I want to debunk that claim by describing two events in which **group opposition** not only remained unpunished, but actually produced results.

In **1939**, Hitler authorized a **euthanasia program** called T-4 (after the address of its headquarters in Berlin, Tiergartenstraße 4). It targeted institutionalized people with mental illnesses and disabilities. The victims were killed by lethal injection or gassing. The program's organizers tried to keep the killings secret, but there were too many people involved to conceal the actions.

News of the killings of handicapped people upset many Germans. Relatives of some of those murdered launched protests of various kinds. But the most concerted protest came from the Protestant and Catholic clergy in the summer of 1941. By then, about 75,000 people had been killed in the program in Germany alone. In **August 1941**, the Catholic Bishop of Münster, **August von Galen,** took a public stance against the killings. He gave a sermon condemning the killings as a crime against humanity. Galen's sermon was reprinted in secret newsletters, hand-copied, distributed all over Germany and even abroad. Nazi leaders were furious but did not dare take action against Galen. He was too well-known and too popular.

Late in **August 1941,** Hitler gave an order to halt the euthanasia program. It was a victory for the opposition, albeit somewhat hollow, as the T-4 killers had already made their quota.

The second incident involved a group of **German Gentile women** in Berlin who were married to German Jewish men. In **early 1943**, in preparation for Hitler's upcoming birthday in Berlin, Goebbels planned to remove the last Jews from the city. Police arrested these men and locked them in a building on the Rosenstrasse (street of roses). From there they were to be deported and killed.

In a spontaneous show of disobedience, the gentile wives of those German Jewish men gathered in the Rosenstrasse to protest the arrest of their husbands and demand their release. Sympathizers joined them, and soon there were several thousand people milling about. Hitler and Goebbels were furious, but they did not dare order police to open fire on the crowd of Germans. Instead they allowed the men to be released. Many of the internees of the Rosenstrasse survived the war.

The two events described show that opposition to the Nazi regime was possible, and raises the possibility that the Holocaust could have been avoided had the German population stood up against the perpetrators of the atrocities. It forces us again to consider Goldhagen's contention of "Hitler's willing executioners" (see page 30, footnote 17).

Armed resistance by Germans against the Third Reich or opposition to the core ideologies of the Nazi regime had become extremely difficult by the time World War II started. The time to oppose Nazism had been in the first phases of its rule. But Hitler had foreseen the dangers, and had made every effort to paralyze organizations, e.g., the communists that might have been the focal point of resistance. Nevertheless, after 1938 there arose a conspiracy against Hitler among some top army generals and disillusioned high-ranking Nazi officials. But it was only in the summer of 1944, when Germany was clearly losing the war, that they were emboldened to strike against Hitler in the unsuccessful assassination attempt of July 12. (For a detailed discussion see pages 45–50.)

There was an isolated incident of resistance in the winter of 1942 that was easily and brutally suppressed. A handful of Catholic students at the University of Munich formed an organization they called the **White Rose**. The key figures were a brother and sister, **Hans**

George Feher

and Sophie Scholl. The Scholls and their associates printed a series of leaflets decrying the crimes of the Third Reich. Nazism, they wrote in their last leaflet, had turned German youth into godless, shameless, unscrupulous murderers.

Police caught the Scholls along with three of their friends and one professor. They were tried and convicted for spreading defeatist rumors against the state. The Scholls were executed in **February 1943**. The university remained silent; there were no protests from the administration, faculty or students. After the war, the University of Munich named its main quadrangle after the Scholl siblings. The protest by the White Rose was immortalized in the book "Sophie Scholl and the White Rose," and the movie "Sophie Scholl: The Final Days."

In the territories under German control there were several **partisan resistance** groups, like the one in Yugoslavia that I mentioned earlier. But they made little impact on German might. More serious uprisings, like the one in autumn of 1944 in Slovakia (see page 88) and in Warsaw (see page 51), occurred only after the Germans were on the ropes.

Two **Polish undergrounds** were formed after the Germans defeated Poland in **September 1939**. One was the **AK** (*Armia Krajova*), the **Home Army**, a right-wing organization that took its orders from the Polish Government in Exile in London. This group was well-armed, disciplined, and carried out effective sabotage operations against the Germans. The attitude of the Home Army towards the Jewish resistance fighters was ambivalent at best, but mostly hostile. The reasons were: widespread anti-Semitism, their belief that most Jews were communists, and their low esteem for Jews as fighters. The second Polish underground was a communist group, the **AL** (*Armia Ludowa*), the **People's Army**. They were friendlier toward the Jewish fighters, and even collaborated with them. However, they were rather weak, poorly organized, and altogether not very effective.

Perhaps the most praised and promoted resistance during the war was that of the **French underground**. No doubt there were many acts of heroism carried out by its members. However, according to most historians, the extent and impact of the resistance was greatly exaggerated by the postwar French government in order to divert attention from the extensive collaboration of the French with Nazi Germany.

The defiance of an entire village to the Nazi-dominated Vichy regime, stands out as an example, showing that under courageous and dedicated leadership, resistance was possible and effective. It occurred in Le Chambon-sur-Lignon in southeast France, where the pastor André Trocmé urged his Protestant Huguenot congregation to take in Jewish refugees—the people of the Bible—and hide them from the authorities.[22] Under his leadership Le Chambon became a unique haven for refugees in Nazi-occupied France. When Trocmé was pressed by the Vichy regime to produce a list of Jews in town, he replied: "We do not know what a Jew is. We know only human beings."

In February 1943, Trocmé was arrested and sent to an internment camp near Limoges. He was pressed to sign a commitment to obey all government orders, which he refused to do. Nevertheless, he was released after four weeks. After the release he went underground, but continued to keep the rescue efforts running. It is estimated that between 1940 and 1944, when the war in France ended, between 3,500 and 5,000 refugees were saved from deportation. In January 1971, the Holocaust Memorial Center in Jerusalem, Yad Vashem, recognized André

---

[22] P.P. Hallie, "Lest Innocent Blood Be Shed: The Story of Le Chambon and How Goodness Happened There," Harper & Row, 1979.

39

Trocmé and his wife Magda as Righteous Among the Nations. The rescue efforts at Chambon were made into a movie in 1989 by Pierre Sauvage, "Weapons of the Spirit."

One should note that there were enormous barriers against resistance. A most significant one was the Nazi policy of exacting reprisals. The Germans made entire communities suffer for acts of sabotage and assassinations, on a scale greatly out of proportion to the supposed offense. A case in point was the assassination of **Reinhard Heydrich**, Governor of the Protectorate of Bohemia and Moravia, in **June 1942,** by the Czech underground with the support of the British Special Operations Unit. The Germans responded with total destruction of the town of **Lidice**, near Prague, where they murdered all men as well as many women and children.

The extent of **Jewish resistance** is a topic of controversy, as I have previously mentioned. Some accuse Jews of passivity, and compare their behavior to "sheep led to the slaughterhouse." Others recall their heroism against all odds. I believe that the truth lies somewhere between these two extremes, with both scenarios taking place under different circumstances.

Jewish resistance occurred in many forms. All across German-occupied Europe Jews took to the woods, forming partisan groups to combat the Nazis. One group, led by the **Bielski brothers,** acquired legendary fame. The Bielskis came from Nowogrodek in Bielorussia, where the Germans murdered 4,000 Jews in **December 1941**, among them the parents of the four Bielski brothers. In **March 1942**, the brothers fled to the forest, and established an effective partisan fighting group led by one of them, Tuvia Bielski. By the end of the German occupation the Bielski brothers had assembled a group of 1,500 Jews in their forest camp.

Another resistance group was led by **Abba Kovner**, a 23-year-old poet and member of Hashomer Hatzair. Following the massacre of 10,000 Jews in the **Vilna ghetto** on **October 28, 1941**, Kovner was one of the first to grasp the significance of the massacre. He wrote a proclamation—the first call for an armed resistance. It read: "We will not be led like sheep to the slaughter. It is better to die fighting like free men than to live at the mercy of the murderers. Arise with your last breath!"

Kovner's appeal led to the creation of the first Jewish resistance organization in occupied Europe, the **FPO** (*Fereynegte Partisaner Organizatsye*), the **United Partisan Organization**. It brought together young Jews from the whole spectrum of political organizations, from the far right (the Betar) to the left (Hashomer Hatzair).

In the ghetto, Kovner built bombs, sneaking out through the city sewer tunnels to sabotage German outposts and blow up German trains. After the liquidation of the Vilna ghetto in **September 1943**, Kovner and his group escaped to the forest, where they joined other partisan groups. In 1944 they joined the Red Army in the liberation of Vilna. After the war, Abba Kovner immigrated to Israel and joined the kibbutz Ein Hachoresh.

The most known resistance took place in the Jewish **ghetto of Warsaw** in the spring of 1943. On **April 19, 1943**, the Germans decided to liquidate what was left of the ghetto. Two thousand Germans came, with armored vehicles, flamethrowers, heavy machine guns, and even aircraft. In the ghetto, the Jews had organized with about 500 fighters, under the leadership of **Mordechai Anielewics**. Armed only with gasoline bombs, hand grenades, one or two submachine guns and about ten rifles, they mounted a desperate armed resistance. They had prepared an elaborate system of bunkers and underground passages. Determined to make a stand, they held off the Germans for four weeks.

The SS dynamited and burned down buildings, and smoked out the Jews in the bunkers. The tenacity of the Jewish fighters was astounding, but, not surprisingly, the

Germans eventually gained the upper hand. The last stand of the uprising took place in a bunker on 18 Mila Street, where 120 of the remaining fighters gathered. The Germans injected poisonous gas into the bunker and killed the Jewish fighters, among them their leader Mordechai Anielewics.

The Warsaw ghetto uprising has become a symbol of heroism. It was the first, unprecedented, organized rebellion in an urban area against the Nazis in Europe. The date of the uprising, the 27th of Nissan, is marked in Israel as Holocaust and Heroism Day.

A few months after the Warsaw uprising, rebellions occurred in two concentration camps, **Treblinka** and **Sobibor**. In the summer and autumn of 1943, as the deportations to both camps were winding down, the relatively few Jewish working teams left alive understood that their own liquidation could not be far off. In Treblinka a revolt was organized under the leadership of **Marceli Galewski**, an engineer from Lodz, and master carpenter **Jacob Wiernick**. On **August 2, 1943**, the first shot was fired and the camp was set on fire. As chaos was spreading, hundreds of inmates succeeded in breaking through the fences and escaping. Although during the escape most of them were recaptured or killed, it is estimated that out of the 850 inmates living in the camp at the time of the uprising, 100 succeeded in escaping the German dragnet. Among them were Wiernick and Galewski; but Galewski was unable to go on, and committed suicide.

The uprising in Sobibor involved the rather unique cooperation of Jewish inmates and Soviet POWs. The operation was started by the camp's working Jews in early 1943. However, only in late September, when a young Jewish Red Army lieutenant, **Alexander Pecherski**, who had arrived with a group of Soviet POWs, joined the planning group, were concrete steps rapidly taken. On **October 14, 1943**, the group lured key SS members under fictitious pretexts to various workshops, where they killed them. The main gate was stormed, and more than 300 inmates succeeded in escaping into the surrounding forests. Pecherski and his group crossed the River Bug and joined the partisans.

The uprisings in Treblinka and Sobibor, coming after the Warsaw rebellion, caused a security scare in Berlin. Himmler was convinced that the murder of the remaining Jewish workers and inmates in other camps should be completed as rapidly as possible. He proceeded to implement under the idyllic code name Harvest Festival. Among the victims were 18,400 inmates in **Majdanek**, killed by the SS on **November 3, 1943**.

Hesitatingly, I conclude this section with a disturbing thought that must have crossed the mind of anybody that has thought about the Holocaust. Although the number of escapees in the two uprisings pales in comparison to the number murdered in the camps, it shows that, against all odds, uprisings against the mighty Nazi machinery had a chance of success. That no attempts at uprisings occurred during the height of the 1942–1943 exterminations leaves me in a distressed and troubled "what if …" state of mind.

The war goes on

While the killings in the camps continued with ever-greater brutality and extent, the German war machine kept grinding on. We shall look at three fronts—Stalingrad, North Africa, and Italy—in which Germany suffered its first major setbacks of the war (1942–1943). Germany's invincibility had finally been challenged.

The Battle of Stalingrad

In 1941, German successes on the Eastern Front fell short of a complete victory and destruction of the Soviet army. The German army was bogged down and stopped in its advance by the harsh Russian winter conditions. By mid-1942, the Germans renewed the offensive by launching a two-pronged attack. One entered the **Caucasus** with an eye on the oil fields, and the other moved toward **Stalingrad** (now called Volgograd) on the lower Volga River.

Hitler instructed **General von Paulus** to take Stalingrad, and Stalin ordered his army to defend the city at all costs. Fighting was extraordinarily fierce with staggering losses on both sides. At one stage the German situation became desperate, and von Paulus pleaded with Hitler to let him withdraw and save his forces. Hitler refused. Instead, he promoted von Paulus to Field Marshal pointing out that no German field marshal had ever capitulated. In **December 1942**, the Soviet army surrounded the Germans and on **January 31, 1943**, von Paulus capitulated. The Soviets took 91,000 German prisoners; there were hundreds of thousands dead on both sides. (For a detailed account, see page 60.)

The victory of the Red Army at Stalingrad marked a significant departure from the way the war had been going for Germany. Nevertheless, although Stalingrad was an important military and symbolic turning point, the outcome of the war was still far from a forgone conclusion. A month later, in **February 1943**, the Germans mounted a successful counteroffensive at the southern part of their Eastern Front.

One outcome of the German defeat at Stalingrad was a reassessment of the allegiance of the governments of Romania and Hungary toward Germany. Their armies had also suffered a large number of casualties at Stalingrad and were now looking for ways to get out of the war. Suddenly, partnership with Germany looked more like a liability than an advantage. As a consequence, Romanian and Hungarian leaders became less willing to turn over Jews to the Germans to be killed. Not that they became suddenly more humanitarian, but they realized that their treatment of Jews might play an important part, should they negotiate peace terms with the Allies. Thus, the German setback at Stalingrad had the unanticipated effect of prolonging and maybe even saving the lives of some Romanian and Hungarian Jews.

However, in territories occupied by Germany, the situation of the Jews post-Stalingrad became even more catastrophic. German bureaucrats, SS men, and guards who were involved in the killing of Jews, found a new reason to step up their efforts. For them it was clearly preferable to be in the camps overseeing mass murder of unarmed people than to face the Red Army on the Eastern Front. And so the killings continued unabated. By the **end of 1943**, few Jews remained alive in German-occupied Eastern Europe, most of them in hiding or fighting in partisan units.

The fighting in North Africa

Africa had been the focus of fascist Italian ambitions ever since 1935, when Mussolini's forces invaded Ethiopia. In **1940,** the Italians suffered severe setbacks in their fight against the Allies, and requested German help. Germany responded in **1941** by forming the **German Africa Corps** under the popular **General Erwin Rommel** (1891–1944), the "Desert Fox."

Rommel's successes in Africa during 1941 and 1942 were phenomenal. He captured all of North Africa and his armies came within a few hundred miles of the British Mandate of Palestine. Living at the time in Palestine, I remember our anxieties as we followed Rommel's advances. Hitler had promised the Grand Mufti of Jerusalem, Haj **Amin al-Husseini**, to drive the British out and slaughter the Jews in Palestine. Fortunately, the Germans were stopped before they could accomplish that grisly goal. Had they not, there would be no State of Israel today, nor would I be here to write this book.

In late **November 1942**, the British 8th Army, under **General Bernard Montgomery** (1887–1976), defeated Rommel's German-Italian forces at **El Alamein**. At the same time, the American and British landed 100,000 troops in Morocco and Tunisia under the command of **General Dwight Eisenhower**. Soon, Allied troops pushed the Axis forces back into Tunisia. In **May 1943**, the last Axis outpost in Africa fell to the Allies, who took 230,000 prisoners; about half of them were German. It represented the second major setback for Germany in 1943. (For a more detailed account, see pages 56–57.)

The fighting in Italy

In **July 1943**, Allied forces landed in **Sicily** and advanced northward through the Italian peninsula. The Italian fascist government, Germany's longest-standing partner, retreated to the north of Naples. After more than 21 years, Benito Mussolini's regime collapsed. In **July 1943**, the Italian king, **Victor Emanuel**, assumed supreme command, had Mussolini arrested, and formed a new Italian government under **Pietro Badoglio**. Germany had lost its ally.

The Germans took severe countermeasures. They occupied Rome, disarmed Italian soldiers and placed them in POW camps. By **December 1943**, the Germans had interned 725,000 Italian soldiers, and had sent 615,000 Italian men to Germany as forced laborers. The Germans managed to free Mussolini by using a special paratroop unit, and install him in a puppet state in northern Italy. Not until **April 1945** did the German forces in northern Italy capitulate. That month, Italian partisans killed Mussolini and his mistress as they tried to flee to Switzerland.

Events in Italy had devastating effects on Jews, not only in northern Italy but also in Yugoslavia, Albania, Greece, and France, countries in which the Germans had divided occupation duties with their Italian partners. Italians tended to be fairly mild occupiers compared to the Germans, especially when it came to genocide of Jews. In contrast to the leaders in Slovakia and Vichy France, who cooperated eagerly with the Germans, Italians had refused to turn over their Jews for killing. Now, with the Italians out of the way, the Germans were free to proceed with the annihilation of the Jews.

Germany's setbacks during 1943 sowed the seeds of their final defeat, described in the next section.

1944–1945. Killing frenzies in the wake of German defeat

If the Germans were to lose the war, Hitler once said, they would "bring down with them a world in flames." Hitler tried his utmost to keep that promise. At the beginning of 1944, many Germans still hoped to win the war; by the end of that year, few had such illusions.

The death throes of the Third Reich were deadly for the Jews. Even as defeat became more and more certain, mass murder continued in the ever-shrinking territories that Germany controlled. As the Germans abandoned killing centers and camps in areas they lost to Allied and Soviet advances, they sent the inmates that were still left alive on murderous treks known as **death marches**. (See page 51.) It seems that the final aspiration of the Nazis was that their defeat be accompanied by the maximum extent of carnage.

The Soviet advance

The Soviet army made rapid advances in 1944. In **June 1944**, on the third anniversary of the German attack, the Soviets launched a massive and successful offensive against the Germans. The German army of about 3 million men faced 6 million Red Army soldiers. In spite of the Red Army's superior manpower, the Soviets suffered a staggering death toll. Even at the end of 1944, the Germans were killing four Soviets for every casualty of their own. But the Soviets had a seemingly inexhaustible supply of replacements, and they prevailed. The German army was inexorably driven westwards.

Allied bombing of Germany

Allied raids on Germany peaked during 1944. American planes made some 750,000 sorties that year, and dropped 1.4 million tons of bombs on Germany. Germany's petroleum and chemical industries were hit hard and by early 1945, the flow of fuel and ammunition to the German front had almost stopped. Allied raids destroyed about 5 million dwellings and killed at least half a million civilians.[23]

Nevertheless, the German war machine demonstrated remarkable resiliency to the assaults from the air. German factories set new records for production of tanks and armaments. Their military output in 1944 was more than five times the country's 1939 level. This achievement was largely due to the organizational skill of **Albert Speer** (1905–1981), Hitler's minister of armament and war production. Speer used massive slave labor to accomplish the task. In 1939 there were about 300,000 forced laborers in Germany. By 1944 that number had skyrocketed to 7.5 million people, brought to Germany from the conquered territories. Speer was tried at Nüremberg, and served 20 years in prison. Unlike the other Nazi leaders, he was repentant and regretted his role in Germany's crimes.

D-Day: Allied landing in Normandy

On **June 6, 1944**, the western Allies landed in Normandy in northwestern France. **D-Day**, as it became known, was the greatest amphibian assault ever. Four thousand Allied ships landed 175,000 troops, after 10,000 aircraft dropped 10,000 tons of explosives on the German defenders of the French Coast.

By **July 1944**, after hard fighting and heavy casualties, Allied forces began to drive the Germans eastwards. On **August 25, 1944**, the Allies liberated Paris, and the following month, under the leadership of General Dwight Eisenhower, crossed the German border.

Hitler and Goebbels instructed the German press to blame the Jews for the war, and admonished the German people to fight the "aggressor" to the last man. They described for the German people their own version of what Allied victory would mean: "Jewish poison, Bolshevik slaughter and rape, capitalist exploitation, and Anglo-American imperialism." Hitler proclaimed: "Any people that allowed itself to be conquered is unworthy to wear the mantle of the master race."

In **September 1944**, Hitler added 1.5 million men to his army by extending the ages of mobilized men to be from 15 to 60 years. On **March 19, 1945**, Hitler gave what became

---

[23] When, in the 2006 war against Hezbollah, Israel *by mistake* dropped a bomb on a house in Lebanon that killed 50 civilians, there was an outcry throughout the world. Compare this with half a million *intentionally* killed civilians by the Allies. What hypocrisy!

known as the **Nero Order**. He instructed Germans fleeing before the advancing Allies to destroy everything and leave nothing to the enemy.

The conspiracy to eliminate Hitler: the assassination plot of July 20, 1944

The conspiracy to eliminate Hitler and the Nazi regime started in earnest in 1938, and culminated in the assassination plot to kill the Führer on July 20, 1944. During the years 1938–1944 the conspiracy saw peaks and troughs of activity depending on Hitler's successes and failures, and witnessed the vagaries of circumstances that could have easily changed history. I shall describe the events as they developed.[24]

The opposition to Hitler started with a number of high-ranking civilian officials who began their careers as enthusiastic supporters of Hitler, but became disillusioned by their Führer's policies. Among them was **Karl Freidrich Goerdeler**, who served as Price Controller under Hitler; he broke with the Nazis in 1936 over their frantic rearmament policies, and resigned. The light came a little later, in 1938, to the financial wizards **Johannes Popitz**, Prussian Minister of Finance, and **Dr. Schacht**, President of the Reichsbank. **Ulrich von Hassell**, who had been ambassador in Rome, was the foreign affairs advisor to the resistance leaders. There were a number of members of venerable German families that joined the resistance. Among them were: **Gunt Helmuth von Moltke**, great-grandson of the famous Field Marshall; **Ewald von Kleist**, a descendant of the great poet; **Pastor Dietrich Bonhoeffer**, a descendant of an eminent Protestant clergyman; and **Fabian von Schlabrendorff**. There were former trade union leaders, such as **Julius Leber**, **Jacob Kaiser** and **Wilhelm Leuschner**. Two Gestapo officials, **Arthur Nebe** and **Bernd Gisevins,** became valuable aides as the conspiracy evolved.

This group, whose members came from various backgrounds, formed a loose organization without a strong leader, and without a strategic plan for action. However, on one point they were clear: To topple Hitler, forces were needed that only the Army possessed. But their efforts to interest the army generals in the cause met initially with little success. Prior to 1938, the generals had little reason to oppose Hitler, since he supported their build-up of a strong army. It was only in May 1938, two months after the annexation of Austria, when Hitler issued a directive to the High Command to prepare plans to conquer Czechoslovakia by force if necessary, that the conspirators succeeded in enlisting the Army to their cause. The generals believed that Germany was not yet ready to wage a war and that Hitler was leading Germany to a ruinous end. Foremost among the opposition to the Führer's grandiose plans for aggression was **General Ludwig Beck**, Chief of the Army General Staff. Beck was a highly respected personality and became the leader of the conspiracy. Other high-ranking generals who joined the conspiracy were: **General Erwin von Witzleben,** who commanded the troops in Berlin; **General Erich Brockdorff-Ahlefeldt**, commander of the Potsdam garrison; and **General Erich Hoepner**, who commanded an armored division in the south of Berlin. **General Hans Oster**, in the Intelligence Bureau of the High Command, had the task of bridging the gulf between the military and civilian conspirators.

In **mid-summer of 1938,** Beck wrote a memorandum to Hitler urging him to call off preparations for war, and pointing out that Germany was defenseless in the West and would be overrun by the French, who had a treaty obliging them to defend Czechoslovakia. But his

---

[24] W. Shirer, "The Rise and Fall of the Third Reich," Simon & Schuster, 1959.

plea fell on deaf ears. On **August 4,** Beck called a **secret meeting of the generals** and laid out to them the situation. Although the generals agreed with him, no decisive action was taken, mainly because of lack of courage and equivocation on the part of **General von Brauchitsch**, Commander in Chief of the Army. On **August 15,** Hitler called a meeting of his top generals, and reiterated his determination to solve the Czech question by force. None of the generals dared to say a word opposing him.

Beck saw that he was defeated by the spinelessness of his fellow officers, and he **resigned on August 18, 1938**. He was succeeded by **Franz Holder,** who had served as Beck's deputy and shared his views. As the new Chief of the General Staff, he now became the **key figure in the plot** to overthrow the dictator of the Third Reich.

The plan of the plotters, developed toward the **end of August,** was to **seize Hitler** as soon as he issued orders to attack Czechoslovakia, and try him on charges that he tried to recklessly launch Germany into a war that they were bound to lose. The conspirators assumed that France and Britain would honor their pact with Czechoslovakia and declare war if Germany attacked. To ascertain whether this assumption was correct, and to strengthen the resolve of Britain and France to fight by apprising them of the plot against Hitler, the conspirators sent emissaries to London.

Thus, on **August 18, General Ewald von Kleist** was dispatched to **apprise the British Foreign Office of the situation,** and to urge them to issue a warning to Germany of the consequences of its planned aggression. But the British government did not act. Only **Winston Churchill enthusiastically supported** and encouraged the plotters, but he was still in the political wilderness, and not in the government. Additional emissaries sent on **August 21** and **September 2** were equally unsuccessful in swaying the British government. Finally, in a desperate effort to induce the British to stand firm, the plotters used the counselor of the German Foreign Office, **Theodor Kordt,** to **inform Chamberlain** that Hitler planned to attack Czechoslovakia on **October 1, 1938,** and that the Army was ready to strike against Hitler the moment the order to attack Czechoslovakia was given. Alas, he also failed to convince the great appeaser, Chamberlain, to stand firm. Instead, **Chamberlain** was contemplating desperate measures to meet Hitler's demands by **sacrificing Czechoslovakia**. In the meantime, the **French cabinet** was hopelessly **divided** on whether they should honor their obligation to Czechoslovakia.

On **September 15,** Chamberlain met Hitler at Berchtesgaden and informed him that, for the sake of peace, Britain and France were, in principle, ready to cede the Sudetenland to Germany. On their second meeting at Gothenburg on **September 2,** to discuss the details of the handover, Hitler demanded that the Sudetenland be occupied at once by the German army and all the Czechs be evicted without compensation, leaving behind their property, their industries, infrastructure and fortifications intact. Hitler clearly wanted to humiliate the Czechs and expose the spinelessness of the Western powers. When Chamberlain pointed out to Hitler that the Czechs would not accept these conditions, Hitler replied: "In that case we shall be at war."

As expected, the Czechs refused to accept Hitler's latest demand, and called for a general mobilization. Chamberlain, upon returning home, encountered for the first time strong opposition in the cabinet to yielding to Hitler; and the French finally saw the light and declared that they would honor their treaty with Czechoslovakia and come to its aid should Germany attack. Britain and France mobilized. **War seemed inevitable**.

For the generals, the time had come to carry out their plot to remove Hitler, and save the Fatherland from plunging into a war it was doomed to lose. They met at noon on **September 28** to discuss the final details of their **move against Hitler** when they heard the news that Chamberlain, Daladier, and Mussolini were coming to **Munich** to discuss the situation. Hitler, apparently, in the face of the mobilization in Britain, France, and Czechoslovakia, got cold feet and called for this final conference. This turn of events forced the generals to call off their plans to overthrow Hitler; they couldn't possibly proceed with it while negotiations were going on.

The agreement reached at Munich gave Hitler all he demanded. It allowed the German Army to march into the Sudetanland on **October 1, 1938**, as the Führer had always said it would. Chamberlain (and Daladier) had cut the ground from underneath the conspiring generals, and had saved Hitler and the Nazi regime. All the conspirators could do now was to wait for a new chance to present itself.

In the summer of 1939, the drums of war were sounding off again in Germany. This time it was Poland that Hitler planned to attack. On **August 14**, he called a meeting of the generals in which he laid out his plan to **attack Poland** by **September 1, 1939**. Nobody dared to speak up opposing the plan, not even General Holder who had been one of the ringleaders 11 months before in the plot to overthrow Hitler. Holder seemed to have been as keen as Hitler to smash Poland, and was not interested, at the moment, in getting rid of the dictator. General von Witzleben, who was to have led the uprising in Berlin against Hitler the year before, had been transferred and was in no position to act in Berlin. General Beck, Holder's predecessor as Chief of the Army General Staff and acknowledged leader of the conspiracy, wrote a letter to General Brauchitsch opposing the attack on Poland, but the Army Commander in Chief did not even acknowledge it. Brauchitsch had a long talk with Holder, who assured him that Hitler would never permit a World War and therefore there was no need at the moment to try to overthrow the Führer.

And what about the civilian faction of the conspiracy? Some of them—Goerdeler, von Moltke, and von Schlabrendorff—went to London to inform the British leaders that Hitler was planning to attack Poland at the end of August. The conspirators saw that the British leaders, including the appeaser Chamberlain, had changed their stance since the days of Munich, and were now committed to declaring war against Germany if it attacked Poland. But the conspirators did not act, although the conditions for action against the Führer had now been fulfilled. They seemed to have been paralyzed by Hitler's complete hold on Germany—the Army, the police, the government and the people. They couldn't think of anything they could do to undermine Hitler's grip on Germany.

Thus, no attempt was made by the conspirators to prevent Hitler from launching World War II by attacking Poland on **September 1, 1939**.

Towards the end of **September 1939,** having conquered Poland, Hitler decided to **attack the West**. This threw the Army High Command into a fit. The generals tried to convince the Führer that the Army, after the Polish campaign, needed time to be refitted and reorganized. In response, Hitler convoked the generals on **October 7, 1939**, and told them to prepare an **attack through Luxembourg, Belgium, and Holland,** to begin on **November 12**. The conspirators, convinced that such an action would be disastrous, once again came to life and started to discuss ways to remove Hitler.

General von Hammerstein, an implacable foe of Hitler, had been given a command in the West. He invited Hitler to visit his headquarters, with the intention to arrest him during the visit. But the Führer smelled a rat and declined the invitation.

Time was getting short. The plot had to be carried out before **November 12, 1939,** the planned date of attack; otherwise, the plotters feared that it would not be possible to get a decent peace agreement after Germany had violated Belgium and Holland. It is worth noting that the conspirators harbored no scruples about violating neutral countries, nor were they concerned with the immoralities and atrocities committed by the Nazi regime; their sole motivation was to save Germany from defeat, and assure a peace agreement which would allow a new Germany to flourish.

General Holder, Chief of the Army General Staff, was again a key figure of the plot, as he had been at the time of Munich. But he was hesitant and confused, and deferred to the Commander in Chief, General von Brauchitsch. Brauchitsch brought a memorandum to Hitler on **November 5, 1939,** pointing out the reasons why he and his **generals opposed an attack** in the West. But Hitler was adamant and furious, accusing Brauchitsch and the Army of being cowards who did not want to fight. Brauchitsch left the Chancellery in shock, a broken man. That was the end of the attempt to depose Hitler. It had failed as ignobly as the two preceding ones. Hitler postponed the attack in the West thirteen times; it was finally carried out in May 1940.

With **Hitler's successes** in the West in 1940, conquering Denmark, Norway, Belgium, Holland, and France, and his initial successes in June 1941 on the Russian front, the **conspiracy fell dormant.** However, when Hitler's army suffered severe **setbacks** in Russia during the **Winter of 1941–42,** and Rommel was retreating in North Africa, the **hopes** of the anti-Nazi conspirators were **ignited again.**

Several of the most renowned generals were blamed by Hitler for lost battles, and were summarily dismissed and publicly humiliated. The conspirators were now convinced that the Officer Corps would react, not only to the shabby treatment they had received, but also to the madness of their Supreme Commander leading them to the brink of disaster.

The plotters believed that, since the war was not yet lost, **an anti-Nazi regime could still get favorable peace terms,** which would leave Germany a major power with some of Hitler's gains—such as Austria, the Sudentenland and western Poland—untouched. One cannot help but feel suspicious of the constant **concern of the German resistance leaders on getting a favorable peace agreement** with the West, **and being so hesitant in getting rid of Hitler** until they got it. If they really considered Nazism to be such a monstrous evil as they contended, they would have tried to overthrow Hitler regardless of how the West might react.

In the **summer of 1941, General von Tresckow,** adjutant to Field Marshal Beck, fighting on the Russian front, **hatched a plan to seize Hitler** on **August 4,** during his trip from the airport to headquarters at the front. But the plotters were still amateurish and had not counted on the Führer's security arrangements. Surrounded by his bodyguards, Hitler declined to use one of the army's cars. It was at this time that the plotters came to the conclusion that the only way to get rid of Hitler was to kill him.

No serious attempts on Hitler's life were made in 1942. **In March 1943, von Tresckow** conceived a new plan he called **Operation Flash.** The plan was to **plant a bomb on the plane Hitler was scheduled to take on March 13, 1943,** returning from a visit to army headquarters in Smolensk. The plotters prepared an explosive package that resembled a couple of brandy bottles, and at dinner Tresckow asked Colonel Brandt, who was in charge of Hitler's party, whether he could take back a present of brandy to his good friend General Stieff. The unsuspecting Brandt said he would be glad to.

The parcel was handed to Brandt as he boarded the plane, with the timer of the bomb set at 30 minutes. The conspirators waited with pounding hearts for the great news to come over the airways. Alas, they waited in vain. After two hours, a routine announcement said that Hitler had landed at his headquarters in Rastenburg. The **detonator** mechanism **had clearly failed**. The plotters were deeply shocked. Not only because the assassination attempt had failed, but they feared the consequences that would follow the discovery of the bomb. That night Tresckow called up Colonel Brandt and told him that a mistake was made, and that he would arrive the next day and bring the really good brandy. That was done, and the bomb was never discovered. But another **plot to eliminate Hitler had failed**.

At the **end of 1943,** a young officer, lieutenant **Colonel von Stauffenberg, joined the anti-Nazi plotters**. Disillusioned about how Hitler conducted the war, in particular the battle of Stalingrad, he became convinced that the Führer must be eliminated, and he was willing to do the job. His dynamic personality, clarity of mind, and organizational talent infused new hope into the conspirators. Stauffenberg succeeded in having some of the **top generals join the plotters**. Among them were: **General Olbricht**; his chief, **General Wagner**, who was Quartermaster of the Army; **General Fellgiebel**, Chief of Signals; **General von Hase**, Chief of the Berlin command, who could furnish the troops to take over Berlin; and, to the surprise of the resistance leader, the popular **Field Marshall Rommel** made himself available to the resistance movement. Stauffenberg was **less successful** with **General Fromm** who commanded the Replacement Army in Berlin, and **Field Marshall Kluge**. They both blew hot and cold, and could not be definitely counted on.

Stauffenberg was involved with the training of the Replacement Army, and was periodically **summoned by Hitler,** who was keen to replace his losses in the East. Stauffenberg had several opportunities to plant a bomb during these meetings, but was waiting for Himmler and Goebbels to also be present. But time was getting short, with the impending Allied invasion in Normandy and the Russian advances in the East. It was therefore decided to **plant a bomb during the staff meeting** at Rastenburg on **July 20, 1944**, whether the number two and three men were present or not. Stauffenberg arrived at Rastenburg around noon, and sought out **General Fellgiebel**, head of communications of the High Command. He instructed him to flash the news of the bombing to the conspirators in Berlin so that action there could begin immediately, and then to disconnect all communications with the outside world. Stauffenberg then entered the conference room, took his place close to Colonel Brandt and Hitler, and **put his briefcase containing the bomb under the heavy wooden table**. The timer on the bomb was set at 10 minutes. While everybody was listening attentively to the report of General Hensinger on the perilous German position on the Russian front, **Stauffenberg sneaked out** and made his way to his car. He **witnessed the tremendous explosion** and was **convinced that everybody in the conference room must be dead** or dying. He raced to the airport where his plane was waiting, and took off.

Staufferberg's plane had no communication facilities and the two and a half hour flight must have seemed to him an eternity. He **arrived in Berlin at 3:45pm** and raced to the phone to call Olbricht. To his utter consternation, **he found out that nothing had been accomplished** during the first crucial hours. Although Olbricht did receive a phone call from Fellgiebel, the connection was bad and the conspirators **were not sure whether Hitler was dead**. Everyone was waiting for Stauffenberg to return.

Contrary to Stauffenberg's firm belief, which he imparted to the conspirators, **Hitler had not been killed**, nor seriously wounded. As survivors later testified, Brandt, irritated by the briefcase at his feet, had shoved it to the far end of the sturdy oak table. That maneuver had saved Hitler's life (but not Brandt's). But none of this was yet known in Berlin, as the communication with Rastenburg was still cut off.

Three precious, vital hours during which the Führer's headquarters had been shut off from the outside world, **had been lost**. The conspirators should have occupied the ministries, arrested the top Nazi officials, taken over the broadcasting stations, and flooded the airways with a proclamation of a new government. But none of this was done.

Stauffenberg tried to save the situation and **started to give orders,** which belatedly moved the conspirators to action (without orders a German officer seems lost—even on such a crucial day). A little after **4pm,** General von **Hase,** the Berliner Commandant, **ordered Major Remer,** Commander of the crack Guard Battalion, **to seal off the Ministries and the SS Security Main Office, and arrest the Propaganda Minister Goebbels**. He accomplished the first task by 5:30 pm, but failed in the second. Goebbels, confronted with an arrest, told Remer that Hitler was not dead. In fact, he placed a call to Rastenburg, and the **Führer** himself **talked to Remer, ordered him to fight the rebels,** and promoted him on the spot to Colonel. Remer obeyed, imparting a fateful blow to the plotters. At about the same time, **General Fromm,** Commander of the Home Front and a key figure in the conspiracy, **learned that Hitler was alive** and well. He immediately switched sides, with catastrophic results to the conspiracy.

By **8:30pm,** the **Nazi High Command sent out messages** from the Führer to all army units abroad. Field Marshall von Kluge, who was in France, had been on the verge of joining the conspiracy, but now **changed his mind**: Another key general was lost from the conspiracy.

Shortly after **9 pm,** the conspirators were struck dumb at **hearing on the radio** that the **Führer would broadcast to the German people** later that evening. Shortly afterward, the SS came to life and **arrested the ringleaders** of the plot. **The revolt was over**.

Hitler's revenge on the plotters was swift and cruel. There was a wild wave of **arrests,** followed by gruesome **torture,** humiliating **show trials,** and **death sentences** carried out by slow strangling while the victims were suspended by piano wires from meat-hooks brought from slaughter houses. The estimated **number of death sentences** carried out is **5,000**. A good many **army officers committed suicide**. Among them were generals **Beck, Tresckow, Stulpnagel,** the military governor of France, and two field marshalls: **Kluge** and **Rommel**. Rommel, being the most popular general in Germany, was not publicly implicated in the plot and was given the option to commit suicide (faked as a stroke) with the promise of a hero's state funeral. And that is what happened.

The **revolt of July 20, 1944, had failed because** of the inexplicable **mistakes** made by the leaders, the **weakness of character** of two key generals, **Fromm** and **Kluge,** the **blind obedience to authority**—so highly valued in German society that it prevented many officers from joining the revolt against Hitler, even when they strongly disagreed with his views and conduct—and the **bad luck** that Hitler survived the assassination attempt. And lastly, it failed because the **majority of the German people**, in spite of their suffering and imminent defeat, **still believed in Hitler** and saw him as the savior of their country.

I want to conclude this section by reiterating and emphasizing **a common misconception regarding the motives** of the conspirators. At first blush they seemed to be driven by the noble and heroic goal of ridding Germany of its tyrannical, barbaric, and inhumane regime. But on closer inspection, these were not the reasons for the resistance: it was, rather, **the fear of the defeat of the German Army,** and the desire of an honorable peace agreement with the Allies so that Germany could still play a dominant role in post-war Europe.

The Polish uprising in Warsaw

In **August 1944,** the underground non-communist Polish Home Army decided to liberate Warsaw from the Germans: Drawing on an armed force of about 25,000 people, the Home Army launched a large scale uprising, hoping that the Red Army, which was rapidly approaching Warsaw from the east, would help defeat the Germans. But the Red Army stopped at the east bank of the Vistula River and waited: Stalin preferred to let German forces wipe out the anti-communist elements in the city to clear the way for his own takeover. The overwhelming German forces crushed the revolt by **October 2, 1944.** On Hitler's order, Warsaw was leveled —totally destroyed. In the process, the Germans killed some 170,000 people. It was an act of revenge, unique even in the gory history of World War II that typified the killing frenzies of the last stages of Hitler's war.

Germany's allies and the Jews of Hungary

The year 1944 brought dramatic changes within the countries that had been partners in the German war effort. In **mid-August 1944,** Finland signed an armistice with the Soviet Union and withdrew from the war. By autumn, **1944,** the Soviets occupied Romania and Bulgaria. Both of these countries' governments signed armistice agreements with the Soviet Union and declared war on Germany.

Hungary, with its pre-war Jewish population of 750,000, played a special role in the Holocaust. I discuss the situation of the Hungarian Jews, and the valiant effort to save them by the Swedish diplomat Raoul Wallenberg, on pages 173–177. I shall briefly summarize here the fate of the Hungarian Jews.

Although Hungary was allied with Germany since the summer of 1941, the Hungarian leader, **Admiral Miklos Horthy,** successfully resisted handing over the Jews of Hungary to the Germans. In **March 1944,** German forces occupied Hungary, their ally, to prevent the Hungarian government from capitulating to the Allies. Horthy was kept on as Regent. Overnight, the situation of the Hungarian Jews changed. German and Hungarian collaborators worked together, under the supervision of Adolf Eichmann, to round up and deport a large proportion of Hungary's Jewish population to Auschwitz-Birkenau. Between May 15 and July 9, 1944, some 437,000 Hungarian Jews were deported. On Horthy's orders, all deportations were stopped after July 9. However, on **October 15, 1944,** Horthy's regime was overthrown, and Hitler installed a Hungarian fascist regime, headed by the Arrow Cross Party. Adolf Eichmann returned to Budapest and the deportations were resumed. Only about 125,000 Hungarian Jews survived the war.

The death marches

In the **fall of 1944,** as the Germans retreated on both the Eastern and Western Fronts, they began to evacuate many of the camps and killing centers from the territories they had occupied. They sent the inmates under guard, marching toward places farther from the ever-advancing front. The half-dead prisoners made their way through Polish, German, and Czech countrysides. Because of the large numbers killed and dying on the way, these treks came to be known as **death marches.** They continued right up until Germany's surrender on **May 8, 1945.** In all, an estimated 300,000 people died in the forced marches.

The collapse of the Third Reich

In **December 1944**, Germany attempted a final, desperate, onslaught in the West. It was called the Ardennes offensive or, by the Allies, the **Battle of the Bulge**. It failed, but only after it had cost many lives on both sides. By early **March 1945**, the German Western Front in the West had collapsed and the Allied forces were advancing in the north, center, and south. In the last six months of the war more German soldiers died than in the preceding four years. In 1940–1941, about 160,000 German soldiers died. In 1944 that number had increased to 600,000.

In the territories occupied by Germany the situation unraveled quickly. In **January 1945**, Hungary signed an armistice agreement with Moscow and declared war on Germany. **March 1945** brought a successful partisan offensive by Tito's forces in Yugoslavia. By **April 1945**, the Red Army was in Vienna, and German forces in Italy capitulated at the end of that month. In early May, Czechs revolted against German occupation in Prague.

Country	Pre-war Jewish Population	Estimated Murdered	% Killed
Austria	185,000	50,000	27
Belgium	66,000	25,000	38
Bohemia/Moravia	118,000	78,000	66
Bulgaria	50,000	0	0
Denmark	8,000	60	0.8
Estonia	4,500	2,000	45
Finland	2,000	7	0.4
France	350,000	77,000	22
Germany	565,000	142,000	25
Greece	75,000	65,000	87
Hungary	825,000	550,000	67
Italy	44,500	7,500	17
Latvia	91,500	70,000	77
Lithuania	168,000	140,000	83
Luxembourg	3,500	1,000	29
Netherlands	140,000	100,000	71
Norway	1,700	762	45
Poland	3,300,000	3,000,000	91
Romania	609,000	270,000	44
Slovakia	89,000	71,000	80
Soviet Union	3,020,000	1,000,000	33
Yugoslavia	78,000	60,000	77
Total:	**9,793,700**	**5,709,329**	

The estimated number of Jews murdered and the pre-war Jewish population in each country. Modified from: http://history1900s.about.com/library/holocaust/bldied.htm.

The end of the Nazi regime came in a disorderly, chaotic, and cowardly way. On **April 19, 1945**, Hitler finally realized the war was lost. Holed up in his Berlin bunker, he dictated his last will and political testament. Consistent until his end, he blamed the loss of the war on "international Jewry." He described the annihilation of the Jews of Europe as his greatest achievement. On **April 22, 1945**, Hitler fell into a depression. He could not bring himself to negotiate peace with the Allies, and decided that Göring was the man for the job. When Göring heard about it, he assumed he was to take over. Outraged by that presumption, Hitler denounced Göring as a traitor and had him arrested by the SS. A few days later, Hitler got word that Himmler toyed with the idea of arranging a separate peace with Britain. Infuriated, Hitler ordered the arrest of the SS leader as well. Himmler committed suicide after he was captured by the Allies, and Göring committed suicide in his prison cell after he was convicted and sentenced to death at the Nüremberg trials.

On **April 30, 1945**, Hitler committed suicide together with his wife Eva Braun, whom he had married the day before. Beside him was the loyal Goebbels, with his wife and their six children, dead by their own hands. On **May 8, 1945**, **Admiral Karl Doenitz** signed the document of unconditional surrender of Germany.

Thus ended "The Thousand Year Reich," after 12 years of Hitler's power and terror. The Nazi revolution that had promised a new awakening brought instead destruction, suffering and death of hitherto unknown proportions. The balance sheet is awesome: Of the 55 million who died in "Hitler's war," 4 million were Germans, with another million reported missing. An estimated 27 million Soviet citizens were dead, as well as 1.5 million Yugoslavs, 1 million Poles, and scores of other people from all over Europe. Close to 6 million Jews were murdered in Europe; their countries of origin are shown in the table on page 52. But these are mere statistics, horrendous numbers that are difficult to internalize. It is people like you and me that were murdered, not statistics. And behind each death lies a personal tragedy.

Hitler's mistakes that saved the world

In concluding the section on World War II, I want to discuss more fully the events that led to the defeat of Germany. In the initial phases of the war the Armies of the Third Reich seemed invincible and the situation for the Allies looked extremely grim. Hitler, through shrewd maneuvering, deceit, and daring aggression backed by a gigantic and efficient fighting force, had conquered the European continent by 1941: from the Arctic in the north, to North Africa in the south, and deep into Russia in the east. Britain, relatively weak and poorly armed at the beginning of the war, was standing alone, headed by a resolute and effective Prime Minister, **Winston Churchill**. In May 1940, Churchill had succeeded the naïve, weak, and appeasing **Neville Chamberlain,** who had contributed in no small measure to Hitler's early conquests (see page 17). How did it come about that in 1941–1942 the tide started to turn and the Third Reich began its downward slide until its final defeat in 1945? The downfall of the Third Reich can be traced to several strategic and tactical mistakes that Hitler made during the war. Some of them were merely damaging, others proved fatal. In the following pages I shall describe these mistakes as they occurred, in chronological order.[25] [26]

The missed opportunity to destroy a large part of the British Army at Dunkirk

Towards the **end of May 1940,** the German Army had conquered Belgium, had broken through the French defense lines, and had routed the British Expeditionary Forces as well as some French units, into a small area around the port of **Dunkirk** on the northern shores of France. The German Panzer tank divisions were heading toward Dunkirk, and threatened to encircle and destroy the Allied forces. In the midst of this evolving catastrophic defeat of the Allied forces, Hitler unexpectedly ordered a halt to the operation for several days. This enabled the British to **evacuate 338,000** men (mostly British troops) in hundreds of boats and ships, thereby saving a large part of the British Army to fight another day. It was called The Miracle at Dunkirk. The Germans had missed an opportunity to significantly degrade the fighting capabilities of the British Army.

Hitler's sudden order to stop the advance came as a complete surprise and shock to the German commanding generals and, although most of them were strongly opposed to it, they carried it out as the Führer demanded. What motivated Hitler to issue the order? Historians and the surviving German generals have debated this question for years. We know, for

---

[25] W.L. Shirer, "The Rise and Fall of the Third Reich," Simon and Schuster, 1959.

[26] B.H. Liddell Hart, "History of the Second World War," G.P. Putnam's Sons, 1970.

from the discourse with his surprised generals at headquarters that summer, the notes of which survived the war. He spoke with admiration of the British Empire, of the necessity of its existence, and of the civilization that Britain had brought into the world. Therefore, one possible argument is that Hitler wanted to make an honorable peace with Britain that acknowledged German dominance over the continent. By capturing the Allied forces at Dunkirk, the British might have felt that their honor had suffered a stain, which they must wipe out by continuing the fight. No doubt, the upcoming battle with the Soviet Union was already germinating in Hitler's mind, and a peace with Britain would free his forces in the West to be used in the fight against the Soviets. Another argument given was the haunting personal experience of Hitler during the First World War, when the German armored divisions were bogged down in the marshes of Flanders. Hitler did not want to repeat the calamity and jeopardize his Panzer divisions. And then **Field Marshall Göring** appeared at the crucial moment and reassured Hitler that his air force would accomplish the encirclement by closing the sea side of the pocket, destroying the enemy troops from the air, thereby preventing possible losses to Germany's armored forces. But he overestimated the effectiveness of the Luftwaffe, and they could not wipe out the British. We shall, of course, never know which of the arguments motivated Hitler to give the halt order, but what is clear is that it enabled the British Army to survive, regroup, and fight another day.

The Battle of Britain: Hitler's miscalculation and Göring's two tactical mistakes

After the fall of France at the end of May 1940, Hitler felt that the war in Europe was essentially won and victory over England was inevitable. He believed that the severe shortages of food caused by the siege, together with the bombing of the ports, storage depots, airfields, military installations, and civilian population, would break the will of the English people to resist, and force the government to capitulate. So confident was he, that on **June 15** he ordered a partial **demobilization of the army from 160 to 120 divisions,** and no serious consideration was given to an invasion. He clearly underestimated the resilience of Churchill and the British people. When Churchill persistently rebuffed all German peace proposals, Hitler belatedly ordered, on **July 16,** the preparation of a preliminary **plan for an invasion of England** "if necessary." He had missed the opportunity to strike after his conquest of France, when England was weak and demoralized after the debacle at Dunkirk. In the meantime, the British forces had time to reorganize and to regain their strength.

On **July 31, 1940,** Hitler set the date for an **invasion on September 15**[th], assuming that by that time the Luftwaffe would have complete air superiority over the Royal Air Force. The outcome of the Battle of Britain depended now on the ability of the RAF to withstand the assaults of the Luftwaffe.

August 12, 1940, brought the first great **battle in the skies**. Heavy damage was inflicted on British radar installations, but the Germans did not pursue the destruction of this vital asset of the RAF. On **August 15,** the **Luftwaffe suffered severe losses**—105 planes, against 34 for the RAF. At this rate, in spite of their numerical superiority, the Germans could not drive the RAF from the skies.

Now Göring made the first of his two tactical mistakes. The success of RAF Fighter Command against the numerically superior attacking forces was based on its use of a sophisticated network of radar stations, which was far superior to the German electronic devices. The British could follow the course of German aircraft from the moment they took off the ground in Western Europe. This enabled Fighter Command to know exactly where and when the aircraft could be attacked. But instead of continuing to destroy the British radar stations, which on August 12 had been so damaging, Göring decided on August 15, the day of his first major setback, to **abandon the targeting of radar** stations and instead concentrate exclusively on the destruction of the RAF planes. This enabled the British to repair the damaged radar stations and use them effectively throughout the Battle of Britain.

From **August 24 to September 6, 1940,** the Germans sent a thousand planes a day to try to destroy the RAF. Though the RAF fighters put up a valiant fight, the German preponderance in sheer numbers began to tell. The RAF lost 466 fighter planes during that period and, more importantly, it lost a quarter of its pilots. Exhaustion had set in among the remaining pilots. The **RAF was at a breaking point**. A few more weeks of this and Britain would have lost the defense of its skies. An invasion of England would have been the inevitable consequence.

And then, suddenly, Göring made his second tactical mistake. On September 7, the **Luftwaffe switched** from attacking the RAF **to massive night bombing of London** and other cities. Though great damage was inflicted onto the British cities, the **RAF fighters were reprieved** and able to recover their strength and morale.

What caused Göring to make the fateful decision to abandon his successful attacks on the RAF? Ironically, it was due to a minor navigational error made by his pilots who, on the night of **August 23,** dropped their bombs, by mistake, on London, and not on their intended military targets. The British retaliated and bombed Berlin the next evening and on following nights. This came as a great shock to the German people. To boost their morale, Hitler and Göring felt obliged to retaliate by bombing English cities.

The battle in the skies continued, with heavy losses incurred on both sides. But the RAF held its ground. In a conference on **September 14**, Hitler admitted that "the enemy recovers again and again and, in spite of the successes of the Luftwaffe, air superiority had not been achieved." He therefore **postponed the invasion indefinitely**. On **October 12, 1940,** the Nazi warlord admitted failure, and called off the invasion until spring of 1941—if then.

Thus, a small number of British fighter pilots had thwarted Hitler's invasion and had preserved England to conquer the continent at a later date. Hitler's failure to conquer Britain had far-reaching consequences, both by pinning down some of his forces in the West while fighting the Soviets in the East, and by preventing his conquest of British-dominated North Africa.

Hitler's failure to realize the importance of conquering Egypt and the Suez Canal; his meager support of Rommel in North Africa

After the defeat of the Italian army by the British in Libya, North Africa, in the spring of 1941, Hitler felt obliged to pull his muddling partner, Mussolini, off the hook (as he had done earlier in Greece). It was not part of a major strategic plan; it was merely meant to save his friend from further humiliation. He sent a light armored division and some Luftwaffe units to North Africa under the command of **General Erwin Rommel**, a dashing, resourceful, and brilliant tank officer. Rommel succeeded beyond all expectations, and in his early victories posed a severe threat to the British Army. But Hitler did not capitalize on the early victories and Rommel was ultimately defeated.

Here is how the events evolved: Rommel with his German Panzer division arrived in Libya (Cyrenaica) on the **last days of March 1941,** and initiated an aggressive campaign against the British. In 12 days he was a **few miles from the Egyptian border**. The British hold on the eastern Mediterranean, including Egypt and the Suez Canal, had suddenly become gravely endangered. **Hitler did not seem to fully realize what a blow it would be for the British** if they lost the Mediterranean. Others, of course, did. Churchill sent an urgent cable to president Roosevelt pleading for America to enter the war. The German High Command also saw the opportunities that seemed to have eluded Hitler. **Admiral Erich Raeder** appealed to Hitler to prepare a decisive offensive against Egypt and the Suez. In his words: "The conquest of North Africa would be more deadly to the British Empire than the capture of London." And Rommel pleaded for reinforcements to continue his advance. But the Führer was preoccupied with the upcoming Russian campaign and decided that **Russia must be eliminated first,** before expending more resources in the Mediterranean. Hitler did not appreciate the larger strategy of the situation, thereby forfeiting a victory in North Africa while the British were still very weak.

The following months saw an inconclusive series of skirmishes and battles. In **November–December 1941, the British** launched on **offensive** and pushed the Germans a few hundred miles west. But Rommel bounced back with his customary resilience, and by January recaptured half of the lost ground. At the **end of May 1942 he resumed his offensive** and forced the British army to retreat toward the Egyptian border. By the end of June, Rommel was deep inside Egypt at El Alamein, as he had been a year before, only **65 miles from Alexandria**. It seemed that nothing could now prevent Rommel from delivering a fatal blow to the British, and then sweep north to capture the great oil fields of the Middle East, and then to the Caucasus to meet the German army in Russia, which was advancing to that region. It was one of the darkest moments of the war for the Allies. But **Hitler**, as we have seen before, **still did not grasp the global potential** of the situation and did not send the exhausted Rommel the much needed supplies and reinforcements. All he did was award the daring warrior a field marshal's baton. Another opportunity, the last one, for a German victory in North Africa was lost.

Rommel resumed his **last offensive** at El Alamein on **August 31, 1942**. But the British had received, in the meantime, strong reinforcement under the leadership of a new very gifted commander, **General Bernard Montgomery,** who was able to repel the attackers. The Germans held out until **October 23, 1942**, when Montgomery **launched** an all-out **attack**. Rommel's situation was hopeless and he asked Hitler for permission to withdraw. But Hitler ordered Rommel to stand his ground and show his troops that "there is no other way but victory or death." Rommel tried to follow orders, but on **November 4**, at the risk of being court-martialed for disobedience, Rommel decided to **retreat to Tunis** and save what was left of his forces (10,000 men out of a total of 43,000). It heralded the end of what started out as such a promising campaign for Rommel to conquer North Africa.

On **November 8, 1942**, Allied troops, under the command of **General Eisenhower,** landed in western Africa, and four days later they had successfully advanced to Algiers. In response, Hitler and Mussolini ordered a quarter of a million German and Italian troops to seize Tunisia to prevent it from being captured by Eisenhower. Initially, the Axis forces were successful in defending Tunisia; but the two armies, the British advancing from the east and the US forces from the west, were able to **defeat the Axis** forces in the **spring of 1943**. Every German soldier and tank that had been rushed to Tunisia, as well as the remainder of

Rommel's men, were captured. Ironically, had Hitler sent a fraction of that force to Rommel earlier, the outcome of the war in North Africa would most likely have been quite different. Furthermore, the loss of such a large force greatly weakened Germany's ability to defend southern Europe, which facilitated the **invasion of Sicily** by the Allies on **July 13, 1943**.

The fateful delay in starting the war with Russia

Some historians argue that Hitler's great mistake was to open a second front in the East while, in the West, Britain remained unconquered. Others, on the other hand, point out that if Hitler had not made some tactical mistakes in the Russian campaign, he might have conquered Russia, and then, with his newly captured resources, turned again to the West to face the British. I want to describe some of these tactical mistakes in the next two sections.

The attack on Russia, code-named **Operation Barbarossa**, had been set for May 15, 1941. To avoid jeopardizing Barbarossa, Hitler needed to bring the Baltic states into his camp. He had no trouble with Hungary, Bulgaria, and Romania; but the **Yugoslavs were not as readily accommodating** as their neighbors. On **March 25**, the Yugoslav Premier and Foreign Minister surreptitiously met with Hitler and Ribbentrop in Vienna, where, under threats and promises of territorial gains, they signed up Yugoslavia to the Tripartite Pact (Germany/Italy/Japan). **On March 26, 1941,** after the Yugoslavs returned to Belgrade, their **government was toppled** by a popular uprising of their own armed forces (which were hostile to Germany). Thus, **the agreement** that had been made in Vienna **was annulled**.

The coup in Belgrade threw Hitler into a wild rage. He took it as a personal affront and, in his fury, made sudden decisions that would prove disastrous to the fortune of the Third Reich. He raged about the **revenge** he would take **on Yugoslavia**; he would raze Belgrade to the ground and destroy Yugoslavia militarily and as a nation. And then Hitler announced the most fateful decision of all: "The beginning of the **Barbarossa** operation has to **be postponed** by up to four weeks." This postponement of the attack on Russia in order that the Nazi warlord might vent his personal spite against a small Balkan country that had dared to defy him, was probably the most **catastrophic decision** in Hitler's career.

On **April 6, 1941**, the German army fell on Yugoslavia with all its might while Belgrade was razed to the ground by the Luftwaffe. On **April 17**, the **Yugoslav** army surrendered at Sarajevo. Hitler had attained his short-term objective, without realizing how costly his successful revenge would turn out to be.

On June 22, the day in 1812 that Napoleon had crossed the Niemen River on his way to Moscow, **Hitler's** armored, mechanized, and hitherto invincible **army** crossed the Niemen and **penetrated** swiftly **into Russia**. In most places along the borders the Russians were not even deployed for action, and were overrun before they could organize resistance. Within a few days, hundreds of Soviet planes were destroyed on the ground, while armies were encircled and hundreds of thousands of Russian prisoners were taken. But by the middle of July, the Russians began to put up a mounting resistance such as the Germans had never experienced before. In spite of this, the German army continued its advance, albeit considerably slowed down. **On October 3, 1942, Hitler proclaimed,** in a speech to the German people, the **collapse of the Soviet Union**: "I declare it today and I declare it without any hesitation."

By **mid-October,** the autumn rains commenced and the battlefield turned into a sea of mud. The great **German army**, moving on wheels, was **slowed down** to a crawl, and in places bogged down. Worse was to follow. Heavy snow came early that winter. By the beginning of November, sub-zero temperatures set in. Under these conditions the Germans had no chance against the Russians, who were far better equipped and trained in fighting in deep snow and sub-freezing temperatures. Any **hope of conquering Russia that winter was gone**. Belatedly, Hitler and the High Command realized that the three to four weeks they thought were needed for final victory had been lost in the revenge campaign against Yugoslavia.

Hitler's decision to fight on three fronts rather than concentrate on the battle of Moscow

Within three weeks of the opening of the campaign against Russia, the **German army was only 200 miles from Moscow**. In the north the Germans were moving rapidly through the Baltic states toward Leningrad. In the south they advanced toward Kiev, the capital of the Ukraine, the much-coveted breadbasket; and further on lay the Caucasus with its oil fields.

The German army was fighting on a thousand-mile over-stretched front, and its swift advance left the German fighter plane bases too far back to provide effective cover at the front. The Germans greatly underestimated the strength of the Russian colossus and its resolve to fight even when encircled. The Germans also encountered, for the first time and to their astonishment, the Russian T-34 tank that was so heavily armored that the shells of antitank guns bounced harmlessly off it.

At this point in time, **mid-July, 1941**, there arose the first great **controversy in the German High Command**. The issue was simple but fundamental. Should the central army, the most powerful of the three German armies, push on the 200 miles to Moscow, or should the thrust of all three armies proceed simultaneously? In other words: was Moscow the prize goal, or Leningrad, or the Ukraine and the Caucasus?

The army **High Command** was strongly **in favor** of concentrating all their efforts to **capture Moscow**. They pointed out to Hitler that besides the psychological value of capturing the enemy capital, Moscow was a vital source of armament production, and the center of Russian transportation and communication systems. But **Hitler**, the former corporal who was now their Supreme Commander, did not listen to their arguments and **overruled his generals**. He had his hungry eyes on the food belt and industrial areas of the Ukraine, and the Russian oil fields just beyond. Neither did he want to give up the capture of Leningrad in the north. To accomplish these aims, several divisions from the central army had to be detached and sent north and south. **Moscow can wait**. This, as General Staff Chief Holder noted in his diary, "was the greatest blunder of the Eastern campaign."

Thus, the central army, deprived of its Panzer divisions, was forced to cool its heels for two months, 200 miles from Moscow. Belatedly and reluctantly, Hitler gave the order on **September 5, 1941,** to **resume the drive on Moscow**. But it was not until October 2 that the divisions could be brought back to the central army, refitted and made ready for the assault.

In the **first half of October**, the German army succeeded in advancing **within 40 miles of Moscow**. But the autumn rains had begun and the **German army got bogged down** in the quagmire of mud. This was followed by heavy snow and sub-zero temperatures that caught the German army without adequate winter clothing, and with their mechanized equipment poorly functioning at the sub-freezing temperatures. In contrast, the Russian army was much better prepared for winter fighting, and possessed the indomitable will to fight to the last man. For the first time, signs of doubt and despair crept into the minds of the High Command and their troops, and the ghost of Napoleon's Grand Army began to haunt their dreams.

On **December 1, 1941,** the Germans launched a desperate **final all-out attack** on the heart of the Soviet Union. But **they stumbled** on steely resistance, and suffered a crushing defeat with enormous losses. For this winter, the German offensive was over. Moscow had not been taken, nor Leningrad, nor the oil fields of the Caucasus. And the main reason for this failure was the wrong decision Hitler had made in July. (See previous section.)

The Battle of Stalingrad; Hitler repeats his mistake of 1941 and pays dearly for his refusal to permit his army to retreat

After the defeat of the German army during the grim winter of 1941–42, the German troops were retreating step by step. But by spring of 1942, fresh troops were brought in and plans were made to **resume the offensive in the summer of 1942**. By now, Hitler realized that he could not destroy all of the Red armies simultaneously, and he decided to concentrate on taking Stalingrad on the Volga, and conquering the wheat fields in the south and the oil fields in the Caucasus.

In **mid-July 1942,** the **Germans** had advanced **close to Stalingrad** and Hitler had to make a decision: whether to attempt to capture it, or divert some of the troops in a quest to capture the oil fields in the Caucasus. Stalingrad, at that point, was relatively undefended and could have been easily captured, but Hitler could not resist the smell of oil and, against the strong advice of his commanders, ordered the **detachment of some divisions** to fight in the Caucasus. By the time Hitler realized his mistake and brought the troops back from the Caucasus to Stalingrad a fortnight later, the Russians had reinforced the defenses of the city. **Hitler had repeated the mistake** he had made a year earlier in the battle for Moscow.

On **July 28**, one of the mobile spearheads reached the western bend of the Volga at Stalingrad. But it took another three weeks to overcome the stubborn Russian resistance to establish a bridgehead across the river. On **August 23,** the Germans began the final stage of their **advance on the city**. Attacks followed attacks, but each one was checked by the Russians. To Hitler, the capture of Stalingrad had become an obsession, a question of personal pride. It hypnotized him into a state in which he lost sight of strategy. (Perhaps his obsession was fueled by the fact that the city bore the name of his arch-enemy.)

The chief of the army staff, **Holder, urged Hitler to call off the offensive**, especially as winter was approaching. This advice infuriated Hitler to such an extent that he **dismissed Holder** and replaced him with a younger man, **Kurt Zeitzler**.

In the middle of September, the Germans penetrated into the suburbs and factory area of Stalingrad. But the German army was not trained for street fighting, and the defenders fought with the ferocity of men whose own homes were at stake. All **through October 1942 bitter street fighting** continued, with the **Germans** making slow progress while suffering **staggering losses**. The German troops were exhausted. The time for a Russian counter-attack was ripe.

The **Russian counter-offensive** was launched on **November 19, 1942**. The Russians attacked the German flank at the Don River west of Stalingrad, in a **pincer movement** from the north and the south aiming to **isolate the German army**. The over-stretched and over-exposed flanks were manned by the satellite armies: the Hungarians, the Italians, and the Romanians, who were of doubtful fighting quality and inadequately equipped. An overwhelming Russian army broke through the Romanian lines; in the north and in the south the Soviet armies were threatening to pierce the front.

The new chief of staff, **Zeitzler, urged Hitler** to permit the army **to withdraw** before being encircled. This threw the **Führer** into a tantrum: "**I won't leave the Volga,**" he stated; and that was that. This was one of several similar fanatical orders to the army to hold fast, regardless of their perilous situation. It led to heavy losses in men and arms, and to the demoralization of the commanders and their troops. As I shall describe, it lost Hitler an entire army at Stalingrad.

On **November 25, 1942, the pincer was closed** 40 miles west of Stalingrad. The German army led by **General von Paulus** was now encircled. At this point, the Germans still had a fighting chance of breaking out, but again Hitler forbade it. The German army followed Hitler's orders to continue to fight, but their effectiveness and morale were sapped by hunger, cold and disease.

On **January 7, 1943, the Russians presented Paulus an ultimatum** to surrender. Paulus radioed Hitler and asked for permission to comply. His request was curtly dismissed by the Supreme Warlord. After the **expiration of the ultimatum,** the Russians unleashed an artillery barrage of 5,000 guns. Within six days the German pocket had been reduced by half. On **January 24,** the Russians once more gave the Germans a chance to surrender. **Paulus** renewed his **plea to Hitler**: "Further defense senseless, collapse inevitable. Request permission to surrender." **Hitler's reply: "Surrender forbidden.** Army will hold their position to the last man and the last round." It was the death sentence of thousands of his men. On the **last day of January,** the horrible **agony of Paulus' army came to an end**. The radio operator at army headquarters sent a last message: "The Russians are at the door of our bunker." Thus ended the Battle of Stalingrad.

The toll on the German troops at Stalingrad was enormous. Of the conquering army of 285,000 men, all that was left, after two months, were 91,000 German soldiers who had been taken prisoner. The rest had been slaughtered. And of those 91,000 prisoners, only 5,000 were destined to see the Fatherland again. Most of those men could have been saved, if it hadn't been for Hitler's stubborn refusal to permit retreat.

But even more severe than these horrendous losses was the effect on the morale of the entire German nation. The **myth of the invincibility of the German Army had been broken. Stalingrad** was the **greatest defeat the German Army** had ever suffered. Coupled with Rommel's defeat at El Alamein, and the Allied forces landing in Africa, it marked the turning point in World War II. **The high tide of Nazi conquest had begun to ebb and it would never flow back again.**

The failure of the Germans to mount a concerted effort to produce the atom bomb

There is little doubt that if Germany had been successful in producing an atom bomb, Hitler would not have hesitated to bomb England and any other enemy that stood in his way —a terrible, frightening scenario to contemplate. Germany's failure to produce the bomb can be to a large part attributed to the Nazi politics and the totalitarian atmosphere that prevailed. On the one hand, the **anti-Semitic racial policies** of the Third Reich caused some of the most eminent scientists—e.g., **Einstein, Fermi, Szilard, Teller,** and **Wigner**—to leave Europe. (All of them became deeply involved in the development of the atomic bomb in the United States.) In addition, the ridiculous dubbing "Jewish science" that caused the repudiation of Einstein's

Theory of Relativity by notable physicists such as **Lenard** and **Stark** (both Nobel laureates) resulted in a generation of young scientists with an inadequate grasp of modern physics.

On the other hand, the **authoritarian regime** of the Third Reich precluded the free interchange of ideas that is at the core of scientific progress. As a result, the ideas of the high-level physicists who still remained in Germany, in particular **Heisenberg**, were accepted without questioning. And in particular, Heisenberg mistakenly became convinced that it was not possible to produce an atomic bomb.

To fully understand what happened in Germany, I want to describe the **wartime activities (1939–45)** on the so-called **Uranium Project**, and to give a bit of background. Most of the information comes from the records of the American mission, **ALSOS,** headed by the physicist **Samuel Goudsmit**.[27] [28] It was set up in the **autumn of 1943,** and its members closely followed the Allied troops as they occupied German-held territories. Their target was to intern and interview German scientists as soon as a territory was captured. I start with some background history.

In **December 1938,** the German scientists **Otto Hahn** and **Fritz Strassmann discovered the principle of fission,** i.e., that the bombardment of uranium by neutrons breaks up the atom, with an enormous amount of energy being released in the process. Physicists immediately began to wonder whether the fission process released further neutrons that could, in turn, cause other uranium nuclei to split, and thus produce a **chain reaction**. The importance and the practical application of this discovery were immediately realized. In England, France, Germany, and the United States, physicists alerted their governments about the potential use of this newly discovered phenomenon for the **production of energy,** and possibly **a bomb** with an extraordinarily large explosive power.

To understand the progress made by the Allies (to a large part by the United States) and the Germans in the development of an atomic bomb, some technical background is required. Let me start with the fission process. When a uranium atom is hit by a neutron it breaks up into two pieces (fission). The sum of the masses of the two pieces is smaller than the mass of the parent uranium atom. This difference in mass corresponds to a large release of energy according to Einstein's famous relationship $E=mc^2$ (E=energy, m=mass, v=velocity of light). Accompanying the fission is a release of several neutrons that can, in turn, produce more fission, that releases more neutrons, resulting in a **chain reaction**. When uncontrolled, this process results in an explosion.

Let's look at it now in more detail. Uranium has **two** main **isotopes,**[29] U235 and **U238**, with abundances of 0.7% and 99.3% respectively. Unfortunately, the fissionable isotope is the less abundant U235. The probability that U235 will capture a neutron (called the cross-section) is large for slow (i.e., low energy) neutrons. But the fission process produces fast (i.e., high energy) neutrons that have a low probability of being captured by U235 (and are mostly absorbed by the U238) and this does not result in further fission. Unless, that is, these fast neutrons are slowed down, which can be done by collisions with an inert substance (called a **moderator**). Graphite (carbon) and heavy water (D_2O) are moderators of choice. To sustain a chain reaction in a uranium pile (also called a **nuclear**

---

[27] Samuel A. Goudsmit, "ALSOS," Tomash Publishers, 1986.

[28] Paul L. Rose, "Heisenberg and the Atomic Bomb Project," University of California Press, 1998.

[29] Isotopes have different masses but the same chemical properties.

reactor) the number of slow neutrons produced must be larger than the number lost (by escaping from the surface of the reactor or being absorbed). As the size (mass) of the reactor increases, the number of neutrons produced increases faster than the number that is lost. The reactor is said to reach **critical mass** when the conditions for a chain reaction are obtained (i.e., the number of slow neutrons produced is larger than that of slow neutrons lost).

An important point realized early by the Allies, but only belatedly by the Germans, was that a self-sustaining **chain reaction by slow neutrons in U235**, although capable of producing controlled energy in a reactor, would be **too slow to produce an effective explosion**. What was needed in an **atomic bomb** was a **fast chain reaction**. This can be achieved utilizing the fast neutrons to produce fission in U235, if the reactor is highly enriched in U235 (since the cross-section for capture of fast neutrons by U235 is small).

In summary: A uranium reactor utilizing slow neutrons can be built even with naturally occurring (i.e., unenriched) uranium by using proper moderators. But **in a bomb** utilizing fast neutrons, **the uranium must be highly enriched in U235**.[30]

At the **beginning of 1940,** an important discovery was made by **Seaborg** and his coworkers at the Radiation Laboratory in Berkeley. They found that when U238 captures a fast neutron, a new transuranic element, which they called **plutonium (Pu 239)**, is formed. They predicted Pu239 to be as **fissible** as U235. Thus, an alternate material had been discovered that could be used to produce an atomic bomb.

After the discovery of fission in December 1938, fear gripped the nuclear physicists all over the world. They realized that whoever developed the atomic bomb first would win the war. It prompted the two Hungarian emigré physicists Szilard and Wigner to convince **Einstein** to write, in **August 1939,** the famous **letter to President Roosevelt** advocating a high-priority program to develop the atomic bomb. The letter was favorably received by the President, and the US government supported the nuclear research unflinchingly and generously, with increasing amounts of funds throughout the war.

The original work in the United States focused on **obtaining reliable data**, e.g., on **cross-sections** for the capture of neutrons with varying energies by the two isotopes, U235 and U238 that were required to design a reactor or a bomb. Experiments were also performed on **the separation of U235**, and the production of **heavy water** and the procurement of **highly purified graphite** as moderators. After the discovery of **Pu239** at the beginning of 1940, experiments were made to **purify it** and measure its properties. By the **end of 1941,** the general theory of chain reactions was well understood, and the **critical mass of the atomic bomb had been calculated** to be within practical limits. A landmark feat was achieved by Fermi and his group on **December 2, 1942,** at the University of Chicago, where they produced a **self-sustaining chain reaction** in a reactor using natural (unenriched) uranium with graphite as a moderator. It was an awesome moment—**the first time that atomic energy was harnessed by man**. It not only boosted the confidence of the scientists that their calculations had been correct, it provided them with the means of **producing Pu239 in the reactor** as a possible alternate fissionable material.

The various research projects dealing with the uranium problem were performed in different places in the United States, and were coordinated by larger and larger

---

[30] Note that the claim of the Iranians to have to enrich uranium to 20% U235 for building a nuclear reactor for peaceful purposes makes no sense, and clearly indicates their goal of making an atomic bomb.

organizational units as the number of projects and people increased. As confidence in producing an atomic bomb grew, it was decided to make an all-out effort to produce one. The existing organizations were insufficient for such an effort and, in **June 1942,** plans for a new, huge organization called the **Manhattan Project** were drawn up. It represented a collaborative effort between scientists, engineers, industry and academia, with the Army playing an important role in the procurement of material and the engineering phase of the work. This mammoth enterprise was headed by the able administrator, **General L.R. Groves** of the Corps of Engineers. The group leaders of the different projects all reported to him. The group responsible for designing and building the atomic bomb was based at **Los Alamos** in New Mexico, and was headed by the theoretical physicist **J.R. Oppenheimer**.

When reading the Smyth Report,[31] published at the end of the war, which describes in detail the work on the atomic bomb, one is impressed by the scope, foresightedness, and systematic pursuit of the goal. For example, different approaches to solving problems were pursued simultaneously, not sequentially, in order to save time. This was the case with the separation of U235, where three different methods (diffusion, electromagnetic separation, and centrifuging) were pursued. Also, the separation of U235 and Pu239 as possible fissionable fuels for the atomic bomb were both pursued simultaneously. To get an idea of the scope of the projects, the plant that produced Pu239 was located in a relatively uninhabited area at **Hanford** in the state of Washington. At its peak productivity it had a population of 60,000 people, all engaged in the plutonium production.

The crowning success of this intense effort of thousands of people came on **July 16, 1945,** when a **test atomic bomb** was exploded at **Alamogordo** in the remote New Mexico desert. It was an explosion of enormous power, confirming all expectations. On **August 6, 1945, a U235 atomic bomb** was dropped **on Hiroshima,** and a few days later a **Pu239 bomb** was dropped **on Nagasaki.** The Japanese capitulated—the war was won. The event heralded a new era—the atomic age—in which mankind had acquired a tool of unimaginable power. How it will be used in the future is a political and social question whose answer will determine the future of our civilization (see Epilogue page 248).

Let me now switch to describe the **efforts by the German physicists** to build an atomic bomb. Were they closely following on the heels of the Allied successes? Not by a long shot, as shown by the captured documents and interviews of the German scientists, as well as the secret recordings of the conversations among the leading 10 scientists interned after the war. They didn't even succeed in building a nuclear reactor with a self-sustained chain reaction, a feat that the Americans achieved in December 1942, two-and-a-half years before the end of the war. The **fear of the Allies** that the Germans might beat them in acquiring an atomic bomb, thought understandable at the time, **had,** in fact, **no basis.**

Following the discovery of fission in December 1938, German nuclear physicists, like those in other parts of the world, realized the potential of fission as a tool to produce energy and, ultimately, a weapon of mass destruction. They formed the **Uranium Club,** centered around the leading, brilliant, nuclear physicist, **Werner Heisenberg.** The first couple of years, their work proceeded along lines similar to those pursued by the Allies, except that the several projects performed at different universities and institutions were poorly coordinated

---

[31] H.D. Smyth, "Atomic Energy for Military Purposes," Princeton University Press, 1945.

and were often in competition. Different governmental agencies—e.g., the Ministry of Education, the Postal Service, the Army and Navy, the SS—supported the various groups.

In 1940, Heisenberg presented to his colleagues a calculation of the critical mass of a uranium bomb. He **concluded that several tons of purified U235 would be required** to produce a bomb. This convinced Heisenberg and his group that an atomic bomb lay beyond the reach of practicality. Not only didn't they have the means to separate U235 in such quantity, but even if they had, a bomb of that mass would not be deliverable by plane. Alas, the great **Heisenberg had made a fundamental error** in his calculation, to which he and his colleagues adhered throughout the war. Here one must stress the hierarchical nature and hero worship of the German mindset. Heisenberg had attained such an iconic stature among German physicists that nobody contemplated questioning his results. In their self-confidence and belief in their scientific superiority, the German scientists became complacent and convinced that there was no danger the Allies would produce an atomic bomb.

As a result of Heisenberg's fatal mistake, the German scientists shifted their **emphasis** from making a bomb **to constructing a uranium reactor** with a self-sustaining chain reaction. They were aware of needing a moderator to slow down the neutrons (see previous section) and correctly considered graphite and heavy water as prime candidates. And now a second mistake, this time an experimental one, derailed their project. The highly respected experimental nuclear physicist **W. Bothe made a mistake** in measuring the cross-section for capture of neutrons in **graphite**, which made this material **unfit for** a reasonably sized **reactor**. (The error is believed to have been due to the low purity of the graphite used.) The scientists therefore decided to **use heavy water,** which they imported from a plant in Norway. When **British** intelligence got wind of the heavy water deliveries to Germany, they **bombed and destroyed** the **heavy water plant in Norway**. With the limited amount of heavy water at hand, and discarding graphite as a moderator, the **Germans** were **unsuccessful** in achieving the limited goal of **producing** a functioning **nuclear reaction**.

Interesting and reliable insight into the scientific world, political thinking, and moral stance of the German scientists comes from the **secret recordings of the conversations** of the 10 leading **nuclear scientists** interned **from July to December 1945 at Farm Hall**, near Cambridge, England. When the scientists heard on the **6pm BBC news on August 6**, 1945, that the Allies had dropped an atomic bomb on Hiroshima, they did not believe it. Heisenberg repeated his old erroneous calculations showing that tons of pure Uranium 235 would be needed for a bomb. They believed it was all a piece of propaganda, and that probably what the Allies had dropped was a conventional, but very large, bomb. But when at **9pm, BBC** had a more detailed **report of the** immense **devastation** caused **by the bomb**, doubts and consternation set in. In the intellectual arrogance and conceit of their scientific superiority, the Germans could not conceive that the Allies had succeeded where they had failed. Recriminations started to be voiced: the chemist Hahn, who had discovered fission, accused Heisenberg and his physicist colleagues of being second raters, a remark that must have riled the proud Heisenberg for the rest of his life. After a day or two, when the dust had settled, the common concern started to focus on how to save their scientific reputation. They produced a **hypocritical memorandum,** signed by all 10 scientists present, claiming they never intended to produce an atomic bomb for Hitler. It was too terrible and inhumane a weapon to use. They further claimed how morally responsible their action was, compared to the immoral use of the atomic bomb by the Allies. What imaginary self-justification and self-delusion! They conveniently forgot the zeal and enthusiasm with which they pursued the atomic bomb project the first couple of years before Heisenberg, with his erroneous calculation, showed that an atomic bomb was impractical. This "moral" version of why the German scientists did not produce an atomic bomb persists in certain (German) circles to this day. This stance is epitomized by **Heiseberg's preposterous assertion in 1970 that he**, von Laue, and Hahn **had falsified their calculations** to prove to the German government that an atomic bomb is not attainable. Conveniently, von Laue and Hahn were no longer around to repudiate this absurd claim; they had died in 1962 and 1967 respectively. How sad that such a brilliant scientist as Heisenberg could stoop so low in a vain attempt to preserve his scientific superiority. But Heisenberg is not unique among people of great accomplishments who show no correlation between genius and moral integrity.

And so it happened that **Germany was far from producing an atomic bomb,** and was **not even able to construct a functioning atomic reactor**. But it remains an open question whether Germany could have mounted an effort comparable to the Manhattan Project to produce an atomic bomb—even if the German physicists had analyzed the problem correctly.

What would have been the fate of Europe if Hitler had won the war?

Hitler came close to winning the war in Europe. Had Germany acquired the atomic bomb, or had Hitler not made the mistakes described in the previous sections, he might have succeeded in conquering Europe, and perhaps even other parts of the world. How would Europe have looked under Hitler's domination? Although there is no explicit blueprint of the "New Order" that Hitler would have imposed, it is clear, from the actions of the Third Reich and the pronouncements of Hitler and his henchmen, what a hellish nightmare it would have been.

The conquered people by a Nazi-ruled Germany would be made the slaves of the German master race, and the resources of their countries would be ruthlessly exploited for the benefit of Germany. Some parts of the population would be considered Untermenschen (subhuman) who had no right to live, and would therefore be exterminated. Among them would be the remaining Jews and the Roma. The Slavic people, who were also considered to be subhuman, would be forced to toil in the fields growing food for Germany while being allowed to keep for themselves just enough to barely subsist on. The great cities of the east —Moscow, Leningrad, Warsaw—would be permanently erased, and the culture of the Russians, Poles, and other Slavs would be stamped out. Formal education would be denied to them, and their elite (the intelligentsia) killed off. The scenario that I described here is not an idle speculation, but is based on the behavior of the Nazi regime during the war, which I want to describe now in more detail.[32]

On **October 2, 1940, Hitler outlined his thoughts** and intentions to Hans Frank, the Governor of occupied Poland: The Poles are born for low labor; it is necessary to keep the standard of life low in Poland and it must not be permitted to rise...; They should be used by us merely as unskilled labor; The laborers needed by the Reich could be procured from them; The Polish gentry must cease to exist, they must be exterminated wherever they are; As for the Polish priests, they will preach what we want them to preach; If any priest acts differently we shall eliminate him; The task of the priests is to keep the Poles quiet, stupid, and dull. These guidelines were faithfully executed by Frank during the war years.

---

[32] W. Shirer, "The Rise and Fall of the Third Reich," Simon & Schuster, 1959.

On **July 16, 1941**, barely a month into the Russian campaign, **Hitler** summoned the Nazi elite to his headquarters to **remind them of his aims in the newly conquered lands**. At last, his goal of achieving a vast German Lebensraum (living space) was in sight. The way to proceed was: first, to dominate it; second, to administer it; and third, to exploit it. Then Hitler spelled out specific steps: the Baltic countries will be incorporated into Germany; the Crimea will be evacuated and settled by Germans; the German colonies on the Volga will be annexed and the Baku oil fields will become a German concession. Field Marshall Göring added that the vast eastern territory has to be pacified as quickly as possible. The best solution would be to shoot anybody who looked sideways. Göring's approach is also clear from a remark he had made earlier to Count Ciano, Foreign Minister of Italy: "This year between **20 and 30 million Russians will die** of hunger, and it is well that it should be so."

The obsession of the Germans that they were the master race and that the Slavs must be their slaves is made clear by **Erich Koch**, Reich Commissar for the Ukraine, in a **speech** in Kiev on **March 5, 1943**: "**We are the Master Race** and must govern hard...I will draw out the very last of this country. I did not come to spread bliss.... The population must work, work, and work.... We must remember that the lowliest German worker is racially and biologically a thousand times more valuable than the population here."

Concerning the **exploitation** (more appropriately called looting) of the conquered territories, the Germans showed themselves to be most thorough and efficient at it. Besides goods, art objects, services, and manpower, they seized the gold and foreign holdings in their national banks. It is estimated that the amount the Germans extracted from the conquered nations during the war amounted to 140 billion marks (40 billion dollars, corresponding to a present-day value of approximately 1 trillion dollars). Art treasures were looted on specific orders from Hitler and Göring, who thereby greatly augmented their "private" collections. According to an official German report, some 137 freight cars loaded with 31,303 art objects, including 1,083 paintings, were transported to Germany until July 1944.

But all this plunder of material goods does not compare with the **inhuman brutality** with which the Nazis treated their enemies. Here, Nazi degradation sank to a level seldom, if ever, witnessed in all of human history. Millions of decent, normal people were driven into forced labor, millions more tortured and tormented in prisons and concentration camps, and millions more—among them 6 million Jews—were massacred in cold blood or deliberately starved to death. By the end of September 1944, some 1.5 million civilian foreigners and 2 million prisoners of war were deported to Germany to toil under inhuman conditions for the Third Reich. Of the almost 6 million Soviet war prisoners, only about one million were found

Corpses in Bergen-Belsen[33] (April 1945). Source: Shoah— The Holocaust, The American-Israeli Cooperative Enterprise.

alive when Allied and Soviet troops liberated POW camps. The rest had died in German captivity—from starvation, freezing to death, diseases, and execution.

The actions of the Nazi rulers during the war described in this section may be viewed as the beginning of Hitler's New Order—the debut of a Nazi gangster empire stretching from the Atlantic to the Ural Mountains. Fortunately for mankind, it was destroyed in its infancy. It is noteworthy that the fall of the Third Reich was not brought about by any revolt of the German people against inhumanity and barbarism, but by the defeat of the German Army by the Allied forces.

The situation at the end of the war

The liberation of concentration camps

As Allied troops moved into German-held territories during the last stages of the war, they encountered shocking scenes. They found mass graves, abandoned camps, boxcars full of corpses, human skeletons, piles of bones, and some emaciated prisoners barely alive. The images captured by photographers and journalists who accompanied Allied forces horrified people back home, just as they stunned and sickened soldiers who saw them firsthand. The questions they raised have almost become clichés: How could human beings do such things to other people? How can we go on living in a world where crimes and suffering of such magnitude are possible? While you ponder these weighty questions, let me tell you two stories that personalize these horrors.

On **April 11, 1945,** the Americans liberated the concentration camp Buchenwald. One of the American officers was Rabbi Hershel Schechter who, when he saw a pile of corpses, broke down and cried. Suddenly, he noticed a small boy, about eight years old, crawling amid the corpses. The Rabbi stopped crying and tried to comfort the boy by laughing and pretending to be cheerful. He asked the boy how old he was. "Older than you," answered the boy. The Rabbi fearing the boy was deranged, asked him to explain. "You behave like a baby. First you cry, a minute later you laugh. I don't remember when I last cried or laughed, but certainly not at the same time. You tell me who is older." The Rabbi was deeply moved, took him under his wing and arranged for his immigration to Palestine. The boy became the Chief Rabbi of Israel. His name is **Israel Lau.**

The second story describes a personal experience I had with Leo, a survivor of a concentration camp. Leo was a fellow student of mine at the University of California, Berkeley, in 1947. It always amazed me how tense and nervous Leo became before an exam—after all that he must have suffered in a concentration camp, barely two years earlier. Perhaps it is a good sign I told myself. He may have suppressed or made peace with his past and had become a normal, well-adjusted person. Unfortunately, I don't think that was the case as evidenced by the story he told me one day: After they were liberated from the concentration camp, the inmates were put on a train, which they were not allowed to leave. Their diet was very limited and controlled while their digestive system recovered. As a consequence they were always hungry. At one of the train stops they saw a vendor selling hotdogs. They opened the window of the train, climbed out and demanded some hotdogs. The vendor asked whether they had any money to pay for them. "Can you imagine, the chutzpa of this German, asking us, recently liberated from a German concentration camp, for money?" exclaimed Leo, clearly still enraged by the memory of it. "So what did you do?" I asked. "Well what do you think

---

[33] My uncle and aunt, Gyula and Irene Kučera, with their son Karol, were inmates in Bergen-Belsen. Karol survived; his parents did not.

we did? We beat the vendor to death on the spot and divided the hotdogs among us," replied Leo. A shiver ran down my spine. But Leo showed no trace of remorse or shame. He clearly still felt that was the just and appropriate action.

I recently read that 31% of US soldiers who returned from Iraq had serious psychological problems (i.e., post-traumatic syndrome). And their experience must pale in comparison with what survivors of a concentration camp must have experienced.

The plight of the survivors

One might have hoped that the arrival of Allied forces and the collapse of Nazi Germany would stop the violence and misery unleashed by Nazi Germany. Alas, this was not to be the scenario that evolved.

For many survivors of World War II, the suffering continued. Alone, without family or friends, many surviving Jews had nowhere to go. Many Jewish orphaned children no longer knew their birth names or where they came from. Jews had seen their Gentile neighbors turn against them, denouncing them to the Nazis, and stealing their possessions. How could they now go back as if nothing had happened? Nevertheless, some of them did return, and faced terrible disappointment and suffering.

In Poland, Ukraine, Hungary, Slovakia, and elsewhere, Jewish survivors who returned home to search for family members or reclaim their property were often met with violent hostility from the new "owners." Some Jews were attacked and beaten; some were killed. Within a year after the war, more than 1,000 Jews were murdered on Polish soil—by Poles.

One of the leaders of the Sobibor revolt, **Leon Feldhendler**, was killed after the liberation. **Yaakov Waldman**, one of the very few who survived Chelmno, was killed by Poles immediately after the war. One of only two survivors of Belzec, **Chaim Hirszman**, was killed in Lublin on the day he gave evidence to a Polish war crime tribunal about what he had witnessed at Belzec.

The climax of post-war killing in Poland came on **July 4, 1945**, when a group of Jewish survivors gathered in **Kielce** on their way to Palestine. They were attacked by a local mob and 42 of them were killed. Within 24 hours of the Kielce pogrom, 5,000 survivors left Poland in search of a haven elsewhere. They crossed the border to Slovakia and reached the capital, Bratislava (my birthplace). There they were confronted by anti-Jewish demonstrations—the old and familiar story. They continued their wanderings westward, toward the British and American occupied zone of Germany.

Many of the Jews who did not want to return to their places of origin were housed in camps for **displaced persons (DP)**, set up by the United Nations Relief and Rehabilitation Administration (**UNRRA**) of the newly created United Nations. By late 1946, about 150,000 Jews lived in DP camps in the US zone in Germany. The Jewish DP camps were sites of intense Zionist activity, urging the survivors to leave Europe for Palestine, illegally, if necessary, as the British allowed only a trickle of Jews to immigrate to Palestine. Many Jews preferred to wait for visas to the United States, Canada, or Australia; others opted for a quicker solution, such as relocation in South Africa, South America, or the Caribbean. About 20,000 Jews remained in Germany after the last Jewish **DP camp closed in 1957**.

Looking back at the Holocaust, we often vow: "NEVER AGAIN." But for Jews hounded out from Polish towns by pogroms in 1945 and 1946, a more apt slogan might have been: "STILL?!" As one dispirited, down-beaten survivor put it (with a smidgen of humor still left in him): "Oh God, we are so tired of being your chosen people. Please, God, choose somebody else for a change."

A final remark on the efforts of the Allies and the German authorities to mete out justice to the perpetrators of Nazi crimes: To do this was important for both practical and psychological reasons. It made it possible to effect a separation between Nazis who needed to be punished, and Germans who could be integrated into a peaceful world. Psychologically, it was important for the surviving victims to see the criminals, their past tormentors, brought to justice. It provided an acknowledgement of their suffering, and helped restore a measure of confidence in the justice of the world around them.

The top 21 perpetrators of crimes were tried by the **International Tribunal in Nüremberg** during 1945–1946. Half of them received death sentences, and the rest received prison sentences of varying lengths. Lower-ranking Nazis were tried by different courts during the following years. But the German courts did not live up to the task of meting out justice. Many of the German judges had been Nazi sympathizers. They released the Nazis convicted by the Allied court prematurely. And, in dealing with their own cases, the German judges argued that the laws against genocide could not be applied because the crimes were committed before these laws were adopted by the United Nations Convention in 1948 (see page 179). This failure of the German judicial system to adequately process the perpetrators of Nazi crimes should be called **the second guilt of the Germans**. It is only today's third generation of Germans that seem to have internalized the enormity of the crimes committed by its grandparents.

Many Nazis used connections in Turkey, the Middle East, South America, and the Vatican to get themselves to safety and escape justice. For example, **Franz Stangl**, former commandant of Sobibor and Treblinka, fled to Argentina. Also **Adolf Eichmann** found refuge in Argentina, until he was kidnapped by the Israeli Mossad and brought to trial in Jerusalem in 1961. **Josef Mengele**, the vicious doctor of Auschwitz, made his way to Argentina and then to Brazil, where he died in 1979.

The German authorities, under the leadership of **Chancellor Adenauer**, made genuine efforts to materially compensate the survivors of Nazi persecution. This is in contrast to the Austrian, Slovaks, Hungarians, Romanians, and other past partners of Nazi Germany, who did nothing of the sort. Although the German compensation was important for many survivors to start new lives, no amount of restitution could make up for their suffering and the killing of 6 million Jews, and the trauma of the survivors, their offspring, and the whole Jewish community.

2. THE HISTORY AND FATE OF THE JEWS OF SLOVAKIA

The history of European Jews varies from country to country, although it encompasses a discernable common theme of anti-Semitism, pogroms, persecutions, and ultimately the deportation to death camps. Having been born and raised (until age 17) in Slovakia, that little country (50,000 square kilometers) in central Europe that is bordered to the west and north by the Carpathian Mountains, and to the south by the fertile lowlands of the Danube, I want to describe the history and fate of the Jews in Slovakia in some detail.[34] I realize that I am straying from the main topic of the Holocaust (although some of the background may be of relevance), but I could not resist the temptation to use this opportunity to delve into the history of my ancestors in Slovakia.

I am dividing the narrative into three epochs: 1) the early history, up to the formation of Czechoslovakia in 1918; 2) the period between the two World Wars, 1918–1938, during which the Jews were relatively well-off in the liberal, democratic Republic of Czechoslovakia; 3) the fateful years 1939–1945, during which severe persecutions culminating in mass murder—the Holocaust—occurred. I left Slovakia in April 1941, and have, therefore, experienced the persecutions committed during the first years of the last period. The situation of the Jews in postwar Slovakia, as well as the fate of the leaders that participated in the annihilation of the Jews, is briefly discussed at the end.

Early history

The **Romans** crossed the Danube in the **second century A.D.,** and occupied a narrow strip of southern Slovakia that included my birthplace, **Bratislava.** They called it **Posonium,** from which the Hungarian name **Pozsony** is derived. The German name is **Pressburg,** which I shall use interchangeably with Bratislava. The Roman ruins of that period are still visible in the vicinity of Bratislava, and I remember them well from my childhood. There are indications that Jews followed the Roman legions to the region, first as slaves and soldiers, and later as merchants. When the Romans left, the Jews apparently left as well, there being no evidence of Jewish settlement in the region until the 9th century. Jews are mentioned among the inhabitants of the **Great Moravian Empire (833–907),** which encompassed most of Slovakia. In the **11th century, Magyars** conquered Slovakia, and it remained part of the **Hungarian kingdom** for about 1,000 years—**until 1918.**

Both the crusades in the late 11th century, and the harsh persecution by the Bohemian **King Vratislav II,** led to the migration of Jews from Bohemia, Germany, and Austria, to Hungary, where they found refuge; some of them settled in Slovakia. In **1241,** the **Mongols** (also known as **Tatars**) invaded Hungary, wreaking havoc and destruction. After the expulsion of the Mongols, the Jews made a major contribution to rebuilding the economy. In appreciation of their efforts, **King Bela IV** granted the Jews, in **1251,** a **privilege**: a document promising them protection against attacks by Christians, a permanent legal status, and other benefits. A letter from King Bela IV refers to Jews in the cities of **Pressburg** (Bratislava), **Senica, Trnava, Pezinok, Nitra,** and **Trenčin.**

---

[34] I used many sources for this section: The most useful were the articles by Livia Rothkirchen and Ladislav Lipscher in "The Jews of Czechoslovakia," Volumes I and III, published by the Society for the History of Czechoslovak Jews, 1968, 1984; and Joan Campion, "Gisi Fleischmann and the Jewish Fight for Survival," Dvorion Books, 1983.

From the **13ᵗʰ century** on, the Jews were wards of the king, and paid taxes to the royal treasury. They lived primarily in cities, on separate Jewish streets allotted to them by the authorities. Most Jews made their living in finance and commerce; some held positions in public administration or were involved in the minting of coins. Nitra, a major administration and economic center in the Middle Ages, had the oldest Jewish community in Slovakia. The Jewish community in Pressburg was founded in the **13ᵗʰ century** by Jewish refugees from Bohemia, Germany, and Austria. In the **14ᵗʰ century,** the Pressburg community numbered 800 people, and was the largest in the Hungarian kingdom. In the late 14ᵗʰ century **Rabbi Isaac of Trnava** was the leading Torah sage in Hungary, author of the "Sefer Haminhagim" (the Book of Customs), which described the religious practices of the Jews in Hungary.

In the **15ᵗʰ century**, the situation of the Jews worsened as the Christian population turned increasingly to religious extremism. Anti-Jewish riots broke out in several places. In **1491,** the authorities in Trnava initiated a **blood libel**[35] against the Jews, and on **August 22, 1491**, twelve men and four women were burnt at the stake. After the Turks defeated the Hungarians in **1526** and occupied Budapest, Pressburg became the capital of Hungary. The Hungarians expelled the Jews from Pressburg, Trnava, and several other locations. By the end of the **16ᵗʰ century,** the old Jewish communities of Slovakia had disintegrated and the continuity of Jewish life in Slovakia was severely disturbed.

A new immigration of Jews began in the **mid-17ᵗʰ century** and intensified during the **18ᵗʰ century**, giving rise to the Jewish communities of Slovakia that existed until the Holocaust. The Jewish immigrants came mainly from the neighboring countries of Moravia, Poland, and Austria, where new anti-Jewish edicts were proclaimed. Jewish refugees settled in **Nitra County in 1649,** and later in the counties of **Pressburg** and **Trenčin**. As Jews resettled Slovakia, a dichotomy occurred between Jewish ethnicities and cultures. The Jews in the west tended to be more educated and more open to the influences of the surrounding, gentile culture. The Jews in eastern Slovakia followed Hassidic customs, spoke Yiddish, and resembled the Jews of Poland and Galicia.

The living conditions of the Jews deteriorated significantly during the reign of **Empress Maria Theresa (1740–1780)**. She promulgated various edicts and even threatened to expel the Jews from the Austrian Empire. In **1749,** the Jews were subject to a special **tolerance tax**, a heavy burden for the Jewish families. However, the situation of the Jews improved when Maria Theresa's son, **Emperor Joseph II (1780–1790),** instituted changes and innovations in the governance of the Empire. In **1783,** he issued an **Edict of Tolerance** for the Jews of Hungary. The Jews were granted permission to work in almost any occupation, and live in most parts of the empire. Following the Edict of Tolerance, the Jewish settlements expanded and new communities were founded. Jews became financially well-off, and flourished spiritually and culturally. During that time the Jewish community in Hungary attained a population of 80,000, half of it residing in Slovakia.

In the early **19ᵗʰ century**, the Jewish population of Slovakia continued to grow vigorously. The increase in the Jewish population and the improvement in their economic condition were accompanied by a thriving religious life and the emergence of the first

---

[35] These were allegations, which first surfaced in the 12ᵗʰ century, that Jews murdered Christian children to use their blood for ritual purposes on Passover.

Torah Centers. The most important of them was the **Pressburg Yeshiva**, headed by **Rabbi Moses Sofer (Schreiber)** (1768–1839), known as **Hatam Sofer**, who was considered the leading halachic[36] authority of his day. After his death in 1839, the Yeshiva was headed by Hatam Sofer's descendants—Abraham Wolf Sofer, Simha Sofer, and Akiba Sofer—who continued to direct the Pressburg Yeshiva until the eve of World War II.

The Jews of Slovakia suffered considerable hardship when the **Hungarian Revolution** of **1848–49** was crushed by Austria. To penalize the Jews for their role in the revolutionary movement, the Austrian government imposed heavy taxes on the Hungarian **Jewish** communities. During the following decade, Jews founded their first elementary and high **schools**. Some of them, such as the ones in **Nové Mesto nad Váhom** and **Liptovský Svätý Mikuláš,** had such high standards that some of the non-Jewish families enrolled their children there.

In **1867** Austria and Hungary established a **dual Monarchy** (the Austro-Hungarian Empire), and Hungarian became the only language of instruction in the Hungarian part of the Monarchy. The Jews, who had used German for their everyday language, had to switch to Hungarian. To the Slovaks the switch to Hungarian was a source of acute resentment, which gave rise to increased national conscience. There is evidence of Jewish sympathy with Slovak national sentiments. The roster of the **Matica Slovenská** (Slovak Academy), which was established in **1863,** contains a number of Jewish names. Nevertheless, the Slovak nationalists did not consider the Jews as working for their cause.

After the establishment of the dual Monarchy, the Hungarian government passed the **Emancipation Law**, which granted full civil and religious rights to the Jews. Paradoxically, anti-Semitic activity increased in Slovakia. The Slovakian intelligentsia, which advocated a Slovakian national revival, regarded the Jews as tools of the hated Hungarian regime, and accused them of working for the "Magyarization" of their country. The church was actively involved in stirring up hatred of the Jews. In **1882,** a gathering of 200 priests in **Topolčany** urged the Hungarian parliament (fortunately, to no avail) to revoke the equal rights that it had granted to Jews in 1867.

In **1867** the government established a **Hungarian Jewish Congress,** to which all Jewish congregations of Slovakia were invited. However, frictions developed within the Jewish community, which split the Jews of Hungary, and hence of Slovakia, into two opposing groups: the **Neolog** congregation, representing the liberal "modern" elements, and the **Orthodox** congregation. This rigid separation and constant internal dissension had a detrimental effect on the prestige of the Jews and Judaism in the eyes of the rest of the population. The unfortunate split persisted until the outbreak of World War II. Our family belonged to the Neolog group, and I must shamefully admit that we looked down, with derision, on the Orthodox community.

In **1894** the Hungarian government passed the **Compulsory Education Law**, which provided for unified educational standards throughout Hungary. It had a pronounced effect on the social status of the Jews. In Slovakia, Jews began to appear prominently in the fields of law, medicine, education, journalism and commerce. By that time there was a large number of wealthy Jewish industrialists and merchants in Slovakia. About one-third of the Hungarian state budget for industrial development was channeled into Slovakia with the result that, to a large extent, it was the Jewish merchants who introduced Slovak regional

---

[36] Halacha = religious law

products (such as cotton, embroidery, cheese, wines and liquor) into the international markets. All this brought a reorientation of the urban Jewish middle class, who turned **from Vienna,** the "Imperial City," **towards Budapest,** the capital of Hungary. It, no doubt, also provided the driving force for my grandfather to change his name at the end of the 19th century, from the German *Weiss* (White), to the Hungarian translation *Fehér*.

In **1896,** the Hungarian Parliament passed an act (**Article XVII**) placing the Jewish faith on an equal level with Christian religions. This law met with resentment and opposition, and gave rise to the establishment of a new, strongly anti-Semitic clerical party in Slovakia, the **Ľudová Strana** (People's Party), that in later years was to play an important role in the destruction of Slovak Jewry.

Simultaneously with the political awakening of the Gentile masses of Slovakia, the Jews made their first contact with Zionism. In **1897,** the writer **Samuel Bettelheim** from Bratislava, established the **Ahavat Zion Society,** the first Zionist group in Hungary. It is noteworthy that out of 13 Zionist groups formed in Hungary following the first Zionist Congress in Basel (1897), eight were in Slovakia. Moreover, Bratislava was the site of the first **Hungarian Zionist Convention,** held in **1903.**

On the eve of World War I, the Jewish population of Slovakia numbered 140,000. It was quite diverse, comprising several groups that differed in their way of life, religiousness, origins, and cultural background. They spoke four different languages (Hungarian, German, Slovak, and Yiddish), and belonged to various socioeconomic classes. The Jews fought in World War I with the Austro-Hungarian Army, as my father did, and many of them distinguished themselves on the battlefield; about 10,000 Jews lost their lives in the war.

1918–1938. The period between the two World Wars

The **Republic of Czechoslovakia** was established on **October 28, 1918,** after the dissolution of the Austro-Hungarian Empire. It united within its boundaries three different regions: the Czech lands (Bohemia and Moravia) on the west, Slovakia in the center, and the Sub-Carpathian Ruthenia (*Podkarpatská Rus*) to the east. The Jewish population in each of these areas had a distinct and different character. But they were united on one cardinal issue: their loyalty to the republic and its venerated president-philosopher, **Tomas G. Masaryk,** who held office between 1918 and 1935. Masaryk was loved and respected by all; I remember, as a 13-year-old boy in 1937, people crying openly in the streets when Masaryk died.

The liberation of Slovakia after World War I, unlike that of Bohemia and Moravia, was filled with great turmoil, military interventions, and political upheavals. These lasted from the end of October 1918 until the signing of the **Minorities Treaty** with Austria at **St. Germain-en-Laye** on **September 10, 1919,** and the **Trianon Treaty** with Hungary on **June 4, 1920.** This stormy period caused hardship and suffering to broad sections of Slovak Jewry. Having harbored anti-Semitic sentiments for decades, Slovak rioters gave vent to their hatred in **November 1919,** by plundering Jewish property and endangering Jewish lives. These excesses became known as the **November pillages.**

Once peaceful conditions set in, Jews, together with all other law-abiding citizens, endeavored to give their best to the development of the country. Czechoslovakia during the interwar years became a bulwark of democracy and was widely acclaimed as such in the

Western world. It was the only country in Europe where the Jewish population was recognized and accorded minority rights. In each of the **parliamentary elections** in **1929** and **1935,** two representatives of the **Jewish Party** were elected to Parliament.

In the Czech lands, the Jews numbered 118,000 (1% of the population). Although religious practices had declined greatly, Czech Jewry preserved a distinct consciousness of its heritage of 1,000 years of settlement. The Jewish community was split into a number of factions: Czech Jews, German Jews, and nationalists (Zionist Jews). They held adversary positions and were engaged in continuous debates and challenges.

In Slovakia, which was formerly a province of Hungary, the Jews numbered 137,000 (4.1%) of the population. In the 1930 census, 73,000 described themselves as Jewish, 44,000 as Slovak, 10,000 as German, and 10,000 as Hungarian. The great divide in internal Jewish affairs dates back to the Hungarian Jewish Congress of 1869 (see previous section), which split the congregation into the more secular Neologs, and the traditional religious Orthodox to which two-thirds of the Jewish population belonged. Western and central Slovakia had a well-established middle-class Jewish population, embracing professionals, businessmen, and "gentrified" estate owners. The Jews of eastern Slovakia were more akin to the Sub-Carpathian Jewry, for whom religion was the essence of life. The Jews of this region were mostly poor, and barely eked out a living.

The **Jews of Sub-Carpathian Ruthenia** numbered 110,000 (15% of the population). They were the least assimilated of the Czechoslovak Jews. One-half of **Mukačevo** (where my aunt Malcsi and her family lived), and one-third of the capital, **Užhorod**, were Jewish. It is noteworthy that the founder of the **Hassidic movement, Israel Baal Shem Tov (1698–1760),** was born in this region. Ruthenia also boasted two **Hebrew high schools** (gymnasia), one in Mukačevo and the other in Užhorod. In a census taken in this region in 1941, under Hungarian occupation, about 6,000 Jews claimed Hebrew as their mother tongue—an unusual phenomenon in those days.

Czechoslovakia's concession to Jewish nationalism was unprecedented. Tomas Masaryk and a large number of leading intellectuals openly supported Zionism. In 1926, Czechoslovakia established diplomatic relations with the British Mandate in Palestine and opened a consulate there. **In 1927, Masaryk visited Palestine** and was hosted in the new settlements of Beit Alpha and Sarid, which were established by Czechoslovak immigrants. Later on, a settlement in northern Israel was named **Kfar Masaryk** in his honor.

Masaryk's attitude towards Zionism is shown in the following incident that occurred in **1934**. That year Masaryk visited the old synagogue in Brno, the Capital of Moravia. It was the last day of Chanukah and the candelabrum (chanukiah) was lit with nine candles. The president inquired why eight candles were standing in a row with the ninth standing to the side. The rabbi explained that the ninth candle is the Shames (servant) that lights the other eight but does not belong to them. Masaryk replied with a sigh: "This ninth candle seems to me to symbolize the Jewish nation. The other eight candles represent the nations of the world that derive the light from you, whereas you stand aside without participation. You must stop being servants and become masters of your own Jewish state in Palestine." The Jewish congregation was shocked. The president of the republic was advising them to leave the land that they had inhabited for a thousand years! Masaryk continued: "I know you are good citizens but in the eyes of the masses you are not equals. With the rise of Hitler, things will get worse, even in Czechoslovakia. The poison of racial hatred

74

undermines even the noblest soul. With heavy heart I repeat: leave Czechoslovakia before it is too late." Thus spoke Masaryk in 1934. Too few heeded his advice.

There was considerable Zionist activity in Czechoslovakia. The **12ᵗʰ and 13ᵗʰ Zionist Congresses** took place in **Karlovy Vary** (Karlsbad) in **1921** and **1923**, respectively. Under the leadership of **Dr. Oskar Neumann**, the first Zionist youth rally took place in Nitra on September 7, 1924. Until 1938, the Slovak Zionists were part of the Czechoslovak Zionist Federation. In 1938, the Zionists of Slovakia formed an independent Zionist organization headed by Dr. Oskar Neumann. It was in that year that I joined the leftist Zionist youth movement, **Hashomer Hatzair**. There were other Zionist youth movements, covering the entire political spectrum: **Betar** on the right, **Maccabi Tzair** in the center, and the religious group **Mizrachi**. Between 1932 and 1936, 3,200 Jews emigrated from Slovakia, most of them to Palestine.

There was a large number of Jewish sports clubs, whose members were among the leading athletes of Czechoslovakia. The swimming club **Bar Kochba, Bratislava (BKB)** (which my sister and I joined in 1935), won the Czechoslovak championship in 1937. Another well-known sports club was **Makabea, Bratislava**; my father competed for them. A sign of significant sports activities in Czechoslovakia was that the **Maccabi World Congress** took place in **1929 in Moravská Ostrava** where it was decided that the first Maccabiah in Palestine would take place in 1932.

The cultural activities of the Jews in Czechoslovakia were significant. The German-Jewish community contributed a whole range of great writers, scholars, and musicians, some from the pre-World War I generation. They included, among others, **Sigmund Freud, Gustav Mahler, Franz Kafka, Franz Werfel, Max Brod, Hugo Bergmann** (who, incidentally, was the uncle of my sister Erika's first husband, Franz). The educational system in Czechoslovakia was one of the best in Europe, and the Jewish minority benefited from it. About 20% of all university students were Jews, although the ratio in the overall population was only 2.5%. Jewish academics were appointed professors at the Czech and German universities in Prague, and at the Slovak University in Bratislava.

Notwithstanding the prosperity and relative freedom of the Jews during the interwar period, sporadic anti-Semitic outbursts did occur in Slovakia. These were mainly provoked by the clerical, fascist, **Slovak People's Party** (*Slovenská Lǔdová Strana*) (**SLS**), whose leader was **Andrej Hlinka**, from **1923** until his death in **August 1938**. He was succeeded by **Jozef Tiso**. In addition, the ethnic Germans, a minority in Slovakia, formed the **German Party** (*Deutsche Partei*) (**DP**) under the leadership of Franz Karmasin; this DP contributed its share to the anti-Semitic excesses.

As I mentioned at the beginning of this section, the November pillages occurred shortly after the establishment of the republic in 1919. On **November 20, 1920**, serious **anti-Semitic demonstrations** took place at the Komensky University in Bratislava, provoked by the Volksdeutsche (ethnic German) students of the medical school. Hitler's rise to power in 1933 not only emboldened the German **Sudetendeutsche Partei (SDP)** in Bohemia, but also the anti-Semitic Slovak nationalistic parties, which advocated more and more openly the establishment of an independent Slovakia—or at least a Slovakia with a much wider autonomy and self-rule. The signing of the **Czechoslovak-Soviet Treaty of Assistance** on **May 16, 1935,** aroused strong criticism by the Slovak People's Party. It was a signal for agitation against what they called Judeo-Bolshevism. In **1936**, the Slovak nationalistic leaders coined the slogan[37] "**Na Slovensku po slovensky**" (In Slovakia speak Slovak). It was aimed primarily at the Czechs residing in Slovakia, but it contained unmistakable overtones of anti-Semitism. In April of the same year, anti-Jewish demonstrations took place in Bratislava on the occasion of the showing of the film "Golem." In **March 1937, Karol Sidor**, one of the leaders of the SLS, proposed, in the Foreign Committee of the Chamber of Deputies, that the Jews of Slovakia be transferred to Birobidjan in the Soviet Union, as "they are communists anyway." Karol Sidor incited the crowd during a rally, calling Jews, "notorious poisoners of Christian wells." A Trnava printing house issued a brochure of 80 pages, which treated the Jewish question with open enmity.

It was the year **1938**, which turned out to be a watershed in the worsening situation of the Jews in Slovakia. On **February 8**, Franz Karmasin, the head of the German Party (DP), met secretly with Andrej Hlinka, head of the SLS, to coordinate future tactics against the Jews. The **Annexation** (*Anschluss*) **of Austria**, on the **12th and 13th of March 1938**, and the resulting proximity to Bratislava of the German occupation army, caused a great shock to the Jews and everybody else—except the leadership of the SLS, which welcomed it.

The decisive events that ended the integrity of the Czechoslovak Republic followed in quick succession. It started with Chamberlain's journey to Germany and the signing of the **Munich Agreement on September 28, 1938**. On **October 5, 1938, President Beneš resigned** and went into exile in England. On **October 7**, a new Slovak government was set up under the catholic priest, **Monsignor Jozef Tiso**. Czechoslovakia, now officially called **Czecho-Slovakia** (hyphenated!), became a Federal state embracing autonomous Slovakia.

The establishment of a totalitarian, single-party regime in autonomous Slovakia made the situation of the Jews very precarious. On **October 16, 1938**, a meeting took place between Field Marshal **Göring** and Ferdinand **Ďurčanský**, the Slovak Minister of Foreign Affairs, with the participation of Šaňo **Mach**, the Slovak Interior Minister, and Franz **Karmasin**, head of the German Party. The Slovak leaders declared that the "**Jewish problem**" in Slovakia would be solved in a manner similar to that in Germany.

The first move of the autonomous Slovak government in domestic policy was to exclude Jewish students from the Bratislava University; the exclusion of Jews from high schools followed a few months later.

Hitler, trying to soften up Hungary to prevent its opposition to his anticipated invasion of Czechoslovakia, convened, on **November 2, 1938,** a meeting in Vienna in which he allocated a large portion (a third) of the Slovak territory to Hungary. It included a population of 850,000, among them about 40,000 Jews. The feelings of disappointment and dismay of the Slovak population turned to hatred against the Jews, who were held responsible for the loss of the territories because they used the Hungarian language as their vernacular.

The newly established **Hlinka Guard** (*Hlinková Garda*), and the **Voluntary Defense Squadron** (*Freiwillige Schutzstaffel*) of the ethnic Germans, became the police force of the

---

[37] The Slovaks coined a large number of catchy slogans that were plastered all over towns and shouted during demonstrations. Some examples: "Slovensko Slovákom, Palestina Židákom" (Slovakia for Slovaks, Palestine for kikes), "Češy peši do Prahy" (Czechs! Go on foot to Prague), "So Sidorom proti Židom" (With Sidor against the Jews); and later on: "Tiso, Tuka, jedna ruka" (Tiso and Tuka go hand in hand), "Šaňo Mach, Židom strach" (Šaňo Mach: Jews! Have fear!); and after Hlinko died in 1938: "Hlinka, otec, sladko spí; Slovnsko už netrpý" (Father Hlinka sweetly sleeps; Slovakia no longer suffers).

new order. Beating up Jews and Czechs became the order of the day, which, unfortunately, I experienced personally. Slovak leaders now openly demanded that property "stolen" by the Jews be returned to the people. Many Slovaks saw in these demands an easy avenue towards satisfying their greed.

On **October 25, 1938**, Franz Karmasin, the leader of the German minority, became a member of the Slovak Diet. In reality, he was a liaison officer between the Slovak leaders and the Third Reich. He played an important role in the anti-Jewish policies of the new regime.

A new Jewish central organization came into being, the **Jewish Central Office for the Land of Slovakia** (*Židovská Ústredna Úradovna pre Krajinu Slovenska*) (**ZUV**). It incorporated all Jewish cultural and economic institutions and organizations.

The anti-Jewish excesses in Slovakia intensified. A boycott of Jewish shops was organized. The pattern of the German Kristallnacht was repeated in **Trnava**, where in early **December of 1938,** the synagogue was badly damaged by the mob. The most gruesome plight was that of the "stateless," who had been born in the territory ceded to Hungary. These people, among them many Jews, were forcefully taken in the middle of the night, placed on trucks and sent to the Hungarian border. This campaign was organized with the help of **Adolph Eichmann,** who came from Vienna in November to give the Slovaks a helping hand. The Hungarians refused to admit the expellees, so that hundreds of families stayed for weeks in the no-man's land, inadequately clothed and without food, before they were finally admitted to Hungary.

On **December 18, 1938**, the first election to the Slovak Diet took place. It was organized along Nazi lines with only one list of candidates being presented to the electorate. The establishment of this government, with strong ties to, and sympathies with, Nazi Germany, heralded the dawn of the darkest phase in the history of Slovak Jewry.

1939–1945. The fateful years

Slovakia declares independence on March 14, 1939; the anti-Jewish laws

In **March 1939**, Tiso was summoned to Berlin by Hitler, who encouraged, or, more precisely, pressured him to break off completely from Czecho-Slovakia, and promised him full protection of mighty Germany.[38] Upon Tiso's return from Berlin, **Slovakia declared independence on March 14, 1939,** with Monsignor Jozef Tiso as its president. Under his leadership, Slovakia became the staunchest and most loyal of Nazi allies; in effect it was a puppet state of Germany.

High on the list of priorities of the new Slovak government was the "Jewish problem." A prerequisite of its solution was to determine who should be considered a Jew. On **April 18, 1939**, the government issued **Ordinance #63**, according to which a Jew is anybody who: 1) had professed Judaism, even if he or she had converted after October 30,

---

[38] This was cunningly engineered by Hitler who, the following day, occupied the Czech and Bohemian territory—but not Czechoslovakia, as that state had ceased to exist with the break-off of Slovakia the day before. This fact was used by Chamberlain to renege on the British commitment made at Munich to safeguard the borders of Czechoslovakia. He proclaimed that since Czechoslovakia no longer existed, the agreement no longer applied.

1918; 2) had at least one Jewish parent;[39] 3) was married to, or was living in, an extramarital relationship with, a Jew.

The second part of Ordinance #63 dealt with restrictions in the number of Jews in certain liberal professions. The number of attorneys permitted to practice law (and represent only Jewish clients) was restricted to 4% of the total number of attorneys. A similar restriction to 4% was imposed on Jewish physicians. This represented a tremendous reduction, as 50% of all the attorneys and physicians of Slovakia were Jewish. The practice of other professions, such as public notary, was forbidden to Jews.

The laws affecting the education and school attendance of Jewish students imposed a particularly severe hardship. A decree enacted on **June 13, 1939**, restricted the number of Jewish students at public schools to 4% (**numerus clausus**) of the total student body. A few months later, the law was changed to exclude Jews altogether from public schools (**numerus nullus**). These laws affected me directly. At the beginning of the summer I qualified as the one Jew who was admitted to the technical high school, but, by September, I was barred from entering the school.

The reaction of most of the Jewish community, during the early stages of the Slovak State, was an unrealistic optimism. They were convinced that the services of Jewish businessmen and professional people were, in the long run, indispensable to the Slovak economy. They hoped that, before long, the anti-Semitic zeal of the new regime would abate. An even more dangerous illusion, prevalent among the Slovak Jews at the time, was that Germany would lose the war in a short time. How wrong they were, and how fatal their mistake turned out to be!

However, some people were more far-sighted, and a few were proactive in trying to alleviate the plight of the Jews. Thus, in April and **May, 1939, Dr. Robert Füredi**, head of the Central Jewish Relief Committee of Slovakia, **Dr. Oskar Neumann**, president of the Slovakian Zionist Organization, and **Gisi Fleischmann**, a member of its executive committee, set out for London and Paris to arouse the conscience of the world to the plight of Nazism's victims. But their pleas fell on deaf and indifferent ears. Britain guarded its Palestine Mandate with protective jealousy, admitting refugees only grudgingly and in a trickle. The United States, meanwhile, felt no compunction about turning away shiploads of desperate refugees from its own shores (e.g., see page 108).

It was discouraging to watch the disgraceful unwavering coldness of the US State Department and the British Foreign Office, in whose corridors spiritual brutality wrapped itself in the veneer of legality, of regulations, and of reasons of State. This experience was to repeat itself on other occasions during the war.

Meanwhile, the pouring of refugees into Slovakia increased with every triumph of the Nazis. In 1939, they came from Germany, Austria, and the German-controlled Protectorate of Bohemia and Moravia. A typical refugee situation was that of two groups that arrived in Bratislava. One group left Vienna on **December 20, 1939,** and was supposed to go by steamer down the Danube to the Black Sea, and proceed on to Palestine by ship as **illegal immigrants (Aliya Bet).** But when the group arrived in Bratislava, the ships were not available. The stranded people were interned, together with Austrian Jews who had been

---

[39] Note that this was slightly more lax than the Nüremberg Laws of Germany, according to which one Jewish grandparent was sufficient to mark the offspring a Jew. The Slovak law was later changed to conform more closely to the Nüremberg Laws.

residing as foreigners in Slovakia, in an abandoned munitions factory called **Patronka,** in the outskirts of Bratislava. The parents of my best friend, **Hugo Lustig,** who were Austrian citizens, were among the internees. I remember visiting them and bringing them food parcels that my mother prepared. Hugo had immigrated legally with the Youth Aliya to Palestine in 1939.[40]

Another group, that had arrived from Prague, and was stranded in Bratislava because the ships were not available, was housed in a building called **Slobodarna**, a cheap hotel near the railroad station. All the refugees in the camps had to be supported by Bratislava's **Central Jewish Relief Committee**, whose resources were being stretched very thin.

The main reason for the unavailability of the ships was that the British were buying them up to prevent the illegal immigration to Palestine. Finally, on **September 4, 1940**, the two groups began to leave, ironically, on four German ships flying the Nazi swastika. This happened because Germany had decided to bring back to Germany the "Volga Germans" that resided in Bessarabia (a region that had been ceded by Romania to the Soviet Union). Rather than let the ships that went down the Danube to the Black Sea (to pick up the Volga Germans) go empty, the Germans were happy to accept even the despised Jews as passengers, especially since the Jews were made to pay huge fares. In addition, the Germans had the satisfaction of complicating British relations with the Arabs. All four ships arrived safely at the Black Sea, where the passengers transferred to freighters carrying them to Palestine. But that's another story.

According to the statistics of the Central Jewish Office, 7,000 Jews left Slovakia during the period from **March 14, 1939, to the end of 1941**. About half of them went to Palestine, the rest were dispersed among 23 other countries. It is during this period that my sister (in **September 1939**) and I (in **April 1941**) left Slovakia.

In 1940, one year after the restrictions of Ordinance #63 went into effect, further steps were taken to eliminate the Jews from the economy of the Slovak State. On **April 25, 1940**, the **Aryanization Law #113** was passed. Under this law, Jewish owners of businesses had to take on Aryan "partners," but were still allowed, and often even asked, to continue to participate in the management of the business as low-paid employees. This was the case of my father's business. The Aryanization Law was meant to satisfy the anti-Semitic sentiments of the Slovak population, while not disrupting the country's economy by precipitously depriving it of its Jewish workers and experts.

Effective **July 1, 1940**, rent-control laws were no longer applicable to apartments or workshops rented by Jews. This meant that Jews could be evicted at the whim of the landlord. It was in **December 1940** that we were evicted from our apartment on Gajova 9, a modern building owned by the Magnezit Company, one of whose directors was Mr. Horňak, the father of my good friend Tomy. In addition, Jews were forbidden to own radios, telephones, cars, and were banned from restaurants, parks, public gardens, and places of entertainment. Jews were required to deposit all securities and valuables in their possession with the authorities.

The Third Reich, as expected, played a decisive role in Slovakia's internal affairs. On **July 8, 1940**, **Hitler** and the German Foreign Minister, **Joachim von Ribbentrop**, met

---

[40] As I was writing this, I received an unexpected phone call from Hugo (now Gershon) Lustig in Israel. He expressed his pleasure in having met me and my family in Jerusalem and asked whether I could send him any written material on my work and life. I sent him, among other pieces, this write-up.

with the Slovak delegation headed by President **Tiso** in Salzburg. At the meeting Ribbentrop forced a reorganization on the Slovak government along the lines of the National Socialist regime of Nazi Germany. **Ferdinand Ďurčanský,** who had been Minister of the Interior and Foreign Affairs and who tried to preserve independence from Germany, was replaced by two fanatically pro-Nazi politicians, **Alexander (Šaňo) Mach** to serve as Minister of Internal Affairs and **Vojtech Tuka** as Prime Minister and Minister of Foreign Affairs. SS-Hauptsturmführer **Dieter Wisliceny**, a subordinate of Eichmann, became the "advisor on Jewish affairs" to the Slovak government. He was to play a crucial role in the execution of the "Final Solution."

On **September 3, 1940**, the Slovak parliament adopted **Law #210**, which authorized the government to take any action it deemed necessary in matters of Aryanization, liquidation of Jewish enterprises, and expropriation of Jewish assets. These laws greatly benefited the Slovak middle class, which took over stores, workshops, and other enterprises. The result was increased wealth of this segment of the population, which predisposed it favorably towards the government during the war years.

The agency that was created on September 16, 1940 to implement the anti-Jewish laws was the **Central Economic Office** (*Ústredný Hospodárysky Úrad*) headed by **Augustin Moravek**. It was given the status of a "central authority" within the Prime Minister's office.

The creation of the Jewish Office, and the clandestine Working Group

A central authority was also created within the Jewish community to coordinate the enforcement of government orders. On **September 30, 1940**, the Slovak government **(decree #234)** dissolved all Jewish organizations, including the Central Jewish Relief Committee, and in their stead established the **Jewish Office** (*Ústredna Židov*). It was headed by a "Jewish elder" (*starosta*) who was personally responsible to the Central Economic Office that appointed him. A debate ensued among the Jewish leaders whether to cooperate with the new office, which was clearly designed to be a tool against the Jews. They concluded that this agency was a fact of life that could not be avoided, and decided to join it and try to accomplish whatever good might be possible through it.

Shortly after the establishment of the official Jewish Office, a secret underground group called the **Working Group** (*Pracovná Skupina*) was formed. It became the core of Jewish resistance to Nazism in Slovakia. The acknowledged leader of the Working Group was the valiant woman **Gisi Fleischmann**; others included the orthodox **Rabbi Michael Dov-Ber Weissmandl, Rabbi Armin Frieder**, the Zionist leader **Dr. Oskar Neumann, Ondřej Steiner, Dr. Albert Winterstein, Dr. Tibor Kováč,** and **Viliam Fürst**.

The Working Group was able to establish secret contacts with several high officials in the Slovak government. The most important was the contact with **Josef Sivak**, the Catholic Minister of Education and Culture. He kept the Jewish leaders informed about planned anti-Jewish measures. Other officials were approached, in most cases with bribes. Notable among these was **Dr. Isidor Koso**, head of the president's bureau. Among the clergymen who offered help was the papal nuncio in Bratislava, **Monsignor Giuseppe Burzio,** who willingly acted as a conduit for conveying messages to the outside world. Another helpful cleric was **Father Pozdech**, whose heart belonged to the now dismembered Czechoslovakia rather than the independent Slovakia.

In **September 1941**, a comprehensive ordinance called the **Jewish Code**, which was drafted by Interior Minister Šaňo Mach, was adopted by the Slovak parliament. It contained 270 articles and was essentially a replica of the Nüremberg Laws of Nazi Germany. The code recognized the **racial** principle of Jewishness and, therefore, no longer recognized any conversions. Anybody with at least one Jewish grandparent was considered a Jew.

Under the Jewish Code, all Jews above the age of six were required to wear the **yellow Star of David**. This order took effect on Rosh Hashanah (the Jewish New Year), **September 22, 1941**. The Jewish Code authorized the Central Economic Office to expel Jews from any city, and to resettle them elsewhere in Slovakia. An order was issued to expel most of the Jews from Bratislava by the end of 1941. The **expulsion** started the night of **October 27, 1941**. By **March 1, 1942**, 6,700 (about half of the Jewish population of Bratislava) had been resettled.

Until the end of 1941, although Jews lost their property, civil liberties, and human rights, they were still allowed to live in Slovakia, and the deportations and mass killings had not yet started. This was about to change in the following months.

The strategy of the Nazis, carried out by Adolf Eichmann in each occupied country, was to strip the Jews of all their possessions, thereby making them a burden to the local governments and creating an acute "Jewish problem." The Germans provided a convenient solution, which most of the governments, some of them willingly, some with hesitation, accepted without resistance: the deportation of the Jews to the east. This approach was also adopted by Dieter Wisliceny, a deputy of Adolf Eichmann, who was in charge of the solution of the "Jewish problem" in Slovakia. By the **end of 1941**, the stage was set in Slovakia for the **deportations** to be considered and implemented.

The first wave of deportations, March 26 to October 1942

In the **autumn of 1941**, Interior Minister Šaňo Mach set up a department within his ministry, known as Department 14, headed by **Dr. Anton Vašek**, whose task was to deal with the deportation of Jews. At the same time, President Tiso and Prime Minister Vojtech Tuka requested Reichsführer-SS Himmler's aid in solving Slovakia's "Jewish problem." When Eichmann, Himmler's deputy, demanded 500 Reichsmarks (about 20 dollars at the time) for each Jew deported, to pay for "job training of unskilled workers," the Slovaks eagerly complied.

On **March 6, 1942**, Premier Tuka reported to the Council of States, one of the highest authorities in the Slovak government, that deportations of Jews would begin in March 1942, and would be completed by August 1942.

In preparation for the deportation, the Ministry for Internal Affairs adopted a series of organizational measures. All Jews were ordered to register and report to their district boards for physical examination. This was followed by the second phase: the concentration of Jews at specific locations. These were at the Patronka near Bratislava, in **Sered** and **Novaky**, and the military barracks in **Poprad** and **Žilina**.

On **March 26, 1942**, the first deportations of 1,000 Jewish girls to the death camp in **Auschwitz** took place. Further transports **between March 26 and April 5, 1942**, involved only young men and women, a total of 8,000 people. The elimination of much of the youth from the Jewish population reduced the chance of active resistance from the rest of the Jews. After **April 11, 1942**, entire families were deported.

In the middle of the deportations, on **May 15, 1942**, the Parliament passed **law #68,** giving legal sanction to the deportation. This implicated the Slovak Parliament directly in the physical annihilation of Slovakia's Jewish population. Law #68 sanctioned the deportation and specified those who would be exempt from it. The exemptions included: individuals who had been baptized before March 14, 1939 (the establishment of the independence of Slovakia); Jews who were married to non-Jewish spouses prior to September 10, 1941 (the effective date of the Jewish Code); and those exempted by President Tiso. The law further stated that Jews deported from Slovakia would lose their Slovak citizenship, and their property would be confiscated by the State.

After **October 20, 1942**, the deportations stopped. At this point a total of about 60,000 Jews had been deported, out of Slovakia's total population of 90,000. It should be pointed out that of the 90,000, about 7,000 had fled to Hungary (many of whom returned in 1944), others were living in Slovakia with forged Aryan documents or were exempted from deportation by the law discussed in the previous paragraph. Thus, a total of about 20,000 Jews remained in Slovakia at the time.

The reaction to the deportations

What was the reaction of the population to the deportations? Were there dissensions within the government? What was the position of the clergy? What actions did the Jewish Office and the Working Group take to try to ameliorate the situation of the Jews? I shall address these questions in turn.

The initial anti-Jewish laws promulgated during 1939–1941, which deprived the Jews, step by step, of their property and participation in the economic life of Slovakia, were received by the majority of the Slovak population with satisfaction and even enthusiasm. It gratified their greed as they derived material benefits from those actions, and it satisfied their pervasive anti-Semitic feelings. However, the brutalities associated with the deportation of the Jews in 1942, knowledge of which kept trickling down from Poland, started to foment moral indignation among the general population. The Slovak people began to have second thoughts: the brutalities seemed beyond justification. And they did not yet know about the mass murders at Auschwitz. A case in point was Mr. Jablonka, one of the Arisators of my father's business, who was a rabid anti-Semite and treated my father very badly. He became a changed man after he returned from a stay in Poland where he witnessed the atrocities perpetrated on the Jews. From that point on, he behaved civilly and kindly to my father.

This change in mood of the Slovak population was perceived by Eichmann and his henchmen. To allay the concerns of the population, both non-Jewish and Jewish, Eichmann initiated a spate of correspondence from the deportees to relatives and friends in Slovakia. In **August 1943**, 2,500 letters and postcards from the concentration camps reached Slovakia, all of them saying essentially the same: "We are working and we are well." Little did the Slovaks suspect that, by the time the letters arrived, the writers had been murdered.

To further obfuscate the truth, **Fritz Fiala**, editor of the viciously anti-Semitic German newspaper **Der Grenzbote** (The Border Messenger), was sent to prepare a report on the alleged living conditions of the deported Jews. Fiala was accompanied on his "tour of inspection" by Dieter Wisliceny. His fictitious story, made believable with the inclusion of carefully contrived pictures, appeared to confirm that the deportees were indeed alive and treated well.

The psychological results of these campaigns of lies produced the expected results. It allayed the fears and soothed the conscience of a large segment of the Christian Slovak population. It also fooled many of the remaining Jews, some of whom actually welcomed the prospect of deportation, with its hope of a reunion with their dear ones.

However, the Slovak government was not convinced by these rather primitive and transparent strategies, and kept putting pressure on Eichmann to have a Slovak commission visit a concentration camp. Eichmann finally agreed to have a **Slovak delegation** inspect the concentration camp in **Terezin** (*Theresienstadt*), and had the camp spruced up for the occasion. This so-called "Potemkin village" approach was also used to fool the International Red Cross.

The members of the Slovak government and Parliament, with very few exceptions, offered very little resistance to the passage and enforcement of the anti-Jewish laws. Among the exceptions were: **Dr. Josef Sivak**, Minister of Education, who issued many letters of protection to Jewish teachers; **Dr. Gejza Fritz**, Minister of Justice; and **Dr. Mikuláš Pružinský**, Minister of Finance, who did not dismiss the Jewish employees in his department. An important opponent of the deportation was **Dr. Karol Sidor**, a fervent anti-Semite, who, nevertheless, thought that aping Nazi politics would hurt his country. As a result, he fell from grace, had to resign, and was made ambassador to the Vatican.

One memorable event occurred on **March 26, 1942**, the day the first deportation took place. On that day the deportation issue appeared on the agenda of the Slovak Council of State. The debate was opened by a motion submitted by **Dr. Ján Balko**, Deputy Governor of the Slovak National Bank. It dealt with the ethical and moral aspects of the deportation of Jews from Slovakia. Among other things, Balko said: "Is it justifiable to treat Jews in this manner? Can we permit this violation of the laws of nature and God?" In view of the prevailing anti-Semitic passions, it represented a remarkable and singular act of bravery. Not surprisingly, the motion did not pass. Although the delegates were aware that the harsh anti-Jewish measures were at variance with their basic religious beliefs, their lack of courage, and fear of being branded "Jew-lover," as well as their ingrained, traditional anti-Jewish prejudices, made it easy to rationalize and accept the deportation of Jews as an inescapable fact, imposed on them by the mighty Reich.

After the German defeat at Stalingrad in **February 1943,** and the downfall of fascism in Italy in **June 1943**, many Slovak officials feared for the survival of the Slovak State. They became more cautious, and some even attempted to cover up their past anti-Jewish behavior. On **September 3, 1943**, three governmental committees, under the leadership of the Speaker of the Parliament, **Dr. Martin Sokel**, met and issued a statement, warning that the brutal solution of the "Jewish problem" would have severe consequences abroad on the image of the Slovak State. They stated: "Political, common sense demands that we should have respect for public opinion in neutral states, beginning with the Holy See...." It was an attempt by the Parliament to rehabilitate, as it were, the remaining Jews.

The increasing negative attitude of the Slovak people and the government, forced the Germans to ease off. Thus, the Slovak government was able to resist the German pressure, and the deportations were not resumed.

The Church, as always, played an important part in the politics of Slovakia. One just has to look at the power attained by some of the clergymen. The priest Andrej Hlinka was the co-founder and leader of the Slovak People's Party, which ruled during the fateful years, 1939–1945, and the President of Slovakia during this period was Monsignor Josef Tiso. A large percentage of the members of the parliament were clergymen. Thus, the Church bears a heavy responsibility for the mass murder of the Slovak Jews. It brings to mind the Catholic Church's responsibility for the brutalities during the Inquisition, and its anti-Semitic incitements throughout the ages. What an incongruity, considering Christ's teachings of loving kindness!

Although the Church condoned most of the government's anti-Jewish laws, it objected to some, in particular those that dealt with the non-recognition of baptized Jews, and those that involved excessive brutality. But their protests were mostly meek and ineffective. This is reminiscent of the behavior of **Pope Pius XII**, who never openly condemned the actions of Nazi Germany.

The first instance of opposition from the Catholic bishops to anti-Jewish law was provoked by the Jewish Code. At a conference in **Nitra** on **October 7, 1941**, the bishops drafted a memorandum pointing out that the Jewish Code was based on racism, a doctrine rejected by the Church. However, they made it clear that the Church was not opposed to the basic intent of the Code. Their concern was only with the legal status of the Jews that had converted to Roman Catholicism. But the bishops did not take any action, and quietly accepted a noncommittal promise from President Tiso that he would grant appropriate exemptions.

By the **middle of 1942**, during the height of the deportations, the Church began to realize that if it did not protest against the crimes perpetrated against the Jews, it, too, might also end up as a victim of Nazi brutality. A steadily-growing number of clergymen interceded with the Slovak authorities on behalf of the Jews. Also, the Vatican, through its nuncio in Bratislava, Monsignor Giuseppe Burzio, exerted a steady pressure against deportation. In addition to the prevalent Roman Catholic Church, the Evangelical bishops of Slovakia issued a statement in **August 1942**, condemning the deportation as not being in conformity with the fundamentals of humaneness, and the basic principles of Christianity.

The following year, on **March 8, 1943**, the Catholic hierarchy issued a pastoral letter, signed by all Catholic bishops of Slovakia, warning the government against measures "which would deprive our citizens of their personal and material freedom." A bit late, as the majority of Jews had been already deported and most of them were no longer alive. On **May 5, 1943**, the Vatican handed to the Slovak ambassador a note expressing its unhappiness with the Slovak intentions to resume deportations. This pronouncement, as well as the previous ones, had no real teeth to it. How much more effective would it have been if the Pope had threatened Tiso with excommunication the previous year! It might have saved tens of thousands of Jews.

The main official function of the Jewish Office was to enforce the anti-Jewish laws that were passed. In this task it had little freedom, and had to follow orders from the Slovak officials. These activities, understandably, evoked criticisms and resentment from the Jewish community. The development of this situation was probably intended by the Slovak government, and was in line with the fiendish Nazi scheme of pitting Jew against Jew (e.g., the notorious Jewish kapos—overseers in the concentration camps). Fortunately, there were other areas of activity in which the Jewish Office had more freedom, and was able to make positive contributions to the welfare of the Jews.

One of the important achievements of the Jewish Office was their officially-sanctioned **rescue efforts**. One of them was the release of inmates from Polish concentration camps. Following the conquest of Poland in 1939, the Germans set up concentration camps in Silesia for Jews who were living in the Protectorate of Bohemia and Moravia. However, the Germans were willing to release those internees who could prove that they could enter another country. The Jewish Office went into action and obtained Slovak entry permits for the internees. They arrived in Slovakia on **February 1940** (long before the deportations from Slovakia started), and were placed into camps set up for them.

Another of the activities of the Jewish Office was to provide subsistence to the Austrian and Czech internees that were housed in Patronka and Slobodarna, as described earlier (see page 79). The Jewish Office was also involved in **organizing illegal immigration** (Aliya Bet) to Palestine during the period that the Slovak government had no objections to Jews leaving the country.

Much useful work was done by the Jewish Office under the direction of Dr. Oscar Neumann, who supervised the **vocational training** of youth in agriculture and the trades. Those who were successful in immigrating to Palestine greatly benefited from this training. Others, who were placed into labor camps in Slovakia (to be discussed later), also benefited from it. After the deportations started in March 1942, the training office was dismantled and replaced by the reclamation office, whose job was to find legal grounds to **prevent individual deportations**. This office was headed by Dr. Tibor Kováč, who had to deal with Dr. Koso, head of the president's bureau, and Dr. Vašek, head of the feared Department 14. Kováč and his colleagues at first had no idea that the stakes they were playing for were those of life and death. Koso and Vašek, at this point, very likely also did not know, but they also did not want to know, and made a point of not inquiring about the fate of the deportees.

The Jewish Office also served as a bridge between the Jewish community and the Slovak government. As such, it tried on several occasions, albeit mostly unsuccessfully, to **protest and plead** on behalf of the Jewish community. For instance, when the members of the Jewish Office first learned about the deportation plan late in February 1942, they wrote a letter to president Tiso pointing out its illegality according to international law, and its economic consequences for Slovakia. In the letter they appealed to Tiso's humane and religious sentiments. Tiso was not moved by any of the arguments, and sent Augustin Moravek, chairman of the Central Economic Office, and Dieter Wisliceny, to inform the Jewish Office that the deportation plans were official.

Last but not least, the Jewish Office provided an umbrella organization, a cover, for the **clandestine operations** of the Working Group (see page 80). The activities of the Working Group proceeded along several lines: 1) establishing contact with, and providing help to, the deportees in Poland; 2) organizing and facilitating the shuttle of Jews between Slovakia and Hungary, depending on which country was safer at the time; 3) bribing key Slovak officials to stop or at least delay the deportations.

Rabbis Weissmandl and Frieder of the Working Group led the effort of helping the deportees as much as possible. Non-Jews were sent as emissaries to Poland, to bring information and take material aid to the refugees. They were, of course, paid sizable sums of money for their risky undertaking. In **November 1942**, one of the messengers confirmed, without a doubt, that the Nazi goal was the annihilation of the entire Jewish people. The horrors of Auschwitz, however, still remained unknown. It was at that time that my parents in Bratislava received a letter, smuggled out from the concentration camp Opole, written by my aunt Malcsi, asking for help and describing the horrors of the camp.

After the deportations of Jews from Slovakia had stopped in autumn of 1942, the Working Group concentrated on receiving Jews from Poland. The number of Jews who escaped from Poland to Slovakia during 1943 was about 2,500. That Working Group organized help for the transients and facilitated their illegal crossing to Hungary

One plan that unfortunately fell through at the last moment involved 10,000 Polish-Jewish children who were to go to Palestine. The Working Group's negotiations with Wisliceny were progressing well until the **Grand Mufti of Jerusalem**, who was residing in Berlin, got wind of the planned action. He lodged a strong protest with Himmler, on the grounds that these Jewish children would grow up and add to the Jewish strength in Palestine. Himmler thereupon cancelled the plan.

In **March 1944**, German troops invaded Hungary. Until then, the situation of the Jews in Hungary had been far better than in Slovakia; the Working Group was active in organizing and facilitating the passage of Slovak Jews into Hungary. Most of them crossed the border illegally. It was in **April 1941** that I crossed into Hungary on my way to Palestine. In **1942**, several of my cousins and friends attempted to flee to Hungary. Two of my cousins, **Herta** and **Gerti**, were caught on the Hungarian side of the border and were returned to Slovakia. They were immediately deported, and perished in the concentration camp. My cousin **Ilse** and several of my friends, among them **Ula** and **Andrej Fabry**, and **Josef Mayer**, were successful in entering Hungary. After **March 1944**, the situation of the Jews in Hungary became much worse than in Slovakia. There were about 7,000 Slovak Jewish refugees in Hungary who wanted to return to Slovakia. The Working Group went again into action and helped them to return. It should be mentioned that many were helped by the selfless efforts of **Dr. Ján Spišiak**, the Slovak ambassador in Budapest, who defied the law and instructions, and issued Slovak passports and "letters of protection."

Efforts to save the remaining Jews from deportation: the Europa Plan and the establishment of productive labor camps

By the summer of 1942, there remained only some 20,000 (out of 90,000) Jews in all of Slovakia. The Working Group worked hard to save the remaining Jews from deportation. In **June 1942**, they managed to **bribe Dr. Anton Vašek**, (head of Department 14, which dealt with the deportations) so effectively that a number of transports which had been scheduled to leave Slovakia found it impossible to do so because of "technical difficulties." While the Slovak authorities were, temporarily at least, kept in check, it was necessary to also keep the Germans calm. To do so, the Working Group decided to bribe Dieter Wisliceny with the sizeable sum of 40,000 dollars. Wisliceny flew to Berlin to consult with his bosses, Eichmann and Himmler. When he returned to Bratislava, he did not press for an immediate renewal of the Slovakian deportations. Perhaps Himmler already wondered what would happen if Germany lost the war, and may have thought there was safety in sparing Jewish lives. The opposition to the deportation by the majority of the population and clergy, and the fear of many members of the government of possible repercussions after the war, made the Tiso government decide to stop the deportation. **No transports took place for the next two years.**

Encouraged by the success of the briberies that the Working Group thought had staved off the deportation of the remaining Slovak Jews, Rabbi Weissmandl of the Working Group conceived a plan of awesome dimensions—the so-called **Europa Plan**. It was to end the deportation of **all** remaining Jews in Europe. The idea was to buy out the remnants of European Jewry. Wisliceny was approached, and he passed the proposal via Eichmann to Himmler. In **September 1942**, Wisliceny was empowered to offer 2 million dollars to save the lives of the remaining 1 million Jews still alive in Europe, excluding the Jews of Poland.

A feverish effort was undertaken by the Working Group to raise the money but obstacles arose at every step. The Yishuv (the Jews of Palestine) offered to put up 100,000 dollars if the Joint Distribution Committee raised the rest. But Allied currency restrictions forbade the transfer of money to Axis countries. Furthermore, some Jewish leaders feared that they would be accused of helping the Nazi war effort with the money, and of putting the rescue of their own people before a total support of the Allied victory. After protracted negotiation, **Soly Mayer**, the Joint Distribution Committee representative in Switzerland, made the unrealistic offer to put the 2 million dollars the German demanded into a blocked account, payable to Wisliceny after the war. Not surprisingly, the offer was turned down. Instead, Wisliceny made the counter proposal that 200,000 dollars be paid to him for every month without deportation. This offer was turned down by the agencies in New York. Gisi Fleischmann of the Working Group wrote in exasperation, "We do not understand the directives coming from America because they are dead rules and instructions. They have no soul, no understanding of sorrow and pain."

In **August 1943**, after a year of unsuccessful negotiations, Himmler, who oversaw Wisliceny's negotiations with great interest, cancelled the Europa Plan. A great opportunity to save 1 million Jews had been squandered.

A plan to stop the 1942 deportations, the brainchild of engineer **Ondřej Steiner** of the Working Group, was to establish **labor camps** that would turn out economically useful products (furniture, textiles and the like) which would benefit the Slovak economy. In **April 1942**, Steiner proposed this idea to Dr. Koso, who reluctantly agreed with him and sanctioned the **establishment of the camps**. Saňo Mach, the Interior Minister, opposed the plan, but lost out to Koso.

The task of the Working Group was to establish the camps as quickly as possible and make them such an economic asset that the Slovak government would hesitate to do without them. To accomplish this task, money was again of essence. Gisi Fleischmann set off at once for Budapest to obtain the funds from the rich Hungarian Jewish community. She was not successful. The Hungarian leaders insisted that every step of the money transfer must be undertaken legally. Since some of the money was needed to pay for some questionable arrangements, like bribes, such an approach clearly could not work. The short-sightedness and lack of imagination of the Hungarian Jewish leaders was mind-boggling and frustrating to the Working Group. Fortunately, the Jewish Agency in Istanbul came forth with a large part of the necessary funds.

Three main camps were set up: the one in **Sered,** which had one of the most modern and productive carpentry shops in the country; another in **Novaky,** which had tailor workshops; and one in **Vyhne,** where the main industry was construction work on state-organized baths nearby. Several of our friends, among them **Eva** and **Brco Klug, Shmuel Givoni,** and my cousins **Karol Kučera** and **Trude Gerö,** with her son **Tomy,** were in the camp in Sered. In addition to work performed at the camps, there were numerous cultural activities, including academic and vocational courses. The three camps sheltered from 3,000 to 5,000 people who were not subject to deportation. The first-rate manufacturing activities of the camps not only saved thousands of lives; they dispelled, to a large degree, the anti-Semitic misconception that Jews were incapable of doing physical work.

In addition to the camps described above, which represented self-supporting economic units run internally by Jews, there was another type of labor camp set up by the Slovak government as early as 1940. These were military camps where Jews were treated as quasi-military personnel under the jurisdiction of the Department of Defense. They were assigned to the **Sixth Labor Battalion** (*Šiesty Prápor*) and given special blue uniforms to distinguish them from the non-Jewish personnel. Our friends from the BKB swimming club, **Palo Blum** (Borsky) and **Laci Rotter,** among others, belonged to this group. In 1943 this group was dissolved, and its members were incorporated into the other Jewish camps.

On **April 21, 1944,** two weeks before the deportation of Jews from Hungary started, two young Slovak Jews, **Rudolf Vrba** and **Alfred Wetzler,** managed to escape from Auschwitz to Slovakia. They wrote a detailed report for the Working Group on the organization of the camp, the number of victims, and the plan for the annihilation of the 700,000 Jews of Hungary. A copy of the **Vrba-Wetzler report** was sent to various individuals and organizations throughout the free world. The copy that was sent to the Hechalutz Center in Geneva was accompanied by an appeal from Rabbi Weissmandl that the Allies bomb the deportation routes and crematoria in Auschwitz. The World Jewish Congress and the Jewish Agency for Palestine presented the appeal to the governments of the United States and Great Britain, but to no avail (for details, see page 157).

The Slovak uprising, August–October 1944

A fledgling partisan movement started in Slovakia in **1942,** when a group of 25 people, of whom 18 were Jews, was organized. The leader of the group was **Ernst Lipkovič,** a Slovak Jew, who was the only one with military experience, which he had acquired as a member of the International Brigade in the Spanish Civil War. Over the next two years the partisan movement grew, and in the **spring of 1944** they began to organize an armed revolt in eastern Slovakia against the Slovak government of Tiso. In the Sered and Novaky camps, clandestine underground groups were formed, to be ready when the time became ripe. On **August 29, 1944,** the **Slovak National Uprising** erupted. The guards in the Sered and Novaky camps fled; and the leaders of the Jewish underground movement declared all the inmates to be free and called on them to join the uprising, which the majority of the inmates did. On **September 1, 1944,** the partisans liberated the camp at **Vyhne,** whose able-bodied inmates also joined the revolt. The fighting spirit of the Jewish unit under the command of **Lieutenant Imrich Mueller (Ivo Milén)** is worthy of special mention. The unit was cited for bravery and its determined resistance to the German troops, which were numerically and technologically superior. The total number of Slovak partisans that were active in the resistance was 16,000. Of these, 10% were Jews. About

20% of all the Jews that fought in the partisan forces were killed. Among them was my friend **Josef Halasz.**

A special place among the Jewish fighters in the Slovak uprising was held by the four Palestinian Jewish parachutists, **Haviva Reik, Zvi Ben Yaakov, Rafael Reiss,** and **Chaim Chermesh**, who had joined the British army in Palestine. They were dropped over the area liberated by the partisans in **Banská Bystrica,** with the objective of establishing contact between the British military command and the insurgents in Slovakia. They were captured through an unfortunate incident. After escaping a German encirclement, they heard shouts in Russian and ran towards the sounds. The Russians turned out to be under the command of **General Andrei Vlasov**, who had defected to the German side. The Russian handed the parachutists over to the Germans, who executed three of them. Chermesh was successful in escaping, joined another partisan unit and, in 1945, returned to Palestine.

The Slovak government had been incapable of suppressing the uprising on its own, and asked the German army for help—a disastrous step for the remaining Jews. On **August 29**, German troops crossed the western border into Slovakia. After two months of bitter fighting, the Germans suppressed the Slovak uprising and Slovakia came effectively under German rule.

The second wave of deportations, September 1944 to March 1945

As the German troops fought the Slovak resistance and gradually occupied Slovakia, the SS began their activities. In each of the occupied areas, Jews were herded and concentrated into the former labor camp of Sered. The SS commandant of the Sered camp was now the notoriously brutal **Alois Brunner,** who had previously overseen the deportation of Jews from France and Greece. He replaced Dieter Wisliceny, and was the new man in charge of the "Jewish problem" in Slovakia.

Brunner transformed Sered into a German concentration camp and made it into a staging area for deportation to other, mostly extermination, camps. The first transport in the new wave of **deportations** left Sered on **September 30, 1944**. Brunner also ordered the immediate, but orderly, liquidation of the Jewish Office, entrusting this task to two of its members, Gisi Fleischmann and Dr. Tibor Kováč, both of whom were also members of the underground Working Group. Gisi Fleischmann was caught passing a clandestine message to the Jewish community in Hungary, and was arrested. She was immediately sent to Sered, from where she was deported to Auschwitz, where she perished. The other leading members of the Working Group survived the war; most of them settled in Israel.

Before long, protests from abroad against the resumption of the deportations began to reach Slovakia. On **October 24, 1944**, the **Swiss consul** in Bratislava handed a memorandum to the Slovak government warning that the deportations would have an adverse effect on Swiss-Slovak relations. The **archbishop of Uppsala** interceded "on behalf of the unfortunate Jewish brethren." The **Vatican**, too, instructed its representative in Bratislava to protest the deportations. **Carl Burckhardt**, president of the Red Cross, also asked Tiso to stop the deportation. But all Tiso did was pass these protests on to the German envoy in Bratislava, claiming that he had neither the means nor the power to stop the deportations.

The number of Jews living in Slovakia in 1941 was 89,000. During the first wave, March–October 1944, 59,000 Jews were deported. Only 600–800 of them were alive at the end of the war. During the second wave, September 1944–March 1945, 12,000 Jews were deported. Among them were my cousins Karol Kučera and Trude Gerö with her son Tomy. Another 3,500 Jews were shot on the spot following their arrest by the German security forces. Thus, about 80% of the Slovak Jewry was annihilated.

Epilogue

The post-war fate of the leaders that participated in the annihilation of the Slovak Jews

After the war, Jozef Tiso, the president of Slovakia during the fateful war years, was tried by the **National Court of Justice** in Bratislava. Tiso's defense was based on *ad majora mala vitanda* (in order to avoid greater evil), a phrase used by Pope Pius XII in a letter to the bishops of Berlin on April 30, 1943, explaining why he refrained from openly condemning the Nazis. Tiso stated to the court in 1947: "I have always employed every possible means to fight evil; only when the nation was menaced by an even greater evil did I give way, in order to avoid that greater evil." This greater evil, Tiso claimed, would have been the loss of Slovakia's independence, because, if they had resisted the Reich's demands, Germany would have occupied the country. This argument, which would have absolved Tiso and his government of their guilt, requires some discussion and refutation.

Ever since its founding in 1918, long before its rise to power, the Slovak People's Party had advocated the elimination of the Jews from the social and economic life of the country. When Slovakia became an independent state, before the Reich began to intervene in the internal affairs of Slovakia, the Slovak government, **on its own initiative**, devised and implemented a number of strong anti-Jewish measures.

In areas **other** than the "Final Solution" of the "Jewish problem," Tiso successfully resisted pressures from the Reich. For instance, he thwarted the effort of the Germans to participate directly in his government, rejecting the demands of Franz Karmasin that he assign certain government positions to Germans. Tiso was also able to resist German demands to relocate, i.e., exchange German and Slovak populations between the north (Spiš) and the west (Záhorie). Thanks to Tiso's intervention, the German High Command abandoned its plan to evacuate the entire population of eastern Slovakia when the Russian army moved close to the area. Finally, when the Slovak government decided to discontinue the deportations of Jews in the autumn of 1942, Slovakia was able to withstand German pressure to resume deportations. Thus, it seems that Tiso was able to withstand German demands, and it was only when Tiso agreed with their demands that he remained silent and passive and did not try to resist.

On **April 15, 1947**, the court condemned Tiso to death by hanging. Besides Tiso's, 55 death sentences were handed down (more than in Germany and France), 29 of which were carried out. The fate of the main participants in the mass murder of Slovak Jews are listed (alphabetically) below:

Alois Brunner, b. 1912 in Rohrbrunn, Austria. SS-Hauptsturmführer, Eichmann's assistant. Organized deportation of Jews from Austria, Greece, Bulgaria, and France. Arrived in Bratislava in September 1944 to complete the deportation of the Jews. In 1954, sentenced to death in absentia in Paris. Given asylum in Syria, where he lived under an assumed name.

Ferdinand Ďurčanský, b. 1906 in Rajec. Professor of Law at Komensky University in Bratislava. Minister of Justice, 1938–1939. Minister of Foreign Affairs 1939–1940. Tried to preserve independence from Germany and was, therefore, dismissed from his post. Fled to Italy in March 1945. Sentenced, in absentia, to death. Emigrated to Argentina in 1947. Moved to Munich in 1952, where he died on March 15, 1974.

Adolf Eichmann, b. 1906 near Cologne. SS-Obersturmbannführer (Lt. Col.), head of the Jewish section of the Gestapo, working under Heinrich Himmler. Organized, and was responsible for, all the deportations of Jews in Europe. After the war, escaped to Argentina. In May 1960, he was kidnapped by the Israeli Security Service (Mossad). In April 1961 he was tried in Jerusalem. Found guilty and hanged on May 31, 1962.

Andrej Hlinka, b. 1864 in Stará Černová. Catholic priest. Co-founder in 1913, of the Slovak Nationalistic People's Party (SLS), which, after 1925, was named after him (HSLS). It was the leading party when Slovakia proclaimed independence in 1939, and remained so for the rest of the war. Died a natural death on August 10, 1938, in Ruženberok.

Franz Karmasin, b. 1901 in Olomouc. Co-founded in 1928 the Carpathian-Ruthenian German Party (KdP). Deputy in the Czechoslovak Parliament 1935–1938. Founder of the German Party in Slovakia (DP). Elected undersecretary for the affairs of the German minority in Slovakia in October 1938. In 1943, became Hauptsturmführer of the SS. Actively participated in the deportation of Slovak Jews. After the war, fled to Germany. In 1947, was condemned to death in absentia. The government in Prague was unsuccessful in its request to have him extradited from Germany. Died June 1970, in Steinebach am Wörthsee, Bavaria.

Isidor Koso, b. 1896 in Veselé nad Váhom. Lawyer. Was Director of the Ministry of the Interior 1938–1944; director of the President's Office 1944–1945. Helped organize the Aryanization process and the confiscation of Jewish assets. Was a co-author of the Jewish Code. Sentenced in Bratislava to 18 years imprisonment, 12 of which he served in forced labor. Died in 1978.

Alexander (Šaňo) Mach, b. 1902 in Slovenský Meder. Commander of the fascist Hlinka guard, head of the Slovak Secret Police and Minister of Internal Affairs of the Slovak State. He and Tuka most aggressively pressed for the deportation. Mach was condemned to 30 years in prison by the National Tribunal in Bratislava. He was granted amnesty in 1968. Died October 15, 1980, in Bratislava.

Augustin Moravek, b. 1901 in Trnava, Slovakia. Protégé of Prime Minister Tuka. Head of the Central Economic Office 1940–1942. The office dealt with the Aryanization and confiscation of Jewish property. Moravek resigned on June 30, 1942, under a cloud of suspicion of corruption. Rather than face trial, he fled in 1943 to Hungary. His subsequent fate remains unknown.

Karol Sidor, b. July 16, 1901 in Ružomberok. After Hlinka, the most influential leader in the SLS. After Hlinka's death in 1938, Tiso assumed the leadership of the SLS, and Sidor was sidelined. In June 1939 he became the Slovak representative in the Vatican for the remainder of the war. In 1950 he emigrated to Canada, where he died October 20, 1953.

Jozef Tiso, b. 1887 in Veľká Bytča. Catholic priest. Deputy Leader of the Slovak People's Party (SLS) 1930–1938. After Hlinka's death in 1938, Tiso was head of the SLS, and President of Slovakia, October 1939–April 1945. Sentenced to death April 15, 1947, by the National court (Národný súd), for "internal treason, treason of the Slovak National Uprising, and collaboration with Nazism." Hanged April 18, 1947.

Vojtech Tuka, b. 1880 in Štiavnické Bane. Professor of Law in Pécs and later at Bratislava University. Secretary of the SLS. Prime Minister and Minister of Foreign Affairs of the Slovak Republic 1940–1945. Was the moving spirit (with Mach) behind the deportation of Slovak Jews. Condemned to death by the National Tribunal in Bratislava. Executed on August 20, 1946 (despite having suffered a stroke, which left him in a wheelchair).

Anton Vašek, b. 1905 in Hrubá Borša. Lawyer. April 1942–September 1944, head of Department 14 of the Ministry of Interior under Šaňo Mach. His department was in charge of deportations and he was nicknamed "King of Jews." September 1944–April 1945, Chief Notary of Bratislava. Sentenced to death by the National Tribunal of Bratislava. Hanged in 1946.

Dieter Wisliceny, b. 1911 in east Prussia. SS-Hauptsturmführer, Eichmann's deputy. By 1940, advisor on Jewish affairs to the Slovak government. Organized mass deportation from Slovakia (also from Greece and Hungary) 1942–1944. Condemned to death. Hanged in Bratislava February 27, 1948.

The situation of the Jews during the postwar period, up to the present

I wish I could finish this section with a short and happy ending like, "After the war, civil liberties, human rights and restitution of confiscated properties were accorded to the remaining Jews, and they took their rightful place as equals among the population...." Alas, it would not be true; indeed, the picture is not a pretty one, neither during the immediate postwar years (1945–1948), nor during the communist regime (1948–1983); or, for that matter, the present isn't too rosy either. Echoes of the past are ever-present in today's Slovakia.

In the **spring of 1945**, after the termination of hostilities in Europe, the Jewish survivors returned from the woods and other hiding places, from concentration camps, the Allied armies, and countries of exile. To their great disappointment and distress, they did not experience a warm welcome either from the Slovak population or the government: The postwar government of Czechoslovakia was indifferent to the plight of the Jews; the local government in Slovakia was outright hostile to them; and the anti-Semitism of the Slovak population was still rampant.

The struggle for the return of Jewish property to the rightful owners was long and bitter. When the Czechoslovak government passed a **restitution law in May 1946**, the implementation by the Slovak authorities was hamstrung by red tape and various excuses. The great hostility towards restitution from the Slovak Gentile population induced the authorities to slow restitution proceedings, and occasionally even to stop them.[41]

During these early postwar years, anti-Semitism in Slovakia at times reached almost wartime proportions. Numerous **spontaneous pogroms** and outrages occurred in several places. Among them in **Prešov (summer of 1945)**, **Topolčany (autumn of 1945)**, and **Bratislava** (summers of **1946** and **1948**). The main initiator of these excesses was the old fascist-clerical Slovak's People Party, which officially was banned, but against which the authorities took only minimal actions. During the winter of **1945**, Ukrainian nationalists murdered Jews in the villages of **Ulič** and **Kolbasov** in eastern Slovakia.

The one area in which the Slovaks proved helpful was in offering active assistance to the Zionists that organized illegal transport of Jews to Palestine. The Slovaks did not help for altruistic reasons, but for their desire to get rid of the Jews. In **1948–1949**, some 11,000 Slovak Jews immigrated to Israel (among them my parents) and another few thousand moved to other countries.

The **communist takeover** in Czechoslovakia in **1948** coincided with the establishment of the State of Israel. Czechoslovakia was among the first to recognize the fledgling state, and backed it by providing essential military support, training pilots, and putting airfields at the disposal of the Haganah. These actions contributed significantly to Israel's victory in the War of Independence against the Arabs. It should be remembered that in those early days, Slovakia's powerful neighbor, the Soviet Union, was also an early supporter of the State of Israel. The motivation, again, was not love of the Jews, but hatred of the British, who subsequently were forced to leave the Middle East.

During that decisive, but brief, era of friendship between the communist regime and the Jews, Czechoslovakia made it possible for about 20,000 Jews to emigrate to the newly established state. Alas, this friendly relationship did not last long. The change in policy of the Soviet Union towards Israel in the early 1950s brought about a change in attitude of the Czechoslovak government towards the Jews. The Jews were excluded from political, economic, and cultural life, and many were imprisoned and tried.

The most notorious of these trials was against the Secretary General of the Communist Party of Czechoslovakia, **Rudolf Slánský**, and several other high-ranking officials. Historians regard the **Slánský trial** as a manifestation of Soviet-style anti-Semitism, considering that Slánský and 10 of the 14 accused were Jewish. Under coercion and torture, all of them confessed to the trumped-up charges that they were guilty of "Trotskyite-Titoist-Zionist activities." Eleven of them were executed and three obtained lifetime sentences. (All three were **exonerated in May 1968**.) It was during the Slánský trial that several of my friends, who had been loyal members of the Communist Party, became disillusioned with communism.

New hope for Jews (and others) evolved during the **Prague Spring of 1967**, which incidentally coincided with Israel's phenomenal victory in the Six Day War. The euphoria did not last long. **Dubček's** reformist policies were quashed on **August 21, 1968**, when the **Warsaw Pact armies** invaded and **occupied Czechoslovakia**. The ensuing two decades can be described as government-sponsored chicanery of the most sordid nature,

---

[41] In the case of my father's business, the arisators (Aryan partners, page 79) returned it to him voluntarily. My father gave half of it to one of the arisators, Mr. Mičura, who had saved my parents' lives.

accompanied by virulent anti-Semitism. In concert with the Soviet Middle East policy, Israel and world Jewry were vilified, and diverse restrictions were imposed on the Czechoslovak Jews (e.g., the community or individuals were not permitted to have contact with Jewish organizations in the west).

After four decades of suppression, a new era was ushered in by the **Velvet Revolution of November 1989,** which overthrew the communist regime. Hope emerged that under the leadership of President **Vaclav Havel**, who struggled all his life for human rights, the country would be steered to new heights of freedom and democracy. Unfortunately, the age-old rift between Slovaks and Czechs resurfaced, and the Slovaks broke off from the Czech lands. On **January 1, 1993,** the **independent State of Slovakia** was established.

And what is the present situation of the Jews in Slovakia? If I had to put it succinctly, I would say: tolerable but not satisfactory. Let me illustrate it by a few recent incidents.

In 2007, the highest clerical authority of Slovakia, **Cardinal Ján Korec**, a staunch defender of ex-president Tiso and his actions during the war, expressed his support for Tiso in a broadcasted interview. This is by no means an exceptional case; there is a strong nationalist movement in Slovakia to exonerate Tiso and to proclaim Andrej Hlinka a Slovak national hero. Fortunately, so far, these attempts have not succeeded.

In January of 2007, **Rabbi Baruch Myers** and his 12-year-old son were verbally attacked by two youths as they left the synagogue in Bratislava. "Jews to the gas chambers," they shouted. Also a sign of the anti-Semitic feelings of the Slovak population is the frequent desecration of Jewish cemeteries and anti-Semitic graffiti. It is distressing and incongruous that anti-Semitism can take hold and flourish in a country whose total Jewish population at present is only about 3,000.

Recently, I was asked by a visiting scientist/entrepreneur colleague (non-Jewish) from Bratislava whether I would consider returning to live in Slovakia. My forceful negative reply, invoking the past and present situation, elicited an unexpectedly hostile and defensive reaction, after which an uncomfortable silence ensued. My colleague has not spoken or communicated with me since. He was born after the war, but I can't help wondering what his parents did during the war years.

3. THE REACTION OF THE FREE WORLD AS SIX MILLION JEWS WERE MURDERED

A discussion of the Holocaust must include more than the description of the actions of the perpetrators and the victims. It must include the reactions of the countries of the free world that were not under German domination. Throughout the previous sections I deplored the inaction and apathy of the governments that could have helped save the lives of the victims of the Holocaust, but, by and large, did not. In this section, I want to dwell in more detail[42] on the evil of silence and inaction, with particular emphasis on the government of the United States.

The early years of Hitler's regime and the Roosevelt administration

Hitler's appointment as chancellor of Germany on **January 30, 1933,** coincided with the 51st birthday of **Franklin D. Roosevelt**. Five weeks later, on **March 5**, Roosevelt took the oath of office as the 32nd President of the United States. Thus, two administrations, half a world apart, with totally different agendas, goals, and methods of attaining them, started out simultaneously. Little did anybody suspect that a decade later they would engage each other in a brutal war.

The rumble of Nazi jackboots, and their acts of brutalities against the enemies, in particular Jews, was not foremost on the mind of the government and the people of the United States. The attention of the Americans was focused on a more immediate menace— the greatest economic depression in American history, an acute crisis with 12 million people unemployed.

Notwithstanding the severe economic problems, the State Department followed in detail the happenings in Germany. On **March 9, 1933**, US ambassador to Germany **F.M. Sackett** wrote: "Democracy in Germany has received a blow from which it may never recover." The US consul in Berlin, **G. Messersmith,** reported in detail on the new Nazi measures: the dismissal of Jews from public office, the firing of Jewish performers (including the conductor **Bruno Walter**), the boycott of Jewish shops, and the escalation of beatings and murders of Jews following Reich Minister Göring's announcement that the police would no longer be expected to protect the enemies of the Reich.

In the weeks and months after Hitler assumed power, the United States government refrained from any protest to the German government, except when some storm troopers accidentally beat up several American citizens on the street.

Whereas the State Department remained silent, the newspaper editors did not: **The Post-Standard** in Syracuse said, "The whole weight of world disapproval should be summoned to stop this tragic situation, to impress upon the rulers of Germany that the world will not permit a return to the dark ages"; **The Providence Journal** agreed, "If there ever was a time in recent history for marshalling world opinion against such brutality, the time is now"; **The Daily Oklahoman** wrote, "Humanity, to say nothing of Christian duty, would call insistently for an American protest."

---

[42] I used several books as source material for this section. Two of them I found particularly instructive: Arthur D. Morris, "While Six Million Jews Died," The Overlook Press, 1998; David. S. Wyman, "The Abandonment of the Jews," The New Press, 1984.

On **March 20, 1933,** representatives of the **American Jewish Committee** and **B'nai Brith** visited the Secretary of State **Cordell Hull,** and requested that the United States protest the persecution of the Jews in Germany. Hull, who had been reading all the diplomatic dispatches and newspaper accounts, replied that first he had to ascertain the facts. He finally proclaimed that "I shall continue to watch the situation closely with sympathetic interest, but outside intercession has rarely produced the results desired, and has frequently aggravated the situation."

Variously phrased, this was the central theme of American policy toward Nazi Germany for years to come.

On **March 30, 1933, George Gordon,** chargé d'affaires in Berlin, reported that the situation was rapidly taking a turn for the worse, and proposed that the State Department intercede and officially protest the German actions. Hull remained adamant and refused to act. He furthermore stated that he believed the acts of terror and atrocities had been exaggerated. Hull's stated belief was, of course, contradicted by virtually every diplomatic communication of the period.

Among the 4 million Jews in the United States there was great apprehension, and sporadic rallies were held across the nation. The largest **rally** occurred at Madison Square Garden in New York **in 1933:** 20,000 people participated inside, and 35,000 outside. It was an inter-religious meeting, a rare event in those days, during which Bishop **W.T. Manning** expressed Protestant indignation at the events in Germany, and **Bishop F.J. McConnell** spoke for the Catholics. **Senator Robert Wagner**[43] of New York lambasted the Nazis' racist policies. The White House maintained a discreet silence, neither approving nor criticizing the expression of public sentiment.

As the Nazi drive gained momentum in 1933, there was an increasing demand by the public for the United States to tell the German government that the excesses taking place in Germany caused revulsion and horror in the United States. On **April 19, 1933,** the lawyer **Samuel Untermeyer** forwarded a resolution of protest passed by the **Federal Bar Association** and signed by the nation's leading lawyers, asking President Roosevelt to send their message to the German authorities. The White House's reply was that State Department policy forbade the transmission of messages from private individuals or organizations. It was clear that Roosevelt did not consider the formal protest a proper move. As he told **W.E. Dodd** in **July 1933,** before he assumed his ambassadorial duties in Germany: "The German authorities are treating the Jews shamefully, but this is not a governmental affair, and we can do nothing about it."

The silence of the US government was made more conspicuous by the fact that the British Parliament had already debated and condemned Nazi inhumanity. Additional fuel to the demand for a strong US statement came on **April 22, 1933,** from a first-hand description by The New York Times correspondent of the Dachau Concentration Camp. **Dr. Jonah B. Wise,** of the **Joint Distribution Committee,** put it candidly and succinctly at a town hall meeting in New York: "It is difficult for Americans to understand the silence

---

[43] R. Wagner was well known for sponsoring important labor laws, one of them being the **Wagner-Wheeler Law**. George Wheeler, the co-sponsor of the law was the uncle of my first wife (Doris). During the McCarthy era, in the early 1950s, he was being harassed by the McCarthy committee. He left the United States and asked for political asylum in communist Czechoslovakia, where he lectured at the Charles University in Prague. In the 1980s, disenchanted with the communist regime, he quietly returned to the United States. I met him in 1982, at the celebration of the 100th birthday of his mother (Nana).

of President Roosevelt in the face of the greatest human disaster of our time…. I am aware of the niceties of the diplomatic procedures, but in a crisis such as exists in Germany today, diplomatic discretion must yield to moral indignation."

All this public clamor for action was to no avail.

One organization that was particularly vocal in prodding the US government to break the silence was the **American Jewish Congress**. It was led by Dr. **Cyrus Adler**, a distinguished scholar who had taught Semitic languages at John Hopkins University and later became president of the Jewish Theological Seminary. On **May 3, 1933**, Dr. Adler wrote to Secretary of State Hull, pointing out that the British, French, and Australian governments had expressed their abhorrence of Nazi policies, and added: "The problem should not be treated as an internal German question, and we should not limit our concern to American citizens but revert to our earlier liberal tradition that what is human concerns us all." Adler called Hull's attention to the successful "interferences" in the internal affairs of other nations in the past.

One such episode occurred in **1849** when the charge of **ritual murder** was brought against the Jews of Damascus, which at the time was part of the Ottoman Empire. Many Jews were imprisoned, tortured, and murdered. **President Van Buren** made a strong representation to the Sultan of the Ottoman Empire who, as a result, ordered the judges of Constantinople to release all Jews accused of ritual murder. Another example of American intervention occurred in **November 1857**. Learning that Jews were excluded from certain Swiss Cantons, **President Buchanan** ordered his Secretary of State to "use all means in your power to effect the removal of the odious restrictions." On **October 25, 1859**, Swiss **President Furrer** sent President Buchanan a note informing him that "the Council of Zurich is disposed to change the legislation respecting the Israelites, in the interest of humanity and progress."

Even as the United States was torn by civil war, and one might have expected its humanitarian instincts to be postponed to a more propitious time, President Lincoln's Secretary of State, **W.H. Seward**, was so concerned about the **Jews of Tangier**, that on **December 6, 1863**, he ordered the US consul "to exert all proper influence to prevent a repetition of the cruelties to which the Jews in the Moorish Empire had been subjected." Subsequently, the Minister of Foreign Affairs notified the US consul in Tangier that "the murderers of Jewish families are now in prison, and their punishment should deter the commitment of such crimes in the future."

American protests were not restricted to the protection of the Jews. In **1915** the US ambassador to Turkey, **Henry Morgenthau,** father of the future Secretary of the Treasury, intervened with the Turkish authorities on behalf of the persecuted Armenians. It is believed that this action moderated the strength of the Turkish assault.

The American Jewish Committee's attempt to change the attitude of the United States government by citing these events, unfortunately failed. The State Department claimed that there was no analogy between these past events and the plight of the Jews under Nazi rule.

Failure of the US government to protest was the first in a long series of refusals to respond. The American response to Nazi racism can best be described as a coordinated series of inactions and apathy, in contrast to the past traditional defense of humanity. To add insult to injury, the refusal to interfere in German domestic policies was accompanied with the denial to grant asylum to the victims, as discussed in a later section.

To boycott or not to boycott: the 1936 Berlin Olympics

The participation of the American athletes in the 1936 Olympic Games in Berlin posed a moral challenge to the United States. The Olympic Games were to be a vast spectacle enhancing the international prestige of the Third Reich, and offered a unique opportunity to propagandize the Nazi regime. The issue had been hotly debated since 1933, and there were indications that the United States might withdraw because of Germany's treatment of the Jews in general, and its Jewish athletes in particular. This would have dealt a severe blow to the prestige of the Nazis.

In **November 1933** the **Amateur Athletic Union (AAU)** voted almost unanimously to boycott the games. However, the **American Olympic Committee (AOC)** was the organization responsible for US participation in the Olympic games. Its membership was made up of important businessmen and retired generals who were annoyed at the AAU for interfering in an issue that belonged in the AOC's jurisdiction. Two days after the AAU vote, the AOC adopted a more temperate resolution, though it insisted on the principle of equal treatment of Jewish athletes. It agreed unanimously to consider the anti-Semitic situation only as it related to sports, but not to terror in the streets and concentration camps.

On **September 12, 1934**, **Representative Celler**, who consistently opposed US participation in the Olympics, stated in the House of Representatives: "How can a Jew who is jeered in the street be cheered in the arena as a champion?" Notwithstanding these sentiments, **Avery Brundage**, president of the AOC, announced on **September 27, 1934**, that the United States had accepted the German invitation to participate in the Olympics.

On **April 28, 1935**, German Minister of the Interior **Wilhelm Frick** gave advanced notice of the upcoming Nüremberg Laws, which, among other restrictions, would deprive German Jews of their citizenship. But Brundage and the AOC seemed blind and deaf to the fact that German Jewish athletes couldn't possibly be given equal opportunity to compete for a country in which they were not citizens.

Any hopes that the German government might moderate its policies were shattered on **July 15, 1935**, when 200 Nazis attacked Jews on the Kurfürstendamm, in the heart of Berlin. The Nazis swarmed through cafés, restaurants, and movie theaters, assaulting men and women who looked Jewish, shouting "the best Jew is a dead Jew," smashing windows and leaving a trail of bleeding victims.

Two weeks after the Kurfürstendamm riots, **Jeremiah T. Mahoney**, the former New York State Supreme court Justice, now head of the AAU, repeated the stand of the AAU to withdraw from the Olympic Games in light of the new reports of violence. Avery Brundage replied that he knew of no racial or religious reasons for such an action—a complete denial of the facts.

A few days after Brundage's remarks, the high-jumping champion of Würthenberg, **Gretel Bergmann**, was denied participation in the Olympic Games. But this fact did not move the AOC to change its mind.

The US representative on the **International Olympic Committee (IOC)**, **General Sherrill**, was becoming increasingly short-tempered with those who were against US participation. He warned that if US athletes saw their ambitions frustrated by the Jews, a wave of anti-Semitism would sweep the country. General Sherrill's view on politics is worth noting. He praised Mussolini as "a man I had long known and admired...."

As the controversy continued, the American embassy in Berlin decided to see for itself whether Jewish athletes in Germany were treated fairly, as Mr. Brundage had been led to believe. **Ambassador Dodd** reported the results of the investigation on **October 11, 1935.**

Jews had been barred from open competition, denied the use of sports facilities, and their letters of protest to the Olympic Committee had not even been answered. To compound the problems of the Jewish athletes, the new statute of the Reich League of Physical Exercise stated that in order to qualify, members must be ideologically (*weltanschauliche*) fit, which excluded the 30,000 members of the Jewish sport clubs.

A final, climactic meeting of the AAU took place on **December 8, 1935,** in New York. President J.T. Mahoney persisted in opposing participation in the Olympics, but Mr. Brundage, whose AOC committee had primacy over the AAU, proclaimed that the United States would participate in the Olympic Games, with or without the cooperation of the AAU. During the meeting it was revealed that a questionnaire had been sent to 140 US athletes, who were potential participants in the Olympics. All, except one, a Jewish sprinter named **Herman Neugass**, were in favor of participation. After a tense five-hour session, the AAU voted to participate in the Olympics, defeating Mahoney by a mere two votes. Mahoney resigned as president and was immediately succeeded by Brundage. Ironically, after the Olympics, the AAU acknowledged the moral judgment of Jeremiah T. Mahoney, and once again elected him as president of the AAU, by an overwhelming margin over Avery Brundage. A case of closing the barn door after the horses had escaped.

President Roosevelt did not take a public position. Had he expressed opposition to the US participation in the Berlin Games, he might have tipped the balance in favor of the boycott.

The refusal of the United States to withdraw from one of the great propaganda festivals in Nazi history was one of a series of decisions that played into the hands of Adolph Hitler. It was yet another example of the shameful, acquiescent cooperation of a spineless world.

And so the stage was set for the Nazis to proceed with the pageantry of the Olympic Games, with the participation of the United States and all the other countries. Anti-Jewish signs were removed from the streets and the press was ordered to refrain from making anti-Jewish pronouncement for the duration of the games. But even as the games went on, German engineers were supervising the construction of the **Sachsenhausen concentration camp,** just 18 miles north of Berlin.

In the United States, dissent, at least was expressed, and the situation was openly and extensively discussed. In the other countries of the free world, opposing voices to participation in the Olympic Games were not even heard.

Since the decision had been made by the United States to participate in the Olympic Games, it was up to the individual athletes to decide whether to follow their conscience or further their sports career. In addition to Herman Neugass, mentioned above, three other American Jewish athletes refused to go to Berlin: high-jumper **Syd Koff,** and Harvard track and field stars **Norman Cahners** and **Milton Green**. Only one non-Jewish American athlete, speed skater **Jack Shea,** joined the boycott. The most spectacular boycott was that of the entire Long Island University Blackbirds basketball team, which had several Jewish players.

There were four Jewish-American athletes that were on the US team in Berlin: the baseball player **Herman Goldberg**, the basketball player **Sam Balter,** and the runners **Sam Stoller** and **Marty Glickman**. Both Stoller and Glickman were scheduled to run in the 4x100-meter relay. But only hours before the event they were replaced by two other runners. Glickman has claimed that Coach **Dean Cromwell**, who was responsible for the switch, was motivated by anti-Semitism. That Cromwell was a racist is supported by his remarks to explain the success of the Afro-American athletes in Berlin: "...the black athlete's ability to sprint and jump was a matter of life and death to him in the jungle."

Interestingly, **Afro-Americans** were against the boycott. They argued that white America was hypocritical to condemn racism in Germany while fostering it in the United States. This point of view was succinctly expressed by the Afro-American sprinter **Mark Robinson,** the brother of the famous baseball player Jackie Robinson. On his return from Berlin, he remarked: "At least in Germany we didn't have to sit in the back of the bus."

There were a number of Jewish athletes from other countries participating in the Berlin Olympics. Twelve garnered medals, seven of them won by Hungarians. Two "token" Jews (actually half-Jews) were permitted to compete for Germany, to assuage the concerns of the IOC. One was **Rudi Ball**, an ice skater, who participated in the Winter Olympics in Garmisch-Partenkirchen; the other was blond, blue-eyed fencer **Helen Mayer,** who won the silver medal. When she mounted the medalists' podium she gave the stiff-armed Heil Hitler salute.

There were many individual Jewish athletes from all over the world who refused to go to Berlin. A case-in-point was the refusal by **Dr. P. Steiner, Dr. A. Abeles**, and **H. Baderle** of our swimming club, Bar Kochba Bratislava (BKB), who were members of the Czechoslovak Olympic swimming team. For their refusal to participate in the Olympics, the BKB was fined, and forbidden to participate in swim meets for a year. This restriction was lifted after a few months, and in the summer of 1937 BKB triumphed as winners of the Czechoslovak championship in Prague—with its honor intact.

There were several interesting cases of non-US Jewish athletes who refused to go to Berlin. One was the Canadian athlete **Sammy Luftspring**. In a letter to the Toronto Globe he wrote, very presciently: "Germany would exterminate its Jews if it had the opportunity."

And then there is the sad case of the two cousins, Jewish gymnasts **Gustav** and **Alfred Flatow**. They were among 10 athletes selected to compete for Germany in the first modern Olympic Games in Athens in **1896**. Gustav garnered two gold medals, and Alfred three gold and one silver medal. Alfred Flatow remained prominently active in German gymnastics until expelled by the Nazis in 1933. He was, nevertheless, invited as an honored guest of the 1936 Olympic Games. He declined the invitation. In **1938** Alfred fled to the Netherlands, where his cousin Gustav lived. When Germany occupied the Netherlands, both Flatows were arrested and deported to the Theresienstadt concentration camp, where they perished. In **1997,** Berlin honored Alfred and Gustav Flatow by giving the name Flatowallee (Flatow-alley) to a street near the Olympic Stadium. The following year, a stamp honoring the Flatows was issued.

As was the case with the 1936 Olympics in Berlin, there were discussions about boycotting the 2008 Olympics in **Beijing**. China, of course, cannot be compared with Nazi Germany. But it denies basic civil rights to its citizens; it provides advanced weaponry to rogue regimes such as Syria, North Korea, and Iran; it supports the terrorists of Hamas and the genocidal regime of Sudan; and it is engaged in a brutal repression in occupied Tibet. But a boycott of the games was never seriously considered, and not a single athlete refused to participate in the games.

At one stage, the idea seemed to have taken hold that the heads of state should boycott the opening ceremonies in Beijing. This would have avoided penalizing the athletes. But, finally, the idea was dropped, and President Bush, as well as 80 other heads of state (the most ever to have attended any Olympics), participated in the opening ceremonies. Self-interest and expediency triumphed again over principles.

The only Olympics ever boycotted by the United States was the one in **Moscow in 1980,** following the invasion of Afghanistan by the Soviet Union. Ironically, this was done by President Carter, one of the least effective and least successful of US presidents in modern times.

The Evian Conference

Q: What do you do if you don't want to do anything, but you want to look like you are doing something?

A: You call a conference.

That, unfortunately, characterizes the Evian Conference on the refugee problem. Here is the chronology of events.

On **March 22, 1938,** 10 days after the German occupation of Austria, President Roosevelt, responding to mounting pubic pressure, invited 33 governments to participate in a conference to discuss possible cooperative efforts to aid the emigration of refugees from Germany and Austria. The invitation contained a statement that sowed the seeds of failure right from the start. It said that no country "would be expected or asked to receive a greater number of emigrants than is permitted by its existing legislation." The same day that the conference was announced, Roosevelt made that point unequivocally clear by assuring the American public that the conference would not result in an increase or revision of US immigration quotas.

There was an instant, massive, enthusiastic reaction from religious, civic, and other groups. The **Federal Council of Churches** of Christian America "hailed with appreciation" the US proposal for the conference. The **American Jewish Committee** characterized it as "a splendid act," and **William Green**, president of the American Federation of Labor, stated that "refugees have proven themselves through the years to be our finest citizens...."

The reaction to Roosevelt's proposal might have been less exuberant had the public known the motives behind it. It was the State Department's strategy to counteract the outcry of the public that demanded action on behalf of the refugees. Secretary of State Cordell Hull, and Undersecretary Sumner Welles, decided that it would be preferable to get out in front and guide the pressure, primarily as a tactic to forestall attempts at liberalizing immigration laws. And Roosevelt could claim that he had placed the United States in a leading humanitarian role on the refugee issue. Furthermore, a conference would be months in planning, would silence the critics of apathy, and, if all worked well, would divert refugees from the United States to other countries.

The conference was scheduled to take place **July 6–13, 1938,** at the Royal Hotel in Evian, a luxurious resort on the French shore of Lake Geneva. Switzerland had not been willing to host the conference, as it did not want to alienate Hitler. It was also embarrassed because it had begun to restrict immigration of Jews from Germany and Austria. **Thirty-two nations** would attend; only Italy and South Africa had declined, and the latter was sending an observer. Roosevelt chose not to send a high-level official, such as the Secretary of State; instead, Myron C. Taylor, a businessman and close friend of Roosevelt, represented the United States at the conference.

There was much maneuvering and press coverage taking place before the conference. The **Veterans of Foreign Wars** passed a resolution disapproving the admission of any refugees to the United States. In contrast, the press, by and large, exhorted the conference attendees to come up with practical solutions to solve the refugee problem. Perhaps Anne **O'Hare McCormick**, columnist of The New York Times, put it most succinctly: "It is heartbreaking to think of the lines of desperate human beings around the consulates in Vienna and other cities, waiting in suspense for what happens at Evian. ...It is a test of civilization.... Can America live with itself, if it lets Germany get away with its policy of extermination?" But these lofty sentiments were offset by many Americans who were reluctant to welcome Jewish refugees in the middle of the Great Depression. They believed that refugees would compete with them for jobs and resources allocated to the needy.

Even before the conference started, it was clear that the United States and Britain, to whom the others looked for leadership, had utterly disparate viewpoints. The US representative **Myron Taylor** advocated relief for millions of refugees through a new **Intergovernmental Committee (IGC)**. **Lord Winterton**, the head of the British delegation, advocated an expansion of the League of Nations High Commission for Refugees (a doddering, ineffective relic).

On **July 6, 1938**, the Evian Conference was called to order, with Myron Taylor, the US representative, being elected its president. Taylor was the first speaker at the conference. He deplored "...the fate of millions of people as this conference convenes. The time has come for governments to act, and act promptly and effectively in a long-range program of comprehensive scale.... If the present situation is permitted to continue, there is catastrophic human suffering ahead, which will result in general unrest and international strain."

Alas, Taylor's words were not followed by action. During the nine-day meeting, delegate after delegate rose to express sympathy for the refugees; but most countries, including the United States, Britain, France, Australia, and Canada, offered excuses for not letting in more refugees. Only one country, the **Dominican Republic**, offered to grant sanctuary to 100,000 Jews, a relatively large number for such a small country. Unfortunately, the outbreak of World War II, the following September, prevented the full utilization of this offer.

The **United States**, with its tradition of asylum, its vast land mass, and its unlimited resources, made only one concession at Evian: it agreed, for the first time, to accept its full, legal quota of 27,370 immigrants annually, from Germany and Austria.[44]

The US representative, Myron Taylor, was in favor of liberalizing American immigration policy; but he lacked the power to do so, and was unable to change the State Department's mindset. However, he was successful in overcoming British objections and establishing, at Evian, the **Intergovernmental Committee on Refugees**, an organization independent from the impotent League of Nations High Commission for Refugees. Unfortunately, its leaders consisted of the same personalities that had dominated the Evian Conference. They would accomplish just as little.

The United Kingdom chose caution and pragmatism, subordinating humanitarianism to British national interests. Lord Winterton, head of the British delegation, said at the conference: "It has been the traditional policy of the British government to offer asylum to persons who, for political, racial or religious reasons, have had to leave their own countries. However, for economic and social reasons, the traditional policy of granting asylum can only be applied within narrow limits…. The question of Palestine stands upon a footing on its own, and cannot be taken into account at this meeting." It should be noted that Lord Winterton was chairman of the recently formed Committee to Defend Arab Interests in the Commons. Lord Winterton also supported the view of his ambassador in Berlin, who stated: "Germany's policies towards the Jews, however uncivilized and deplorable, is Germany's own business."

Colonel White, Australia's chief delegate, proclaimed: "It will no doubt be appreciated that, as we have no real racial problem, we are not desirous of importing one." This, in spite of Australia's vast spaces of land, a small population, and a need of workers. Before arriving at Evian, White had spoken at several meetings in England, encouraging British immigration to Australia. Brits yes, Jews no. White's speech at Evian was perceived as the most depressing of all delegate speeches. The Australian government's final decision was to allow only 300 landing permits per month to be granted to Jews.

Canada had a tight immigration policy from the 1920s, admitting only those that had the funds to set up and sustain themselves. A number of Canadian officials in high positions were anti-Semitic, including the Prime Minister **Mackenzie King** and the Director of Immigration **Frederick Blair**, who feared that "Canada was in danger of being flooded with Jewish people." Mackenzie King's political attitude can be gleaned from a remark he made to an American diplomat about his meeting with Hitler in Germany in 1937. He described Hitler as being sincere and "sweet," and having the face of a good man. He did not agree with Hitler's methods but could understand his motives. He said Hitler might come to be thought of as one of the saviors of the world.

---

[44] The quota was not filled the previous years because of the complex regulations and bureaucratic hurdles that were intentionally put in place by the US government to reduce the flow of immigrants. An example was the requirement to obtain a declaration from the German police (the Gestapo!) that the visa applicant was not a criminal. This was difficult to obtain since, in the eyes of the Nazis, all Jews were criminals.

I encountered a similar difficulty in 1950 when I wanted to change my student visa to an immigration visa. I needed a written statement from the police department in hostile, communist Czechoslovakia, that I was not a criminal. Fortunately, my cousin Dr. Karol Kučera, a lawyer in Bratislava, knew the right people and was able to obtain the required document.

Hume Wrong, the chief Canadian delegate at the conference, was advised by Mackenzie King to say as little as possible, and under no circumstances make any promises or commitments. Wrong made a short speech saying that Canada sympathized with the Jewish refugees, but that it was already doing all it could. Only 5,000 refugees were admitted into Canada during the entire 1933–1945 period. Only after Mackenzie King finished his tenure as prime minister in 1948 were the Canadian immigration laws liberalized.

New Zealand was unwilling to lift its restrictions. **Columbia, Uruguay** and **Venezuela** wanted only agricultural workers. The **Peruvian** delegate pointedly remarked that the United States had given his country an example of "caution and wisdom" by its own immigration restrictions.

France stressed that, having taken in 200,000 refugees, it had reached its saturation point. **Nicaragua, Honduras, Costa Rica,** and **Panama** issued a joint statement saying they could not accept "traders and intellectuals." **Argentina**, with a population one-tenth that of the United States, reported that it had welcomed as many refugees as the United States, and could not be counted on for large-scale immigration.

The **Swiss** delegate, **Dr. H. Rothmund**, Chief of the Police Division of the Swiss Justice Department, said: "Switzerland, which has as little use for these Jews as has Germany, will take measures to protect itself from being swamped by Jews."

The failure of the Evian Conference to effectively address the refugee problem can be best summarized by the comments of **Chaim Weizmann, Golda Meir**—and the German government.

Dr. Chaim Weizmann, who was to become Israel's first President in 1948, commented after the Evian Conference: "The world seemed to be divided into two parts—those places where the Jews could not live and those where they could not enter."

Golda Meir, Prime Minister of Israel from 1969–1974, was among the uninvited delegates from Palestine. She recalled her experience at Evian in her Memoirs: "Sitting there in the magnificent hall and listening to the delegates of 32 countries rise, each in turn, to explain how much they would have liked to take in substantial numbers of refugees and how unfortunate it was that they were not able to do so, was a terrible experience. I don't think that anyone who didn't live through it can understand what I felt at Evian—a mixture of sorrow, rage, frustration and horror."

Responding to Evian, the German government gleefully stated how "astounding" it was that foreign countries criticized Germany for the treatment of the Jews, but none of them wanted to open the doors to receive them. And **Hitler gloated**: "It is a shameful spectacle to see how the whole democratic world is oozing sympathy for the poor treatment of Jewish people, but remains hard-headed and obdurate when it comes to helping them...."

Evian[45] was not only ineffective, it was counter-productive in that it gave Hitler the green light to believe he could do whatever he wanted to the Jewish people because nobody wanted them. By their refusal to take Jewish refugees, the countries that attended

---

[45] Note that Evian is the home of a famous spring, the source of an unexciting table water, and "Evian" spelled backwards is "naïve"; but for the Jewish people it was an extremely costly naïveté.

the Evian Conference condemned the Jews to torture, inhumane treatment, and horrible death.

The reaction to The Night of Broken Glass (*Kristallnacht*)

Hitler, emboldened by the passive response at Evian to his treatment of the Jews, as well as the appeasement by the British and the French at Munich in September 1938, no longer cared about world opinion, and unleashed an unprecedented ferocious attack on the Jews on **November 9, 1938,** following the assassination of a German official in Paris. This orgy of killings, arrests, burning of bookshops and synagogues became known as The Night of Broken Glass or Kristallnacht. (For a more detailed description of the event see page 17.)

The barbarities of Kristallnacht were discussed in the British House of Commons by **Philip Noel-Baker**, a Labor Party member who later won the Nobel Peace Prize. Mr. Noel-Baker called the Nazi atrocities "a lasting memory of human shame," and called for large-scale rescue efforts. But as happened before, and would happen again, words were not followed by action.

The American public also responded to Kristallnacht with outrage. The editorial in the **Hartford Courier** is typical of the attitude of the press: "The people outside Germany who still value tolerance, understanding, and humanity, must not keep silent in the face of what has just taken place."

But the US government, the official voice of those people who "must not keep silent," remained silent.

Propaganda Minister Goebbels, aware of the outcry across the sea, challenged the democracies: "If there is any country that believes it has not enough Jews, I shall gladly turn over to it all our Jews." There were no takers.

On **November 14, 1938**, Assistant Secretary of State **George Messersmith**, whose long diplomatic service within Germany had been marked by eloquent and perceptive reporting, sent a strong memorandum to Secretary of State Hull. He wrote: "Of all the many acts of the German government against innocent and defenseless people, these last are the culmination. Whenever such acts in the past have been committed, we have spoken up and acted. The time has come when it is necessary for us to use action beyond mere condemnation." He suggested that Ambassador Wilson be recalled from Germany "for consultations."

Hull immediately consulted President Roosevelt, and the same day a cable was dispatched to Ambassador Wilson, recalling him to Washington. It was the first time since World War I that an American ambassador to a major power had been recalled, and it created a sensation.

Roosevelt called a news conference on **November 15, 1938,** in which he said that he could scarcely believe that such things would happen in a 20th century civilization. When a correspondent asked if Mr. Roosevelt would recommend to Congress that immigration laws be modified to permit the entry of more refugees to the United States, the President replied that no modifications were contemplated.

The recall of Ambassador Wilson, and the President's brief verbal chastising of Germany, comprised the total response of the American government to the Kristallnacht.

The United States continued its trade relations with the Third Reich, a fact that prompted 36 of the most prominent writers of the United States to send a telegram to the President. Among the signers of the telegram were **Eugene O'Neill, John Steinbeck, Pearl Buck, John Gunther, Edna Ferber, Lillian Hellman, George Kaufman, Thornton Wilder, and Dorothy Thompson**. The cable said: "We feel that the American people and the American government have no right to remain silent.... It is deeply immoral for the American people to continue having economic relations with a country that avowedly uses mass murder to solve its economic problems."

The response of the US State Department was summarized in a statement on the refugee problem that stressed the importance of the Intergovernmental Committee on Refugees, which was floundering in London. It read in part: "It is easy to dismiss the whole refugee problem by saying 'nobody wants any more Jews.' That is unquestionably true, but the problem remains to be solved and this government is committed to solving it. The failure of the Intergovernmental Committee on Refugees would involve a serious loss of prestige for this government."

The humanitarian instincts of the British Foreign Office were also aroused. On **November 17, 1938,** two days after Roosevelt's press conference, **Sir Ronald Lindsey,** British ambassador in Washington, called upon Undersecretary of State Sumner Welles with a novel and imaginative proposal: Britain would be willing to relinquish most of the 65,000 places per year it had in the US immigration quota, in order that they may be used by German refugees to enter the United States. The implications of the offer were staggering. Since only 4,000 British immigrants had arrived in 1938, the unused portion offered vast relief opportunities.

Mr. Welles rejected the offer offhand. He explained that there were insuperable obstacles, and that quotas were established under law and were not the property of the nations to whom they were granted. In invoking "legal" obstacles to reject the British offer, Welles had fallen back on a convenient subterfuge, one that had been used, and would be used until late into the war, to block rescue actions.

There was another proposal, advocated by the Jewish organizations, which involved the mortgaging of future quotas. They suggested that 82,000 refugees, entitled to enter the United States from Germany during a three-year period, be admitted immediately in view of the emergency. German immigration would then be cancelled for the next three years. Thus, the total number of immigrants admitted over a three-year period would not exceed the limit stipulated by law. This proposal was also rejected by the State Department.

It clearly was not a lack of proposals that prevented a solution to the refugee problem, but the hard-headed objections of the State Department to admit more Jews to the United States.

Roosevelt, though unwilling to change US immigration law, seemed to have been genuinely concerned about the immigration dilemma. He wrote on **November 23, 1938,** to Myron Taylor: "The Intergovernmental Committee on Refugees, which your devoted efforts created in Evian, has not yet produced the concrete results I had hoped for. Special efforts must be made to make the committee work really effective. We must produce concrete and substantial results and we must produce them soon."

Roosevelt, unwilling to admit additional refugees, was considering the possibility of large-scale resettlement of the Jews in thinly populated, colonial areas of the world. On

November 3, 1938, Roosevelt wrote to **Isaiah Bowman**, the distinguished geographer and president of John Hopkins University, asking for his assessment of the feasibility of resettling the Jews in any part of the world that had uninhabited, or sparsely inhabited, good agricultural lands.

In **December 1938**, Bowman sent the President a 26-six page summary of worldwide settlement possibilities. He estimated that it would cost 500 million dollars to resettle the refugees throughout Africa, South America, Southeast Asia, and Australia— that is, provided they were accepted by these countries. Roosevelt thanked him but took no further action.

The year 1938 ended without having contributed anything to the solution of the refugee problem.

The tragic voyage of the St. Louis

The attitude of the nations, expressed at the Evian Conference in 1938, was manifested again in the tragic events surrounding the voyage of the St. Louis. It was a voyage that would hold up a mirror to mankind, reflecting its callousness and selfishness.

On **May 13, 1939**, the Hamburg-America's luxurious steamer St. Louis sailed from Germany headed for Cuba with 936 passengers, 930 of them Jewish refugees. All passengers held official Cuban landing certificates. For most of the refugees, Cuba would be a temporary sanctuary en route to the United States; they had quota numbers that would allow them to enter the United States from three months to three years after their arrival in Cuba.

For the passengers of the St. Louis, it was a dreamlike odyssey. Having been treated as subhuman by their Nazi oppressors, and with the memory of Kristallnacht still on their minds, they found themselves suddenly in luxurious quarters, being treated by the unusual German **Captain Gustav Schroeder** and his crew with respect and courtesy. It seemed that Captain Schroeder was trying to make amends, on this one journey, for the entire German nation.

As they sailed from Hamburg that day, they were not aware that eight days earlier, Cuban President **Federico Laredo Brú** had signed a decree invalidating the landing certificates. There were several reasons for this action. The director general of the immigration office, **Manuel Benitez Gonzales,** had come under public scrutiny for enriching himself with the sale of landing certificates. There was also general hostility toward Jewish immigration, the refugees being viewed as competitors for scarce jobs. Furthermore, native anti-Semitism was fanned by agents from Germany in Cuba, as well as by the Cuban Nazi Party.

Shortly before the St. Louis reached Havana, a telegram from Cuban officials notified the Captain of the invalidation of the passengers' landing permits. The fear, which had been dissipated by days of civilized treatment, returned with its old brutal intensity. Captain Schroeder did his best to assure his passengers that he would do his utmost to influence the Cuban authorities to honor the landing certificates.

On **May 27, 1939**, the St. Louis docked in Havana. No one was allowed ashore, and none of the relatives and friends of the passengers were allowed to board the ship. The official Cuban position was that the landing certificates had been sold illegally and were, therefore, invalid.

On **May 28**, the Jewish **Joint Distribution Committee (JDC)** sent **Lawrence Berenson**, a prominent New York lawyer and head of the Cuban Chamber of Commerce in the United States, to negotiate with the Cuban government the landing of the passengers.

President Brú agreed to meet Berenson on **June 1**, but notified Captain Schroeder on **May 31** that the St. Louis must depart the following day. Captain Schroeder urged President Brú to let the passengers ashore, and expressed his fear that a wave of suicides would occur if the ship were forced to leave.

That very day, as if to justify the captain's predictions, **Max Loewe**, a lawyer from Breslau and a World War I hero, slashed his wrists and jumped overboard. He was pulled from the water and rushed in grave condition to a hospital ashore.

Despite the demanded departure of the St. Louis, the President kept his appointment with Berenson. He expressed sympathy for the refugees, but was adamant that the St. Louis sail to the seven-mile limit while they discuss specific terms for the landing of the refugees.

Meanwhile, the JDC asked the US government to offer temporary haven to those refugees who possessed US immigration numbers. This request was unequivocally rebuffed. There would be no compromise with US immigration laws.

On **June 2**, at 11 a.m., the St. Louis sailed for Hamburg, its passengers destined for almost certain annihilation. Hardened newspapermen in accompanying launches wept openly, as hundreds of refugees lined the rails imploring Cuba for mercy and straining for a final sight of loved ones on the dock.

As the St. Louis steamed slowly under the concerned command of Captain Schroeder, Berenson continued to negotiate with the Cuban government. He met with President Brú on **June 4**. The president announced his terms: 500 dollars for each person on board plus full maintenance guarantees—a total sum of about 1 million dollars. The St. Louis would be recalled if the money was available within 48 hours. Berenson replied that it would take time to raise such an amount.

While President Brú and Berenson discussed the cash requirements, the St. Louis hovered off the city of Miami, Captain Schroder trying to delay his return to Hamburg as long as possible. A US Coast Guard cutter shadowed the St. Louis with orders to prevent any refugees from jumping overboard and swimming ashore.

Newspaper descriptions of the scenes prompted **Bishop James Connor Jr.** to write a letter to the Richmond Times Dispatch: "The failure to take any steps whatsoever to assist these distressed persecuted Jews, is one of the most disgraceful things which has happened in American history, and leaves a stain and a brand of shame upon the record of our nation."

While the St. Louis inched along the Florida coast, Berenson received authorization from the JDC to offer the Cuban government 500 dollars per person. On **June 5** President Brú agreed to receive the refugees on the Isles of Pines if, in addition, the JDC provided all the living expenses of the refugees. He set a deadline of noon the following day to have a written agreement of these conditions. Berenson prepared the document the same day and handed it to the president's representative, a major in the Cuban secret service. The major asked if the JDC was willing to give him a gift "after the thing is over." Berenson replied that he would consider a small gift.

Nothing happened. Berenson did not hear from the government and was unable to reach either the major or President Brú. At noon on **June 6**, the Cuban government announced that the deadline had passed and the offer had been withdrawn. The Havana lawyer with whom Berenson had dealt, explained why the offer had been cancelled. He believed that the Cuban government officials had expected a gift of at least 350,000 dollars. It was an unfortunate lack of grasp of the situation, by Berenson and the JDC, which scuttled the agreement.

In the evening of **June 6**, the St. Louis set her course for Europe, under the command of the distraught Captain Schroeder, towards a fate that held out little hope for survival. A committee of passengers sent a cable to President Roosevelt, pleading that the refugees be allowed to temporarily disembark on US soil. There was no reply.

The New York Times editorialized, saying among other things, "The cruise of the St. Louis cries to high heaven of man's inhumanity to man." But there was no general surge of feeling among the American people, all descendants of immigrants, to come to the aid of the unfortunate refugees floating across the Atlantic toward certain doom.

President Roosevelt could have issued an executive order to admit the refugees, but chose not to buck the mood of the nation. A Fortune magazine poll at the time indicated that 83% of Americans opposed relaxing restrictions on immigration.

For Hitler, the turning back of the St. Louis marked a stunning propaganda victory, similar to the one he enjoyed after the Evian Conference the year before. It proved that, in spite of their protestations, the world leaders did not want Jews in their countries any more than he wanted them in his. As an editorial in "Der Weltkampf" put it: "We are saying openly that we do not want the Jews, while the democracies keep on claiming that they are willing to receive them—and then leave the guests out in the cold! Aren't we savages better men after all?"

The JDC, which had failed in its efforts with the Cuban government, rose now to the challenge of saving the passengers on the St. Louis. **Morris Troper**, the JDC European chairman with headquarters in Paris, began a round-the-clock effort to find a haven for the refugees. While Troper negotiated with various relief organizations and governments, Captain Schroeder sailed as slowly as possible to give Troper the necessary time to accomplish his goal. On the St. Louis itself, passengers formed a committee of the most stable personalities, to prevent suicides by constantly patrolling the decks.

As the St. Louis approached the coast of continental Europe, Troper's efforts finally bore fruit. The **Belgian government** was willing to accept 250 passengers who had American immigration papers. On **June 12**, the **Dutch Minister** of Justice announced that Holland would welcome 190 passengers. On the same day, **French Minister** of the Interior **Sarraut** was told that the **British** had agreed to admit 250 passengers. Minister Sarraut promptly agreed to accept a similar number. A tragedy had been averted by a zero-hour rescue.

On **June 13**, Troper wired the good news to Captain Schroeder and the passengers of the St. Louis. The refugees were overcome with joy and cabled a long reply expressing their deepest and eternal thanks. The ship altered its course to land at Antwerp, Belgium, where transportation was provided for the passengers to their countries of asylum.

The odyssey of the St. Louis had a temporary happy ending, but the happiness was not to last for long. The following year Hitler invaded and conquered Holland, Belgium, and France, and most of the refugees (except those in England) perished in concentration camps.

One bright spot illuminates the dark episode of the St. Louis. Captain Gustav Schroeder emerged a hero. He had shown great compassion for the passengers, and had resisted leaving Cuba and the United States as long as humanly possible. On the way back he pledged that if no visas for the passengers were forthcoming, he would scuttle the St. Louis on the coast of England. After the war he was decorated by the West German government for his conduct, and Yad Vashem in Israel honored him posthumously as one of the Righteous Gentiles.

Why didn't the Allies bomb Auschwitz and the railroads leading to it?

This question was debated for decades after World War II. The facts were finally detailed in 1978 in a meticulously researched article in the journal "Commentary" by the historian David Wyman, and further elaborated in his 1984 book, "The Abandonment of the Jews." [42b]

In the **spring of 1944,** the requests to the Allies, by many people and organizations, to bomb the gas chambers and crematoria at Auschwitz and the railway lines leading to them, became ever more pressing and numerous. Three circumstances made these requests timely and important: 1) in mid-April, the Nazis started concentrating the 800,000 Jews of Hungary for deportation to Auschwitz; 2) two Slovak Jews, **Rudolf Vrba** and **Alfred Wetzler** escaped in April from Auschwitz and revealed in full detail the mass murder happening there, laying bare what was to be the fate of the Hungarian Jews; 3) since December 1943, the American Air force occupied the airfield in Foggia, Southern Italy, making it feasible for the first time to strike Auschwitz and the railway lines leading to it.

Vrba and Wetzler fled Auschwitz on **April 10, 1944,** and reached the Jewish underground in Slovakia by the end of April. They wrote a 30-page report detailing Auschwitz's geographical layout, internal conditions, gassing and crematorium techniques, and revealed the plans to exterminate the Hungarian Jews. A copy of the report reached the Jewish leadership in Budapest by **early May**.

In **mid-May**, as deportations of Hungarian Jews started, Jewish leaders in Budapest and the Slovak underground in Bratislava sent pleas to bomb the railway lines through **Isaac Sternbuch**, the representative of the Jerusalem-based **Vaad Hahatzala** in Switzerland. Sternbuch transmitted the message to the Union of Orthodox Rabbis in New York and the military attaché of the American legation in Bern, asking him to transmit the message through diplomatic channels to Washington. By **June 22**, Sternbuch had received neither a reply nor an acknowledgement from the US government. The message seemed to have been blocked either in Bern or in Washington.

During the **third week of May**, Rabbi **Michael Weissmandl** and **Gisi Fleischmann**, leaders of the Slovak Jewish underground, wrote a long letter to Jewish organizations in New York, describing the desperate situation of the Hungarian Jews and pleading for immediate bombing of the deportation routes.

On **June 13**, a copy of the Vrba-Wetzler report reached **Gerhard Riegner** of the World Jewish Congress in Geneva. He summarized the report and delivered it to the representatives of the American and British governments in Geneva, with his own appeal to bomb the gas chambers and railway lines from Hungary to Auschwitz.

It should be noted that during June 1944, the truth about Auschwitz began to appear in the Swiss, British, and American press, and thus became known to the whole world.

On **June 18, Jacob Rosenheim,** of the New York office of the **Agudat Israel World Organization,** addressed letters to high American government officials, informing them of the deportations and the anticipated fate of the deportees. He emphasized again that paralysis of the rail traffic would, at least, slow the annihilation process. His appeals were relayed to **Pehle,** head of the War Refugee Board (see page 118), who passed the information on to **McCloy** of the War Department in Washington.

On **June 24,** the War Department took up the matter and ruled against the proposed bombing, stating that the suggestion was "impractical" and "could be executed only by diversion of considerable air support essential to the success of our forces...." It further stated that "...after due consideration of the problem, we believe that the most effective relief of victims of enemy persecution is the early defeat of the Axis."

The rejection of the bombing was not the result of a thorough analysis, but was based on a confidential War Department policy made in Washington five months prior to the June 24 meeting. This policy, which effectively removed the War Department from participating in rescue and relief efforts, was espoused over and over again, whenever requests for action were submitted to the government. And there were many such requests, in addition to the ones described. Perhaps one, sent directly to President Roosevelt, warrants mentioning:

Late in **July,** the **Emergency Committee to Save the Jewish People of Europe** wrote to President Roosevelt directly, calling for the bombing of the deportation railways and the gas chambers and crematoria in Auschwitz. The letter emphasized that the railways were also used for German military traffic and that an attack on Auschwitz could open the way for inmates to escape and join the resistance forces. Both actions would thus assist, not hamper, the Allied war effort. Nothing at all came of this request either.

While Pehle was pressing McCloy unsuccessfully, representatives of the **Jewish Agency for Palestine** were attempting, with equal futility, to interest the British in a similar scheme. Dr. Chaim Weizmann had first discussed the proposed bombing with **Mr. Eden** in **July 1944.** Months later Weizmann was informed that the suggestion had been turned down "...because of the great technical difficulties involved."

Let us now examine the validity (or, rather, invalidity) of the reasons given by the US War Department to reject the proposals to bomb Auschwitz and the railway lines leading to it. As already mentioned, the two main reasons were "impracticability" and "diversion of air power essential to the success of our forces" (i.e., presumably needed elsewhere).

First, one has to realize that from March 1944 on, the Allies controlled the skies of Europe, the German air force having been defeated. Thus, US bombers were never deterred from bombing a target because of probable losses in air combat. Hence, the fear of losses could not be part of the "impracticability" (which, incidentally, was never explained or spelled out).

Second, prime German targets in 1944 were various German oil installations,[46] many of them located in the vicinity of Auschwitz. As a matter of fact, as early as **January 1944**, Allied bombing strategists were analyzing Auschwitz as a potential target because of the synthetic oil and rubber installations near the camp. The huge **Blechhammer oil-refining complex**, only 47 miles from Auschwitz, also came under careful study, as well as a group of eight synthetic oil plants in Upper Silesia not far from Auschwitz.

On **June 26**, 71 Flying Fortresses attacked the oil refineries near Auschwitz, and on **July 7**, 452 bombers attacked again. On **August 20**, 127 Flying Fortresses escorted by 100 Mustang fighters dropped 1,300 500-pound bombs on the factory areas of Auschwitz, less than five miles to the east of the gas chambers. Again, on **September 13**, 96 Liberator bombers rained destruction on the factory areas of Auschwitz. All these aircraft could have easily bombed the camps and the railroad lines, which they crossed on the way to their targets. So, the main argument of the War Department that "diversion" was required to bomb the camps, was clearly bogus.

Could the death factories have been located from the air, and could aerial bombing have been precise enough to knock out the mass-murder buildings without killing a large number of Jewish inmates? The answer to both questions is a definite YES.

Detailed descriptions of the structures and the camp's layout had been supplied by Vrba and Wetzler, and were in Washington by early July. Beginning in **April 1944**, detailed aerial reconnaissance photographs of Auschwitz were available at Air Force headquarters in Italy. Furthermore, the four extermination buildings were easily recognizable; they were 250–340 feet long, and high chimneys towered over them. And weather conditions in the Auschwitz region were excellent for air operation throughout August and most of September.

As to the required accuracy for hitting the buildings, there were several alternatives. Mitchell medium bombers, which flew at lower altitudes than the heavy bombers and therefore were more accurate, could have been flown with one of the missions to Auschwitz. An even more precise alternative would have been the use of P-38 Lightning dive-bombers. They had proven their capabilities on **June 10, 1944,** when they very effectively attacked the oil refineries in **Ploesti**, Romania, making a 1,255-mile roundtrip from their bases in Italy. The distance from Auschwitz and back was 1,240 miles. And even if there was a danger of accidentally harming some of the inmates it was worth taking the risk, as all of them were doomed to death.

The basic reason given by the War Department for its rejection of the bombing proposals was that military resources could not be diverted to non-military objectives. The logic of this position was extremely forceful in a world at war. But the policy was not as ironclad as the War Department indicated in its replies to the bombing requests. Exceptions were often made for humanitarian reasons. For instance, the Allied military moved 100,000 **non-Jewish, Polish, Yugoslav,** and **Greek** civilians to camps in Africa and the Middle East and supplied them with food, shelter, and medical care. The war effort could also be deflected for other purposes, such as the preservation of art. **Kyoto**, the ancient capital of Japan and a center of culture and art, was taken off the target list by Secretary of War **Stimson**. On another occasion, McCloy, Deputy Secretary of the War

---

[46] Most war historians agree that the high attention given to the destruction of oil facilities was one of the most decisive factors in Germany's defeat. Loss of oil gradually strangled the Third Reich's military operations.

Department, prevented the planned bombing of **Rothenburg**, a German town known for its medieval architecture. But, potentially saving millions of Jews did not seem to be in the American government's interest. To the American military, European Jews represented an extraneous problem and an unwanted burden.

Decades later, many high-ranking American politicians admitted the mistake and the erroneous arguments of the War Department that led to the rejection of the bombing requests. One of them was Senator **George McGovern**, the 1972 Democratic nominee for president. In 1944, he was a 22-year-old B-24 pilot who participated in the bombing raids on the German oil installations. In a **2003** videotape interview,[47] he made several telling comments on the bombing issue, among them: "Franklin D. Roosevelt was a great man and he was my political hero. But I think he made two great mistakes during World War II. One was the internment of Japanese Americans; the other was the decision not to bomb Auschwitz. There is no question that we should have attempted to go after Auschwitz. There was a pretty good chance we could have blasted those rail lines off the face of the earth, which would have interrupted the flow of people to the death chambers, and we had a pretty good chance of knocking out the gas chambers and ovens. The administration's "diversion" argument was just a rationalization. How much of a diversion would it have been, when we were already flying over the area?"

Other VIPs added their voices to condemn the inaction. President **George W. Bush,** on his visit to Israel's Yad Vashem Memorial on **January 11, 2008**, viewed an enlargement of an aerial reconnaissance photograph of Auschwitz that was taken in the spring of 1944. Mr. Bush turned to Secretary of State **Condoleezza Rice** and remarked: "We should have bombed it."

President **Bill Clinton** remarked at the opening of the US Holocaust Museum in Washington DC on **April 22, 1993**: "As our fragmentary awareness of Nazi crimes grew into indisputable facts, far too little was done.... As the Allies attacked Germany, rail lines to the death camps were left undisturbed."

If the arguments given by the War Department to refuse the bombing requests were faulty—a mere excuse or, as McGovern had put it, a rationalization—then what were the **real reasons** behind the refusals? Was it perhaps anti-Semitism, which was known to be prevalent in the State and War Departments? This is likely to have been a contributing factor, but the basic reason was the broad policy of the Roosevelt administration to refrain from taking action to rescue Jews from the Nazis. The policy is also evident from the other events discussed in this chapter, e.g., the St. Louis incident, and the attitudes at the Evian and Bermuda (see next section) conferences. The United States did not want to deal with the burden of caring for large numbers of refugees who, they feared, would flood the country. Great Britain felt similarly about it. The result was that the Allies turned away from one of history's most compelling moral challenges.

The Bermuda Conference

In **early 1943**, Whitehall and Washington were flooded with ideas and proposals, accompanied by thousands of signatures on petitions, urging actions on the refugee problem and the plight of those persecuted by the Nazi regime. Proposals included a direct

---

[47] "They Looked Away," 2003 DVD directed by Stuart G. Erdheim, and narrated by Mike Wallace.

appeal to the Axis powers to release the Jews; the temporary suspension of the American immigration quotas; a concerted Allied effort to convince the neutral countries to open their borders to escaping Jews; the demand that the British revoke their White Paper of 1939 that severely limited Jewish immigration to Palestine; and the application of pressure on the International Red Cross to provide the same safeguards for imprisoned Jews as for prisoners of war (the Red Cross had, in effect, accepted the German designation of Jews as "stateless" criminals and had denied them these safeguards).

In Washington the deluge of requests fell on the lap of Assistant Secretary of State **Breckinridge Long**, whose responsibilities encompassed all refugee affairs. His importance in blocking most rescue efforts warrants a brief description of the man. Long, an avowed anti-Semite, sixty-one years old in 1943, was a descendant of a politically prominent Missouri family. His career and fortunes were enhanced by marrying the wealthy granddaughter of Francis Blair (the Democratic nominee for Vice-President in 1868). His wealth enabled him to contribute substantial funds to the presidential campaign of Woodrow Wilson who, in **1917,** repaid Long by appointing him **Third Assistant Secretary of State**. Long, similarly, contributed generously to the presidential campaign of Franklin D. Roosevelt in 1932. On **April 20, 1933**, Roosevelt appointed **Long** as the **Ambassador to Italy**.

The new ambassador was greatly impressed by what he saw in Italy. He rhapsodized Mussolini and his government, praised the Italian efficiency, cleanliness, and morale, and was impressed by the fascists in their dapper uniforms. As for Italy's aggression against Ethiopia, which was strongly condemned by the League of Nations, Long saw nothing wrong with it, and counseled against American economic measures to halt Mussolini's assault.

Long was recalled from Rome in **1936** (some said for ulcers, others said for his verbal indiscretion). Roosevelt praised him for his splendid record. In **January 1940**, Long was appointed **Assistant Secretary of State** with responsibility for 23 of the department's 42 divisions. The divisions under Long's supervision dealt with everything that was connected with relief for the Jews of Europe, e.g.: visas for visitors or immigrants; funds for food, clothing or medicine; appeals to the International Red Cross for humane treatment of Jews.

With Long supervising the Visa Division, there would be no reform in the cumbersome procedures of granting visas. Roosevelt was afraid the Jewish issue was a political liability and, by his inaction, helped to doom European Jewry. But if Roosevelt personally was sympathetic to the victims of Nazism, Long was not. In suppressing the influx of Jews, Breckinridge Long claimed to protect the nation against an invasion of radicals and foreign agents. Thus, at the **beginning of 1943**, as suggestions for handling the relief of the Jews poured into Washington, Long sat firmly in command under **Secretary of State Cordell Hull** and **Undersecretary of State Sumner Welles,** with full support from the White House, "protecting the Republic" from foreigners (Jews) seeking asylum.

Perhaps the most appalling contribution Long made to the restrictive immigration policy during the war was an intra-departmental memo he circulated in **1940**. He wrote: "We can delay, and effectively stop for a temporary period of indefinite length, the number of immigrants into the United States. We could do this by simply advising our consuls to put every obstacle in the way, and to require additional evidence, and to resort to various administrative devices that would postpone and postpone and postpone the granting of the visas."

In Britain the reaction to the Nazi extermination of European Jews was more widespread, and cries for action more forceful than in the United States. The main impetus came from members of the Parliament and Christian Church leaders. The outrage was not quite enough to liberalize its Palestine policy, but enough to consider other alternatives. On **January 20, 1943**, the British Foreign Office sent a memorandum to the American State Department proposing an **international conference** to consider the ever more pressing refugee problem.

In Washington, the responsibility for dealing with the British overture fell to Breckinridge Long who delayed a reply in the hope of squashing the British efforts. Thus, a month passed without an American response to the British suggestion. On **February 20, 1943**, **Richard Law**, the British Undersecretary of State for Foreign Affairs, pointed out that his government would be unable to postpone (beyond the following week) its reply to the demands to help the Jews. The threat that Britain would make a unilateral announcement regarding help to the Jews finally prompted the US State Department to act. On **February 25, 1943**, Secretary of State Hull stated that intergovernmental action was obviously necessary. He proudly pointed out that the United States had initiated the Evian Conference in 1938, which had established an Intergovernmental Committee on Refugees. He failed to add that the Evian Conference simply confirmed the unwillingness of the world to accept the Jews and that the Intergovernmental Committee was, for all practical purposes, defunct.

Hull suggested a conference to take place in Bermuda[48] with the proviso that the United States would be bound by its immigration laws, and that the refugee problem should not be confined to persons of a particular race or faith. Thus, it seemed from the start that the Bermuda Conference would be as much of a fiasco as the Evian Conference had been five years earlier.

During the months preceding the Bermuda Conference, new detailed reports on German atrocities against the Jews became known, but the American government made great efforts to stem the flow of this information. Here is what happened:

On **January 21, 1943**, **Gerhard Riegner**, the representative of the World Jewish Congress, provided the American legation in Bern with a new and detailed description of Nazi atrocities. He reported, among other things, that Germans were killing 6,000 Jews each day in Poland. **US Minister Harrison** sent the report to Rabbi Wise, via the State Department. The same day, Harrison received a cable from the State Department, initialed by Sumner Welles, saying that, in the future, Harrison should not accept reports submitted for transmission to private persons in the United States. Harrison was astounded. The United States and Britain had publicly pledged, in December 1942, to come to the aid of the Jews, and to punish war criminals. To do that, continuous information about Nazi atrocities was required. Yet the United States was instructing him to reject one of his most

---

[48] Bermuda was chosen because wartime regulations restricted access to the island. This ensured that no demonstrations or lobbying would take place, and allowed control of the number of reporters and private representatives. Members of the Joint Distribution Committee and the World Jewish Congress were not permitted to attend.

fertile sources of information. Harrison regretfully and apologetically notified Riegner that new regulations prohibited future private communications.

Upon receipt of the Riegner report, **Rabbi Wise** organized a "Stop Hitler Now" rally to be held on **March 1, 1943,** at Madison Square Garden. Seventy-five thousand persons attempted to enter the Garden, which seated only 21,000. **Dr. Chaim Weizmann,** president of the World Zionist Organization, addressed the crowd: "The world can no longer plead that the ghastly facts are unknown and unconfirmed. Expressions of sympathy without accompanying attempts to launch acts of rescue become a hollow mockery. Let the vast territories of the United Nations give sanctuary to those fleeing from imminent murder. Let the gates of Palestine be opened to the fleeing Jews."

An eloquent resolution was adopted at the rally, which Rabbi Wise forwarded to Sumner Welles. In an accompanying letter he wrote: "It is a source of deepest regret that despite the December 1942 declaration by the United Nations, little or nothing has been done to implement the declaration, and that the Nazi extermination has proceeded at an accelerated tempo.... I ask you to take action which may aid in saving the Jewish people from utter extinction."

Ironically, while these events took place in the United States, great technical breakthroughs to facilitate the mass murder of Jews were accomplished at Auschwitz. Engineer **Pruefer** of the firm **I.A. Topf & Sons** had designed and tested new furnaces. The gas chambers had been enlarged to hold 2,000 people, tightly packed. The prussic acid (Zyklon B) was solidified into pellets that were tossed into the gas chambers asphyxiating the victims within 15 minutes. This was a great "improvement" over the more primitive killing methods used earlier. The first improved crematoria were ready on **March 13, 1943**, a month before the Bermuda Conference.

The Bermuda Conference opened on **April 19, 1943**. The American delegation was led by **Dr. Harold Willis Dodds**, president of Princeton University, after several other candidates had turned down the job. Among them was Myron Taylor (who had led the delegation at Evian), Supreme Court **Justice Owen Roberts,** and **Charles Seymour** (president of Yale University). The American delegation included **Congressman Sol Bloom** of New York, whose intellectual resources and courage on refugee issues were notably deficient. When Rabbi Wise complained that Bloom was not an appropriate representative of American Jewry, Breckinridge Long replied that he was a representative of America.

The US State Department drew up guidelines for the American delegation: They were **not** to limit the discussion to Jewish refugees, **not** to promise US funds for the refugees, **not** to bring refugees across the ocean, **not** to expect any changes in the US immigration laws, **not** to establish new agencies for the relief of refugees since the Intergovernmental Committee already existed. The **British** added some "don'ts" of their own: They would **not** consider direct appeal to the Germans, **not** exchange POWs for refugees, **not** lift the blockade of Europe for the shipment of relief supplies to the refugees, and **not** consider changing their immigration policies with respect to Palestine.

The New York Times editorialized that the goal of the conference seemed pitifully inadequate to counter Hitler's war of extermination, and appeared to be designed to assuage the conscience of the reluctant rescuers rather than aid the victims.

The opening speeches by Mr. Law and Dr. Dodds corroborated the Times' prophecy. Law proclaimed that victory in the war provided the only real solution to the refugee problems, and the persecuted people should not be led to believe that aid is coming to them. Dodds reiterated this point and added: "The problem is too great to be solved by the two governments here represented." Only the opening speeches by Law and Dodds were released to the press. The remainder of the conference was shrouded, at the time, in secrecy.

When Sol Bloom suggested, during the conference, that the United States and Britain make an effort to admit refugees in large numbers, Dr. Dodds silenced him with the reminder that the delegates were bound by US policy. When Bloom questioned Britain's closed-door policy in Palestine, Dodds cut off the discussion.

While diplomatic niceties were practiced in Bermuda, a harsh drama was taking place in Nazi-occupied Poland. On the same day the Bermuda Conference opened, the Germans launched their final assault on the **Warsaw ghetto**. They moved against the 60,000 Jews remaining from the original 500,000 inhabitants. While the United States and Great Britain were ruling out inconvenient methods of rescue at Bermuda, the ghetto fighters were simplifying the refugee problem by their heroic death. They fought against German armor with a handful of revolvers and rifles. The outside world contributed nothing to their fight.

On the fifth day of fighting, the citizens of the embattled ghetto addressed a desperate appeal to the free world: "This is a fight for your freedom as well as ours, for your dignity and honor as well as ours. All of us will perish in the fight but we will never surrender.... The heroic uprising of the doomed sons of the ghetto should at last awaken the world to deeds commensurate with the gravity of the hour."

It did not.

Thus, **April 19, 1943** marked not only the opening of the Bermuda Conference, but the beginning of the end of the Warsaw ghetto. It was also the eve of Passover, the holiday celebrating the exodus of Jews from bondage in Egypt. But, in 1943, the events in Bermuda and Warsaw did not lead to the Promised Land. The Red Sea did not part.

After the Bermuda Conference, the United States and Britain issued a brief statement: "The delegates were able to agree on a number of concrete recommendations which will lead to the relief of a substantial number of refugees of all races and nationalities. Since the recommendations involve military considerations, they must remain confidential."

Most observers believed that the confidentiality was imposed to conceal the poverty of concrete results and thus avoid embarrassment.

The main "confidential" recommendation proposed an expansion of the existing Intergovernmental Committee on Refugees, i.e., the expansion of a committee whose efforts in the past had epitomized failure.

The Bermuda Conference has faded from memory, along with the exercises in diplomatic futility. Even those who participated, and were major actors in it, deplore its outcome. **Richard Kidston Law**, later to become **Lord Coleraine**, who headed the British delegation to the Bermuda Conference, recalled in 1965: "It was a façade for inaction. We said the results of the conference were confidential, but in fact there were no results that I can recall."

Although one cannot calculate how many Jewish victims resulted from the Bermuda Conference's inaction, one man's death was clearly related to that event. That man was **Szmuel Zygielbojm**, the Polish Jewish labor leader who had escaped across Germany after the murder of his wife and two children. On **May 12, 1943**, thirteen days after the adjournment of the Bermuda Conference, Zygielbojm committed suicide in London. He left a farewell note addressed to the President and Prime Minister of the Polish government-in-exile: "I cannot live while remnants of the Jewish population of Poland are perishing. My friends in the Warsaw ghetto died with weapons in their hands. It was not my destiny to die together with them but I belong to them in their mass graves. By my death I wish to make my most profound protest against the passivity with which the world is looking on and permitting the extermination of the Jewish people. I was unable to do anything during my life, perhaps by my death I shall contribute to the arousing from lethargy of those who could and must act to save the handful of Polish Jews still alive."

The War Refugee Board

There was one powerful man in Washington, **Secretary of the Treasury Henry Morgenthau**, who was greatly disturbed by the behavior of the State Department with regard to European Jewry. In particular, he was upset by the misleading statements made by Breckenridge Long during a congressional hearing that took place at the **end of 1943**, in response to questions raised by **Peter Bergson**, leader of the activist Jewish **Revisionist Zionist** group. Morgenthau documented the State Department's inaction, obstruction and misrepresentations, and presented the findings to President Roosevelt on **January 16, 1944**. In response to Morgenthau's memorandum, Roosevelt established the **War Refugee Board (WRB)**.

In the preface of the report Morgenthau wrote: [49]

> One of the greatest crimes in history, the slaughter of the Jewish people in Europe, is continuing unabated. This government has for a long time maintained that its policy is to work out programs to save the Jews. Yet, the record shows that certain officials in our State Department utterly failed to take any effective actions to prevent the extermination of the Jews in German-controlled Europe. The procrastination of these officials is well known. Although they used devices such as calling conferences (e.g., at Evian and Bermuda) to explore the refugee problem, in fact nothing has been accomplished.

> The best summary of the situation is contained in one sentence of a report submitted on **December 20, 1943**, by the Committee on Foreign Relations of the US Senate: "We have talked, we have sympathized, we have expressed our horror, the time to act is long past due. "

> There is a growing number of responsible people and organizations who have ceased to view the failure of the State Department to act as the product of simple incompetence. They see plain anti-Semitism motivating the actions of the State Department officials. If nothing is done about it, there is a danger that it may explode into a nasty scandal.

Morgenthau then proceeds to document two specific cases:

I: World Jewish Congress proposal to evacuate thousands of Jews.

On **March 13, 1943**, the World Jewish Congress representative in London sent a cable to their offices in Washington stating that it was possible to rescue Jews provided funds were put at the disposal of the World Jewish Congress in Switzerland. On **April 20, 1943**, the State Department received a cable from Bern relating to the financial arrangements in

---

[49] I greatly abbreviated, and in some instances paraphrased, the content of the report.

connection with the evacuation of the Jews of Romania and France. The question of financing the evacuation of the Jews was first called to the attention of the Treasury Department on **June 25, 1943**. A conference between the State Department and Treasury Department dealing with this matter was called on **July 15, 1943**. The following day the Treasury Department advised the State Department that it was prepared to issue a license for the transfer of funds.

It was not until **December 18, 1943**, after having interposed objections for five months, that the State Department suddenly instructed Minister Harrison to issue the necessary license. This, no doubt, was in response to my having made, on **December 18, 1943,** an appointment to discuss the matter with Secretary of State Cordell Hull.

Breckinridge Long, who is in charge of these matters in the State Department, knew that his position was indefensible and took the precipitous action before my pending conference with Hull. Hadn't I made the appointment with Hull, the State Department officials would never have taken action on this matter, or would have delayed it so long that any benefits which it might have had would have been lost.

II: Suppression of facts regarding Hitler's extermination of Jews.

On **October 5, 1942**, Sumner Welles, Acting Secretary of State, sent a cable to Minister Harrison in Bern, requesting all the evidence which he might secure from the World Jewish Congress officials Riegner and Lichtheim, concerning Hitler's plan to exterminate the Jews. On **November 1942** and **January 21, 1943**, Harrison forwarded documents from Riegner confirming the facts of the extermination of the Jews. On **February 10, 1943**, a highly significant cable, initialed by Sumner Welles, was dispatched to Harrison. It suggested that in the future he not accept reports submitted by Riegner. It was an attempt by State Department officials to stop the Government from obtaining further information, and countermanded the Department's previous requests for evidence on Hitler's plans to exterminate the Jews.

The State Department, being aware of the potential explosive nature of the cable, made every effort to prevent the Treasury Department from obtaining a copy. We were advised that it was a departmental, strictly political, communication and that a copy could not be furnished to the Treasury.

At the Conference in Secretary Hull's office on **December 20, 1943,** in the presence of Breckinridge Long, I asked the Secretary for a copy of the cable, which he promised to furnish to me.

On **December 20, 1943**, Breckinridge Long sent me a paraphrased version of the cable omitting important sections. However, one of the men in my department was able to obtain a copy of the original.

Morgenthau concluded the report with these words:

The facts I have detailed in this report, Mr. President, came to the Treasury's attention by accident as part of a routine investigation of the licensing of the transmission of funds to the World Jewish Congress. How many others of the same character are buried in the State Department's files I have no way of knowing. Judging from the almost complete failure of the State Department to achieve any results, the strong suspicion must be that there are not few. This much is certain, however: The matter of rescuing the Jews from extermination is a trust too great to remain in the hands of men who are indifferent, callous, and perhaps even hostile.

Roosevelt reacted sympathetically to Morgenthau's memorandum. He knew that it contained political dynamite; if it were made public, the damage to the prestige and good faith of his administration would be incalculable.

During the **January 16, 1944** meeting with the President, Morgenthau with his two assistants, **Randolph Paul and John Pehle,** presented a suggested draft of an executive order establishing a War Refugee Board (WRB).[50] Roosevelt reacted to it enthusiastically, and on **January 22, 1944,** only six days after the meeting with the Treasury officials, Franklin D. Roosevelt announced the establishment of the War Refugee Board. John Pehle, the thirty-four-year-old assistant to Morgenthau, was named acting executive director.

The executive order creating the WRB began by stating: "It is the policy of this government to take all measures within its powers to rescue the victims of enemy oppression who are in imminent danger of death, and to afford such victims all possible relief and assistance consistent with the successful prosecution of the war."

For the first time since Hitler's accession to power in 1933, US policy called for the rescue of the innocent. It was late, very late in the war. At least 4 million Jews had perished during the period of Allied apathy, and the German machinery of destruction was now in full operation.

Why had it taken the United States so long to affirm principles as old as the nation itself? In the years **between 1933 and 1944,** the American tradition of sanctuary for the oppressed was replaced by a combination of political expediency, diplomatic evasion, isolationism, indifference, and raw bigotry, which played directly into the hands of Adolph Hitler.

Could the WRB accomplish anything significant so late in the war? Few thought that it could. The acting director, John Pehle, was one of the few. Three days after the establishment of the Board, Pehle sent a cable, over the signature of Cordell Hull, to all US embassies and consulates, ordering, that "action be taken to forestall the plot of the Nazis to exterminate the Jews of Europe." The practice of suppressing unpleasant information had ended. The message specified that "communication facilities should be made freely available to carry out the policy of this government."

The objectives of the WRB were to aid the victims of Nazism while pressing the Allies and neutrals to take forceful diplomatic actions on their behalf. Crucial to the success would be its **field representatives** assigned to US embassies in the neutral nations of Europe: **Turkey, Portugal, Switzerland, Spain,** and **Sweden.**

One of the field representatives, **Ira A. Hirschmann,** assigned to the US embassy in Ankara, Turkey, was particularly effective, and his actions warrant a brief description. Hirschmann had received his diplomatic training as a department store executive in New York, working in turn for Lord and Taylor, Saks Fifth Avenue and Bloomingdale's. But Hirschmann's horizon went beyond retailing. He was appointed by Mayor La Guardia to the Board of Higher Education of New York City, and served as first chairman of the Board of Directors of The New School of Social Research.

Hirschmann participated in the Evian Conference of 1938 as a private observer. Disgusted by the hypocrisy of Evian, he decided to concentrate his energy on rescue work. He took a leave of absence from Bloomingdale's and volunteered to serve the WRB in Turkey.

The strategic significance of Turkey lay in its accessibility to refugees from Nazi-controlled **Hungary, Romania,** and **Bulgaria.** Working closely with representatives of the **Jewish Agency for Palestine,** who were operating covertly in Istanbul, Hirschmann

---

[50] The establishment of such an entity had been vigorously advocated during the previous month by a small, vocal, and effective Jewish group led by Peter Bergson (see page 129).

organized transport of Jews from Constanza in Romania to Istanbul. Between April and August 1944, 4,000 Jews were evacuated from the Balkans. From Turkey, the refugees were transported by train through Syria and Lebanon to Palestine (the route I took three years earlier).

In Washington, John Pehle fired off hard-hitting messages to the Axis powers, threatening retribution for their war crimes. This struck terror in the Romanian officials who had banished the Jews to concentration camps in **Transnistria**. Ira Hirschmann exploited this Romanian fear. He met on **March 14, 1944,** with **Alexandre Cretzianu**, the Romanian minister to Turkey, and pointed out to him the terrible fate that awaited his countrymen who would be judged war criminals. Then Hirschmann pressed Cretzianu to request his government to release the Jews from the Transnistrian concentration camps. By this time only 48,000 had survived, of the 185,000 who had been deported. Cretzianu agreed to recommend to his government that the camps be evacuated and the Jews protected. In return, Hirschmann promised to obtain four US visas for the Cretzianu family.

On **March 17, 1944**, the American embassy was notified that the Romanians had begun the transfer of Jews from the Transnistrian camps, and on **March 20,** the Red Cross in Bucharest conveyed the message that the safe return of the 48,000 Jews had been completed. Thus, the activities of one man, backed by concerned men in Washington, saved close to 50,000 lives.

Using similar techniques, Hirschmann pressured the **Bulgarian government** through **Nicholas Balabanoff**, the Bulgarian Minister Plenipotentiary to Turkey, into revoking its anti-Semitic laws. Balabanoff conveyed Hirschmann's message to his government, and on **August 30, 1944,** the Bulgarian cabinet announced that the laws would be revoked.

Another effective member of the WRB was its representative in Switzerland, **Roswell McClelland**, a thirty-year-old Quaker. Having lived in unoccupied France in 1941, he had established many contacts with the **French Resistance movement**. He was able to relay money from the Joint Distribution Committee to help them sustain a clandestine printing press in Southern France, which turned out massive quantities of false documents. He also shipped large quantities of medicine and sanitary supplies to France. In addition, McClelland dispatched funds to partisan fighters in Slovakia who liberated 1,500 Jews from the concentration camps in **Sered** and **Novaky** (see page 88) in the **autumn of 1944.**

For Jews who could not stay hidden in France, McClelland helped to organize escape routes across the Pyrenees into Spain. The hazardous, 15-hour trek through the mountains was conducted by Spanish Republican and French guides, who led at least 1,000 hunted men, women and children to safety.

The US government's attitude towards the refugee problem was incongruous (perhaps hypocritical would be a better word). On the one hand, by creating the WRB, the government affirmed its intention to take all measures within its power to rescue the victims of enemy oppression. On the other hand, the government refused asylum to the victims.

The WRB came up with a proposal to rectify this incongruity. Being aware of the strong opposition to immigration in Congress, the State Department, and the American public, the Board suggested the establishment of **emergency camps**, which they called "**free ports**,"[51] where refugees could be interned like POWs and repatriated to their homeland after Germany's defeat. This operation would take place outside the immigration system, thereby avoiding any question of altering quotas or visa procedures. If such a step were to be taken, not only would a key haven become available, but the WRB would gain leverage for its attempts to persuade other nations to do the same.

In **March 1944**, the WRB drafted a memorandum to President Roosevelt explaining the situation and outlining its proposal. Before the memorandum could go to the White House, it needed the approval of the Secretaries of War (Stimson), State (Hull) and Treasury (Morgenthau). After many discussions and delays, the recommendation went to the White House on **May 8, 1944**. Morgenthau and Pehle saw Roosevelt on **June 1, 1944**. Pehle repeated the main points of the memorandum, emphasizing the strong public support for the plan. The President accepted the proposal and agreed to bring 1,000 refugees over from Italy. The same day Pehle found a camp offered by the War Department in northern New York, near the town of **Oswego** on the shores of Lake Ontario. On **June 8**, Roosevelt approved the camp, and on the following day announced his decision at a press conference.

The WRB's original objective was to have many free ports to offer refuge to all oppressed people escaping Hitler. Alas, Fort Ontario remained the only free port—a mere token payment to decency. While the immigration quotas of the United States allotted to countries of occupied Europe went 91% unfilled (55,000 unused slots that year), the **United States** opened its gates to **1,000 fugitives** from extermination. Compare this to **Sweden**, a country one-twentieth the size of the United States, which had welcomed **8,000 Jews** from Denmark eight months earlier.

In the United States, two reactions greeted the President's decision of establishing a free port. One was gratitude, combined with disappointment that the step had been so limited. To this group belonged the majority of the press, all Jewish and many non-Jewish organizations, and many renowned private citizens. The other was anger and indignation. To this group belonged restrictionists and anti-Semites who wrote angry letters to the President, members of Congress, and journalists. No one in this group believed that the refugees would go back; and many saw the arrival of 1,000 Jews as a wedge opening the door for hundreds of thousands more to arrive. Many in Congress were indignant at Roosevelt's use of executive power to bring Jews in.

The refugees, 982 of them, arrived from Italy one **August morning in 1944**. They came from different nations, predominantly from Yugoslavia, Austria, Poland, Germany, and Czechoslovakia. Many of them had survived concentration camps. Ninety percent of them were Jewish.

Life at Fort Ontario was not easy. Families lived in barracks that had been partitioned into small apartments that lacked individual bathrooms and had only the barest furnishings. The refugees were allowed to leave the camp and go to the nearby town of Oswego for up to six hours at a time. No one was allowed to travel beyond Oswego. Visitors could come to the camp but not stay overnight. The restrictive living in the camp caused a serious deterioration of the morale of the refugees. The tension of being surrounded by freedom, close enough to touch it, yet not being free themselves; the uncertainty about the their

---

[51] This name for the emergency camps is in analogy to the free ports where foreign goods that arrive are destined for shipment to other countries, and stored only temporarily.

future; the frustration due to their inability to obtain employment, to become self-supporting and begin to rebuild their lives—all this took its toll.

When the war ended in **May 1945**, the future of the Fort Ontario refugees hung in the balance. The plight of the millions of displaced persons in Europe was emerging as a serious problem. Food, clothing, and shelter were in short supply. Against that background, it seemed unimaginable for America to insist on the return of the 1,000 refugees to Europe. But they could not be kept at Fort Ontario indefinitely, either. Finally on **December 22, 1945, President Truman** ruled that the refugees could enter the United States under the barely-touched immigration quota. Thus, 18 months after their arrival, the refugees officially entered the United States as immigrants.

Although Fort Ontario could hardly be counted among the success stories of the WRB (War Refugee Board), it was not a complete failure. There were other frustrations, difficulties, and failures that the WRB encountered. The relationship of the WRB with the **International Red Cross** was particularly acrimonious and frustrating. The WRB appealed to the Red Cross time and time again to take aggressive action to obtain humanitarian treatment for the Jews being persecuted so viciously by the Germans. However, request after request from the WRB met with the same answer: the Red Cross could not interfere in the internal affairs of a belligerent nation. John Pehle and the WRB did not accept this explanation. On **March 23, 1944,** they proposed to the Red Cross that it urge Germany to place concentration camp inmates on a status equal to that of prisoners of war; and, also, demand the right to ship and distribute food packages to inmates of the camps. Once again, the State Department obstructed the WRB's message by holding it up for over a month, until **April 29**. On **May 17, 1944**, Red Cross **president Max Huber** replied: "The steps which the WRB wished the Red Cross to take would go far beyond the limits of their traditional capacity."

The International Committee of the Red Cross did not become aggressive until the end of 1944, when Nazi defeat seemed inevitable. Only at this point did the Germans give the Red Cross access to the concentration camps. Then, utilizing funds provided by the Joint Distribution Committee and transmitted via the WRB, the Red Cross organized a massive distribution of food parcels, which undoubtedly saved several thousand inmates from starvation.

Another setback of the WRB occurred in **Spain**. There, the US ambassador, **Carlton Hayes**, firmly refused to permit the assignment of a WRB representative to his embassy. Hayes refused to ask the Spanish Government to cooperate in implementing President Roosevelt's policy with respect to refugees. Hayes' attitude dashed the hope of the WRB to use Spain as a major escape route—a conveyor belt—to move thousands of refugees to freedom. Hayes' lack of intervention emboldened the Spanish police to turn over to the Germans any refugees caught at the border.

Pehle complained to both the President and Secretary Hull about the reluctant and obstructionist ambassador, but they refused to take any action. The WRB had no choice but to ignore the ambassador and to clandestinely circumvent him in its rescue efforts. Hayes agreed only late in 1944 to accept a WRB representative, but by that time France was in Allied hands, and rescue through Spain was no longer necessary.

In spite of these setbacks, the balance sheet of accomplishments of the WRB was impressive. In a little more than a year, the WRB saved **tens of thousands of lives**. It assisted in the wartime concealment and support of additional thousands of potential victims of the Nazis. More than that, the WRB gave hope to the oppressed, stirred the apathetic, encouraged the active, and breathed new life into the forgotten American tradition of helping the oppressed. One cannot but wish that it had been established earlier, during a period when the apathy and inaction of the US government and its people made them silent bystanders to the cruelties and genocide of the Nazis—millions of lives might have been saved. The WRB stands out as a gesture of atonement for these past failures.

Summing up

Szmuel Zygielbojm, the Polish Jewish Labor Leader, in despair over the mass killings of Jews, committed **suicide in 1943** in London. In his farewell letter he wrote: "The responsibility for the crime of murdering the entire Jewish population falls, in the first instance, on the perpetrators, but indirectly it is also a burden on the whole of humanity, the people and the governments of the Allied states which thus far have made no effort toward concrete actions for the purpose of curtailing this crime. By the passive observation of the murder of defenseless millions and the maltreatment of children, women and old men, these countries have become the criminals' accomplices."

How can we understand the dismal failure of the world, most notably, the United States and Great Britain, when confronted with one of history's most compelling moral challenges? The other countries quieted their conscience by pointing to the behavior of the United States, "the beacon of democracy and humanitarianism."

The main reason for inaction or, worse, obstruction of rescue efforts, was rooted in the unshakable policies of the governments. The US State Department and the British Foreign Office had no intentions of rescuing large numbers of European Jews. On the contrary, they feared that Germany would release thousands of Jews forcing the Allied governments to take them in, a situation that the two great powers did not want to face. The US Congress' unequivocal opposition to immigration, the Christian Church's almost total silence, the press' burial of news about the death factories in the back pages of their newspapers, the general apathy, indifference, selfishness, and wide-spread anti-Semitism— all contributed to the formulation of the closed-door policy and to its acceptance by the public.

And, most important, President Roosevelt failed to speak up on the issue. He was reluctant to accept the political risks of humanitarian measures on behalf of the foreign Jews, and remained passive in the face of the mass murders. His inaction in the face of such a momentous and historical event as the systematic annihilation of European Jewry, emerges as the worst failure of his presidency.

Only when his administration stood on the brink of a nasty scandal over its rescue policies, did Roosevelt give in to the prodding of Secretary of the Treasury, Henry Morgenthau, and establish, in 1944, the War Refugee Board. However, he gave it little power and cooperation, and it was the Jewish Joint Distribution Committee that funded 85% of its work. The British resented the WRB, dismissed it as an election-year tactic, and tried to obstruct its work. It is to the credit of a few dedicated people, like John Pehle, Ira Hirschmann and Roswell McClelland, that the WRB achieved successes far in excess of expectations for such a small, poorly-supported group.

Because of the State Department's obstructionist policies, only 21,000 refugees were allowed to enter the United States during the three-and-a-half years of war with Germany. This represents a mere 10% of the number that could have been legally admitted under immigration quota during that period.

To ease public pressure, the US government pretended to care about the refugee problem by initiating two international conferences, at **Evian (1938)** and **Bermuda (1943)**. These conferences produced no effective solutions to the refugee problems. The participating diplomats and statesmen spent more time inventing reasons not to save the Jews than trying to find a way to save them. The two conferences were not only useless: they were counterproductive, by providing fodder for the German propaganda machine.

There were many rescue proposals submitted to the administration. They were turned down using rationalizations and outright lies. Here are several examples:

1) The administration asserted that shipping was unavailable. This was a lie. In **1943**, American vessels carried 1,400 non-Jewish Polish refugees to the American West Coast. In **March 1944**, the British, claiming shipping shortage, backed out of an agreement to transport 630 Jewish refugees to North Africa, while providing ships to move thousands of non-Jewish refugees from Yugoslavia to Italy and Egypt. In **November 1943**, Breckinridge Long told the House Foreign Affairs Committee that lack of transportation was the reason the State Department was issuing so few visas. This was not true. Three Portuguese liners sailed every six weeks from Lisbon to US ports, and dozens of other Portuguese and Spanish passenger ships crossed the Atlantic on a less regular basis. Furthermore, US Liberty ships that took troops to North Africa were sailing empty on their return trips.

2) Another stock excuse for inaction was the claim that Axis governments planted agents among the refugees. This problem, if it existed, could have easily been handled by security screening. It is significant that Army intelligence found not one suspicious person among the 982 refugees who arrived at Fort Ontario.

3) Another rationalization took the high ground of nondiscrimination. It asserted that helping Jews would improperly single out one group for assistance when many other people were suffering under Nazi brutality. Equating the genocide of an entire race with the oppression of other Europeans is absurd.

4) A related excuse for inaction was the assertion that special help for the Jews would stir up anti-Semitism and invite charges that the war was being fought for the Jews.

5) An often-used argument for rejecting rescue proposals was the claim that they would detract from the military effort and thus prolong the war. This excuse was used to justify the refusal of the Allies to bomb Auschwitz. In reality, none of the rescue proposals infringed upon the war effort.

Related to the last point was the Roosevelt Administration's mantra that the only way to help the Jews was to win the war as quickly as possible. As if there were a choice between winning the war and rescuing the Jews. In fact, there was no conflict between the two and they could have been—indeed, should have been—carried out simultaneously. The long-held administration's view—expressed in the slogan "rescue through victory"—proved to be faulty. When victory came, there was virtually no one left to rescue.

A consequence of the government's attitude was that the United States itself evacuated a mere 1,000 Jews to Fort Ontario and another 1,000 to North Africa, while

Britain and the United States evacuated 100,000 non-Jewish (Yugoslav, Polish, and Greek) refugees.

The Holocaust was not only a Jewish tragedy. It was a tragedy for Western civilization and all humankind. Most Americans and the world did not see it that way, and considered it a strictly Jewish problem. That explains, in part, why the United States and the rest of the world did so little to help.

Has the dismal failure of the American response to the European Jewish catastrophe taught us a lesson? I believe it did. The mistakes and omissions made in the past are universally acknowledged, and there is now a commitment at the highest level of the American government to take action when confronted with outbreaks of massive persecutions. When the Indo-Chinese refugees, the "boat people," in the 1970s, confronted the world, President Carter and Vice President Mondale pointed out that in the Nazi era the United States and the other democracies had "failed the test of civilization." They called on the nation not to "re-enact their error." In time, 800,000 Indochinese reached safety in the United States. Another instance is the response (albeit slow) of the Clinton Administration to the atrocities committed in former Yugoslavia.

The record, unfortunately, is not perfect. In Rwanda the response was too slow to prevent genocide; and in Darfur, rescue has yet to be provided.

A clear instance of affirmation to uphold American civic responsibilities and not compromise moral principles, are the words of three US presidents chiseled in stone on the outside wall of the Holocaust Memorial Museum in Washington DC:

> Out of our memory of the Holocaust we must forge an unshakable oath with all civilized people that never again will the world fail to act in time to prevent this terrible crime of genocide.
>
> – Jimmy Carter

> We must make sure that from now until the end of days all humankind stares this evil in the face. And only then can we be sure that it will never rise again.
>
> – Ronald Reagan

> Here we will learn that each of us bears responsibility for our actions and for our failure to act. Here we will learn that we must intervene when we see evil arise.
>
> – George H.W. Bush

Let us heed these words as we remember and mourn the six million Jews that perished in the Holocaust.

I want to conclude with a few general and personal remarks:

I express here strong criticism of the behavior of the Allied governments during the Hitler era. Am I perhaps guilty of judging past events by present day moral standards, rather than those that prevailed at the time? I don't think so. Americans 70 years ago were not members of some distant culture, with different basic values from their present ones with regard to human responsibility for assisting other human beings in desperate need of help. There has been no moral revolution between 1940 and now, endowing present-day Americans with moral standards superior to those that prevailed two generations ago. If America had been an amoral wasteland during World War II, the Secretary of Treasury, Henry Morgenthau, would never have written the report to President Roosevelt when he uncovered the scandalous behavior of the State Department. And Roosevelt's reaction to the report, the establishment of the WRB, would never have occurred. It is not that basic moral values were different then from now, but that most people simply did not live up to their values.

Having justified the criticism in general, I have to admit to a very uncomfortable feeling in criticizing the United States. Being an immigrant myself, who gained so much by being admitted to this country, I am immensely grateful to America for providing me with a higher education, the possibility of pursuing a scientific career, and a comfortable life for me and my family. Am I not biting the hand that fed me? In a way, it is like children criticizing some of the opinions and attitudes of their parents without diminishing their love and respect for them. And isn't this what makes democracy work: to be able to disagree and criticize openly, without being in any way unpatriotic? Consider, for instance, the quotations of the three presidents who certainly cannot be accused of being disrespectful of the United States. They criticized their own country for past failures and learned a lesson from them for better governance in the future.

And lastly, the failure of the world to avert the tragedy of the Holocaust, points clearly and emphatically to the importance for the Jews to have their own state. Had a Jewish State existed in 1939, the fate of the Jews would have had a vastly different outcome. Not only would a Jewish State have provided a safe haven for all Jewish refugees, it might have helped the war effort by contributing to the Allied nations its manpower and military resources.

The existence of the State of Israel gives teeth to the oft-repeated pledge "**Never again.**"

4. THE RESPONSE OF THE JEWISH COMMUNITY IN THE UNITED STATES DURING THE CRITICAL YEARS OF GENOCIDE

In the preceding chapter, I described the reaction of the free world to the atrocities committed by Nazi Germany and some of the efforts made by the Jewish organizations to alert the American public to the dangers that faced the Jews in Europe, including the demonstrations and suggestions for alleviating the situation (see pages 106 and 110–113). Neither the demonstrations nor the suggestions bore fruit, and there is a general feeling that the Jewish organizations could, and should, have done more to save the Jews of Europe. In this section I want to explore this point in more detail, with particular emphasis on the last three and a half "genocide years" of the Nazi regime.

When the United States entered the war (in **late 1941**) and in the **first half of 1942**, sporadic reports of Nazi atrocities against the Jews reached the West. However, they were perceived as unconfirmed rumors, and the extent of the escalating catastrophe was not comprehended. British high officials knew, from German messages decoded in 1941, of the mass murder of Jews in Poland and in the occupied Soviet territories. However, this information remained strictly secret to prevent the Germans from knowing that their **Enigma code** had been broken. Added to the lack of knowledge of the mass killings, was the American Jews' veneration of President Roosevelt, which resulted in the acceptance of his policies that gave the rescue of Jews a low priority. Furthermore, there was the fear of an anti-Semitic backlash that might occur if pressure were exerted on the government by Jewish organizations. Unfortunately, this attitude prevailed even after the extent of the mass killings became common knowledge. As I shall describe, at times the Jewish leaders overstepped the limits of subservience, thereby adding to the hardship of ghetto inhabitants, and impeding forceful rescue efforts.

The tepid response of the mainstream Jewish organizations, including their leader Stephen Wise

The most influential leader and spokesman of the American Jewish community was **Rabbi Stephen Wise** (1874–1949), who, as a child, emigrated from Hungary to New York. He was ordained as a Reform rabbi and held strong, liberal, political convictions. After meeting Herzl at the 2nd Zionist Congress in 1898, he became an ardent Zionist and, in 1936, became president of the **Zionist Organization in America**. Wise founded the **American Jewish Congress** in 1920, and, in 1936 was instrumental in the creation of the **World Jewish Congress** that he led during the critical World War II years. Wise was a personal friend and ardent (some say blind) supporter of President Roosevelt, and served on his **Advisory Commission on Political Refugees** (1938–1945).

In a display of unconditional Americanism, Rabbi Wise decided to impose a complete embargo on all aid sent to Jews in occupied Nazi territories, in compliance with the US government's economic boycott of the Axis powers (whereby food packages were seen as assistance to the enemy). Telegrams were sent to representatives of the World Jewish Congress in Europe with strict orders to halt any shipment of packages to the ghettos. Wise justified this cruel decision by proclaiming that "we will not put our interests before those of our country."

Wise's attitude is clearly expressed in a letter of **September 1940** to **Otto Nathan**, one of Roosevelt's economic advisors: "Cruel as I may seem, as I have said to you before, Roosevelt's re-election is much more important for everything that is worthwhile and that counts, than the admission of a few people to the United States, however imminent their peril."

Another incident showed Rabbi Wise's deference towards the US State Department to the detriment of the Jewish cause. At the end of **July 1942**, a German industrialist, **Eduard Schulte**, well connected to high Nazi officials, traveled to Zürich and informed **Gerhard Riegner**, the head of the Geneva office of the World Jewish Congress, of Hitler's plans for the total extermination of the European Jews by the end of the year (see pages xxx). Riegner sent the now famous telegram through the US and British delegations to the World Jewish Congress headquarters in New York and London. Rabbi Weis received the ominous news, but was asked by the US Secretary of State **Sumner Wells** not to publicize the report. Wise complied with the request. It was not until **November 1942**, as further information about the German extermination campaign was accumulating in Washington, that Sumner Wells gave Wise the green light to publicize the report. Thus, many precious months were unnecessarily lost before the world was made aware of the Nazi extermination program.

Mainstream Jewish leaders continued to accept Roosevelt's **"rescue through victory"** approach, which justified the administration's low priority given to rescue efforts lest they detract from the main goal of winning the war. But as **1943** wore on without evidence that Allied victory was imminent, and given Wise's inability to persuade the administration to launch a serious rescue effort, a growing segment of the Jewish population demanded stronger initiatives to be implemented. Wise's leadership was challenged by the more forceful **Rabbi Abba Hillel Silver,** of Cleveland, who became co-chairman of the **American Zionist Emergency Council**. But the strongest challenge to the low-pressure tactics of Rabbi Wise came from a small but effective and vocal group of right-wing Revisionist Zionists led by **Peter Bergson** (a.k.a. **Hillel Kook**).[52]

The forceful approach of the Revisionist Zionists under the leadership of Peter Bergson

Hillel Kook (1915–2001), a nephew of Ashkenazi Chief Rabbi Abraham Isaac Hacohen Kook, was born in Lithuania and moved at age 10 with his family to Palestine. In the early 1930s, he joined the Revisionist Zionist movement and its military arm, the **Irgun Zvai Leumi (IZL),** a radical Jewish underground militia. In **1940,** Kook accompanied the leader of the Irgun, **Ze'ev Jabotinsky,**[53] to the United States, and changed his name to Peter Bergson to spare his prominent family any embarrassment that might ensue from his forthcoming political activity.

The original task of Jabotinsky and Bergson in the United States was to raise funds to purchase arms for the Irgun fighters in Palestine. After Jabotinsky's death in **August 1940,** Bergson and his comrades decided to forge an entirely different political path, and to focus

---

[52] For a detailed description of Bergson and his activities, see "A Race Against Death," D.S. Wyman and R. Medoff, The New York Press, 2002.

[53] Ze'ev Vladimir Jabotinsky (1880–1940), was a Russian Zionist orator and activist who played a crucial role in establishing, under British auspices, a Jewish Legion that helped capture Palestine from the Turks during World War I. Troubled by the cautious response of the Zionist leadership, he established his own more militant wing of Revisionist Zionists, and, in 1935, seceded from the World Zionist Organization. Later, he established an underground militia, the Irgun Zvai Leumi, commonly known as the Irgun.

exclusively on establishing a Jewish army to fight Nazi Germany. They formed the **Committee for a Jewish Army** and organized rallies in Manhattan in **June 1941** and in Washington DC in **December 1941**. In **February 1942**, Bergson persuaded Representative **Andrew Somers** of New York to introduce a congressional resolution endorsing the creation of a Jewish army. Although the resolution never came to a vote, it signaled that there was now a Jewish organization that, unlike the others, was ready to press its agenda on Capitol Hill, with or without the approval of the Roosevelt administration.

When the mass killings of the Jews became known and made public in a State Department-approved press conference held by Rabbi Wise on **November 24, 1942**, the press was still hesitant to report it adequately, as evidenced by the fact that the leading newspaper, The New York Times, reported on it with a small note on page 10. This apathetic response to the news of the extermination jarred the Bergson group, and made them move rapidly to rearrange their agenda. The rescue of European Jews became Bergson's top priority, with the Jewish army goal taking a backseat for the moment.[54]

Bergson's tactics were the diametric opposite of the conservative, kid-glove diplomatic approaches of the mainstream Jewish organizations. He used direct—and often bombastic—appeals to the American public and members of Congress to demand the rescue of Jews from Nazi terror. He placed hard-hitting, full-page ads in major newspapers, with headliners such as: "Action, Not Pity," "This is Strictly a Race Against Time," "Help Prevent 4 million People from Becoming Ghosts," "How Well are You Sleeping?" It startled Americans, who were accustomed to Jewish groups that spoke in soft tones, if they spoke at all. Bergson also organized marches, demonstrations with a lot of pageantry and "hoopla." It was all part of a tireless battle he waged against the prevailing indifference of the population, trying to rouse the conscience of the nation and prod the Roosevelt administration to rescue Jews from Hitler.

The Bergsonites planned to hold a mass rally at **Madison Square Garden** on **March 9, 1943**. Stephen Wise and the American Jewish Congress, fearful that their leadership might be usurped, hastily arranged a mass meeting at the same location for **March 1**, under the banner "Stop Hitler Now." The reaction of the public to the rally was enthusiastic. Twenty thousand jammed Madison Square Garden, while tens of thousands stood outside. The roster of speakers included AFL President **William Green**, New York City **Mayor La Guardia, Stephen Wise,** and World Zionist Organization President **Chaim Weizmann**.

The rally, which to a large extent had been organized as a reaction to the activities of the Bergsonites, brought public attention to the plight of the Jews in Europe and the need for action. One immediate effect was a change in the editorial position of the N.Y. Times, which had previously advocated the "rescue through victory" approach. In the wake of the rally, a N.Y. Times editorial now asserted: "The United Nations governments have no right to spare any efforts to save lives." The US government including the State Department, sensitive to unfavorable publicity, felt the need to act. On **March 3, 1943**, it announced that it planned, with Britain, to hold a conference on the refugee problem. This became known as the **Bermuda Conference** (see page 113).

---

[54] Whereas the Bergsonites never succeeded in convincing the US government to form a Jewish fighting unit in the US Army, in Great Britain the lobby of the Jewish Agency in London finally succeeded. In **August 1944**, Prime Minister **Winston Churchill**, moved by the slaughter of Hungarian Jews, consented to the creation of a **Jewish brigade**, composed of Palestinian Jews, which reached a strength of 5,000 soldiers. They saw action during the final months of the war, and when the war ended they played an important role in helping survivors emigrate to Palestine.

Meanwhile the Bergsonites, not to be outdone, adopted a uniquely dramatic approach for the **March 9, 1943** event at Madison Square Garden. They organized a pageant, **"We Will Never Die,"** to publicize the plight of European Jewry. **Ben Hecht,** the well-known Hollywood screenwriter (among his screen credits are "Gone with the Wind" and "Wuthering Heights"), provided the script and recruited the prominent actors **Paul Muni, Edward G. Robinson,** and **Stella Adler. Kurt Weil** provided the score, and **Moss Hart** directed the production. The two opening performances on March 9, 1943 were viewed and enthusiastically received by 40,000 people. The following month it was performed in Washington DC, with **Eleanor Roosevelt,** hundreds of members of Congress, cabinet members and Supreme Court Justices attending. The pageant struck a major blow at the wall of silence surrounding the Nazi genocide, and aroused public consciousness about the plight of European Jewry.

Unfortunately, the success of the pageant "We Will Never Die" further exacerbated the conflict between the established Jewish groups and the Bergsonites. When the American Jewish Congress announced its March 1 rally, the Bergsonites offered to stage the pageant as a joint project. Stephen Wise and the Congress rejected the proposal. Worse was to come; the non-cooperation of the mainstream Jewish organizations turned into obstruction. Local sponsors of the pageant at other locations were pressured by the Jewish organizations to cancel the performance. They were told that the pageant was the handiwork of irresponsible extremists who were trying to undermine the established Jewish leadership. The attempts to stop the performance were largely unsuccessful and only showed the ugly face of the intra-Jewish fighting. Stephen Wise even urged (unsuccessfully) NY Governor **Thomas Dewey** to declare March 9 an official day of mourning for European Jewry, and to cancel the New York City pageant. It is ironic, sad, and a disgrace, that although the goals of the mainstream Jewish organizations and the Bergsonites were the same (i.e., the rescue of European Jews and the establishment of a Jewish state after the war), the differences in approach and the animosities between the two groups prevented them from joining forces in a collaborative effort to attain these goals.

The conference that was announced by the US administration on March 3, 1943, took place in **Bermuda in April 1943**. As described earlier, it produced no tangible results except for a huge disappointment. The Bermuda Conference had raised hopes for Allied action to rescue Jews, but these expectations were shattered. The Bergsonites reacted with a full-page ad in The New York Times, declaring: "To 5 million Jews in the Nazi Death-Trap Bermuda Was a 'Cruel Mockery.'" Senator **Scott Lucas** (D–Illinois), a US delegate to Bermuda, denounced Bergson as an ungrateful alien, and urged the State Department and the FBI to investigate whether Bergson could be drafted or deported.

In the **spring and summer of 1943**, grass root dissatisfaction with the mainstream Jewish leaders' caution and vacillations escalated. The more aggressive approach of the Bergson group was beginning to strike a responsive chord in the Jewish community. The **Independent Jewish Press Service** urged to "scrap our hush-hush mufflers and get ourselves a loudspeaker." A small band of activists had finally made an impact.

In **July 1943**, the Bergson group did what should have been done at Bermuda. They organized a conference to which they invited a panel of experts to discuss detailed plans for rescuing the Jews of Europe. The gathering produced a new organization, the **Emergency Committee to Save the Jewish People of Europe**. It became the new focus of Bergson's activities, deliberately avoiding controversial issues such as the future of Palestine, which he believed would be a distraction from his main goal of rescuing Jews.

American Zionist leaders were outraged and lambasted Bergson for his decision to put Palestine on the back burner. The World Jewish Congress, under the leadership of Stephen Wise, continued to vigorously denounce Bergson in public.

At the **American Jewish Conference** held in **August 1943**, one month after the Bergson Conference, Wise told his audience: "We are Americans first, last, and at all times.... Our first and sternest task, in common with all other citizens of our beloved country, is to win the anti-fascist war" (exactly the line taken by the US government to justify their inaction on the refugee problem).

In **August** and **September 1943** the activities of the Emergency Committee intensified, while, at the same time, **William R. Hearst's** 43 newspapers carried editorials advocating the Emergency Committee's agenda. The administration could no longer afford to neglect these activities, in particular on the eve of the presidential election, and on **August 12, 1943**, Secretary of State **Cordell Hull** agreed, after many unsuccessful attempts by Bergson, to meet with him. The Emergency Committee's central demand was the establishment of a special governmental commission devoted to the rescue of Jews. Hull was non-committal and the Bergsonites continued to press ahead with their campaign. On **October 6**, they organized a march on Washington by 400 rabbis, which attracted substantial media coverage. It was followed by a rally at Carnegie Hall on **October 31**, honoring Denmark and Sweden for the rescue of Danish Jewry.

Until **late 1943**, Bergson refrained from publicly criticizing the popular President Roosevelt. In **November** of that year, Bergson crossed that line with a biting ad proclaiming that "the silence of the Allies was a death sentence of the Jews." On **November 9, 1943**, as a result of Bergson's lobbying, a resolution was introduced in the US Congress to create a commission "to formulate and effectuate a plan of immediate action to rescue the Jews." The sponsors of the bill were Senators **Guy Gillette** (D–Iowa) and Representative **Will Rogers, Jr.** (D–California). The hearings in the House Foreign Affairs Committee began on **November 19, 1943**. Stephen Wise testified at the hearing, criticizing the resolution as "inadequate" because it did not urge the British to open the doors of Palestine to Jewish refugees. That was a shrewd stratagem by Wise, to give the impression that he supported the US rescue action and merely wanted to correct a flaw in the wording of the resolution. But he undoubtedly was aware that his testimony hurt the chances for the passage of the resolution.

As it turned out, the appearances of Bergson and Wise were not the decisive factors in the final outcome. It was the blunder of **Breckinridge Long** that brought the issue to a head. Long presented an array of facts and figures at the hearing that were both wrong and misleading. When Long's testimony was made public, the State Department found itself under attack. As the furor continued and the resolution hung in the balance, the Secretary of the Treasury, **Henry Morgenthau,** entered the picture. Aware of the State Department's misleading statements, he drafted an 18-page memorandum, carefully documenting the State Department's intentional obstruction of rescue. Morgenthau presented the memorandum to President Roosevelt on **January 16, 1944**. Six days later, the President issued an executive order creating the rescue commission thereby avoiding a potentially explosive Senate debate. (It is generally believed that if Roosevelt had not established the commission, the legislation would have passed anyway.) The new commission was named the **War Refugee Board (WRB)**. The head of the WRB was **John Pehle**, an energetic young man who had been Morgenthau's assistant.

The establishment of the WRB was the Bergson group's greatest and most important success. It was the Bergson group that sowed the seed of the WRB, although its ultimate establishment was brought about by other people and events (e.g., Breckinridge Long's misleading statements and obstructionism, and Henry Morgenthau's intervention). The members of the WRB acknowledged and appreciated the Bergson group's crucial role in the board's creation, and maintained a warm rapport with Bergson. They met with him frequently in the **spring of 1944** to discuss specific methods of rescue. Although the WRB made valuable contributions, it could have done much more had the Roosevelt administration given it the support it needed for major rescue operations. But rescue never became more than a very low priority in the Roosevelt administration. In spite of being handicapped by lack of adequate support, it is estimated that the WRB rescued about 200,000 people.

By mid-1944, there was no longer any doubt that Germany was going to lose the war, and Bergson started to look ahead toward the post-war era. In **May 1944** he established the **Hebrew Committee of National Liberation**, made up of the small Bergsonite core group of Palestinian Jews. They regarded themselves as the government in exile for the Jewish state (yet to be established). By setting up the Hebrew Committee Bergson did not intend to jettison the rescue efforts; on the contrary, he hoped that the Hebrew Committee might open up diplomatic contacts that would be of help to the rescue.

What Bergson did not anticipate was the outrage and vehement opposition to the Hebrew Committee by the World Zionist Organization and the **Jewish Agency**,[55] which considered themselves the sole legitimate representatives of the Palestine Jewish community. The ensuing attacks on Bergson forced him to divert a considerable amount of energy to responding to his critics, which took a toll on the Emergency Committee's rescue efforts. Nevertheless, the Emergency Committee continued its rescue efforts, albeit from a weakened position. It launched a nationwide campaign calling for free ports for Jewish refugees. By the end of the **summer of 1944,** one such port was created at **Oswego** with about 1,000 European refugees (see page 122). The Emergency Committee also sent a letter to President Roosevelt in **July 1944,** urging the Allies to bomb the railways to Auschwitz (see page 110). It was the first organization to make this recommendation to the US government.

Conclusion

The general feeling that the mainstream Jewish organizations could and should have done more to save the Jews of Europe is, in my opinion, justified. However, in contrast to the ineffectiveness of the mainstream Jewish groups, there was a relatively small band of active, vocal, and effective Revisionist Zionists under the leadership of Peter Bergson, whose aggressive tactics produced remarkable results. Although the majority of Jews (including myself) oppose the right-wing ideology of the Irgun and Bergson, the saving of Jewish lives supersedes ideology, and all of us owe the Bergsonites a great debt.

---

[55] The Jewish Agency was widely viewed by the Jews of Palestine as their de facto government. The League of Nations, which granted to Great Britain the Mandate for Palestine in 1922, called for its establishment. It was to represent the interests of the Jewish population in Palestine, and advise and cooperate with the British administration.

Epilogue

When World War II ended, the Emergency Committee disbanded while Bergson's Hebrew Committee focused full-force on the campaign for Jewish statehood, building up public and political pressure that contributed to Britain's withdrawal from Palestine. Following the creation of the **State of Israel** on **May 15, 1948**, Bergson returned to Israel and reassumed his Hebrew name, Hillel Kook. He was elected to the first Knesset (Parliament) as a member of Begin's **Herut Party**, serving from 1949 to 1951. Disputes between Kook and Begin soon erupted over issues such as the relation between religion and state, and the country's lack of a constitution. Disillusioned, Kook left Israel in 1951 and immigrated to the United States. He later returned to Israel and permanently settled there in 1970. He passed away on August 18, 2001, a disappointed and embittered man.

5. A BRIEF HISTORY OF THE ESTABLISHMENT OF THE JEWISH COMMUNITY IN PALESTINE—THE YISHUV—AND ITS RESPONSE TO THE HOLOCAUST

As I discussed in the previous chapter, the mainstream American Jewry was, by and large, paralyzed in the face of the Jewish catastrophe in Europe, and displayed an unconditional Americanism vowing not to consider their "Jewish interests" before those of their country. Whereas the attitude of the American Jews can be understood by their fear of being labeled unpatriotic and giving rise to an anti-Semitic backlash, the attitude of the Jewish community in Palestine—the Yishuv—and its leadership was more perplexing and troubling. Indeed, the behavior of the Yishuv during the Holocaust has become one of the most sensitive and controversial issues that have plagued the Israeli public since the end of the World War II. Israelis have been traumatized by feelings of guilt that the Yishuv had failed to do what could have been done to rescue Jews in the Nazi-occupied territories.

But before addressing these questions, I wish to digress and briefly discuss the history of Zionism, i.e., the establishment of the Yishuv that ultimately led to the creation of the State of Israel in 1948.[56] In a sense, this is only tangentially related to the main topic of this chapter, but the events and memories of the past played an important role in determining the behavior and attitudes of the Yishuv during the crucial years of the Holocaust. (Besides, it is such an interesting story that it is worth re-telling.)

Palestine in the pre-Zionist era

After the Romans sacked Jerusalem and burnt it down in 70 A.D., the dispersion of Jews began. But the Jews never forgot Palestine. Wherever they resided, they remembered and longed for their ancient homeland; and Palestine was never without (albeit in a small number) Jewish inhabitants, even during the Crusades, when most of the Jews were slaughtered. So, if we define Zionism as a yearning for Zion, it is as old as the Diaspora. But as a political force, Zionism dates back only to the end of the 19th century.

In 1800 there were about 10,000 Jews living in Palestine, most of them concentrated in Jerusalem and a minority in Safed, Tiberias and Hebron. The majority were pious Jews who had come to the Holy Land to pray and die. Their presence in Palestine was a Mitzvah (sacred duty), bound to speed up the coming of the Messiah. They were poor and were mostly supported by charities from abroad. A few engaged in crafts, mostly masonry. A remnant of this ancient community survives to this day in the Mea Shearim quarter in Jerusalem. The new Jewish colonists who arrived at the end of the 19th and beginning of the 20th century, severely criticized this community; it reminded them of the ghettos of Eastern Europe, the Jews leading a miserable and unproductive life, divorced from the soil.

An exception was a group of orthodox Jews who broke out of Jerusalem in 1879, purchased a stretch of swampy land (near present day Tel Aviv), and established a farming settlement they called **Petach Tikva** (Gate of Hope). But after two years, the settlers, malaria-stricken and not used to farming, gave up and abandoned the settlement. It was resettled by newcomers in 1882 (see page 142).

Palestine in the 19th century was a backward and neglected province of the Ottoman Empire that lagged in development behind its neighbors, Lebanon, Syria and Egypt. In Egypt, the seeds of progress had been sown by Napoleon's expeditionary forces in 1799,

---

[56] Amos Elon, "The Israelis," Holt, Rinehart & Winston, 1971.

and further fostered by the opening of the Suez Canal in 1869 and the takeover by the British in 1882.

During the 19th century, travel to Palestine was becoming easier and safer, and a large number of visitors—pilgrims, artists, and authors—described the rather deplorable situation they found when they arrived in the country. **Herman Melville** visited Jerusalem in **1857**, and wrote that the Jews of Jerusalem were "like flies who have taken up their abode in a skull." **Mark Twain**, who visited in **1867**, did not have nice things to say about Palestine either.

The flip side of this sorry state of affairs was the challenge and opportunity that the underdeveloped ancient land of Israel offered to the Zionist colonizers.

The movements that led to Zionism

Jews were persecuted throughout the centuries. Repressions, pogroms, massacres, and the expulsion from Spain and other countries caused immeasurable suffering, and fueled a search and yearning for solutions that would lead to a life of peace, dignity, and an adequate level of prosperity. The pursuit of these goals gave rise to several movements that ultimately led to Zionism and the establishment of a Jewish State. In the next sections I describe some of these movements that evolved during the last few centuries.

In **1648**, the Cossack leader **Bogdan Chmielnicki** (1593–1657) perpetrated a pogrom in the Ukraine of ferocious intensity in which hundreds of Jewish communities were annihilated and hundreds of thousands of Jews were massacred. The horror of this event sent a shock throughout Jewry, and spawned a **messianic movement** led by **Shabtai Tzvi** (1626–1676). Tzvi was a Syrian Jew who left his native Smyrna in 1654 for Salonika, in Greece, where he declared himself the Messiah. He traveled extensively in the region, to Rhodes, Tripoli, Egypt, Palestine, and Constantinople. Wherever he went he was enthusiastically received by the Jewish masses and heaped with honors. So great was his following, that the Sultan in Constantinople feared an uprising and arrested Shabtai Tzvi. To save his life, the "Messiah" converted to Islam. The disillusionment and shock among his followers was immense.

These events, the Chmielniski pogrom and the disillusionment caused by the Shabtai Tzvi fiasco, prepared the grounds for the formation of a religious and social movement called **Hassidism**. It was founded in the Ukraine by **Israel Baal Shem Tov** (1699–1762), a mystic miracle-worker who preached that all Jews are equal before the Almighty; that sincere devotion, zeal and heartful prayers are more important than great learning; and that God can be better served through joy than by solemnity and intellectualism. Hassidism was enthusiastically embraced by the Jewish masses, who were frustrated by the hierarchical and elitist structure of the rabbinates, and by the Talmudic scholarship and intellectual approach that was inaccessible, incomprehensible, and hence unsatisfying to them.

An important part of the Hassidic movement was the school of thought known as **Kabala**, a mystical philosophy that had its origin in ancient Palestine and Babylon. It appears distinctly in the writing of the Essenes (around the time of Christ) and in the Talmud (4th and 5th century A.D.). The central work in the literature of the Kabala is the **Zohar (Splendor)**, which was compiled by **Moses de Leon** of Spain (1250–1305) at the end of the 13th century. The kabalistic movement reached its culmination in the 16th century in Safed, Palestine, with Rabbi **Isaac Luria** (1534–1572). The Kabala deals chiefly with the nature of God, the creation of the universe, the destiny of man, and the ultimate meaning of the written law. It asserts that the text of the Bible is filled with hidden meanings: that the words contain mysterious concepts that men should strive to uncover. One way to do this is to use the numerical values assigned to each letter of the Hebrew alphabet: adding up the numbers corresponding to the letters in a word renders a numerical value for that word—forming new words with identical numerical values can decode the hidden meaning of the text. The Hassidim considered the Zohar a holy book on the same level as the Bible and the Talmud.

In the century following the foundation of Hassidism, half of the world's Jewry adopted its teachings. Nowadays, Hassidism, although still practiced, has lost its importance as a mass movement.

Another movement, the **Enlightenment (*Haskala*)**, tried to deal with the persecution of Jews. It arose in Germany in the middle of the 18th century. The promoters of the Haskala (called the *maskilim*) believed that Jews were persecuted because they differed from the non-Jews in culture, language and manner. The maskilim believed that if the Jews spoke the language of the land and modernized their ways, they would be treated as equal citizens.

The champion of the Haskala was **Moses Mendelsohn** (1729–1786), philosopher, polyglot, and leading German intellectual. In 1783, Mendelsohn published his German translation of the Pentateuch (the first five books of the Old Testament) written in Hebrew letters, with the purpose of teaching German to the Jews. He was also instrumental in establishing modern Jewish schools in the major cities of Germany. The movement quickly spread to Austria, Poland, and Russia, but was strongly opposed by the leaders of orthodox Jewry who saw in the Haskala a threat to Judaism and a source of assimilation. Indeed, many of the maskilim became estranged from Judaism, and some of them left the Jewish faith entirely (e.g., the composer Felix Mendelsohn, grandson of Moses Mendelsohn).

The maskilim advocated the use of Hebrew instead of Yiddish, and they started a Hebrew quarterly, Ha-Measeph (1784–1831). The Haskala produced the first Hebrew novelist, **Abraham Mapu** (1808–1867). His first literary success was the Hebrew novel "Ahavat Zion" (Love of Zion), followed by several biblical novels written in a romantic style and florid language. Mapu's novels elicited in his readers their longing for Zion, which served as a strong stimulus for the Zionist movement.

Alas, the hopes of the maskilim were not realized. The "modern" Jew was not accepted by the native population as an equal. The governments continued their old ways of persecuting the Jews, decreeing anti-Jewish legislation and, in Russia and Poland, promoting pogroms. Consequently, many Jewish leaders came to believe that the only solution to the Jewish problem was the establishment of a **Jewish National Home**. Thus, the Haskala movement became a potent factor in the initiation of the Zionist movement. It created a stratum of middle-class Jews imbued with their historic tradition, while also cognizant of the political and social ideas of the western world. What seems remarkable (in hindsight) is that it took 2000 years of persecution and suffering to arrive at the Zionist solution of a Jewish homeland.

The Jews of Eastern Europe: the source of the early pioneers

During the second half of the 19th century, Eastern Europe (Russia, the Ukraine, Poland, Lithuania) was a desperately backward land teeming with wretchedly poor, illiterate peasants living under the yoke of autocratic governments. As if it were the Middle

Ages in the 19th century, with rampant poverty and hopelessness, survival was an achievement.

Of the millions of Jews that eked out a miserable existence, about 5 million lived under Czarist rule, and 3 million inhabited neighboring Poland, and Romania (part of the Austro-Hungarian Empire). The majority were descendants of Jews who escaped the 12th century slaughter by the Crusaders in the Rhine and Danube Valleys. Jews in Eastern Europe were required by law to live in the so-called Pale of Settlement, where they lived in tight, isolated clusters. They spoke Yiddish, a German vernacular of the 12th century, with some Hebrew, Polish, and Russian mixed in. Early in the 19th century, Yiddish developed from the unwritten language to a popular vehicle of literary expression. Parallel with the development of Yiddish as a literary language, Hebrew was rediscovered for secular purposes. Although Yiddish was still a richer and more expressive language, Hebrew breathed the magic of past glory and ancient wisdom.

The Jews lived in little townlets, called **shtetls**; there were thousands of them dispersed over Russia, Poland, Lithuania, and the Ukraine. They were communities of shopkeepers, peddlers, artisans, innkeepers, beggars, dreamers, and *luftmenschen* (those living on air). Although there were always representatives of the government (policemen, tax collectors) in the shtetl, the Jewish community handled its own day-to-day affairs. Education—centered on the Bible and the Talmud—was compulsory for boys between ages 5 and 13. This was in sharp contrast to the illiterate Christian peasants surrounding them. The hallmark of these communities was equality between poor, rich, learned and unlearned, i.e., the absence of a social hierarchy. This attitude later played an important role in the social ethos of Zionism.

The Pale of Settlement had been formally instituted by **Catherine II** (1762–1796) following the partition of Poland when 3 million Jews came under her rule. The succeeding Czars ruled by arbitrary edicts, with varying degrees of animosity toward the Jews. **Alexander I** (1801–1825) first permitted Jews to pursue any occupation and to attend Russian schools, only to reverse himself later, ordering the Jews back to the Pale. His successor, **Nicholas I** (1825–1855), promoted further hardships by introducing a special, 25-year-long, military conscription for Jews. His successor, "the liberal Czar," **Alexander II** (1855–1881), reversed his predecessor's measure, freed 40 million serfs, and opened schools and universities to Jews. Anarchists assassinated him in 1881; three of them involved bore Jewish names. The next Czar, **Alexander III** (1881–1904), was the worst. He was completely in the hands of his advisor, **Pobenotsev**, a fanatical anti-Semite who sponsored anti-Jewish riots as a popular diversion from the miseries of daily life. His formula for solving the Jewish problem: "One third emigration, one third conversion, and one third death." At about this time the Russian word **pogrom** (devastation) entered the international vocabulary.

After 1887, Jews were barred from high schools and universities. The children of rich Jews studied in Europe, and the rest studied at home. The Jews studying abroad were exposed to a liberal atmosphere; this played an important role in Israeli politics years later.

In addition to the persecution and political woes came new economic hardships for the East European Jews, brought about by new marketing techniques and the growth of banking and credit. Whereas in Western Europe, Jews participated in these new developments, in Eastern Europe Jews were too isolated in shtetls to do so. Consequently, their middleman position in trade became undermined and obsolete, causing a rapid decay of the shtetl toward the end of the 19th century.

138

George Feher

There were **three avenues** for the East European Jews **to escape** the persecution, oppression, and misery. The **first one** was **emigration**, mostly to America. Between 1800 and 1870, only some 8,000 Jews undertook the long trip. But after the first Odessa pogrom, 60,000 Jews left between 1871 and 1880. After the second Odessa pogrom in 1881, the number rose to 200,000 in the 1880s, and to 300,000 in the 1890s. Between 1900 and 1914, some 1.5 million Jews left Russia for North America. This represented a significant fraction (about 30%) of the Jewish population of Eastern Europe. From Galicia (present day southern Poland: at the time part of the Austro-Hungarian Empire), 240,000 left between 1880 and 1910.

But immigration to other countries also took place. Of particular note is the wave of immigration to Latin America, mostly Argentina, that was conceived and financed by the immensely rich philanthropist **Baron Maurice de Hirsch** (1831–1896).

Baron Hirsch was born in Munich to a wealthy and distinguished family of court bankers. He further enhanced his fortune by initiating audacious financial schemes, among them the building of the Orient Express railway linking Europe (Vienna) with Constantinopole. As Baron Hirsch reached middle age, his interest shifted from business to philanthropy and he used his (and his wife Clara's) vast fortune to alleviate the plight of Jews, mostly in Eastern Europe. After the 1887 edict by Alexander III limiting Jews' access to secondary education, Baron Hirsch devised a plan in which he would provide Russia 50 million francs (10 million dollars) to establish a separate school system for Jewish youth in the Pale. When Russia refused his offer, Baron Hirsch came to realize that emigration was the only way to solve the plight of the Russian Jews.

Baron Hirsch's plan to help the Jews leave Russia was to buy large swaths of land in Argentina and negotiate with the Russian government to grant the Jews permission to emigrate. In his scheme it was essential that the Jews be willing to do manual and physical work. He envisaged the settlers living in cooperative farming settlements, an idea reminiscent of the *moshavim*, the agrarian cooperatives that were later created in Israel. The plan required huge amounts of money, and, in its day, represented a great philanthropic enterprise as well as a great private social project.

Why did Baron Hirsch pick Argentina? In the 1880s and 1890s the Jews that were fleeing Russia were barred by the Ottomans from going to Palestine, and the United States also did not want them. Argentina, on the other hand, had vast territories that needed laborers, and a very open and liberal immigration policy. It was a logical choice for offering a home to the Jews of Eastern Europe.

In order to manage the project, Baron Hirsch founded the **Jewish Colonization Agency (JCA)** in London in 1891; it acquired legal status in Argentina in 1892. Baron Hirsch's plan was to settle the immigrant Jews in farming colonies, the **Colonias Baron Hirsch** as they became known. Baron Hirsch anticipated that in the first year 25,000 Jews would arrive, with an increase of the numbers every year to a total of 3 million in 25 years. The plan fell way short of its goal, and by 1913 the population of the colonies was 26,000 (a third of the Jewish population in Palestine at the time).

In July and August 1891, six ships with immigrants arrived in Argentina. They established the first settlement and called it **Colonia Mauricio**, in honor of Baron Maurice de Hirsch. My wife's grandfather, Salomón Rosenvasser, was one of its founders. Between 1892 and 1913, seven more colonies were established. My wife's great grandfather on her mother's side was a co-founder of **Colonia Clara**, which was established in 1892.

Although the colonies became functional entities, the project did not live up to Baron Hirsch's expectations. The large number of immigrants proposed by Baron Hirsch never materialized, and the effort to create a Jewish home based on agriculture largely failed. The "gaucho judío" never took roots. As was the case in my wife's family, the first generation born in Argentina left for urban centers becoming businessmen and professionals, leaving the land in the hands of non-Jews. Compared to the settlers in Palestine, what was missing in the Argentinean colonization was the idealism and enthusiasm of the Zionists to regain their ancient land of glory and make it into a model, socially just, society.

The **second avenue** of escape was **politics**, with its ultimate goal of revolution. Jews contributed far beyond their proportionate share of recruits to the Russian revolution. Many of the leaders of the revolution—Trotsky, Zinoviev, Kamenev, Sverdlow, Sokolnikov—were Jewish. Half the delegates to the Russian Social Democratic Party Congress in 1903 were Jewish. Lenin greatly appreciated and acknowledged the contribution of Jews to the revolution.

The **third avenue** of escape was **Jewish nationalism**, which was closely related to the second avenue, the social revolution. There were two main movements of Jewish nationalism: the Bund and the Socialist Zionists. The **Bund** was a Yiddish-speaking labor movement within Lenin's Revolutionary Social Democratic Party; it favored cultural and political autonomy within the Socialist Federation. In contrast, the **Socialist Zionists** wanted a country of their own, and became the dominant driving force in the colonization of Palestine. It is the people of this movement, their predecessors, successors, and, most important, the pioneers (*chalutzim*) that left for Palestine, that are described in the next section.

The forerunners of political Zionism

Many people associate the beginning of Zionism with **Herzl's publication** in 1896 of "**The Jewish State**," which was a response to the anti-Semitism generated by the Dreyfus trial in France. This notion is further fostered by the veneration and fame (some think excessive) of Herzl and his contributions. But there were many ideologues and authors who preceded Herzl, some by decades, who advocated the idea of a Jewish State. There was **Yehuda Alkalai's** "The Third Redemption" (1843), **Moses Hess's** "Rome and Jerusalem" (1862), **Zvi Kalisher's** "Seeking Zion" (1862), and **Leon Pinsker's** "Auto-Emancipation" (1882). Let us look in more detail at the main pre-Herzl personalities that shaped the Zionist dream.

Moses Hess (1812–1875), was an assimilated German Jewish Socialist, like his friend Heinrich Heine. In his book "Rome and Jerusalem" (1862), he abandoned assimilation as a solution, and strongly pressed for a Socialist Jewish State. For a time he was a collaborator of Marx and Engels. He advocated a return to "productive" work on the soil, without social hierarchies. Hess's book was largely ignored at the time, particularly in Russia, where hunger, persecution and fear of death (rather than ideologies) provided the driving force for action.

A prominent ideologue of Jewish nationalism in Russia was **Moses Leib Lilienblum** (1843–1910). He was born in Lithuania and moved to Odessa in 1868. Lilienblum started as a teacher at an orthodox religious seminary and later joined the Haskala. After witnessing the Odessa pogrom of 1881, he turned his back on religion, doubted the efficacy of the Haskala, and started to advocate a Jewish National Home in Palestine. He joined the movement **Hovevei Zion** (Lovers of Zion) and, in association with Leon Pinsker (see below), organized a society for the colonization of Palestine. He introduced the well-known little blue collection *tzedakah* boxes to raise funds for the purchase of land in Palestine.

Leon Pinsker (1821–1891) was born in Poland and moved to Odessa where he became a distinguished physician. At first he embraced assimilation but, like Lilienblum, he radically changed his views after witnessing the Odessa pogrom in 1881. He became convinced that the only solution for Jews was to become a nation with its own territory. He joined the Hovevei Zion movement, which paved the way for Jewish colonization in Palestine. In 1882, he published (anonymously) an influential pamphlet "Auto-emancipation—an appeal to his people by a Russian Jew." The same year, the Zionist colonization of Palestine commenced.

The birth of political Zionism

In **1882**, a young Jewish law student by the name of **Theodor Herzl** (1860–1904) was attending the University of Vienna. He was a thoroughly assimilated Jew. His goal was to make a future for himself in German letters, which he succeeded in accomplishing. It took Herzl more than a decade to come to the same conclusion that Lilienblum and Pinsker had arrived at in 1881. In 1895, under the shocking impact of the Dreyfus trial in France, he published a pamphlet "The Jewish State" that attracted widespread attention. Although Herzl was a latecomer to the Zionist movement, he gave it charismatic leadership, an organizational machine, and a place on the map of international politics. Herzl convened the **first Zionist Congress** and established the **World Zionist Organization (WZO)** in Basel in **1897**. He conducted elaborate negotiations with European heads of state and the Sultan, but they came to naught. Not being steeped in the Jewish tradition, Herzl was not interested in the romantic revival of Hebrew, and Palestine was not even his first choice for a Jewish State. When Britain offered him Uganda for Jewish settlement, he accepted it; but the scheme was vetoed by his own Zionist organization.

Herzl's contributions to the World Zionist movement were enormous and he can be justifiably called the **father of political Zionism**, but it should be kept in mind that the roots of Zionism are not in the fin-de-siècle Vienna of Herzl. Rather, it was the left-wing Socialist Zionists of Eastern Europe who created the concept of the "Hebrew peasant," and the Zionist Labor movement that dominated Israel's politics for over half a century.

The practitioners of Zionism: pioneers that immigrated to Palestine and established the Yishuv

While the Zionist ideologues and "theoreticians" were writing books and pamphlets, Zionist groups of young people were forming all over, mostly in Russia, with the intent of realizing the Zionist dream by immigrating to Palestine. Immigration, called Aliya (ascent), took place in several waves, each of them catalyzed by some major external event.

The First Aliya—the BILU (1882–1904)

The terrible 1881 pogrom in Odessa prompted Pinsker to write his influential pamphlet (see previous page) in 1882. The same year, a group of students reacting to the pogrom, gathered in Kharkov (Ukraine) to form the **BILU** movement, initials of *Bet Ya'akov L'chu V'Nelcha* (House of Yaakov, come ye and let us go, Isaiah 2:5). The first year (1882), 300 families from Russia and 450 pioneers from Romania arrived in Palestine. During the 1882–1904 period, about 25,000 immigrants arrived in Palestine.

In March 1882, a young dedicated Zionist from southern Russia, **Salman David Levontin**, arrived in Palestine and together with his uncle and other Lovers of Zion, made a large land purchase (3,200 dunams = 791 acres) located 12 miles southeast of Jaffa, where they established a new colony which they called **Rishon le-Zion** (the First to Zion). The same year the Bilu resettled **Petach Tikva**, established **Zichron Yaakov** on the southern ridge of Mt. Carmel, and **Rosh Pina** in Upper Galilee.

Two more important events occurred in 1882. The **British seized power in Egypt**, a prelude to the extension of their rule into Palestine, which ultimately led to the **Balfour Declaration** in 1917 that guaranteed the Jews a homeland in Palestine. The second important event was the arrival of a young philologist from Lithuania named Elieser Perlman who adopted a new name, **Ben-Yehuda**. He was obsessed with the idea of reviving Hebrew as a spoken language—a difficult task for a language that had remained static over 2,000 years.[57] But his determination and fanaticism proved that Hebrew could become a language fit for daily use.

Initially, the Lovers of Zion denounced private ownership of land as the greatest evil of civilization. However, these idealistic theories soon evaporated, and the new colonies quickly gravitated to private ownership of land, capitalist profit, and exploitation of cheap Arab labor. By 1889, seven years after the founding of Rishon le-Zion, a group of merely 40 Jewish settler families attracted 300 Arab families to work for them. A similar situation prevailed in the other colonies. Of course, they were criticized by visiting Zionists for adopting the ugly aspects of colonialism, but the settlers ignored the gratuitous criticism and advice given by those who themselves were not willing to come to Palestine.

The early settlers had a difficult time. They had no farm experience, the climate was harsh, the work was hard, and the returns meager. A great number of settlers (over half) left Palestine and returned to Russia or re-emigrated to other countries. By 1904, the majority of settlers had begun to doubt the Zionist dream. Even Elieser Ben-Yehuda, the great fanatic of the Hebrew revival, supported those seeking a territory in Uganda or Brazil. It was at this low point in the Zionist enterprise that the second wave of emigration from Russia occurred, and decisively changed the course of events.

The Second Aliya (1905–1914)

The Second Aliya was instigated and fueled by the 1903 Kishinev (Moldavia, previously Bessarabia) pogrom, and the failure of the Russian revolution of 1905. It spanned the decade between 1905 and 1914. About 40,000 people immigrated to Palestine

---

[57] It is probably the only ancient language that has not been transformed by time, and that present-day elementary-school children can read and understand. This is in contrast, for instance, to ancient Greek and Latin, which have evolved into languages that bear little resemblance to their ancient predecessors.

during that period. Although this was a mere trickle compared to the 1.5 million who emigrated to America, it represents the most important Aliya. It revived the Zionist dream and established the social, political, and ideological framework for the next half a century. Among the pioneers of the second Aliya were the future leaders of the Yishuv and the State of Israel, among them: **David Ben-Gurion** (alias Grien), the de facto leader of the pre-State Yishuv and first Prime Minister of Israel; **Yitzchak Ben Zvi** (alias Shimshelevitz), second President of Israel; **Shneour Zalman Shazar** (alias Rubashov), third President of Israel; **Berl Katznelson**, leading ideologue of the Zionist movement; **Shmuel Dayan**, co-founder of the first kibbutz, Degania, and father of the future general Moshe Dayan.

The newcomers of the Second Aliya vehemently protested the colonialism and exploitation of Arab labor practiced by the first wave of settlers. They stuck to the original socialist doctrine, that Jews must build their homeland with their own hands. They were young and idealistic, full of the fervor of Russian revolutionism, which they transposed to Zionism with a tenacity and zeal far greater than that of the First Aliya. They formed the Marxist labor party, *Poale Zion*, in which Ben-Gurion and Ben Zvi played a major role. They considered themselves part of the international proletariat. For many of them, sovereignty and nationhood were less important than the creation of a new, economically and socially just, society.[58]

For many of the pioneers of the Second Aliya, the magic key to self-realization was physical labor. It was the beginning and end of morality. It was like a religion—it was worshipped. The great prophet of the religion of labor was **Aaron David Gordon** (1853–1922), a frail and ailing man who, at age 48, arrived in Palestine and became a manual laborer. He called on his followers to become **"zealots of labor"**; as Jews, they must not live by their wits, but by their sweat.

The young pioneers worked in the fields and drained swamps during the day, and at night sat under portraits of Marx and Herzl, heatedly debating the constitution of the future Socialist Republic of Jewish Palestine.

The resolve of the pioneers not to exploit Arab labor, reinforced their naïve and erroneous judgment concerning the **Arab reaction to the Jewish colonization**. How could the Arabs object to the hard-working Jews improving the land and raising the economic level, thereby enabling them (the Arabs) to live in more comfort and wealth? The fatal misjudgment of the Jews was the neglect of the nationalistic feelings of the Arabs—the very same feelings that the Jews had brought with them to Palestine. In fact, in **1881**, when the Lovers of Zion were forming clandestine clubs in Russia, secret societies in Damascus were distributing pamphlets requesting home rule for the Arabs of Syria, Lebanon, and Palestine. And in **1905**, when the pioneers of the Second Aliya were starting to arrive in Palestine, the Arab nationalist **Naguib Azuri** formed the Ligue de la Patrie Arabe in Paris. He presciently predicted that "the awakening Arab nation, and the Jews trying to reconstitute the ancient kingdom of Israel, are destined to combat one another until one is broken by the other." This statement was made 106 years ago! But few, if any, members of the Second Aliya, apparently, were aware of Azuri's proclamation.

---

[58] What a sad difference between the members of the Second Aliya, who were dreamers moved by ideological convictions, and the majority of contemporary Israelis, who are motivated by self-interest—the "me and now" generation—for whom "Zionism" elicits a yawn at best, and derision at worst.

It is curious how blindfolded and nationalistically egocentric the early settlers, including Ben-Gurion and Ben Zvi, were. In 1917, Ben-Gurion still made the astounding pronouncement that "in a historical and moral sense Palestine was a country without inhabitants." Ben-Gurion's attitude toward the Arab problem, i.e., not giving it the attention that its importance deserved, is illustrated by the fact that in his youth he learned Turkish and English and, in his later years, ancient Greek and Sanskrit. But Arabic he apparently never deemed sufficiently important to learn.

Meanwhile, the Zionists abroad invented their own reality (or rather unreality) by also negating the existence of Arabs in Palestine. Their unrealistic motto was: "The land without people for the people without land." And even among those few that acknowledged the presence of Arabs in Palestine, there was always the expressed assumption that Jewish settlements would greatly benefit the Arabs and will be welcomed by them. Herzl visited Palestine in 1898; in his report on the trip there is not a single word about the Arab population, which at the time amounted to about half a million, 10 times more than the Jewish population. Particularly striking was his foresight, while visiting Cairo, of the blindness of the British to the rising nationalism in Egypt. Yet, he did not foresee the same Arab nationalism in Palestine.

Perhaps the only positive thing one can say about the early Zionist's misjudgment of the looming gravity of the Arab conflict is that, had the Zionist leaders known that the price of a Jewish homeland in Palestine would be the displacement and suffering of so many Arabs, they might very well have withdrawn their plans. Thus, one is driven to the startling conclusion that the root of the Zionist ultimate success was the result of a basic misunderstanding of the situation.

In later years as the conflict with the Arabs escalated and serious Arab riots against the Jews took place, the severity of the Arab conflict started to dawn on the Yishuv and the Zionists abroad. Several attempts to resolve the conflict failed. By 1935 the need to rescue the Jews from Nazi Germany made any efforts of compromise with the Arabs irrelevant. If allowing Jews into Palestine was an injustice to the Arabs, not allowing them in was an even greater injustice to the Jews. The rights of two peoples were (and still are) clashing in Palestine (Israel). Each of the several Arab-Jewish wars after the establishment of the State of Israel further exacerbated the Arab-Jewish conflict. This conflict represents today a most serious threat to the existence of Israel. However, a detailed analysis of this very important problem lies outside the scope of this narrative.

Let's turn now again to the description of the Second Aliya. A characteristic of these pioneers was their puritanical and ascetic attitude. Poverty was cultivated with zeal, food was plain, and luxury was despised. They fanatically rejected the "materialism" and "decadence" of established society: alcohol, movies, ballroom dancing, the wearing of jackets, neckties, and dresses. (A lot of this attitude still prevailed when I arrived in Kibbutz Merchavia in 1941.) They resented the bourgeois institution of marriage and disdained the "small, cheap, secular" kind of happiness. In many respects, they were the hippies of the beginning of the 20th century. But they did not change their values when they became the Establishment; half the members of the first Israeli constituent assembly in 1948 were veteran pioneers (*chalutzim*); a third were members of kibbutzim, although the kibbutz population was only about 5%.

Idealistic, as I described the pioneers of the Second Aliya, they represented only a fraction of the newcomers. A considerable number soon left the country, as had many of the first wave—tired, sick, unable to adapt to the climate and hard work. It is estimated that between 60% and 70% of the newcomers left. By 1918, the Jewish population in Palestine had dwindled from its peak of 90,000 to 50,000. The Third Aliya restored again the population.

The Third Aliya (1918–1923)

The Third Aliya was mainly a result of the **Balfour Declaration** of 1917, the British document endorsed by the League of Nations legitimizing Palestine as a Jewish homeland. The other causes were the dislocations caused by World War I, and the growing disappointment with the Russian Revolution of 1917. In addition, the violent upsurge of peasant anarchists caused a series of pogroms more ferocious than under the Czar. In the Ukraine alone, the number of casualties following the Revolution is estimated to be around 100,000.

The spirit of the Third Aliya was passionately anti-authoritarian: formal government was anathema. The new pioneers wanted to be free people, operating in **communes** (*kibbutzim*) of like-minded enthusiasts, sharing all material possessions and ideals. Utopian, liberal, and idyllic as these ideas sound, there was a certain rigidity and narrow-mindedness in this libertarian system. The rigid principles of personal behavior and thought were imposed by majority decisions with complete intolerance of minority views. As a result, people holding slightly divergent opinions found it difficult to live under the same roof and often left the settlement (as I did in the 1940s, after living one-and-a-half years in the kibbutz).

Members of the Third Aliya, like their predecessors of the Second Aliya, revered manual labor above anything else. In the early 1920s a group of chalutzim established a **Labor Brigade** and named it in honor of **Joseph Trumpledor**, the first Jewish hero killed in an Arab ambush, in 1920.[59] They aimed to create a commune of Jewish workers, essentially trying to convert the country into one great kibbutz. The romance of the Labor Brigade and its road-building gangs lingered for years. Even a brief membership in this select fraternity became a note of aristocratic distinction and a key to political advancement. In 1954, thirty years after the event, half the leading politicians of the ruling Labor Party had been laborers in the Trumpledor Brigade in the 1920s.

The Third Aliya totaled some 35,000 pioneers. One-third of those who arrived soon left. But by 1924 the Jewish population had again grown to 90,000.

The Fourth Aliya (1924–1931)

In the mid-1920s, a political and economic crisis in Poland, and the Johnson-Lodge Immigration Act passed by the United States Congress curtailing mass immigration, spurred Polish Jewish immigration to Palestine, forming the Fourth Aliya. Between 1924 and 1931, approximately 80,000 Jews arrived in Palestine from Central Europe, mostly from Poland. Unlike the Bolshevik-minded immigrants of the previous Aliyot, they were primarily petty merchants and small industrialists with their own capital (at least 1,000

---

[59] Trumpledor (1880–1920) was reputedly the only Jewish officer in the Czarist army. He lost an arm in the Russo-Japanese war (1904) and immigrated to Palestine in 1912. At the outbreak of World War II he organized, together with Vladimir Jabotinsky, a Jewish unit within the British army that participated in the liberation of Palestine from the Turks.

pounds to satisfy the requirements of the British Mandate). They established the first semblance of an industrialized urban Jewish community in Palestine. Many of them left during the 1926–1927 depression, when those leaving exceeded the number of those arriving. By 1931, there were 190,000 Jews in Palestine (about 20% of the population).

The Fifth Aliya (1932–1940)

The Fifth Aliya can be divided into two periods. The first (1932–1935), covering the beginning of the Nazi persecution, saw the arrival of 144,000 immigrants, and was followed by economic prosperity. During this time the **Youth Aliya** was founded, providing an additional immigration quota for children between the ages of 13 and 17. The second period (1936–1940) coincided with the Arab riots and economic depression. Immigration was restricted by the British Mandate, first for economic, later for political reasons. In 1939, the **McDonald White Paper** recommended that only 75,000 Jews be allowed admission during the next five years. During the second period, 36,000 immigrants entered Palestine, including 15,000 illegal immigrants (i.e., without government permits).

The Sixth Aliya (1941–1947)

This was a period of struggle against restriction on immigration at a time when rescue of Jews from Nazi Europe was most needed. Many tragic incidents occurred during this period (e.g., the sinking of the Exodus, Patria, Struma). Many of the intending immigrants were interned in Cyprus. Eighty-five thousand Jews arrived during the Sixth Aliya, of whom 28,000 were illegal immigrants. By the time the state of Israel was established in 1948, the number of Jews in Israel had reached 750,000.

Of all the Aliyot, the deepest influence on the social structure of the country was exerted by the Second and Third Aliya. They set a pattern of politics and society, of habits, passions and prejudices that add up to what one loosely calls national character. Politically, it was a fusion of nationalism and socialism. It persisted for many decades but, unfortunately, the country is changing, becoming more materialistic, right-wing, militaristic, and religious.

I want to return now to the main topic of this chapter:

The response of the Yishuv to the Holocaust

The reaction (or inaction) of the Yishuv during the World War II Holocaust, as I discussed at the beginning of this chapter, is an issue of debate to this day. The main questions are: 1) When did the leadership of the Yishuv learn about, and grasp, the Nazi policy of systematically killing all European Jews? 2) Once this fact was understood, what financial and human resources were allocated, and how much effort was expended to help the European Jews? 3) What rescue plans were devised, and to what extent were they carried out? Much has been written about these topics[60] and I shall try to summarize the main events and conclusions.

---

[60] Among the many books, I found these two to be particularly insightful: D. Porat, "The Blue and the Yellow Stars of David," Harvard University Press, 1990; Y. Bauer, "Jews for Sale?" Yale University Press, 1994.

To understand the Yishuv's actions, it will be helpful first to describe the political framework and institutions that prevailed in Palestine before and during World War II. They provided the leadership of the Yishuv and are, therefore, primarily responsible and accountable for the Yishuv's reaction to the Holocaust.

The political infrastructure in Palestine

The most important political body was the **Jewish Agency (JA)**, which in the 1940s was already considered, by the 500,000 Jews then living in Palestine, to be "the government of the state-in-the-making." The task of the JA was defined in 1922, when the League of Nations confirmed the British Mandate over Palestine. The JA was to represent the Jewish people, and to cooperate with the British authorities in the implementation of the **Balfour Declaration of November 2, 1917**, which states: "His Majesty's Government views with favor the establishment in Palestine of a national house for the Jewish people." In parallel with the Jewish Agency, the British offered to create a similar **Arab Agency**, but this offer was rejected by the Arab leaders.

The Jewish Agency dealt with organizing immigration and absorbing the immigrants in Palestine. It founded the Youth Aliya, maintained departments of labor, settlement, and industry, and helped establish the defense forces of the Yishuv.

On **Chaim Weizmann's** initiative, the Jewish Agency for Palestine was officially approved by the 16th Zionist Congress held in Zürich in 1929. Weizmann was elected to head the Agency, but soon was criticized for being too pro-British. When the British published the White Paper in 1930, recommending that Jewish immigration to Palestine be restricted, his position became untenable and he resigned from the Jewish Agency. He was replaced by **Nahum Sokolow** in 1930, **Arthur Ruppin** in 1933, and **David Ben-Gurion** in 1935. Ben-Gurion led the JA throughout the critical years of the Holocaust (till 1948).

The dominant political party in pre-state Palestine was the left-wing labor party **Mapai** (*Mifleget Poalei Eretz Israel*: Land of Israel's Workers' Party). It was established in 1930 as a Zionist-Socialist party, and became the dominant force in pre-state and early post-state Israeli politics. It was responsible for the founding of **Hashomer** and **Haganah**, the first armed groups whose task was to ensure the security of the people and property of the emerging Jewish communities. Mapai was led by David Ben-Gurion from the early 1930s till his resignation in 1953. Mapai led every coalition and owned the Premiership from 1948 until the party merged into the Labor Alignment in 1968.

Another important political force in pre- and post-state Israel was the **Histadrut**, a powerful trade union that organized the activities of Jewish workers. It was founded in 1920; the founding members were strict socialists who were profoundly influenced by the Russian-Jewish socialist tradition characteristic of the Second Aliya (1904–1914). In 1920, membership in the Histadrut numbered approximately 4,000. By 1927, Histadrut membership rose to 25,000, encompassing 75% of the entire Jewish Palestine labor force. But the Histadrut was more than a trade union; it provided the Yishuv with social services and security, and was involved in land settlement and in all economic and cultural issues. It was a great colonizing agency that contributed to the formation of the Israeli State. As Israel's first prime minister, David Ben-Gurion, who was also the first secretary general of the Histadrut, put it, "I doubt whether we would have had a state without the Histadrut."

The **National Council** (*Vaad Leumi*) was founded in **1920** (the same year as the Histadrut and the Haganah) to conduct Jewish communal affairs. It comprised representatives of all major factions of the Yishuv, with 20 to 40 members who met at least once a year. It concentrated on internal affairs rather than politics, i.e., education, healthcare, welfare services, and religious matters. It was also involved in internal defense and security matters, and organized recruitment to the British forces during World War II. Its chairmen during the years of the Holocaust were **Yitzhak Ben Zvi** (1939–1944) and **David Remez** (1944–1948).

In addition, there were several minority religious and militant organizations. Among them was the **Revisionist Party**, an extreme nationalist group whose policies called for the use of force to establish a Jewish state on both sides of the Jordan. (The Haganah, in contrast, was a defense force.) The Revisionist Party espoused a more liberal, non-socialist economic structure and a more zealous defense policy than the labor movement. The military wing of the Revisionist Party was the *Irgun Zvai Leumi* (National Military Organization) also called **Etzel**, a Jewish right-wing underground movement, founded in 1931. The spiritual leader of the movement and commander of the Irgun was **Vladimir Jabotinsky** (see page 145, footnote 59) who died in 1940. Begin, who arrived in Palestine with the Polish army (fighting alongside the British) in 1942, became the leader of the Irgun in 1943.

Among the daring actions of the Irgun was the blowing up of the wing of the King David Hotel in Jerusalem on July 22, 1946, killing 91 British soldiers and civilians, and the capture of the British prison in the coastal town of Akko (Acre) on May 4, 1947. Irgun's violent activities led to the execution of many of its members by the British; in retaliation, Irgun executed British army hostages. An even more extreme terrorist group called **Lehi** (*Lohamei Herut Israel*: Fighters for Israel's Freedom), also known as the **Stern Gang,** split off Etzel in 1939.

Politically, the Irgun was the precursor of the *Herut* (Freedom Party), founded by Begin in 1948. Herut later morphed into the Likud Party, which achieved an overwhelming victory at the polls in 1977, and Begin, as prime minister, formed his first government. It heralded the decline of the Labor Party and the socialist ideology that had dominated the Yishuv from the time of the first settlers.

In addition to the Revisionists, there were also several religious minority parties opposing the dominant secular, socialist institutions. The two main ones were: *Agudat Israel* (Israelite Union), and **Mizrachi** (*Merkaz Ruchani*: Religious Center). Agudat Israel had its beginning at a conference that took place in 1912 at Kattowitz. It represented the interests of the ultra-orthodox constituency of the Yishuv. Its Labor wing established strictly religious agricultural settlements in Palestine, outside the framework of the Zionist movement. They argued that the Jews constitute a religious community defined by the Torah and were largely hostile to the establishment of a Jewish state. The Mizrachi movement was founded in 1902 in Vilnius as a Zionist organization. In the British Mandate of Palestine the movement developed into a political party, Mizrachi, with its own trade union, **Ha-Poel Ha-Mizrachi,** founded in 1921.

It should be pointed out that the religious parties in Mandatory Palestine represented a small minority, but their influence has been steadily growing and in present day Israel they wield considerable power: In view of the instability of the Israeli government, their relatively small number of seats in Parliament is able to topple the government, which makes them exert a disproportionate influence on the legislation that is passed.

Besides the institutions that operated in Palestine, there were several worldwide organizations that kept close relations with the Yishuv, and were active in rescue work. The most important of these are:

The **World Zionist Organization (WZO)**, founded by Theodor Herzl as the Zionist Organization (ZO) at the first Zionist Congress, held in Basel, Switzerland, in August 1897. It served as the supreme Zionist institution, whose objective was the creation of a Jewish homeland in Palestine. The WZO's headquarters was located, over the years, in different capitals of Europe. After the creation of Israel on May 14, 1948, the headquarters were permanently moved to Jerusalem. During the critical years of the Holocaust, **Chaim Weizmann** served as president of the WZO (1935–1946). The supreme advisory and supervising institution of the WZO is the **Zionist General Council**, also called the **Zionist Action Committee (ZAC)**, in which the different Zionist parties are represented.

The **World Jewish Congress (WJC)**, an association of Jewish organizations throughout the world, whose goal is to "assure the survival and to foster the unity of the Jewish people." It is actively involved in religious, legal, political, and relief matters. The first WJC convened in Geneva, Switzerland in 1936; 280 delegates represented the Jews of 32 countries under the leadership of **Stephen Wise** and **Nahum Goldmann**. Its headquarters are located in London and New York.

The American Jewish **Joint Distribution Committee (JDC)**, popularly known as The Joint, the world's leading Jewish humanitarian assistance organization, and the chief agency of American Jewry for the relief of distressed Jews in foreign countries. It works in more than 70 countries to alleviate hunger and hardship, and to rescue Jews in danger. It was very active in relief efforts during the Holocaust. The JDC was organized in 1914 through the efforts of wealthy Americans under the leadership of the banker, philanthropist, and Zionist **Felix Warburg**. Originally, its goal was to relieve the sufferings of Jews during World War I; it gained great importance during the rise of Nazism and during World War II. It receives its funds from the United Jewish Appeal.

The information-gathering process

Obtaining information about the condition of the European Jewry, as well as passing information to them, became increasingly difficult after World War II broke out on September 1, 1939. Not only did Germany try to prevent any information from leaking out, but the mandatory British government imposed increasingly strict censorship on the press and postal services in Palestine; only the British news service, Reuters, was allowed to be quoted.

To overcome these difficulties, several Jewish organizations established offices in Geneva, Switzerland, and set up a network of couriers dispersed over Europe. As early as **November 1939**, the JA established an office in Geneva run by **Richard Lichtheim**, a veteran German Zionist. The **World Jewish Congress** was represented by **Gerhard Riegner** and **Abraham Silberschein**. Other Yishuv officials, among them **Chaim Barlas**, head of the Immigration Department of the JA, and **Nathan Schwalb**, of the Zionist Jewish movement *Hechalutz*, also had offices in Geneva, and sent detailed information on the situation of the Jews in Europe to their headquarters in Palestine. After **September 1940**, Barlas moved to Istanbul, which became a center of information as well.

Information was also obtained from many refugees who succeeded in escaping from Europe during the war, including some from concentration camps, who brought eyewitness reports of the atrocities committed. The atrocities described were so horrendous and unprecedented, that the public was, by and large, unwilling or unable to accept them as fact. I shall give examples of this understandable but unfortunate phenomenon later.

It was also important to get news about events in Palestine out to central European countries. Much of it was conveyed in person by emissaries sent abroad from Palestine. In charge of this operation was **Eliyahu Golomb**, a prominent leader of the labor movement and commander of the Haganah.

The developing situation during the war years

As the war progressed, the situation of the European Jews changed, as did the response of the Yishuv and the world. I shall describe the events year by year as they unfolded.

1939–1940. A big blow to the Yishuv came in **May 1939** with the publication of the **White Paper**, which limited the purchase of land by Jews and restricted immigration to 75,000 over the next five years. The reaction of the Yishuv was to organize **illegal immigration—Aliya Bet**, which had been started by the Revisionists (the Irgun Zvai Leumi) already in 1937.

On **September 1, 1939 Germany invaded Poland, and England and France declared war**, although little was done to stop the advancing German troops, who conquered Poland in a couple of weeks. At the outbreak of the war, Chaim Weizmann declared that the Yishuv was prepared to enlist in the British army to fight the Nazis and support Britain in every possible way. During **1939–1940, 6,500 men and women joined the British army**. Ben-Gurion declared: "We must fight the war as if there was no White Paper, and we must fight the White Paper as if there was no war." By the end of the war, **30,000 Jews** in Palestine had joined the British Army.

With the German invasion of Poland, the killing of Jews began immediately. Reports of the atrocities reached Palestine through Polish refugees who arrived via Lithuania. Among them was **Apolinary Hartglas**, former president of the Zionist Organization in Poland. He was the first to report explicitly, in **February 1940,** on the extermination of the Jews. In **August 1940**, Mapai leader **Dov Hoz** arrived in Palestine from Europe and reported to Mapai headquarters about the destruction of Polish Jewry. But the situation was not discussed formally by any institution, including the Jewish Agency, and the information was not made public. After the war, the JA was heavily criticized for their action (inaction). How can one explain this behavior of the leadership of the Yishuv?

Porat tries to answer this question in her book[61]: She argues that until the end of 1940, the leadership of the Yishuv did not consider itself the center of information about the Jews, and certainly not the central power. That role was delegated to London, the headquarters of the Allied powers. Moreover, the Yishuv saw itself as a small community, at the margins of the war, incapable of undertaking the task of helping the Jews of Europe.

---

[61] D. Porat, "The Blue and the Yellow Stars of David," Harvard University Press, 1990.

According to Ben-Gurion: "This task should not be managed from here." It was an assignment better suited for the World Jewish Congress (WJC), the World Zionist Organization (WZO), and the Joint Distribution Committee (JDC).

Toward the end of 1939, the JA established a **Committee of Four** under the leadership of **Yitzhak Gruenbaum,** a past member of the Polish parliament and one of the most prominent Jewish leaders in Poland in the 1920s. At the beginning the committee focused its attention on the fate of Polish Jewry, but later included the entire European Jewry. Its main task was to gather all information about the Jews in the countries occupied by the Germans. In 1943, the committee was enlarged in size and scope as discussed on page 154.

In the meantime, Aliya Bet continued. From September 1939 until October 1940, 8,500 newcomers arrived, but then the British decided to put an end to it. They exerted diplomatic pressure on countries from which the ships left for Palestine, and British coast guard boats attacked refugee ships. In **November 1940,** three ships carrying 3,500 refugees anchored in Tel Aviv. The British announced that they would send them to their colony in Mauritius in the Indian Ocean. In a desperate attempt to prevent the sailing to Mauritius, the leadership of the Yishuv agreed to attach an explosive to one of the ships, the **Patria**. The ship sank immediately and 200 people drowned. The survivors were forced to board the other two ships and were dispatched to Mauritius until the end of the war.[62] Aliya Bet virtually ceased.

The irony of the situation was that German policy from 1939 to the spring of 1941 was one of expulsion of Jews, not of extermination. If it weren't for the policy of the British and most of the rest of the free world, a large number of Jews could have been saved during that period.

1941. In the **spring of 1941** Britain's military position deteriorated both in Europe, where they had to withdraw from Greece, and in the Middle East and North Africa, where Rommel was advancing eastward. Palestine was in danger of being crushed by a German pincer movement, from Syria in the north, and Egypt in the southeast. The Yishuv responded by enlisting in greater numbers in the British army, and by strengthening the Haganah and training it for guerilla warfare behind enemy lines.

In **February 1941** Ben-Gurion returned to Palestine after 10 months in Britain and the United States. In his view, first priority should be given to formulating a political program that would bring about the establishment of a Jewish State after the war—a rather optimistic attitude in light of the looming danger of Germany occupying Palestine. Ben-Gurion's concentration on post-war goals shifted attention away from the immediate plight of European Jews.

Ben-Gurion's opinion prevailed in the Yishuv institutions. Particularly detrimental to the rescue efforts was the attitude of the Committee of Four, headed by the ineffective **Yitzhak Gruenbaum.** They proclaimed that "everything Hitler did could be undone after the war." This, in spite of eyewitness reports warning that if the present situation in the 40 ghettos of Poland continued, no Jew would survive.

In **1941,** with the Mediterranean blocked, the Balkan states reduced to German satellites, and Lithuania annexed by the Russians, the importance of Istanbul as a source of

---

[62] The parents of my good friend Terry Eisinger were on the Patria and survived the war in Mauritius.

information was increased. Hungary was still independent, and considered a haven for Jews from Poland and Slovakia.[63]

On **June 22, 1941, Germany invaded the Soviet Union** and the murder of hundreds of thousands of Jews by the German Einsatzgruppen, helped by local collaborators, had begun. News of the enormity of these killings did not leak out immediately, and killings were still thought to be in the hundreds. **Moshe Shertok** (later **Sharett**), head of the Jewish Agency's political department, expressed the view that "the suffering was one of the inevitable evils of war, rather than a problem demanding a solution." He agreed with the Allies that only a military victory could end the suffering of the Jews. The gap between what actually was happening and what the Yishuv perceived to be happening had become abysmal. How great this gap was, is illustrated by the Yishuv's response to the **pogrom in Baghdad in June 1941,** during which 500 Jews were reported dead. The Mapai leaders expressed shocked disbelief: "Such atrocities are not committed even in Nazi Germany."

The British censor forbade publication of the violence in Iraq and Europe, lest it inflame Arab violence in Palestine. The British mandatory government pressured **Agronsky** (later **Agron**), editor of the Palestine Post, among others, not to publish information on the much higher toll among the Jews of Europe than had been previously reported. The editors, in retrospect shamefully, acceded to the British government's pressure.

In the second half of 1941, the situation was getting worse. Polish refugees who reached Palestine in **September 1941,** reported that people in the ghettos were dying every minute from hunger. **Chaim Barlas,** Director of the JA's Immigration Department (1926–1948), who was stationed in Istanbul, got word of the atrocities of the Einsatzgruppen. **Eliyahu Dobkin,** head of the Histadrut Immigration Department (1935–1945), told the JA about the cruel expulsion of Romanian Jews to Transnistria, and the shooting of 7,800 Jews in one day in Jaca. But in spite of these reported events, the situation of the Jews was not discussed by the leading organizations of the Yishuv. Between **August** and **December 1941,** neither the JA nor the Mapai Central Committee discussed the subject even once. Finally in **December 1941,** the JA held its first full discussion of the situation of the European Jews. But the full truth of the tragedy had not yet been grasped, and many still hoped that the gravity of the situation was exaggerated. And they confessed at the end of the meeting: "None of us knows what to do to help."

1942. In **January 1942,** a letter from the Soviet foreign minister, **Molotov,** was distributed to foreign ambassadors in the USSR. It listed crimes committed by the Nazis, including those toward the Jews. However, the newspapers of the Yishuv cautioned their readers that the description of the killings was exaggerated, accusing the Soviets of using it as a propaganda tool against the Nazis. At the same time, photographs were circulated in London, showing Jews being murdered by Germans. None of these topics were discussed by the JA or the Mapai Central Committee.

In **February 1942,** the **Struma,** an old cattle boat, packed with 770 refugees, sank in the Black Sea. Only one person survived. After two months of negotiations between the JA and the British, the Struma had been refused entry to Palestine, and then had been turned away by the Turks into the open sea. This incident illustrated the Yishuv's helplessness.

---

[63] It is at this time, the end of April 1941, that I, together with eight others from the Shomer Hatzair, escaped to Palestine through Hungary, Romania, Turkey, Syria, and Lebanon.

Rage against the British reached a new high, and demonstrations took place throughout Palestine. But the discussion in the Yishuv focused on immigration as a solution, with little attention being given to alternate concrete plans to rescue the Jews of Europe.

In **mid-March 1942**, the press in Palestine published information reported by Hungarian soldiers returning from the Russian front, that 250,000 Jews had been murdered by the Gestapo in the Ukraine. In **April and May 1942**, the Yishuv was informed of the murder of 90,000 Jews in Minsk, the liquidation of Estonian Jewry, the killing of 50,000 Jews within a few days in Babi Yar near Kiev, and the liquidation of the Kovno ghetto.

At the **end of May 1942**, the Mapai Central Committee addressed the question of the Polish refugees in the Soviet Union. **Eliyahu Dobkin** told the Committee that about one million Polish Jews had escaped to Russia. Although it seemed like encouraging news that so many Jews had been saved, Dobkin warned that many of them would perish from hunger and disease. He suggested that none of this be made public lest it antagonize the Soviet Union and make it adopt a harder line toward Zionism. (The fear of antagonizing the powers of the free world, be it the British, the American, or the Russian, seems to be a recurrent theme throughout the crucial years.)

By the **end of May 1942**, the Polish government in exile received reports from Poland that 700,000 Jews had already been killed in eastern Poland and occupied Russian territories. This was broadcasted by the BBC in June. On **June 30th, 1942,** the WJC announced on the American broadcasting network, that the number of Jews killed was close to one million. The JA executives met, but what did they discuss? Whether German Jews had the right to publish a German language newspaper in Palestine—a topic completely out of keeping with the horrendous events of the time. At that meeting, Gruenbaum mentioned the murder of hundreds and thousands of Jews, a figure in marked contrast to the million that had already been publicized all over the world.

But the Yishuv was preoccupied with serious concerns nearer to home. In North Africa the German army was advancing toward Egypt, and the fall of Palestine seemed highly possible. Thus, the immediate question for the Yishuv was not whether it could save the Jews of Europe, but whether it could save itself. The Yishuv began preparing to defend the territory with "its back against the wall." The prevalent feeling was that they would fight to the last man, leaving for posterity the "legend of Masada" rather than living "the life of a whipped dog." Fortunately, the German defeat at **El Alamein** in **October 1942** turned the tide, and the danger was averted.

In **July 1942**, information was received about the deportation of Jews from France, Holland, Belgium, Bohemia, Slovakia, and Germany. Churchill delivered a tough anti-Nazi speech promising to punish all war criminals after the war. Thus, the summer of 1942 saw the beginning of international reactions to the murders taking place behind enemy lines.

In **August 1942, Eduard Schulte**, a German industrialist with close ties to the Nazi leadership, defected to Switzerland, and revealed the plan discussed at Nazi headquarters to exterminate 3.5 to 4 million Jews in the autumn. (For a more detailed discussion see pages 167–169). Leaders of the Yishuv received the news with disbelief.

At a meeting of the JA in **October 1942**, Gruenbaum said that "the information is exaggerated." Ben-Gurion vacillated between despair and hope. The whole discussion was disjointed and unfocused with a "Kafkaish" ending when **Eliezer Kaplan**, the treasurer of the JA, allocated 50 pounds to Gruenbaum for telegrams, although Gruenbaum had requested a hundred.

In the middle of **November 1942**, 69 Yishuv members who had been caught in Europe at the beginning of the war arrived home. They had been exchanged for a group of Germans held by the Allies, including some from the Templar colonies in Palestine. The newly arrived brought information of the horrors that were taking place in Europe: the deportations under inhuman conditions, the Jews digging their own graves before being shot, their being buried alive, and the gassings.

When this news reached Palestine, Ben-Gurion and Dobkin proposed that **20,000 Jews be exchanged** for Germans living in the various Allied countries. This plan was immediately and strongly opposed by the British who did not want to send able-bodied Germans to their enemy lines. So the exchange never rose above a trickle. By the end of the war, a mere **800 Jews** had been exchanged.

On **November 22, 1942**, the JA convened for the first time a meeting almost exclusively devoted to European Jewry. The following day they published an announcement in the local press about the slaughter of Jews in Europe, but still held back some of the gruesome details. Even the watered-down versions of atrocities were so horrendous that many were reluctant or unable to believe them. At that meeting **Moshe Shapiro** of the religious Mizrachi party proposed a day of mourning, fasting, praying and public rallies. But the JA rejected the rallies, fearing that the pressure on the British to loosen up on immigration, and to increase their rescue efforts, might hurt the war effort and sour British relations with the JA. But the strong negative reaction of the Yishuv and the press to the tepid approach of the JA prompted it to declare not one, but three days of protests. A hundred thousand people (a fifth of the Jewish population) participated in the processions expressing grief and shock; people broke out crying.

The JA suggested that delegates be sent to the United States, Britain and South Africa, and that representatives of all free Jewry be convened in Palestine to discuss the situation of the European Jews. However, the various political parties were unable to agree on the composition of the delegations and the proposal was never implemented.

After the JA's announcement on November 23, 1942, that European Jews were being systematically exterminated, the Yishuv began to press for a wider and more representative and effective body than the Committee of Four. Ben-Gurion enlarged the Committee of Four to **twelve**, including the religious Agudat Israel, the National Council, and the Revisionist Party, with Gruenbaum again as chairman. The new committee was named the **Rescue Committee** and remained under JA supervision. They had no real power, either politically or financially, and were treated by the JA almost derisively. Ben-Gurion relegated the reports of the Rescue Committee to the end of their meetings and often cut Gruenbaum short. There was no love lost between Ben-Gurion and Gruenbaum. This is not surprising in view of their different backgrounds and personalities. Ben-Gurion derived his power from the Labor movement, whereas Gruenbaum belonged to the General Zionist Party, and had served in the Polish parliament, where he eloquently defended the rights of the Jews. Ben-Gurion despised parliamentary maneuvers and hyperbole—in short he couldn't stand Gruenbaum.

It's no wonder that under these circumstances the Rescue Committee was not a success. In addition to the personality clashes of the two leaders, it was poorly organized and ineffective. It was heavily criticized, and there were recurring demands to replace

Gruenbaum with somebody of greater prestige, influence and effectiveness, who would enjoy the full backing of Ben-Gurion. But nothing was done, and it continued to operate ineffectively for its lifetime of two years.

On **December 17, 1942**, Britain's foreign secretary, Anthony Eden, read a statement in Parliament on behalf of all the Allied governments, in which he declared that the exterminations were verifiable, condemned the barbaric policies of the Nazis, and promised to punish the criminals after the war. The parliament rose to its feet in solidarity. It was a watershed moment, long overdue, in which the extermination policies of the Nazis were finally officially recognized by the free world.

Although the Allied December 17 declaration represented a strong expression of sympathy for the victims, it did not contain any proposals for action. This point was strongly criticized by the British press, Parliament, and the trade unions. Many believed that the JA had missed an opportunity to put greater pressure on the British government when it was vulnerable to public opinion. But whether it would have helped to force the British government to make concessions, remains an unanswered question.

In the absence of Allied help, the Yishuv maintained delegates (emissaries) in the five European nations that remained neutral at the end of 1942: **Spain, Portugal, Sweden, Switzerland, and Turkey**. These emissaries established links between European Jewry and the Yishuv, and worked hard to find means of rescue. Their efforts met with some success, albeit on a small scale, as discussed in a later section.

1943. **In January and February 1943**, a low mood prevailed in the Yishuv. None of the rescue proposals had yet produced results, and the Allies had done nothing since their declaration in December 1942. The public protests were losing their impact: The public was getting tired of assemblies, and public response started to wane. The Yishuv felt helpless; it had no leverage on the free world except the moral admonition that "the blood of the people of Israel will never let you rest."

Added to the general malaise of the Yishuv was its dissatisfaction with the JA's continued stance against taking stronger actions to alleviate the plight of the European Jews. The JA advanced several arguments to justify their position. First was their fear that rallies and strikes could lead to a confrontation with the British who could use it as a pretext for closing recruiting offices, refusing to establish a Jewish Brigade, clamping down further on immigration, and jeopardizing the establishment of a Jewish State after the war. Second was their anxiety that mass demonstrations could rekindle Arab riots. And finally, they argued that demonstrations in Palestine had received little notice in the foreign press and were therefore ineffective. But as logical and realistic as these arguments may have been, the public did not buy them, and a growing gap developed between the JA and the Yishuv. More and more voices were heard along these lines: "We cannot remain silent; Jewish history will never forgive us; our brothers' blood is crying out to us."

Then two events, starting on Passover eve, **April 19, 1943**, shook up the Yishuv and rekindled its involvement: the **Bermuda Conference** on refugees, and the **revolt in the Warsaw ghetto**. (These events are discussed on pages 113 and 40–41, respectively; here I focus on the reaction of the Yishuv.)

At the time the Bermuda Conference was contemplated, Moshe Shertok was in the United States. He asked the State Department point blank: "What do you need a conference for; isn't it a mere cover-up?" Their answer was frank: "Hitler will not release anyone, and if he does, where shall we take the hundreds of thousands of Jews?" It was clear that the Allies would have considered the release of Jews by the Germans exceedingly troublesome, and the conference was going to be a sham—as indeed it turned out to be.

Debates in the Yishuv on what to do on the eve of the **Bermuda Conference** had already begun in **March 1943**. But, as so often happens in Palestinian politics, everybody came up with a different proposal. The Revisionists and Agudat Israel proposed a mass demonstration in Jerusalem. The Histadrut proposed circulating a petition to be signed by every Jew. The JA objected to the petition, arguing that it would be a waste of time and effort. As a result the Bermuda Conference opened without any public event in Palestine. Golda Meir sadly remarked: "What do we want from the Gentiles if the Yishuv itself has not yet tried to move heaven and earth."

Only belatedly, on **June 15, 1943**, ZAC organized a public response: 250,000 adults and 60,000 children signed a petition expressing disappointment with the Bermuda Conference, and demanding immediate action from the Allies. The petition was submitted to the British government together with specific practical suggestions for rescue. It is questionable whether the petition would have had an effect had it been submitted earlier to the Bermuda Conference, but at this stage, two months after the conference, it was completely ignored.

The **Warsaw ghetto revolt** filled Jews throughout the world with pride and agony. The Yishuv pressed for some action to express their feeling of solidarity with the defenders of the ghetto. The Histadrut and ZAC proposed a fundraising effort during a "Warsaw Ghetto Day," and a one-day strike of workers in industry and British army camps. But the Revisionists and Agudat Israel did not consider these activities commensurate with the enormity of the event and rejected them. So, once again, because of dissention among the parties, nothing was done.

1944. As 1944 arrived, not only did JA's tepid response persist, but public response also started to decline. Only the Revisionists, who represented a minority of the Yishuv, continued to advocate strong public protests and actions. The difference in their approaches caused a serious rift between the Revisionists and the majority of the Yishuv. The Revisionists' view was that only direct military action against the British would change their policy on immigration and rescue. In **February 1944**, Etzel detonated explosives in government offices of the Mandate, killing several policemen. Their action proved counterproductive. The British government ceased to issue entry permits to refugees. There was an uproar in the Yishuv, as a result of which the Revisionists' participation in the Rescue Committee was terminated.

In contrast to the actions of the Revisionists, the main effort of the Yishuv went into raising funds for rescue operations. Only with the **German invasion of Hungary in March 1944** was the issue of public protest raised again—for the last time. But Ben-Gurion continued to claim that the issue did not belong to the JA, but to the National Council.

In the **spring of 1944**, Ira Hirschmann, the representative of the **US War Refugee Board** who had been appointed by Roosevelt to conduct rescue operations (see page 120), arrived in Istanbul. To coordinate operations between the War Refugee Board, the US embassy, the JDC, and the various emissaries from the Yishuv, Hirshman created a broad-based council, with Barlas as chairman, and a steering committee headed by himself. This resolved the squabbles that had plagued the rescue mission in Istanbul (see page 158). But it came very late in the war (summer of 1944), and very late in the process of extermination.

The proposal to **bomb Auschwitz,** or the railways leading to it, was first made by **Vrba and Wetzler,** two Slovak Jews who escaped Auschwitz on **April 17, 1944.** The first time the Yishuv was involved in this issue was on **June 2, 1944,** when **Gruenbaum,** head of the Rescue Committee, on his own initiative, approached **Lovell C. Pinkerton,** the American consul in Jerusalem, with the bombing suggestion. On **June 11, 1944,** during a meeting of the JA, executive Ben-Gurion opposed Gruenbaum's proposal to bomb Auschwitz, arguing that they did not know the actual situation in Poland and they believed that Auschwitz was a large labor camp. They soon learned the truth when the JA later received a copy of the eyewitness account, by two Auschwitz escapees (Vrba and Weber), of the mass-murder process taking place. Upon receiving this information, Ben-Gurion and the JA leadership promptly launched an intensive lobbying effort to persuade the Allies to bomb Auschwitz. On **June 30, 1944, Shertok and Weizmann** met with the British undersecretary of the foreign offices, **George H. Hall,** and a week later with **Anthony Eden,** repeating the suggestion to bomb Auschwitz. The proposal received **Churchill's support,** but the British Secretary of State opposed it arguing that the operation was too difficult and risky, and the distance too great. The Americans had rejected the proposal on similar grounds two weeks earlier (for a detailed discussion see pages 110–113).

Early in **June 1944,** the **Allies landed in France,** and later that month **430,000 Hungarian Jews were transported to Auschwitz,** and annihilated in its gas chambers (see page 51). As this tragedy unfolded, the Yishuv stood by helplessly. There was nothing left to do but mourn. The tragic fate of the Hungarian Jews marked a **turning point** in the Yishuv's approach to the rescue of the European Jews. The focus shifted from saving Jews in Nazi-occupied territories, to the areas liberated by the Allies.

Meanwhile, another operation behind enemy lines, albeit small in scale, was finally taking place. The idea of **dropping parachutists,** volunteers from the Yishuv, behind enemy lines, had cropped up periodically since 1940. The British, whose cooperation was needed, were not enthusiastic about the idea. They feared the post-war implications of such an action. They did not want to train members of the Yishuv who could later act against them, and were afraid that the Yishuv would demand a reward for its military aid during the war. Nevertheless, in response to public pressure over the annihilation of Hungarian Jewry, the departure of **32 parachutists** was approved by the British at the **end of August 1944.** They operated in Romania, Yugoslavia, Slovakia, Bulgaria, and Hungary. Twelve of them were captured, seven of them were executed. Thus, the parachutists' mission took place late, was small in scope, and accomplished little. Its main legacy seems to be the creation of national heroes, among them **Hana Senesh,** who was captured and executed in Hungary, and **Haviva Reik,** who succumbed to the same fate in Slovakia.

During 1944, the **number of refugees** reaching Palestine, both legally and illegally was around **5,000**—a small but not insignificant number.

Rescue efforts in the five neutral European countries

As mentioned earlier, by the end of 1942, only five European nations remained neutral: Spain, Portugal, Sweden, Switzerland, and Turkey. In this section, I shall discuss rescue efforts in these neutral countries.

After the German occupation of the Vichy-governed part of France in **November 1942, Spain** agreed to leave the Pyrenees open, mainly for Frenchmen who wanted to leave France to join the Free French Army. But Jews, too, could and did take advantage of this escape route. Despite Spain's sympathy with Germany, it showed a surprising benevolence toward the refugees. It did not limit the number of refugees, and granted protection to several thousand Jews of Spanish origin.

In **April 1944**, the Zionist office in London sent an emissary, **Wilfred Israel, to Lisbon, Portugal**, to help smuggle Jews out of France, Belgium, and the Netherlands. Israel had tried in the past to convince the JA of the "technical and moral" need to open an office in Lisbon—but to no avail. It was only in **April 1944** that the JA finally opened an office in the Iberian Peninsula, and admitted that they had made a mistake in assuming that the fascist Iberian countries could not be counted on for saving Jews. In the last two years of the war, **11,500 Jews** were saved through the Spanish and Portuguese rescue routes.

In **October 1943**, practically all the **Danish Jews** (7,500 people) were transferred to Sweden by boat (purchased by a Jewish emissary) through a swift operation organized by the Danish underground. Another **900 Jews**, half of the Jewish population of Norway, infiltrated Sweden by foot.

Switzerland was not eager to receive refugees, and after mid-1940 (when Italy joined the Axis) was surrounded by Axis states and therefore unable to operate as a transit state. However, the Yishuv emissaries were active in sending **food parcels** from Geneva to Poland and Western Europe. They were sent by regular mail while Jews lived at their regular addresses. When the ghettos were established, the International Red Cross was willing to deliver the parcels to the ghettos until the **spring of 1943**. By the **summer of 1943**, sending parcels became difficult. Fewer and fewer Jews could be located at reliable addresses, and the Allies, fearing that the shipments may fall into German hands, raised objections, and the shipments stopped. It is estimated that **100,000 parcels** reached their destination.

Turkey formed a bridge between Europe and Asia, and between Palestine and occupied Europe. Istanbul, after 1940, became the natural center of rescue operations, and Turkey provided the main route for refugees who escaped from Europe. The JA's emissary in Istanbul was **Chaim Barlas**, director of JA's Immigration Department. Friction developed between his group and the emissaries of other institutions and organizations of the Yishuv who favored more energetic and, if needed, illegal undertakings that were opposed by Barla's cautious approach. Unfortunately, these frictions and quarrels often proved detrimental to the rescue operations. It was only in the spring of 1944 that these problems were resolved.

During the whole of 1943, no massive rescue efforts were successfully implemented; however an estimated **900 immigrants** reached Palestine from the Balkans, Hungary, and Slovakia. They all passed through Turkey, where they received British permits to enter Palestine, as 21,000 permits remaining out of the 75,000 stipulated by the White Paper had still not been used.

Ransom plans: Jews for sale

Starting in **1942**, several plans developed in the satellite governments of **Romania, Slovakia,** and **Hungary** to let out Jews in large numbers, in **exchange for money and goods**.

The Transnistria Affair. In late **December 1942**, a proposal reached the JA, via Turkey, to let 70,000 Jews emigrate from Transnistria (to Palestine and Syria) in return for payment of 100 pounds per capita (i.e., a total of 7 million pounds). These were the survivors of 180,000 Romanian Jews that, in October 1941, had been deported to Transnistria, a region in the Southern Ukraine that had been annexed to Romania by the Germans.

The JA response was first to explore whether Romania was capable of carrying out an action that was opposed to German policy, and whether the Allies would permit the transfer of funds to the enemy. Their conclusion was negative on both points, and they decided to prepare a more realistic plan to be presented to the Allies: return the Jews to Romania, or leave them in Transnistria and provide help to enable them to survive.

In the meantime, negotiations continued between Jerusalem, Istanbul, and Bucharest. A turning point in these negotiations came at the **beginning of February 1943**, when the US State Department, with British acquiescence published a statement prohibiting anybody from negotiating with the enemy to save Jews, as this was considered an attempt by the Germans to extort foreign currency. At the end of **February 1943**, **Chaim Weizmann,** in the name of the JA, asked the British ambassador in the United States, **Lord Halifax**, to look into the Romanian proposal. The answer of the British government was that they considered the affair an unacceptable German blackmail: Britain cannot change its policy on admitting refugees to Palestine—the Jewish problem will be solved only with the victory of the Allies. This British position was reinforced by the pitiful outcome of the Bermuda Conference the following month. Consequently, the JA effectively gave up on the Transnistria project throughout the remainder of 1943. In **March** and **April** 1944, 1,200 refugees arrived in Palestine from Transnistria, and after Romania signed a truce with the Soviets in the **summer of 1944**, 40,000 Jews were allowed to return from Transnistria to Romania.

The Europa Plan. On **March 14, 1939**, Slovakia became, nominally, an independent country under German protection. In **1942**, 58,000 Slovak Jews—two thirds of the Jewish population—were transported to extermination camps in Poland. An underground group of Jews known as the Working Group tried to stop the deportation by bribing the Germans. They paid 50,000 dollars to **Dieter Wisliceny**, Heinrich Himmler's deputy in Slovakia. Thereafter, the deportation ceased until the unsuccessful Slovak rebellion against the Nazis in the autumn of 1944.

Convinced that the bribes paid to Wisliceny had stopped the deportation, the Working Group expanded its goal to **save all of Europe's Jewry** by bribing the Germans, in what became known as the **Europa Plan**. They gave Wisliceny an advance payment of 20,000 dollars, and asked him to transmit the proposal to Himmler. In **November 1942**, Wisliceny reported that Himmler considered the plan favorably, and that for two to three million dollars he would be willing to consider the proposal.

Following these talks, the Working Group contacted the JA, the WJC, and the JDC, asking for their financial help. After initial skepticism and lots of discussions, Schwalb and Berlas finally informed the Working Group, in **June 1943**, that the three organizations had decided to adopt the Europa Plan, and would send 200,000 dollars for the advance payment as requested by Wisliceny. After persuading Roosevelt and later the State Department, the money was deposited into a blocked account in Switzerland, from which money could be withdrawn only after the war. But this was not what Wisliceny had in mind; he wanted cash, in dollars, now—not promissory notes.

At the end of **September 1943**, Wisliceny informed the Working Group that the German government had reneged on their decision to stop the deportations. This marked the end of the protracted negotiations between Wisliceny and the Working Group.

The tantalizing question remains whether the down payment of 200,000 dollars requested by Wisliceny in cash would have stopped the deportation in Europe. Since there is no German documentation that has been found on the subject, this question, unfortunately, cannot be definitively answered. There is, however, circumstantial evidence that Germany had no intention to deviate from the "Final Solution." It was fortuitous, it seems, that the bribe in Slovakia coincided with the stoppage of deportations, because following the deportation of 60,000 Slovak Jews, the Slovak parliament took measures to protect the remaining 20,000 Jews. The stoppage is also consistent with German policy not to annihilate all Jews in one step, in case Germany needed manpower for its labor force. Thus, the premise on which the Europa Plan was based seems incorrect. This underscores the deep gap that existed between reality and the perception of the Slovak Jewish leadership.

Merchandise for Blood. Adolf Eichmann's **Merchandise for Blood** (*Ware für Blut*) was perhaps the best-known ransom plan devised during the Holocaust. It was first presented to the Yishuv emissaries in Istanbul on **May 19, 1944**, by **Joel Brand**, a leading member of the Rescue Committee in Hungary, whom Eichmann had dispatched to Istanbul to present the plan. Eichmann's proposal involved the exchange of 1 million Jews for 10,000 trucks and 400 dollars per capita. However, the Jews would not be allowed to emigrate to Palestine but only to neutral countries.

On **May 24, 1944**, a summary of Eichmann's proposal was dispatched to Jerusalem, where an emergency session of the JA was called by Ben-Gurion and Shertok. The JA meeting centered on three points: 1) Did the Germans really intend to stop deportation? They were now proceeding at an unprecedented pace of 12,000 people a day; 2) What would the Allied reaction be?; 3) What should the JA do? Although most believed that the plan was "fantastic," "satanic," and very "questionable," they felt that even if there was only a tiny chance of success, it should be pursued as a last resort to save the remaining European Jews.

Shertok wanted to talk personally to Brand, but by the end of May 1944 had been unable to obtain a visa to meet with him in Istanbul. At the beginning of **June 1944** the British suggested that Brand meet with Shertok in Palestine, and promised that they would allow Brand to return to Hungary. The Germans agreed to let Brand go to Palestine but he had to return to Budapest within two weeks.

Shertok suspected a trap, and advised Brand strongly against traveling to Palestine, where the British might arrest him. They agreed on a compromise instead; Brand was to meet Shertok near the Turkish border in Aleppo, in Syria (where the British presence was less prominent than in Palestine). Alas, contrary to the promise given by the British, Brand was arrested in Aleppo as soon as he arrived there. After three days Brand was finally allowed to meet with Shertok. After a six-hour meeting, in the presence of British intelligence officers, Brand was transferred to a prison in Cairo, and Shertok returned to Palestine where he reported the content of his discussions with Brand to the JA.

The gist of Brand's account was Eichmann's conditions for the Merchandise for Blood deal, with an added spin by Brand, in whose opinion the German intentions were mainly political: They wanted to use the plan as a way to prepare a meeting of the SS in Budapest with the representatives of Britain and the United States for possible peace negotiations, as Germany saw its defeat approaching.

The JA decided to ask the British to convene a meeting of the chairman of the intergovernmental Committee for Refugees, **Sir Herbert Emerson**, with German official representatives, in a neutral country, to discuss the ransom plan. On **June 15, 1944**, Ben-Gurion and Shertok presented this request to the High Commissioner in Jerusalem. They also requested that Brand be allowed to return to Budapest as had been promised by the British. The High Commissioner didn't try to deny that the British had broken their promise, saying "My answer is very simple: this is war." The High Commissioner conveyed the JA proposal to London, but the meeting never took place.

In the meantime, the Germans insisted that Brand be allowed to return to Budapest. But the British continued to resist the request. On **June 20, 1944**, **Steinhardt**, the US ambassador in Turkey, received explicit instructions from the State Department to cease involvement in the Brand affair. The British Foreign Office immediately followed suit. Thus, the Brand affair effectively ended **June 20, 1944**, but neither the British nor the US governments made their decision public until later in July.

On **July 6, 1944**, Weizmann and Shertok met with Eden, and repeated their previous suggestions: 1) Issue certificates of protection to the remaining Jews, 2) Warn the Hungarians of dire consequences after the war if the deportation did not stop, and 3) Bomb Auschwitz and the roads leading to it. Eden presented the proposals to Churchill who accepted them in principle, but remained adamant not to negotiate with the Germans.

By **mid-July 1944**, the JA finally realized that Eichmann's proposal would not be dealt with by the Allies. As a last resort, Ben-Gurion sent a telegram to President Roosevelt entreating him not to abandon the remnants of the European Jewry. But the desperate telegram produced no concrete results.

The decision of the Allies to condemn Eichmann's proposal was published in the United States on **July 19, 1944**, and all over the world the following day. On the same day, July 20, 1944, when the hope of Brand's mission was definitely extinguished, **Admiral Horthy** declared Hungary's willingness to stop the deportations. It was a reaction to the international pressure of the West, and to the American bombing of the Budapest railway on July 3, 1944, which Horthy attributed to Jewish pressure.

Brand was finally released from prison in Cairo in **October 1944**, and brought to Palestine. He was bitter, and blamed the JA and the Mapai for the failure of his mission. He accused them of being more loyal to the Allies than to their brothers. Brand did not fully comprehend the Yishuv's limited power: how few bargaining chips the Zionist movement had, and how low a priority the Allies assigned to the saving of the Jews.

Shertok summarized the Brand affair as a heart-rending, discouraging effort that occupied his time and energy, and that of his colleagues, for two months. The Allies claimed that their refusal to act was a matter of principle: not to negotiate with the enemy. But a large underlying and unpublicized factor was their fear of having to deal with a flood of Jews in case something came of Merchandise for Blood.

Many also see a positive side to Brand's mission. It may have contributed to creating the international pressure that resulted in Horthy's decision to rescue the remaining 250,000 Hungarian Jews from deportation.

The financial support for rescue efforts

What priority the JA assigned to rescue efforts was a topic of discussion and controversy for years, and to some extent still is. It is, therefore, instructive to look at the problem quantitatively, i.e., what fraction of financial resources was allocated to rescue operations.

The **JA budget** was based on the income from three funds: 1) the **Foundation Fund** (*Keren Hayesod*), established in 1920 to rebuild the land of Israel, which provided 5.5 million pounds[64] during the war; 2) the **Jewish National Fund** (*Keren Kayemet*), founded in 1901 to purchase land in Palestine, which provided 6 million pounds during the war; 3) the **Mobilization Fund** (*Mas Gijus*), established in July 1942 to support soldiers' families and to acquire arms, which raised 2.7 million pounds during the remaining years of the war. From these three funds the JA had to decide what fraction to allocate to rescue efforts.

Throughout the war years the different agencies criticized the JA for failing to allocate funds on a scale commensurate with the size of the catastrophe.

In **February 1942**, **Menachem Bader**, a leader of Hashomer Hatzair and emissary in Istanbul, returned to Palestine and requested funds from the Histadrut for rescuing the Jews of Slovakia and Romania. The Histadrut tried to move the JA to action, threatening that if they did not come up with the money, the Histadrut would start an independent fundraising campaign. The JA finally allocated 75,000 pounds, as a loan to be repaid by the Histadrut.

In **January 1943**, the National Council demanded that the JA immediately allocate 250,000 pounds to investigate rescue possibilities. The Histadrut proposed that two-thirds of the Foundation Fund be allocated to rescue. In the meantime it offered the JA 50,000 pounds, to be matched by the JA. The response of the JA was to offer a mere 15,000—as a loan.

In **mid-April 1943**, a combined **Mobilization and Rescue Fund** (**MRF**) was established with a goal of raising 50,000 pounds a month, of which 20% were earmarked for rescue.

At the **end of April 1943**, a telegram arrived from Warsaw, informing the Yishuv that the ghetto uprising had begun, and asking the JA to send at least 35,000 pounds. The Histadrut upped the amount and asked the JA to send 60,000 pounds. The Histadrut also asked for a week dedicated to donations, during which each worker would contribute one

---

[64] To convert to 2016 dollars, multiply by 40.

day of wages. The response was disappointing. Some workers avoided paying, some demanded proof that the money would reach the Jews in the ghetto. About 27,000 pounds were collected—far short of target.

In the **summer of 1943** the income of the MRF had declined, and it failed to achieve its monthly quota of 50,000 pounds. The timing of this decline was extremely unfortunate, as the Allies had started to advance into occupied areas, in which people were in need of help. Furthermore, some German allies (Hungary, Romania, and Bulgaria) started to consider shifting allegiances. This posed a danger that Germany would invade them and annihilate the remaining Jews; rescue at that moment was of utmost importance.

In view of this situation, the Histadrut persuaded the JA to organize a one-time fundraising appeal for 250,000 pounds, to be called **Diaspora Month**. Ben-Gurion embraced the idea enthusiastically. The start of Diaspora Month was set for **mid-September, 1943**. Alas, the target was not realized, and only one-third (80,000 pounds) was collected. The reason for the failure of Diaspora Month was a decline in public enthusiasm caused to a large extent by the secrecy with which, by necessity, the rescue operations were conducted. This made people doubt that anything was being done.

In **summary**, the total amount spent on rescue operations in **1943** was 320,000 pounds. This represented a small fraction (about 15%) of the total JA budget of 2.1 million pounds spent on defense, land reclamation, and settlements. In **1944**, the JA spent 860,000 pounds on rescue, out of a total budget of 5.2 million (approximately the same fraction as in 1943). The JA was criticized by many, in particular by the Histadrut, for not allocating more funds to rescue operations. It is to the credit of the Histadrut that, if it were not for its initiatives and constant prodding of the JA, the amount allocated to rescue would have been even smaller. In addition, it should be noted that the public support for fundraising was often less than enthusiastic, and the target quotas were rarely met.

Concluding remarks

There are two major points about the Yishuv's response to the Holocaust that are disturbing, and for which it is being criticized to this day: the time gap between the events in Europe and the response to them; and the relatively mild and ineffective response to such a monstrous event as the Holocaust.

The time gap. It is a psychological fact that there are time gaps between receiving information, understanding it, believing it, internalizing it, and finally acting on it. The more unprecedented and horrendous the event, the longer the gaps. And nothing as monstrous as the Holocaust had occurred in the 20th century. In this connection, it is worth remembering Golda Meir's words that one should consider it to the credit of normal "good" people that they did not believe such atrocities could be committed by fellow human beings, and that they had the naiveté to think that the mighty Allies would not stand by idly as such monstrous crimes against humanity were being committed. Alas, we have learned a lesson: Evil exists, and many genocides have been committed since the Holocaust.

The mild and ineffective response. The tepid response was partly due to human failures (personal and institutional squabbles, and the inability to sustain outrage), and partly due to circumstances inherent to the situation (the Yishuv's meager resources, and political dependency on Britain). Although there were some individual leaders, private citizens and a minority party (the Revisionist) who pressed for radical action, the Yishuv at large had difficulties sustaining its outrage and vigilance, and soon continued its daily life as before. Attention was chiefly devoted to donation problems and political factionalism. Except for some transient instances, like during the Warsaw ghetto rebellion in 1943, and the deportation of 430,000 Hungarian Jews in 1944, there was no mass display of outrage over the Holocaust. The Yishuv never launched an extraordinary action—some operation commensurate with the pain and rage over the events that befell the European Jews. I was living in Palestine during the crucial years 1941–1946 and was occupied mainly with my own existential and career problems. I must, therefore, be held responsible and share in the blame for this inaction.

And then there were the squabbles, on personal and institutional levels, that distracted the efforts from rescue operations. During the war, the institutions of the Yishuv had long debates about the relations with the Arabs, the Soviet Union, the political future of the Yishuv, and interparty problems. Few discussions dealt with the plight of European Jewry. In particular, within the Labor movement (Mapai) in the 1940s, much energy was channeled away from the rescue of Jews, towards coping with the challenge of communism and the Soviet Union. Part of the party was more interested in a world of equality without classes than in Zionism. In October 1942, the discussions on this issue at a Mapai conference split the party in two. The energy, the thought, and the dedication that should have been applied to the rescue of Jews were, instead, applied to socialist issues. It is ironic and sad when one juxtaposes the news about the annihilation of thousands of Jewish communities, with the squabbles and splits within the parties and factions that took place on a daily basis.

There were also tensions during the war years between the two main leaders, Weizmann and Ben-Gurion. Weizmann was undeniably the leader most admired by the Zionists before the war, yet from the end of 1938 until the fall of 1944, he stayed in England and the United States, and did not visit Palestine. Although he participated with Shertok in the negotiations regarding rescue efforts and the bombing of Auschwitz, he never appealed directly to Churchill or Roosevelt. He admitted later that he was mostly involved in his scientific work. Ben-Gurion had no confidence in Weizmann's pro-British policies, and his ability to lead in time of crisis, although Ben-Gurion himself was criticized by his colleagues for his relative lack of involvement with the Holocaust.

The influence of Ben-Gurion and the JA, which he led, was enormous. It behooves us therefore to look more closely at this iconic, and at times enigmatic figure. Ben-Gurion, in his pragmatic nature, concluded, after the Bermuda Conference in April 1943, that there was no possibility of saving the millions of European Jews. Consequently, he turned his attention to post-war goals. Ben-Gurion's emphasis on building a Jewish state, rather than focusing on rescue operations, is perhaps best illustrated by the relatively meager financial support allocated by the JA to rescue. (See page 162.)

Not that Ben-Gurion was unemotional about the Jewish tragedy playing out in Europe, as can be seen from one of his bitter and eloquent outcries on the occasion of the 40th anniversary of Herzl's death on July 10, 1944: "Why have you mistreated us so—you lovers of freedom and justice, fighters for democracy, liberty, equality, and socialism? Why have you mistreated the Jewish people, standing by while our blood flows unceasingly, without raising a finger, without coming to our aid, without saying to the slaughter, enough…."

But even as Ben-Gurion despaired about the lack of Allied support for rescue operations, he could not risk leaving the Yishuv isolated in the international arena. The JA was therefore unwilling to fight Britain's policy openly and thereby jeopardize the very existence of the Yishuv's future.

On an emotional level people found it difficult to accept this commonsense, logical argument in the face of continuing annihilation. All the steps taken by the JA were within the "the rules of the game" dictated by Britain: Germans living in Palestine were never taken hostage; the Agency, on British request, did not support the Polish demand in 1942–43 for reprisal bombing of German cities; there were no attempts to broadcast to the Jews under occupation; there were no massive demonstrations or hunger strikes to harass the Allies; there were no hard-hitting exposés about the Allies' indifference; there were no direct contacts with German authorities to discuss ransom offers. In short, Ben-Gurion as a politician had to suppress all impulses to mount an extraordinary response to an extraordinary situation lest his rage against Britain isolate or endanger the future of the Yishuv. This seems to lie at the core of the endless debate about Ben-Gurion's position during the Holocaust.

Having said all this, we need to remember the great difficulties the Yishuv faced at that time and the psychological background that made it difficult to grasp the unprecedented horror of the Holocaust that led to the time gap between event and action. As for the difficulties facing the Yishuv: It was a minority in a country ruled by the British, with their overwhelming priority of winning the war rather than saving Jews. The Yishuv's resources in manpower, money, and arms were small. Unlike the Arabs, it had no oil, no natural resources, no strategic territories, i.e., no bargaining chips or political leverage over the Allies. This point is easily forgotten in the face of present day Israel, with its military might, and a Jewish population 10 times larger than during World War II.

6. THE RIGHTEOUS AMONG THE NATIONS

While the rest of the world looked passively on, or, worse, helped or participated in the Nazi atrocities, many brave individuals inside and outside Germany risked their lives to save Jews. Many saved only one Jewish life, but as the Talmud says: "He who saves one human being is as if he saved an entire world." Others saved hundreds and even thousands of lives.

At Yad Vashem, the Holocaust memorial in Jerusalem, the Avenue and Garden of the Righteous Among the Nations honor and immortalize the non-Jews who followed their conscience and acted according to the most noble principles of humanity to help and save Jews during the Holocaust. Two thousand trees, symbolic of the renewal of life, have been planted in and around the Avenue. Adjacent to each tree, a plaque gives the names of the individuals honored. An additional 20,000 names of non-Jews, recognized by Yad Vashem as Righteous Among the Nations, are engraved on walls in the Garden.

I shall describe the actions of five righteous men (**Schindler, Schulte, Sugihara, Fry, and Wallenberg**) who stand out in my mind. These rare individuals had the capacity and courage to assert their moral autonomy, at great risk and for no personal gain, by resisting the demands of evil governments. I write about them with a sense of awe and admiration. They need to be remembered and celebrated.

Oskar Schindler[65]

One of the best-known cases, in large part due to Spielberg's 1993 movie "Schindler's List," was that of Oskar Schindler. Schindler was a German Catholic who ran a factory that manufactured kitchen utensils outside the edge of the Cracow ghetto. He employed many Jews whom he treated well and protected from deportation. For instance,

Oskar Schindler
1908–1974

when the Gestapo tried to transfer some of his workers to the nearby slave labor camp at Plaschaw, he was able, by bribery and persuasion, to keep them. As Soviet forces approached in January 1945, Schindler transferred his factory to Brünnlitz, taking his Jewish work force with him. While at Brünnlitz, he became aware of a locked wagon marked "Property of the SS" that contained over 100 Jews, starving and freezing, who had been transported from the Birkenau concentration camp. Schindler was determined to save those Jews and convinced the railway official that the wagon was intended for his factory to supplement his labor force. When he broke open the locks, 16 of the Jews had frozen to death. Not one of them weighed more than 35 kgs. The Schindlers fed, guarded, and nursed them to health. Between 1943 and 1945 Schindler saved 1,200 Jews by employing and protecting them in his factory. He died in 1974. At his funeral, on the slope of Mt. Zion in Jerusalem, more than 400 Jews whom he had saved paid him their last respects.

---

[65] Jeremy Roberts, "Oskar Schindler: Righteous Gentile," Saddleback Publication Co., 2000.

Eduard Schulte[66]

A less known figure is that of the German industrialist Eduard Schulte, who fought the Nazi regime by providing valuable information to the allies; he was the first to alert the world to the construction of the extermination camp in Auschwitz.

Schulte was the general director of Giesche, one of Germany's leading mining firms that produced zinc, which is a prime ingredient of brass. Brass was an indispensable material for the German armament program. As one of the leading industrialists, Schulte was invited to a meeting on February 20, 1933, at the residence of Hermann Göring, the president of the new Reichstag. Hitler was also present, and delivered one of his famous rambling and violent speeches. Schulte was consumed by a passionate hatred of Nazism and considered Hitler a raving lunatic. He was convinced that the Nazis would bring about the ruin of Germany. His instincts told him that the Nazi propaganda was fraudulent. When Hitler and Goebbels made their emotional speeches about peace, he knew they were lying. To him the economic policy of the Third Reich did not make sense, unless it was to prepare for a war of expansion and conquest.

Schulte's plan was to undermine the Nazi regime from within. Since he was privy to sensitive inside information in Germany, and he frequently traveled on business to Switzerland, he was able to pass on the information to his contacts there. On August 27, 1939, Schulte conveyed to the Swiss military intelligence the information that Hitler would attack Poland on September 1. Although this information was immediately passed on to Paris and London, Britain and France did not react, and the German forces crushed the Polish army with ease.

In April 1941 Schulte arrived in Zürich, with the startling information that Germany was preparing to attack the Soviet Union. Schulte also supplied important information on the development of rockets at Peenemünde. As a result, the Allies bombed the site. This delayed the production of the rockets (V-1), which were only ready to be launched on June 13, 1944, seven days after the Allied landing in Normandy. Hadn't the Allies delayed the development of the rockets, the results would have been very serious.

Eduard Schulte

I shall now discuss in more detail the passing of Schulte's information on Auschwitz and the "foot-dragging" reaction of the Allies. On July 17, 1942, Himmler visited Auschwitz and, also, the close-by Giesche works where he met with Schulte. Although Schulte thought the Nazi leadership capable of committing any conceivable crime, the Nazi plans for Auschwitz, that he gleaned from Himmler, were so horrendous that he had difficulties believing them. After convincing himself of the veracity of the plans—the contemplated mass killings of the Jews—Schulte took the next train to Zürich to warn the Jews and the rest of the world that measures must be taken to prevent the mass murder.

Schulte passed on his information about Auschwitz to Gerhard Riegner who represented the World Jewish Congress at the League of Nations in Geneva. Riegner met with the American consul in

---

[66] Walter Laqueur and Richard Breitman, "Breaking the Silence," Simon & Schuster, 1986.

Geneva. Riegner met with the American consul in Geneva, who passed the information to the American legation in Bern. There, counselor of legation J. Huddle, and Minister L. Harrison, considered Riegner's story as "war rumors inspired by fear," but sent the information off to Washington. There, the State Department called the legation's message "wild rumors" and asked the legation to refrain from accepting information of this kind. The information on the "Final Solution" was not passed on to President Roosevelt.

Schulte had better luck with the British consul, who immediately informed the Foreign Office in London and asked them to convey the message to Silverman, a member of the British Parliament who also headed the British Section of the World Jewish Congress. On August 28, a month after Schulte had come to Switzerland, Silverman sent a telegram to Rabbi Stephen Wise, president of the World Jewish Congress, a man of great influence in Washington.

On September 28, 1942, a month after receiving the information from London, Wise spoke at a rally in New York against Nazi atrocities but, as promised to US Secretary of State Summer Walls, did not refer to Riegner's report (see page 129). The rally created far greater publicity than any generated previously.

On October 7, the White House issued a press release indicating the extent of the Nazi war crimes. Roosevelt declared that these war crimes would be punished at the end of the war.

In early November 1942, Roosevelt asked Congress to approve a bill to loosen restrictions on immigration for Jews who wished to enter the United States. The bill was defeated, and Roosevelt was not willing to wage a battle over this issue. It is regrettable that Roosevelt did not make a speech about the dreadful fate of the Jews, which, like other of his famous speeches, would have reverberated around the world. Finally, in mid-December, the United States and eleven other nations, joined the British Government in making known and strongly condemning the Nazi killings of Jews.

Schulte had wanted the Allies to attack the death camps in order to prevent the mass murders from taking place. Instead, they issued a tardy and ineffective denunciation of Nazi killings. How many millions of Jews could have been saved if the Allies had acted in a timely and effective manner?!

On December 2, 1943, Schulte received a phone call from his friends in Berlin warning him that the Gestapo was on his trail, and urging him to leave Germany as soon as possible. He arrived in Switzerland a few days later, obtained a medical certificate stating that he was gravely ill, and checked into a clinic. In the meantime, the papers for asylum were prepared and approved, and he stayed in Switzerland for the rest of the war.

In the spring of 1944 the Nazi regime awarded Schulte the War Cross of Merit for "his extraordinary contributions to the German war effort." Schulte's instinct told him that it was a ruse to get him back to Germany to be arrested, and he did not go.

After the war, Schulte was eager to contribute to the rebuilding of Germany. He left Switzerland in August 1945, with high recommendations from the US Office of Strategic Services (OSS). Ironically, in the denazification process that he had to undergo, he was refused clearance for a high governmental position because of the 1944 award that he had been given by the Nazi regime. Embittered, Schulte left Germany in January 1947. He died, a disappointed man, in January 1966, in Zürich, at age 75.

To add insult to injury, the German courts refused to grant benefits to his son Ruprecht and his wife Doris as the heirs of someone who had suffered losses during the Nazi regime. The court claimed that by passing on information to the enemy, Edward Schulte had committed a crime. Ironically, deputy ministers and generals who had blindly obeyed Hitler till the end received substantial pensions, as did widows of the leading Nazis, like Mrs. Göring and Mrs. Heydrich. So much for post-war German justice.

Chiune (Sempo) Sugihara[67]

Chiune (Sempo) Sugihara was appointed Japanese Consul-General in Kovno (Kaunas), Lithuania, in 1939. There, confronted with evil and suffering, he and his wife Yukiko followed their conscience and, defying orders of their government, risked their careers, livelihood, and future, to save the lives of several thousand Jews. Here is their story:

Chiune Sugihara was born on January 1, 1900, in Yaotsu, Japan, to a middle-class father and a samurai-class mother. He graduated from high school with top marks. In 1919, the Japanese Foreign Ministry recruited him and assigned him to Harbin, China, where he studied Russian and German and he later became an expert in Russian affairs. He then served with the Japanese-controlled government in Manchuria, where he was promoted to Vice Minister of Foreign Affairs. Sugihara was disturbed by his government's policy and cruel treatment of the Chinese. He resigned his post in protest in 1934.

Chiune (Sempo) Sugihara
1900–1986

In March 1939, Sugihara was sent to Kovno, the capital of Lithuania, to open a one-man consulate. Lithuania was strategically situated between Germany and the Soviet Union, and he was to report to his government on their respective war plans. When the Nazi armies invaded Poland on September 1, 1939, a wave of Jewish refugees streamed into Lithuania bringing with them chilling tales of German atrocities against the Jewish population.

On June 15, 1940, the Soviets invaded Lithuania and annexed it. In July 1940, the Soviet authorities instructed all foreign embassies to leave Kovno. Sugihara requested and received a 20-day extension: precious little time to put into action a plan to save thousands of Jews. The free world, with very few exceptions, barred the immigration of Jews. Among the exceptions were the two Dutch Caribbean islands, Curaçao and Dutch Guiana (now called Surinam). They did not require formal entrance visas, and the Dutch consul in Kovno was willing to stamp the refugees' passports with entrance permits. There remained one major obstacle: The Soviet authorities agreed to let the refugees pass through the Soviet Union only if, in addition to the Dutch entrance permit, they also had a transit visa from the Japanese (as they would have to pass through Japan on their way to the Dutch islands).

---

[67] Ken Mochizuki, "Passage to Freedom," Lee & Low Books, 1997.

One morning in late July 1940, Consul Sugihara and his family awakened to a crowd of Polish refugees gathered outside the consulate. Desperate to flee the approaching Nazis, they knew that their only chance to freedom was to obtain the required Japanese transit visa. Sugihara was moved by their plight, but he did not have the authority to issue hundreds of visas without permission from Tokyo. He wired his government three times for permission to issue visas to the refugees. Three times his request was denied.

Sugihara, the career diplomat, faced a very difficult choice. On one hand, he was bound by the traditional obedience he had been taught all his life. On the other hand, he was a samurai who had been taught to help those who were in need. It was a choice between the head and the heart. He knew that if he defied the orders of his superiors, he would likely be fired and disgraced.

After a soul-searching discussion with his wife, Yukiko Sugihara decided to follow his conscience: The visas would be signed. For 29 days, From July 31 to August 28, 1940, Mr. and Mrs. Sugihara sat for endless hours writing and signing visas by hand. Hundreds of applicants became thousands as he worked to grant as many visas as possible before being forced to close the consulate and leave Lithuania. And, as Sugihara left for Berlin, and the train pulled out of the station in Kovno, he gave the consul's visa stamp to a refugee, to use it to save even more Jews.

After receiving their visas, the refugees took the train to Moscow and proceeded by trans-Siberian train to Vladivostok. From there they continued to Kobe, where they were allowed to stay for several months, and then were sent to Shanghai, China. As many as 6,000 refugees made their way to Japan, China, and other countries. They had escaped the Holocaust and became known as **Sugihara's survivors**.

Despite his disobedience, the Japanese government needed Sugihara, and decided to postpone disciplinary action until his skills were no longer needed. He served during the rest of the war as Consul-General in Prague and Bucharest. But after the war, the Japanese government unceremoniously dismissed Chiune Sugihara from the diplomatic service. His diplomatic career was shattered and he had to start his life over. At first he worked as a part-time translator and interpreter. For the last two decades of his life, he worked as a manager for an export company with business in Moscow—a poor end for a once rising star in the Japanese foreign service. And all because he dared to save thousands of human beings from certain death.

Today, close to 70 years after those 29 fateful days in July and August of 1940, there are about 40,000 descendants of the Sugihara survivors who owe their lives to one modest man and his wife. After the war Sugihara never mentioned or spoke to anyone about his extraordinary deeds. It was not until 1969 that Sugihara was found by a man he had helped save, Mr. Yehoshua Nishri, economic attaché to the Israeli embassy in Tokyo. The following year Sugihara visited Israel on the invitation of the Israeli government, and, in 1985, he was bestowed the honor of being named one of the Righteous Among the Nations.

Forty-five years after he signed the visas, Sugihara was asked why he did it. He answered: "They were human beings and they needed help. I am glad I found the strength to give it to them."

Consul Chiune Sugihara died at age 86 on July 31, 1986.

Varian Fry[68]

Varian Fry, a 32–year–old Harvard-educated classicist, preppy journalist, and editor from New York City, helped over 2,000 refugees, in the Vichy French zone, to escape from Nazi terror during World War II.

Fry was somewhat of a dilettante until he went to France. Born in New York on October 15, 1907, the son of liberal Protestants, he was a very bright but unruly and rebellious youngster. He was constantly in trouble at boarding school, and also managed to get himself expelled from Harvard for several months; but he was still able to graduate in 1931 with a B.A. in Classical Studies. When they were freshmen at Harvard in 1927, he and his classmate L. Kirstein founded the influential literary magazine "Hound and Horn," to champion modernist authors like Joyce and Eliot.

Varian Fry
1907–1967

In 1935, Fry visited Berlin as a foreign correspondent for the American journal "The Living Age." There he witnessed the brutality of Nazi storm troopers violently beating Jews on the streets. He was appalled and horrified by what he saw, and became an ardent anti-Nazi. In Berlin he met Ernst Hanfstaengl, a German-American Harvard graduate who held a high position in the Propaganda Ministry of the Third Reich. Hanfstaengl told him that the Nazi leaders, Hitler and Goebbels among them, were determined to eliminate the Jews. Upon his return to the United States, Fry wrote about the brutality he witnessed and the dangers of Nazism. But his articles did not get the response they deserved and that he had hoped for. He wanted Roosevelt to speak out; he wanted the churches to take a stand, the pope to threaten "to excommunicate all the Catholics who, in any way, participated in the frightful crimes…."

The fall of France in 1940 was deeply unsettling to Fry. It motivated him to act, and he founded, together with Karl Frank and Harold Oram, the **Emergency Rescue Committee (ERC)**, which sought to save as many refugees as possible. The ERC needed someone to go to Europe to do the rescue work. Fry stepped up to the plate and volunteered. Armed with 3,000 dollars and a list of 200 prominent refugees, he flew to Marseille in August 1940 to assist in any way he could.

After France fell to Hitler, a large number of refugees were suddenly trapped in the unoccupied zone of southern France, where the authoritarian Vichy regime was established. Both Jews and non-Jews were threatened with extradition to Nazi Germany under Article 19 of the Franco-German Armistice—the Surrender on Command clause.

Despite having no training in underground work and no knowledge of forgery, black marketers or secret passages, Fry quickly rose to the occasion. Working day and night, Fry assembled a team of European and American assistants, and established the American Relief Center, a legal organization that also acted as a cover for an illegal underground operation. At age 32, Fry had found his vocation. He discovered reserves of courage and energy in himself that he never knew existed, and he labored to the point of exhaustion.

---

[68] Varian Fry, "Surrender on Demand," Johnson Books, 1997.

Fry and his staff worked feverishly to help the refugees to freedom, against the obstructions of the French, and even of the American authorities. Getting anybody out of France required subterfuge and deceit, a willingness to take risks and break laws. Fry was up to the job. He provided the refugees with either legal or forged documents, gave them financial aid, and directions on how to reach Spain and Portugal through an elaborate network of escape routes. From there, many departed for America or Africa.

One issue that haunted Fry was the question of selection. The number of refugees that sought his help exceeded, by far, the resources at his disposal. He chose people whom he considered most valuable, i.e., novelists, poets, painters, historians, scientists. His greatest efforts went towards those who had been singled out by the Nazis and were in most danger. He also favored refugees who already possessed some of the necessary documents, and who were fit enough to make the arduous journey across the Pyrenees. It was a daunting task to choose and decide between the life and death of a refugee.

Fry had originally planned to stay in Europe one month to save the 200 people on his list. Once there, moved by the suffering around him, he expanded his mission drastically. He stayed for 13 months and saved more than 2,000 refugees, among them many of this century's greatest talents, such as: the writers Hannah Arendt, Lion Feuchtwanger, Franz Werfel, Heinrich Mann; the artists Marc Chagall, Jacques Lipshitz, Max Ernst; the Nobel Prize-winning biochemist Otto Meyerhof. The arrival of these people in the United States significantly changed the character of American culture. They effectively shifted the cultural center of the world from Paris to New York.

Fry was under constant pressure from the American government, which wanted good relations with the Vichy regime, to return to the United States. He repeatedly ignored these entreaties. Shamefully, the US consulate finally confiscated his passport, and connived with the Vichy regime to have Fry expelled from France in September 1941.

When Fry arrived back in New York, he was received with little enthusiasm. He slowly drifted into obscurity, and went into decline. Nothing could ever match the fulfillment, excitement, and sense of power he had felt during that one year in France. He felt unappreciated and drifted from job to job, from journalism to magazine editing, to teaching Latin in high school, which was his last job before his death. On September 13, 1967, two weeks after his divorce from his second wife, Annette, the Connecticut State Police found Fry in bed, dead from a cerebral hemorrhage.

Varian Fry did not receive the recognition he deserved during his lifetime, with one exception. In 1967, shortly before his death, the government of France recognized his contributions by awarding him the Croix de Chevalier de la Légion d'Honneur. Belatedly, his contributions are being recognized more and more. Fourteen years after his death, his own country honored him with the Eisenhower Liberation Medal, and, in 1991, Fry's contributions were officially recognized by the United States Holocaust Memorial Council. In 1995, Fry became the first US citizen to be listed as Righteous Among the Nations at Israel's National Holocaust Memorial, Yad Vashem. On that occasion US Secretary of State, Warren Christopher, planted a tree in Fry's honor, expressed his gratitude to Varian Fry, and acknowledged that Fry's "heroic actions never received the support they deserved from the US government, including, I regret to say, the State Department." In the year 2000, the square in front of the US consulate in Marseilles was renamed Place Varian Fry, and a street in the East-West Berlin Wall area was named Varian Fry Strasse.

Raoul Wallenberg[69]

Raoul Wallenberg was a Swedish diplomat who became a legend through his work to save thousands of Hungarian Jews during the last year of the World War II.

Raoul Wallenberg was born August 4, 1912. His parents came from two of Sweden's most outstanding families, whose members included diplomats, bankers, bishops of the Lutheran Church, as well as artists and professors. Raoul's father, an officer in the Swedish Navy and son of the Swedish ambassador to Japan, died three months before Raoul's birth. In 1919, Maj Wallenberg, Raoul's mother, married Fredrik von Dardel who became the administrator of Karolinska, Sweden's largest and world-famous hospital.

Against the will of his family, Raoul attended the University of Michigan in Ann Arbor, from where he graduated in 1935, together with his classmate, future President Gerald Ford. Although Raoul's degree was in architecture, when he returned to Sweden, his grandfather insisted he study banking and commerce. In 1936, his grandfather arranged a position for him at the Holland Bank in Haifa, Palestine. There he met many Jews who had been forced to flee Nazi persecution in Germany. Their stories affected him deeply, and no doubt contributed to his later rescue activities. In 1939, back in Sweden, Raoul went to work with a Jewish refugee, Koloman Lauer, who was the director of a Swedish-based import and export company (the Mid-European Trading Company) that specialized in food delicacies. Raoul often traveled on business to Hungary, and through Lauer's relatives in Budapest, he came to know the Hungarian Jewish community.

Raoul Wallenberg
1912– ?

In 1944, at the behest of President Roosevelt, the **United States War Refugee Board (WRB)** was belatedly established. Its top priority, after the Nazi occupation of Hungary in 1944, was the rescue of the 750,000 Hungarian Jews. The WRB turned to neutral Sweden, which had an active embassy in Budapest, looking for somebody to be sent to Hungary on its behalf. That person, supported by large sums of money from the WRB, and protected by the Swedish government with a Swedish diplomatic passport, would be empowered to issue Swedish passports to as many Jews as possible.

Raoul Wallenberg was chosen to be the WRB's representative. He turned out to be the right man for the job—a quick thinker, energetic, brave, and compassionate. On July 3, 1944, at age 31, he arrived at the Swedish embassy in Budapest. His primary adversary was SS Lt. Col. Adolf Eichmann, who, by the time Wallenberg arrived in Hungary, had already deported 437,000 Hungarian Jews. There remained 230,000 Jews living in Budapest.

A special department was created in the Swedish embassy in Budapest, staffed primarily with several hundred Jewish volunteers. Wallenberg persuaded the Hungarian authorities to exempt his staff from wearing the yellow star; this allowed his workers much greater freedom of movement—an essential factor in carrying out many of Wallenberg's missions. Wallenberg did not use traditional diplomacy. He shocked the diplomats of the

[69] John Bierman, "Righteous Gentile: The Story of Raoul Wallenberg," Penguin Books, 1995.

Swedish legation with his unconventional methods. Everything, from bribes to threats, was used with success.

Wallenberg's first job was to redesign the Swedish protective passport, the *Schutzpass*, making it a large, flashy, official-looking document. He knew that the Nazis and their Hungarian counterparts were frequently people of little education, who would be impressed by such a document. He then printed huge placards picturing the Schutzpass, and put them up all over the city. This made the Nazis familiar with the document and its authority.

Wallenberg's next step was crucial to his success. In a section of Budapest designated by the Hungarian government as the International Ghetto, Wallenberg purchased 30 buildings from which he flew Swedish flags. These buildings housed, among others, 8,000 children whose parents had been deported. All the inhabitants of these houses were given the full protection of the Swedish government. Following Wallenberg's example, other neutral legations and the Red Cross greatly expanded the number of protected houses. After the war, it was established that about 50,000 Jews living in the foreign houses had survived. Of these, 25,000 were directly under Wallenberg's protection.

On October 15, 1944, the legal Hungarian government of Admiral Horthy fell, and a pro-Nazi government, called the Arrow Cross, was installed. The Arrow Cross gendarmes, an elite, quasi-military corps, were Eichmann's greatest allies in his implementation of the "Final Solution." If possible, they were even more sadistic than their German counterparts.

As the Germans found themselves increasingly on the military defensive, they were less able to supply Eichmann with trains to deport Jews from Hungary. On November 8, 1944, as the Russian army moved closer to Budapest, Eichmann ordered all Jews to be rounded up and marched on foot 125 miles to the Austrian-Hungarian border, for deportation to the death camps. The walk took one week, in freezing cold and snow, with no food or proper clothing. All along the road lay the dead and the dying. Wallenberg, together with Per Anger, second secretary of the Swedish legation, went along the route of the march, giving out food, clothing, fresh water, and Swedish Schutzpasses whenever possible. Wallenberg continued his rescue efforts at the border. He organized Red Cross trucks to deliver food, and set up checkpoints to protect those with Schutzpasses. In many cases, he managed to save Jews from the clutches of the Nazis, with his firm actions and courage as his only weapons. He climbed on the wagons of the transport trains and slipped bunches of the protective passes down to the people inside, and then demanded that the Jews with Schutzpasses should be allowed to leave the train with him.

At the end of November, Eichmann was ordered back to Berlin by Heinrich Himmler, who was preparing to put out peace feelers to the Allies. The marches were halted and Eichmann was instructed to cease all liquidation efforts.

Wallenberg became famous among the Jews of Hungary for his many individual acts of bravery, but it was as a negotiator that he achieved his greatest results. In the first days of January 1945, he got word that a final plan, masterminded by Eichmann before he left Hungary, was soon to be carried out. The plan called for the total massacre of the 70,000 Jews that remained in the ghetto. It was to be carried out by a combined task force of SS men, commanded by the German general August Schmidhuber, and Arrow Cross men.

It was in the last moment that Wallenberg succeeded in averting the massacre. He enlisted the help of Pál Szalay, a high-ranking Arrow Cross man, who was horrified by the atrocities of his compatriots. Szalay was to become Wallenberg's spokesman in negotiations with General Schmidhuber. Wallenberg needed an intermediate, as it was far too dangerous for him to meet personally with the SS leader; he was already wanted by the Gestapo, and there had been several attempts on his life.

Szalay informed Schmidhuber that if the planned massacre took place, Wallenberg would see to it that the general was held personally responsible, and hanged as a war criminal. With the Russian army approaching the city, the general reconsidered. He issued the order that no ghetto action was to take place. It was Wallenberg's last and biggest victory.

When the Russian army entered Budapest they found 70,000 Jewish men, women and children in the ghetto. Another 25,000 people were in the protected houses and an additional 25,000 persons were found hiding in Christian homes.

In all, 120,000 Jews of Budapest survived the "Final Solution." It was the only substantial Jewish community left in Europe. At least 100,000 of them owed their lives directly to one man—RAOUL WALLENBERG.

On January 17, 1945, Wallenberg left for a meeting with the Russian commander, Marshal Rodion Malinovsky, in Debrecen, Hungary. On the way, he was taken into "protective custody" by the Soviet NKVD, later known as the KGB. The Swedish ambassador in Moscow was notified that the Russian authorities had taken measures to protect Raoul Wallenberg. What followed for the next several decades was a series of lies and deceptions on the part of the Russian government, and a series of protests and requests (albeit ineffective and not sufficiently forceful) on the part of the Swedish government to free Wallenberg.

Wallenberg was imprisoned in Moscow, and his mother, Maj von Dardel, was notified in **February 1945**, that her son was safe and would be released soon. She was told that it would be best for Wallenberg if neither she, nor the Swedish government, made a major issue of Wallenberg's absence.

In **April 1945**, Averell Harriman, then US ambassador in Moscow contacted the Swedish ambassador Staffan Soderblom to offer assistance to help determine Wallenberg's fate. Soderblom declined US help or involvement—a major mistake. A second tactical error was committed during a meeting between Stalin and Soderblom on **June 15, 1945**. The ambassador told Stalin that, although he personally felt that Wallenberg was dead, killed by the Arrow Cross; his government had requested that the Soviets initiate an inquiry.

In **February 1947**, a fellow inmate, Bernard Rensinghoff, communicated with Wallenberg in Lefortovo Prison in Moscow by knocking on the wall. Resinghoff was later released and reported that the interrogating KGB commissar told Wallenberg that he was a "political" case, and the proof of his guilt was the fact that the Swedish government had done nothing on his behalf. On **August 18, 1947**, Soviet Deputy Minister of Foreign Affairs Andrei Vishinsky informed the Swedish government that "Wallenberg is not in the Soviet Union and is unknown to us." In **1952**, Stalin ordered the arrest of prominent Jewish doctors. He planned a show trial in which Wallenberg would be charged as an American agent, a clear contradiction of Vishinsky's claim of Wallenberg's non-existence. After Stalin's death in **March 1953**, the trials were stopped. During **Easter of 1956**, the Swedish Prime Minister, Tage Erlander, met with Nikita Khrushchev. He received the stock answer that Wallenberg was not, and never had been, in the Soviet Union. In **February 1957**, the Soviets changed their story: Deputy Foreign Minister Andrei Gromyko notified the Swedish government that Wallenberg had died in prison on **July 17, 1947**.

Strong evidence that Wallenberg was alive in 1961 came from Nanna Svartz, a physician from Stockholm's Karolinska Hospital, and a friend and personal physician of Wallenberg's mother. During a scientific meeting in Moscow, she met Professor Alexander Myasnikov who confided to her that Wallenberg was in a mental hospital, and he had personally examined him. On a subsequent meeting in **March 1961**, Dr. Myasnikov told Dr. Svartz that he had been summoned by Krushchev, who was furious with him for having spoken about Wallenbeg. Myasnikov now claimed that there must have been a misunderstanding: He knew nothing about Wallenberg, and never wanted to talk about the subject again. In **September 1965**, the Swedish press published the Svartz-Myasnikov affair. The Swedish public and press were outraged by the incident. In **November 1965**, Dr. Myasnikov was interrogated again by the KGB. He died under suspicious circumstances; officially, he died of a heart attack.

In **1964**, the Soviet Union offered to trade Raoul Wallenberg for Soviet spy Wennerstrom, who served a life imprisonment in Sweden. Prime Minister Erlander, with the consent of the Cabinet, turned down the offer. Their argument was that the release of Wennerstrom might encourage the recruitment of other spies, and, furthermore, they did not consider the swap equitable, as Wallenberg was not a spy. In my opinion, these are weak arguments, and Sweden missed a great chance to free Wallenberg. At any rate, that episode leaves little doubt that Wallenberg was alive in 1964. This episode was made public in the Swedish press only in **1991**.

In **1979**, General Kupriyanov, living free in Leningrad, expressed his surprise that Wallenberg had not yet been released, as he knew that he had been sentenced to 25 years in prison in either 1945 or 1946, and thus should have been released no later than 1971. Based on the new evidence, Sweden formally re-opened the Wallenberg case. The Russian reply, reverting to the old broken record: "As already stated on innumerable occasions, Wallenberg died July 1947." In **May 1979**, Kupriyanov was interrogated by the KGB, and asked to officially refute his previous statement. He refused. Shortly thereafter, Mrs. Kupriyanov was sent for by the KGB, and told that her husband had died of a heart attack.

In **July 1990**, Wallenberg's brother, Guy von Dardel, was informed that his request to organize an investigating Commission was approved by the Central Committee of the Communist Party. In **January 1991**, approval of the Commission by the Central Committee was abruptly rescinded. After the changes in the Soviet government in **August 1991**, the new head of the KGB, Vadim Bakatin, proposed that a joint Swedish-Soviet commission be appointed to continue archival research on Raoul Wallenberg.

In **January 2001**, after a 10-year investigation, two reports were released: one from the Russian side, and the other from the Swedish side. The Swedish report established that it was not possible to draw any definite conclusions about the real fate of Raoul Wallenberg. The main conclusion of the Russian report was that Raoul Wallenberg died in 1947, and continuing to search for him was pointless. The Swedish working group established the unfortunate disappearance of a series of key documents from Russian archives, suggesting that efforts had been made to cover the tracks of illegal actions by the Soviet authorities. The Prime Minister of Sweden, Göran Persson, concluded: "We must continue with our efforts to obtain new facts which would throw light on Wallenberg's fate—it cannot be said that Wallenberg is dead."

During the first years after World War II, relatively little was written about Wallenberg, as he disappeared into the horrors of the Gulag. After several decades, interest in Wallenberg grew around the world, and the recognition that he deserved started to be accorded to him. In 1966, Wallenberg was honored at Yad Vashem as one of the Righteous Among the Nations. In 1981, he became an honorary citizen of the United States, in 1985 of Canada, and in 1986 of Israel. Commemorative stamps honoring Wallenberg's wartime heroism were issued in Israel in 1983, in Sweden in 1988, and in the United States in 1997. The plaza in front of the United States Holocaust Museum in Washington is named the Raoul Wallenberg Place; in 2001 a memorial was created in Stockholm in his honor; and there are a number of sites honoring Wallenberg in Budapest. All these are poor compensations for the ineffective efforts to free Wallenberg after World War II.

The five examples that I chose, of people who risked their lives to save others, give us hope that all is not lost in these cynical times, when there is so very little for mankind to believe in. The heroic actions of these people represent the silver lining of the clouds of evil that enveloped the world during Hitler's reign. How sad and unfortunate it is, that, in many cases these beacons of light were dimmed by the obstructionist and shabby treatment these unusual people received from their respective governments and the outside world. Have we learned anything from these past experiences? I am not sure; many atrocities have since been committed, in the face of which the world maintained a shameful silence and inactivity.

7. OTHER GENOCIDES: COMPARISONS WITH THE HOLOCAUST

Naming, defining, and criminalizing genocide: a tribute to Raphael Lemkin

Until the Second World War, the phenomenon of genocide was, in the words of Winston Churchill, a "crime without a name." The man who gave the crime a name, and demanded intervention and remedial action, was an obscure Polish-Jewish jurist, a refugee from Nazi-occupied Europe, named Raphael Lemkin.

Lemkin was born on June 24, 1901, near the town of Bezwodne in eastern Poland, which was part of Imperial Russia at that time. He developed a talent for languages (mastering a dozen or so), a passionate curiosity about cultures, and a lifelong obsession with mass killings in history and the contemporary world. "Why?" was the question that consumed Lemkin. Why did states kill their own citizens on the basis of nationality, ethnicity, or religion? Why did onlookers ignore the killing, or applaud it? Why didn't someone intervene? Why is a man punished when he kills another man, while the killing of a million remains an unpunished crime? Lemkin did not have an answer to these questions. But, already as a young man, he hatched a plan. He would stage an intellectual and activist intervention program. He would write an international law that would punish and prevent racial mass murder.

In pursuit of this goal, Lemkin studied law and earned two law doctorates, from the Universities of Heidelberg (in Germany) and Lemberg (in his native Poland). After completing his studies, he rapidly rose to become a public prosecutor in Warsaw in 1925. He also became involved as a Polish representative to the League of Nations.

In 1933, Lemkin drafted a proposal making the destruction of national, racial, and religious groups an international crime, and presented it at an important international conference in Madrid. But he found little support for his proposals among the delegates.

The outbreak of World War II in 1939, found Lemkin in the heart of the inferno in Poland, with Nazi forces invading from the west, and Soviets from the east. After the Polish armed forces were defeated, Lemkin joined the civilian guerilla underground, and in 1940 fled through Lithuania to Stockholm, leaving his parents behind. They, together with 40 of his relatives, perished at the hands of the Nazis.

Lemkin believed that the United States would be receptive to his ideas, and in a position to actualize them in a way that Europe under the Nazi yoke could not. An epic 14,000-mile journey took him across the Soviet Union by train to Vladivostok, by boat to Japan, and across the Pacific to the United States. Here he was offered, and accepted, a professorship at Duke University in Durham, North Carolina.

Up to his arrival in the United States Lemkin used words like "vandalism" and "barbarity" to describe the atrocities committed. These words did not strike a chord with his legal audiences. He then proceeded to use his linguistic resources, searching for a concise and memorable expression. He invented the word "genocide." It appeared first in print in his book "Axis Rule in Occupied Europe," published in November 1944. In the preface of his book he writes: "The practice of extermination of nations and ethnic groups as carried out by the invaders is called by the author (Lemkin) **genocide**, a term derived from the Greek word *genos* (tribe, race) and the Latin *cide* (to kill), as in homicide or suicide."

Lemkin's 670-page book is considered, by most readers, a rather dull treatise, dealing with a multitude of economic changes brought about in Axis-occupied Europe. Only about 3% of this work is devoted to the subject of genocide. Much more significant in popularizing the concept and the word "genocide," was a series of articles Lemkin wrote for leading journals between 1945 and 1948. During these three years, the big, liberal newspapers of the world made his new word famous.

Lemkin now put everything aside and made the passage of a genocide convention (legal brief) the focus of his life. He wrote and rewrote the text of the convention, and lobbied incessantly to bring it before the United Nations. His single-minded perseverance finally bore fruit. The General Assembly of the United Nations met on December 9, 1948, in Paris, and voted unanimously to adopt the Convention for the Prevention and Punishment of the Crime of Genocide. The convention defined acts of genocide, and stated that genocide is a crime under international law.

The Convention laid down the following definition of genocide:

Genocide means any of the following acts committed with the intent to destroy, in whole or in part, a national, ethnical, racial, or religious group:[70]

1) killing members of the group;

2) causing serious bodily or mental harm to members of the group;

3) deliberately inflicting on the group conditions of life calculated to bring about its physical destruction in whole or in part;

4) imposing measures intended to prevent births within the group;

5) forcibly transferring children of the group to another group.

The adoption of the Convention was, at last, a victory for a tireless crusader who had fought his entire adult life against genocide—the world's most heinous crime. Regrettably, in spite of the passage of the convention, genocide continues to be perpetrated, and goes largely unpunished, to this day. Lemkin was spared this disappointment. He died in 1959 of a heart attack, only a decade after his triumph at the United Nations. He died forgotten, penniless, and alone. Only seven people came to his funeral.

Another term, **Holocaust**, was sometimes used to describe the mass murder of people. The term is derived from the Greek word *holokauston*, meaning a complete (*holos*), and burnt (*kaustos*), sacrificial offering to a god. But unlike genocide, which was precisely defined by the United Nations Convention, holocaust never was. Since the 1950s the use of the term Holocaust has been increasingly restricted to describing the extermination of European Jews by the Nazis. In Hebrew, the word ***shoah***, meaning catastrophe, is used. I have been using both words interchangeably throughout.

On the question of the uniqueness of the Holocaust

When I contemplated writing this chapter, I assumed that, among the other mass murders and genocides, the Holocaust was unique. Indeed, the original title of the chapter was "Why is this genocide—the Jewish Holocaust—different from all other genocides?"

---

[70] The Soviets insisted that political groups should not be included among the category of genocidal victims. This proved to be a regrettable deficiency of the resolution.

As I delved into the literature dealing with other genocides,[71] I realized that the question of uniqueness is complex, controversial, and deadly serious. Consequently, I dropped the original glib and light-hearted title, and chose instead the title of this sub-section for the title of the chapter. As I further immersed myself in the literature of genocides, I became more and more disturbed by the manner in which many writers treated the uniqueness of the Holocaust.

Some authors fiercely argue for the uniqueness of the Holocaust with the energy and ingenuity of theological zealots. At times, the treatment of the Holocaust as a "superior" and unique event takes on the semblance of a competition—a vulgar exercise of comparative victimization that deeply violates reverence for other genocides. To me, it seems abhorrent to engage in passing moral judgment on the comparative suffering of victims, differentiating between mass murders of different kinds, and elevating a particular genocide over others.

For a person who lost family and friends, and was personally involved in the persecution (like myself), it is perhaps psychologically understandable to believe (as I did) that one's own people reached the culmination of uniqueness of destruction. It is a deep emotional reaction to a traumatic shock, as one confronts one's searing perception of the Holocaust's reality. But it is not based on rational deliberations, such as one would expect to guide the conclusions of historians and writers like Yehuda Bauer, Steven Katz, Elie Wiesel and others. Alas, it seems that the emotions of these writers clouded their academic objectivity.

I have now come to the conclusion that the concept of "uniqueness" should be jettisoned in the quest for understanding each genocide, and the Holocaust in particular.

There is one more point I want to make: Some people feel that the tremendous tragedy of the Holocaust is diminished when studied together with other genocides. I believe this is an affront, and a humiliating assault on the dignity of the victims of other genocides.

The attitude of not "diluting" the Holocaust with other genocides unfortunately prevails in many quarters, including the State of Israel. For example, a documentary film on the Armenian genocide was banned from Israeli television lest it detract from the Holocaust.[72] Similarly, an effort by some people in Israel's Education Ministry to include the Armenian and Gypsy genocides into the high-school curriculum was squashed by an oversight committee of Israeli historians.

Having strong emotional ties to Israel, these attitudes were extremely upsetting to me, and I almost gave up on writing this chapter. However, since my main goal in writing about the Holocaust is an attempt to understand it, I believe that a study of other genocides may contribute insight. I therefore enlarged the scope of this chapter, and changed the title accordingly.

---

[71] See: Adam Jones, "Genocide," Rutledge, 2007; Alan Rosenbaum ed., "Is the Holocaust Unique?" Western Press, 1996; Ervin Staub, "The Roots of Evil," Cambridge University Press, 1989.

[72] An additional reason for this action is the Israeli concern that it would damage the relations between Turkey and Israel.

A brief history of genocides up to the 20ᵗʰ century

Antiquity

Genocide—the word is new, the deed is ancient. It has been with the human race since time immemorial, its roots lost in distant millennia, and will remain so unless an "archeology of genocide" can be developed.

Mass murders have been described in the earliest historical records. I shall pick a few examples from the first millennium B.C.

One is Agamemnon's pronouncement of genocide against the Trojans (quoted by Homer about 800 B.C.): "We are not going to leave a single one of them alive, down to the babies in their mother's womb—not even they must live. The whole people must be wiped out of existence and none be left to think of them and shed a tear."

A second set of examples is the God-ordered genocides[73] that appear in the revered Old Testament. The trend starts early in the book of Genesis (6:17–19) where God decides "to destroy all flesh with the exception of Noah and a nucleus of human and animal life." Further on in Samuel 15:2–3 the Lord declares: "I will punish the Amalekites for what they did in opposing the Israelites when they came out of Egypt. Now go and attack Amalek, and utterly destroy all that they have; do not spare them, but kill both man and woman, child and infant, ox and sheep, camel and donkey."

Thus, God appears in the Bible, the sourcebook of three major religions, as a despotic, sadistic, genocidal figure—an exemplary case for being tried (in absentia) by the international tribunal at The Hague for "crimes against humanity." Why should we, then, be surprised that succeeding generations continued to commit this crime?

Most wars of antiquity were accompanied by genocides committed by the victors. For example, the destruction of Melos by Athens during the Peloponnesian War (5ᵗʰ century B.C.), and Rome's siege and eventual razing of Carthage (149–46 B.C.), in which 150,000 Carthaginians (half the population) perished. Among Imperial Rome's other victims were the Jews, who were defeated with the conquest and destruction of Jerusalem and their temple in 70 A.D. Also, the followers of Christ were subjected to savage persecution and mass murder during Roman times.

Medieval times

Ironically, the barbarities committed by the Romans against Christians were duplicated by the Christians themselves during Europe's medieval era (9ᵗʰ–14ᵗʰ century). This period produced the Crusades, religiously sanctified campaigns against non-believers. The first Crusade (1096–99) left a trail of blood and destruction throughout the Rhine and Moselle Valleys, as well as in Prague and Hungary. Entire communities, tens of thousands of people, were wiped out. The Crusades culminated in a wholesale massacre of all non-Christians in Jerusalem.

Further genocides arose on the other side of the world. In the 13ᵗʰ century, a million Mongol horsemen, under the leadership of Ghengis Khan, surged out of the grasslands of

---

[73] For other examples of Old Testament genocides, see Chalk and Jonassohn: "The History and Sociology of Genocide," Yale University Press, 1990.

East Asia, committing mass murder, and laying waste to vast territories, extending to the gates of Western Europe.

The genocide of Native Americans

Genocides of the early modern era date from approximately 1492, the year of the fateful (and fatal) discovery of the Caribbean Indians by Christopher Columbus. It was followed by the Spanish invasion, occupation, and exploitation of most of Latin America, resulting in the worst human disaster: a most violent program of human eradication accompanied with an outbreak of deadly diseases in the native population.

The first territory conquered was the densely populated Caribbean island, Hispaniola (today the Dominican Republic and Haiti). The Spanish massacred the indigenous population outright, and those not killed were worked to death in gold mines. As a consequence, Hispaniola's native population collapsed, declining from about 8 million at the time of the invasion to a scant 20,000 three decades later. African slaves were later introduced to replace the native workforce.

Rumors of the limitless wealth of the Aztec empire lured the Spanish on to Mexico and Central America. Soon thereafter, assaults were launched against the Incas in present-day Peru, Bolivia, and Ecuador. At the time, the Incas constituted the largest empire in the world, but with their leader Atahualpa captured and killed, the empire quickly fell, and the conquistadores had a free hand to burn, maim, murder, and massacre their way through South and Central America. As in Hispaniola, those not killed worked in the silver mines under atrocious conditions; they had a life expectancy of three to four months—about the same as those in slave labor camps in the synthetic rubber manufacturing plants at Auschwitz in the 1940s. Although the extermination campaigns of the Spanish began to wane at the end of the 16th century, wars against the Indians continued for centuries. Examples are the extermination campaigns against the Araucano Indians in Chile, and the Querandí in Argentina, in the 19th century.

In North America, contact between Europeans and indigenous people occurred through whaling crews that put ashore at the end of the 16th century. The whalers were generally welcomed by the indigenous coastal people, as were the Pilgrims who arrived at Plymouth Rock, Massachusetts, in 1608. The survival of these settlers through the harsh first winters was primarily due to the generosity of the Indians. However, the settlers responded to this amity with contempt for the "heathens." As more settlers flooded into the northeastern seaboard, they brought with them diseases against which the natives had no immunity. This wreaked havoc in Indian communities, leading to a catastrophic death toll. The Indian population of what is now the territory of the United States and Canada was reduced from about 10 million in the 1600s, to 200,000 by the 1890s.

Although disease was without doubt the most important factor in the decline of the American Indian population, genocidal measures, in the name of war, contributed to it significantly. The first of these was the Pequot War (1636–37) in present-day Connecticut, in which settlers exterminated hundreds of defenseless natives. This created a precedent for later genocidal wars including, for example, the notorious mass killing at Sand Creek, Colorado, in 1864.

There were other genocidal strategies to eliminate indigenous people. Forced relocation of Indian populations often took the form of genocidal death marches, most famously the "Trail of Tears" of the Cherokee in 1838, which killed 30% of the population en route. These are reminiscent of the death marches of Jews (see pages 43, 51).

After 1850, the US policy was to establish reservations for the Indians. Officially, they were designed to protect indigenous people against the onslaught of white settlers. In practice, it was a landgrab that allowed the majority of Indian territories to be made available to white settlers.[74]

Then there were the so-called "residential schools," in which generations of Indian children were incarcerated after being removed from their homes and families. The goal of these schools was to eradicate the Native American Indian identity. It was driven by the naïve, insensitive, and ethnocentric ideology that Indian culture was inferior, and that in order to "advance," the Indians had to shed their tradition, as they "progressed" up the ladder of civilization. But apart from the forcible transfer of the Indian children, there was much that was genocidal in the operation of these schools: Mortality rates—from starvation, diseases, and torture—came close to the death rate in Nazi concentration camps. For example, a study carried out in Canada in 1907 (the Bryce Report), revealed that, of 3,755 native children in the schools in 1907, about 43% would be expected to die by the end of 1910.

The atrocities committed against the Indians described in this section are horrendous. Yet, many people in the Americas object to labeling them as genocide. I don't want to enter into the polemics of this question. Suffice it to say that the injunction of the UN Genocidal Convention against "forcibly transferring children of a targeted group to another group," as practiced in North America, is enough to qualify this policy as genocide.

Genocides against indigenous people were committed in other parts of the world, mostly in Australia. When, in 1788, the first British convicts were dumped on Australian soil, the indigenous population was about 750,000. The census of 1911 showed that the indigenous population had been reduced to 31,000.

The Atlantic slave trade

Another disputed case of genocide is the Atlantic slave trade, which took place between Africa and the Americas between the 16th and 19th centuries. Most people object to calling slavery a genocide; the most common argument being that it was in the slave owner's interest to keep slaves alive, not to exterminate them. However, despite the incentives to preserve the lives of slaves for labor exploitation, the brutalities, killings, and violation of human rights of this institution, were enormous. I have, therefore, decided to include it. The decision was prompted, in no small measure, by the inauguration of Barack Obama as the first black president of the United States. The event was embraced enthusiastically by most citizens of the United States, including myself. I believe that this enthusiasm was not only due to the caliber and appeal of Obama, but also represented an atonement for the crimes committed in the past—a partial lifting of the stain on the record of human rights in the United States.

From 1500 to 1860, about 12 million Africans were loaded and transported under dreadful conditions to the Americas. Probably twice as many were seized in the African

---

[74] By the mid-1870s, the territories of the reservations amounted to 100 million acres containing 170,000 people. In the mid-1980s, the Native American population in the United States was estimated at 1.5 million, with about half still living in 278 reservations.

interior. For the African slaves, the most difficult period was the early part of the process of enslavement: the long journey through the African interior to the coast, and the dreaded Middle Passage (crossing the Atlantic), which lasted from weeks to months, under terrible conditions. Adding to the physical hardship was the trauma of uprooting, and family disintegration. The conditions on the ship were unbelievably cramped. The slaves were arranged in tightly packed horizontal rows, lying shoulder to shoulder, shackled to each other. Cruelty and arbitrary abuse added to the toll of hunger, thirst and disease. About 2 million (out of 12 million) died during the Atlantic voyage.

On arrival in the Americas, the slaves were branded with hot irons (like cattle), given new names, and started on a period of recovery (called "seasoning"). They learned a new language, were coerced into a new work discipline, and sold at auctions to the highest bidder. The slave owners became the absolute masters of their slaves, treating them as they wished, not being subject to any prohibitions by the law.

The slave trade epitomizes the reduction of human beings to the category of things, albeit valuable things. The driving force behind the slave trade was clearly economic. The importance to the economic development of the country (and the well-being of the slave owners) trumped the immorality of the slave system, and delayed its abolishment for centuries.

Can one compare the slave trade to the Holocaust, two events so disparate in space, time, intentions, duration, and outcome?

As I read about the slave trade, some images flashed through my mind showing analogous cruelties that took place centuries apart. The cramped, inhumane conditions during the Atlantic voyage of the slaves brings to mind the cramped, locked cattle cars, lacking food, water, heat, and circulating air, that were used to transport Jews to the Nazi death camps. Although the train trip lasted only 2–4 days as compared to weeks for the Atlantic voyage, in both cases a significant fraction died in transit. The fate at the end of the trip was, of course, quite different in the two cases. For most Jews it meant death within a few hours of arrival, whereas for the slaves it was a relative relief and recovery.

The second set of images compare the branding of the slaves with a hot iron, with the tattooing of numbers on the forearm of the Jews who were not destined for immediate death in the gas chambers upon arrival in Auschwitz.

There is one basic and striking difference that characterizes the slave trade and the Holocaust. For the first three centuries of the slave trade, only isolated voices condemned slavery. In general, slavery was considered an accepted, ordinary, and customary institution. In contrast, the Nazis were cognizant that they were perpetrating morally condemnable deeds, and knew that their actions would be considered a war crime were they to be defeated.

The Vendée genocide

I shall conclude this section with a relatively little-known mass-killing campaign that occurred at the end of the 18th century in Vendée, a region in western France. It has only recently been conceptualized as a genocide.

In 1789, the French Revolution overthrew the despotic regime of King Louis XVI, and executed him in March 1793. Following the execution, a homegrown Royalist revolt against the Republican central authority sprouted in the Vendées, an isolated and conservative region of France. Led by Royalist officers, the Vendéeans scored early victories, and humiliated the central authority. Fueled by the notorious Terror of the Jacobin faction, the revolutionaries in Paris implemented a classic campaign of genocide. Under generals **Carrier** and **Turreau**, they pledged to purge the Vendéeans. Their aptly named "hellish columns" launched a scorched-earth drive against the rebels. The Committee on Public Safety approved that approach, and declared that the people of Vendée were to be "exterminated to the last."

The resulting slaughter targeted all inhabitants of Vendée. An estimated 150,000 people died in the carnage. A post-genocide census showed the generalized character of the killings, the victims being equally distributed among men, women and children. Only with the collapse of the Committee on Public Safety did the genocide in Vendée wane.

Genocides committed during the past century

The 20th century is often called the century of genocides, in which millions of civilians were murdered. The numbers are staggering: the Nazis killed 6 million Jews, as well as an estimated 0.5 to 1.5 million Roma (Gypsies), 3 million Soviet POWs, 2 million Poles, and hundreds of thousands of undesirables. The Khmer Rouge in Cambodia massacred 2 million of its citizens, the Ottoman Turks killed 1.5 million Armenians, and 2 million people died in the Sudanese conflict. Stalin's Soviet empire killed 20 million Russians, and Mao Zedong's policies resulted in the death of 30 million of its citizens. Another number that shows the extent of random killing in the 20th century is the ratio of military to civilian deaths. In 1900, this ratio was 9:1; by the end of the century it was reversed in spite of the horrendous military losses in the two world wars. I shall discuss now some of the genocides in greater detail. [75]

The Herero genocide

The 20th century started with a relatively little-known genocide perpetrated by the German colonial forces against the **Herero** nation in present-day Namibia, in southwest Africa. This genocide provides a crucial antecedent to Nazi mass murder four decades later.

In 1903, some 5,000 German cattle ranchers, using deception and violent coercion, displaced the native population (the Hereros) from their traditional land holdings. In 1904, the Hereros rose up against the Germans, killing 120 of them. This resistance to colonial domination infuriated **Kaiser Wilhelm II**, who dispatched a hardliner, **General von Trotha**, to crush the uprising.

Von Trotha defeated the Hereros at the **Battle of Hanakai** in **August, 1904**, and issued his notorious *Vernichtungsbefehl* (annihilation order). In it he pledged that "within the German border every Herero, with or without a gun, will be shot." The army then chased the survivors into the bone-dry wasteland of the Kalahari Desert. The annihilation order remained in place for several months, until a domestic outcry led the German Chancellor to rescind it. The Hereros were allowed to return from the Kalahari—starved

---

[75] Among the evils committed that are not discussed, are the killing of the Ibo in Nigeria, the Ashe Indians in Paraguay, the Buddhists in Tibet, the mass killing in Uganda, the Argentinian *desaparecidos*," and the death-squad killings in El Salvador and Guatemala.

skeletons—only to encounter a worse fate: internment camps under lethal conditions. The word *Konzentrationslager* (concentration camp) that later played a pivotal role in the extermination of millions, had been coined. According to official German figures, of 15,000 Hereros, some 7,700 (45%) perished in the camps. Following the Herero war, another tribal nation, **Nama**, also rose up in revolt against the German rule. It was similarly crushed with approximately half the population killed.

The Herero genocide provided the ideas and methods later adapted and developed by the Nazis in carrying out the "Final Solution." Like Nazi mass murder, the Namibian genocide was premised on the idea of *Lebensraum* (living space), *Vernichtungskrieg* (annihilation war), and German racial superiority. It is interesting to note that men who would become top Nazi personalities were related to, or personally involved in, the Herero genocide. **Hermann Göring**, who built the first Nazi concentration camp, was the son of the first governor of colonial Namibia. **Eugen Fisher**, who ran the institute that supported Mengele's medical "research" at Auschwitz, conducted racial studies in the colony. **Ritter von Epp**, godfather of the Nazi Party, and Nazi governor of Bavaria between 1933 and 1945, led German troops against the Herero during the genocide.

Namibia gained independence from South Africa in 1990. In August 2004, the centenary of the Herero uprising, the German minister of development, **Heidemarie Wieczorek-Zeul**, issued a formal statement: "We Germans accept our historic and moral responsibility, and the guilt incurred by Germans at the time.... The atrocities committed would have been termed genocide."

The Armenian massacre

In 1915, as World War I raged, the Turkish government (ruler of the Ottoman Empire) began a systematic extermination of the Armenian population. To understand this horrendous event, we must go back in history.

Armenians are one of the most ancient peoples of the Near East, having lived in the Southern Caucasus region for 3,000 years. They converted to Christianity in the first millennium, and by the 19th century formed the largest non-Muslim population in the Ottoman Empire. As the Ottoman Empire ("the sick man of Europe") began to crumble in the second half of the 19th century, and the Armenians became more educated, prosperous, and nationalistic, Sultan **Abdul Hamid II** viewed them as a threat to Ottoman sovereignty. In **1896** he undertook a massive campaign of killing, in which **200,000 Armenians died**. It was the harbinger of the full-scale genocide that was to occur two decades later.

In 1908, a group of liberal-minded officers, **the Young Turks**, toppled the Ottoman Sultan and started a new, progressive regime. But the Young Turk movement was rapidly taken over by a small group of fanatical nationalists, headed by The Three Pashas: **Enver**, **Jemal**, and **Talaat**. The trio began to plot the extermination of the Armenian population. The events of World War I, in which Turkey allied itself with Germany and Austro-Hungary against Britain, France and Russia, gave the triumvirate the opportunity to implement their genocidal plan. They accused the Armenians of being secessionists, trying to claim Anatolia, the heartland of the projected Pan-Turkish state. The Armenians were also accused of being Russian spies, fifth columnists, and nationalists, bent on destroying Turkish national and political integrity.

The massacre began on **April 24, 1915,** with the arrest of 600 religious and intellectual leaders of the Armenian community in Constantinopole. They were taken at night from their beds, imprisoned, tortured, and killed. Armenians in the Turkish army, already segregated, were all killed. The authorities turned next to destroying the remainder of the Armenian population. Armenians, including women and children, were rounded up and marched from Anatolia toward the wastelands of the Deir-el-Zor Desert in distant Syria. In scenes reminiscent of the Nazi deportations of Jews to concentration camps, local people were depressingly eager to exploit Armenians' misery and dispossession. Most of the deported Armenians were either killed on the way to Syria, or died from hunger and thirst in the desert. Of the approximately 2 million Armenians who resided in Turkey in 1914, it is estimated that one half to two thirds perished in the genocide.

The Allies, cognizant of the massacres, threatened the Young Turks with prosecution after the war for crimes against humanity. However, after Turkey's defeat, the Allies took no action other than to prod the Turkish regime to bring to trial those accused of directing and implementing the Armenian genocide. The inaction of the Allies encouraged the Nazi murderers two decades later, and prompted Hitler to make his famous statement to his followers to assuage their fear of repercussions: "Who still talks today about the annihilation of the Armenians?"

In **April 1919,** the Turkish court indicted over 100 former government officials, but only three relatively minor figures were executed. In **1920,** the nationalistic new leader **Mustafa Kemal,** known as **Ataturk,** "father to the Turks," stopped the trials.[76] Denied formal justice by the Turkish government, a number of Armenian militants took the matter into their own hands and settled the score vigilante style. They assassinated Talaat Pasha in Berlin in 1921, and Jemal Pasha in Tiflis (now Tbilisi) in 1922. Enver Pasha was killed by an Armenian, Bolshevik officer during a revolt in Turkistan in 1922.

Of all the genocides, the Armenian one has most often been compared to the Holocaust. Here are some of the similarities and differences:

1) Both Armenians and Jews were ethno-religious minorities of inferior status in their respective host countries.[77] Both rapidly gained social status and prosperity in the second half of the nineteenth century. This caused resentment within the dominant group (which was struggling economically), and resulted in discrimination and persecution. However, it was only wartime circumstances that enabled the Turks in World War I, and the Nazis in World War II, to implement their policies of genocide;

2) The perpetrators of the Armenian genocide were motivated by a nationalist ideology; the victims were a territorial group that had sought autonomy. In contrast, the Nazis were motivated by racism and anti-Semitism. The Jews were not a territorial group, and did not threaten the integrity of the government;

3) The Armenians could avoid deportation and annihilation by converting to Islam. (It is estimated that 200,000 Armenians converted and were saved.) This option (conversion) was explicitly rejected for the Jews by the Nazis, whose racist ideology insisted on maintaining "the purity of Aryan blood";

---

[76] He re-conquered most of the territory that had been declared, in 1918, an independent Republic of Armenia. What remained of Armenia was incorporated into the Soviet Union.

[77] The Armenians had a historical claim on part of Turkey (Anatolia) as their ancestral territory; the Jews, being an immigrant population, had no such claim in Germany.

4) Nazi genocide was aimed at obliteration of the Jewish race on a global scale, rather than a regional scale as was the case with the Armenians;

5) The killers of the Armenians relied on massacre and starvation, whereas the Nazis developed death camps with an extraordinarily sophisticated technology and organization, not seen before or since;

6) The fraction of the population that was murdered, of Armenians in Turkey and Jews in Nazi-occupied Europe, was about the same (60–70%). However, the absolute number of Jews that perished was about five times larger than the number of Armenians;

7) Lastly, there is a big difference in attitudes taken by government towards the two genocides:

Turkey consistently denies the existence of the Armenian genocide and exerts pressure on other countries to do the same. In recent times, however, these denial efforts of the Turkish government have met with decreasing success. The European Parliament, the United Nations, and the International Association of Genocide Scholars, all acknowledge the Armenian genocide. Regrettably, the United States is still holding out. It considers Turkey an important ally and a linchpin of stability in the Middle East, and, so far, has conformed to Turkey's wishes. Although 45 states individually have acknowledged the Armenian genocide, the US Congress has failed to do so.

The Holocaust, in contrast to the Armenian genocide, is acknowledged by the entire world (with occasional exceptions like Iran's ex-President Ahmadinejad). In many countries, denial of the Holocaust is a punishable offense.

Stalin's terror

During the protracted periods of terror and violence unleashed between **1917**, when the Bolsheviks came to power in Russia, and **1953**, when Joseph Stalin died, millions of people (estimates vary from 20 to 40 million) were executed, died in prison or in the **Gulag**[78] (a vast network of brutal labor camps).

<u>The Ukrainian famine.</u> Here I want to focus on the relatively brief period between **1931** and **1933**, during which a man-made famine **killed 5 million** Ukrainians. Stalin used his enormous power to pursue the industrialization of the Soviet Union, in what was perhaps the greatest social and economic revolution in modern history. To finance the industrialization he needed foreign currency, which he tried to obtain by exporting as much grain as possible. The main source of grain was the Ukraine, the breadbasket of the Soviet Union.

The suffering of the Ukrainian people in this process was of little concern to Stalin. On the contrary, the Ukrainian aspiration for independence and the economically autonomous Ukrainian peasantry were perceived by Stalin as threats to Soviet hegemony that needed to be eradicated by any means, including terror. Stalin's twin goal was to lay his hands on Ukrainian grain, and quash Ukrainian nationalism and culture. The fulfillment of the first goal produced a massive famine, which broke the spirit of the Ukrainian people, and proved to be an effective tool to break the renaissance of Ukrainian culture.

---

[78] **Gulag** is an acronym for the Russian term *Glavnoe upravlenie lagerei* (Main camp administration).

Stalin started in **1930** with a purge of Ukrainian academics and political leaders, and initiated a terror campaign against the peasantry. He introduced the forced collectivization of farms into state-controlled entities, called ***kolkhoz***. This simplified the task of the authorities to requisition the grain. The Soviet planners levied and collected an over-demanding amount of grain that left insufficient amounts to feed the local population. This inexorably led to a man-made **famine in 1931**, which grew worse in **1932** and **1933**. The twin evil of forced collectivization and grain seizure caused massive starvation and deaths. Stalin's order to prevent peasants from fleeing the famine-stricken countryside effectively decreed the death sentence on millions who were starving. Of the Ukrainian population of 25 million, about **5 million** of the rural population, and **600,000** in the urban area of the Ukraine, **died** of starvation or related medical problems.

It should be added that the attitude of the Soviets toward the peasants contributed to their brutal treatment. The Soviets held the peasants in thinly disguised contempt. They considered them backward, stubborn, and deaf to argument—an impediment to progress. Among them, the ***kulaks*** (the richer peasants) aroused the greatest Bolshevik hatred. In January 1930, Stalin approved the liquidation of the kulaks as a class. Hundreds of thousands were sent to the Gulag, and 2 million into internal exile to distant corners of the Soviet Union.

And what did Stalin accomplish through forced collectivization and the relentless struggle for industrialization? Even his enemies conceded that he created a powerful industrial state. However, Stalinism ultimately left the Soviet Union with an inefficient system of production. The central planning process distorted production, as industries strove to meet production targets rather than produce what the economy needed.[79]

There is a great difference between the Ukrainian famine and the Holocaust. The deaths due to the famine were not the intent, but rather the consequence, of Stalin's ruthless economic policy. Stalin intended that after the famine there should still be Ukrainians, but no Ukrainianism. Hitler intended that after Auschwitz, there would be neither Jews nor Judaism.

Terror after the famine. In **February 1934**, the Leningrad party chief **Sergei Kirov** was assassinated. Stalin was officially mourning and was a pallbearer at Kirov's funeral, yet the assassination had been secretly engineered by him, who saw in Kirov a popular, upcoming star and competitor. It was a typical Machiavellian ploy. Stalin used the assassination to rid himself of his perceived enemies, labeling them "terrorists," "saboteurs," and "provocateurs." Hundreds of thousands were arrested. Random terror reigned without even

---

[79] This brings to mind an experience during a trip to communist Czechoslovakia in 1960. Driving from Bratislava to Prague, I picked up a hitchhiker who insisted that I take a road that on the map looked considerably longer than the one I had intended to take. He explained: "I was in charge of building the shorter road. We were paid by the mile, with an extra bonus for finishing before the targeted timeline. We hurried and skimped on the cement. As a consequence, the road is now full of potholes."

Another example showing the detrimental effects of the quest for meeting targets involved the production of steel plates. The target in Czechoslovakia was more easily met by producing thicker, half-inch plates. As a result, no thin plates, necessary for the car industry Škoda, were available, and car production for that year lagged. The following year the authorities changed the target and stipulated the fraction of steel plates with a given thickness that needed to be produced. The engineers realized that by not adding silicon (to strengthen the steel), they could roll out steel faster. The result, of course, was a much inferior product. This could not happen in an economy that fosters competition, rather than relying on central planning and arbitrary targets to be met.

a pretense of a rule of law. These excesses were followed by the **Great Purge of 1937–38,** in which 1.5 million people were arrested and half of them executed. The purge displays, better than any other event, the ruthless megalomania and intense paranoia of Stalin.[80] The purge started with the prosecution, conviction, and execution of the old party member **Nikolai Bukharin,** who had questioned Stalin's crash collectivization and crash industrialization. Many of the old Bolshevik guards were convicted "en bloc" during "show trials," and most were executed. Even the NKDV (the precursor to the KGB) was purged, and its leader, **Yezhov,** executed.

During the war years, the excesses were duplicated in occupied Poland and subsequently in the Baltic states, which the Soviets occupied in 1940. The destruction of national minorities was high on Stalin's list of priorities. During the war in 1943–44, under the trumped-up accusation of collaborating with the Germans, the Chechens, Balkars, Tatars, Ingushi, Karachai, Kalmyks, and Meshketians were deported, and their cultures assaulted and repressed.

In the final months of his life, Stalin directed his paranoia against a minority that so far had largely escaped tragedy: Soviet Jews. Those arrested in the so-called "**Doctors' Plot**" in **January 1953** were mostly Jewish. Their fate was anticipated to be similar to that of the victims of the Great Purge. But they were saved by the death of the dictator in **March 1953.**

Is it genocide? To apply the term genocide to the atrocities committed by the Soviets, one is hampered in some cases by the deficiency of the Genocide Convention to include political groups as genocide victims. Nevertheless, a plausible case can be made that the Soviets violated the Genocide Convention for "acts committed with intent to destroy in whole or in part, a national, ethnic, racial, or religious group." In the case of the Ukrainian famine, the expulsion of vast numbers of kulaks to marginal territories of the Gulag, the grain seizure at the height of the famine, the refusal to distribute grain to starving peasants while preventing them from fleeing the famine-stricken countryside, is considered by most historians to be genocidal.

The genocide of the Roma (Gypsies) [81]

The Nazi genocide committed against the Roma paralleled, more than that of any other group, the attempted extermination of European Jews. The Roma and the Jews were the only people killed for the "crime" of existing. But, unlike the Jews, whom the Nazis passionately hated and considered a threat, the Roma were considered an irritant, an antisocial element of society to be gotten rid of. In contrast to the Jews, the Roma were hardly ever mentioned in the inflammatory speeches of Hitler or the attacks by Goebbels. Nevertheless, the fate of both peoples was equally grim.

---

[80] A little-known story showing Stalin's paranoia was told to me in Israel by Dr. Zondek (with whose nephew I roomed in Haifa in the early 1940s). Around 1930, Stalin wanted a thorough physical check-up. Not trusting his own doctors, he summoned Dr. Zondek, who was considered the best internist in Berlin, to examine him. Zondek arrived in Moscow and was confronted with 10 look-alike Stalins that he had to examine, and write a report about. He never found out which of them was Stalin.

[81] Because of the derogatory connotation of the word Gypsy, they are nowadays referred to as Roma. They include many different tribes (e.g., the Sinti in Germany, the Kalderash, the Lovari, the Rudari, etc.) that speak different dialects of the Romani language and share many cultural characteristics.

The horrible Nazi phrase **"lives undeserving of life"** was coined with reference to the Roma, shortly after Hitler's ascent to power. In 1935, marriages between Roma and German Aryans (as between Jews and Aryans) were outlawed. This is ironic, because the Roma originated in Northern India, the cradle of Aryans. The Roma language has roots in Sanskrit and Hindi. The word Roma is derived from *Rom* (man, in Hindi). At the beginning of the 11th century, India came under attack by the Afghan general **Mahmud Ghazni**, who was trying to push Islam eastwards into India. As a result, many Roma emigrated in the 13th century, through Afghanistan to Turkey, Greece, and eventually to all parts of Europe. Because of their dark skin, different (nomadic) way of life, and unfamiliar customs, they were shunned and persecuted throughout the centuries.

In July **1936**, two years prior to the first mass roundup of Jews, hundreds of Roma men were dispatched to the Dachau concentration camp. In **1938**, the first reference to a total solution of the Roma "problem" appeared in a Nazi announcement; 1,000 Roma men were deported to concentration camps. At the end of **1941**, 250 Roma children at Buchenwald became test subjects for the killing efficiency of the infamous Zyklon B cyanide, later used to exterminate Jews en masse.

In **December 1942**, a large number of Roma were deported to Auschwitz-Birkenau, where 20,000 of the 23,000 German and Austrian Roma perished. But the German and Austrian Roma formed an insignificant proportion of European Roma. Germany had, in 1938, a Gypsy population of only 16,000, of which less than 10% survived. The vast majority of Roma lived outside Germany, mainly in Poland, Yugoslavia, Hungary, Slovakia, and Ukraine. It is these regions that had the greatest number of victims. In the Ukraine alone, the German Einsatzgruppen murdered 100,000 Roma.

The estimated number of Roma killed in Nazi-occupied areas varies widely, ranging from 0.5 million to 1.5 million.[82] The reason for this uncertainty is that Roma, being mostly nomads, were rarely included in the census data of the country they lived in. But it is safe to assume that the fraction of the European Roma population murdered roughly equals that of the European Jews. Yet, whereas the Holocaust has been on the conscience of the world since the end of World War II, the Roma murders have been little more than a footnote in the history of Nazi violence. One reason for this is that the absolute number of Roma killed is about five times smaller than that of Jews. In addition, most Roma, before and after the war, were illiterate, and thus unable to match the outpouring of academic analyses of the Jewish Holocaust by Jewish writers and scholars. Finally, and sadly, Roma continue to be marginalized and stigmatized by European societies.[83] To add insult to injury, no assistance was given to Roma survivors, in contrast to the reparation given to Jewish survivors.

---

[82] The figure of 250,000 Gypsy deaths, displayed at the US Holocaust Memorial Museum, is considered by most scholars an underestimate. Several scholars accuse the museum of downplaying all genocides in order to accentuate the uniqueness of the Holocaust.

[83] I have fond memories of Roma from my childhood summers spent in Bolešov (Slovakia), where I played and mingled with them. I also learned a smattering of Roma words, which on one occasion came in handy. In the 1950s I dined with a friend in a Hungarian restaurant in New York City. A Roma woman approached us to read our fortune. I told her *"Nane love"* (in Roma: "I have no money"). But she insisted on reading my palms. When she finished and I refused to pay, claiming to have told her that I had no money, she called the manager. It turned out that she was Hungarian, dressed as a Roma and hadn't understood my Roma remark. In conclusion: *Idyuka, vadyuka, indyuk pindyuk, sakva rakva, jugla, jug. Dyorum, porum lisha pore, nane love, sacre lere, sacra rakva, juglo jug.* (Sorry for any misspelling: my Roma is a bit rusty after 70 years.)

Genocide in Cambodia

Between **1975** and **1979**, close to **two million people**, about a quarter of the Cambodian population, were **killed** by the **Khmer Rouge**, the ruling party during that period in Cambodia. I shall start with a brief history of Cambodia, followed by a discussion of how a relatively small, marginal, communist group—the Khmer Rouge—rose to power, and how its ideology led to genocide. I then discuss the fall from power of the Khmer Rouge and, in the aftermath, the long-delayed quest for justice.

A brief historical background. Cambodia once was a great and powerful nation. The **Angkor Empire** in the **9ᵗʰ to 14ᵗʰ century** was rich, and had conquered vast territories that belong today to its neighbors. A symbol of this glory is Angkor Wat, a magnificent complex of temples and other buildings. It is nostalgically remembered by Cambodians of today, and immortalized by featuring the three towers of Angkor Wat on the national flag.

Cambodia was a country with deep class divisions. It was ruled by a king who had absolute and unquestionable power, and was revered by the population. Absolutism often breeds violence, and this was the case in Cambodia. During the Angkor Empire, people convicted of serious crimes were buried alive; lesser crimes were punished by mutilation (e.g., amputation of limbs). The majority of the population of the Angkor Empire were slaves without any rights whatsoever. The peasantry was ruled by an aristocracy that controlled the land and taxed them heavily.

From time to time, over the centuries, Cambodia was ruled, often brutally, by outsiders. In the **first half of the 19ᵗʰ century**, the **Vietnamese**, the historic enemy of Cambodia, occupied the country. They ruled ruthlessly, and rendered the royal family powerless. In **1863**, Cambodia fell under the sway of the **French**, who wanted a buffer zone between their Vietnamese territory and British-controlled Burma. The Cambodians accepted the French protectorate since it freed them from Vietnamese domination. The price they paid was that their **King Norodom**, became little more than a French vassal. As elsewhere in their empire, France fueled nationalist aspirations in Cambodia by economic exploitation and political subordination. In **1954**, the French lost their Vietnamese territory as well as their protectorate of Cambodia, which became independent, and was ruled by **Prince Sihanouk** (grandson of King Norodom) until he was overthrown in **1970**.

From the above description we see that many institutions and attitudes were deeply rooted in the history and tradition of Cambodia. They include absolutism of the ruler, violence, forced labor (slavery), hatred of minorities (particularly Vietnamese), and nostalgia for their past glory. They all played a role in forming the ideology of the Khmer Rouge, and contributed to the perpetration of genocide under their rule.

The ideology of the Khmer Rouge. The French inadvertently contributed to the formation of the ideology of the Khmer Rouge through scholarships they awarded to Cambodians to study in Paris. All future Khmer Rouge leaders, including Saloth Sar (better known as **Pol Pot**), formed their ideology during their studies in Paris. In the 1950s, the French capital provided the richest environment for revolutionary ferment anywhere in the world. The French Communist Party, which had led the resistance to Nazi occupation, emerged from World War II with a powerful presence in mainstream politics. The party was in its high Stalinist phase at the time, and exerted a great influence on the Cambodians.

Like many communist revolutionaries of the 20th century, notably those in the USSR and China, the future Khmer Rouge leaders developed a visceral hatred of the revolution's enemies. These included the bourgeoisie, professionals, "imperialist stooges" (collaborators with the United States), the religious (Buddhist monks), and the educated class—in effect it included essentially all urbanites. They associated the urban environment with corruption, exploitation, and Western decadence. The Khmer Rouge wanted to establish a utopia of classless peasants. They envisaged a peasant society in which life was simple, ascetic, and communal. (This reminds me of the kibbutz movement in Israel without, of course, the coercion and violence that existed in Cambodia.) The Khmer Rouge regarded the peasants as the guardians of the true and pure Cambodia. Technology was distrusted and to be destroyed, except for some factories producing goods for agriculture. Never mind that in **Mao Zedong's "Great Leap Forward"** an almost identical mentality had produced absurd and catastrophic outcomes. They believed that with proper guidance, people could accomplish anything.

Ironically, despite their idealization of the peasants, no senior Khmer Rouge leader was of peasant origin. Virtually all were city-bred intellectuals. Thus, the genocide they later inflicted on intellectuals and the urban population was profoundly hypocritical. In the final analysis, the Khmer Rouge leaders were petty-bourgeoisie radicals overcome by peasant romanticism.

The Khmer Rouge ideology embraced purity, discipline, and militarism. Like the Nazis, the Khmer Rouge expressed their racism through an obsessive emphasis on racial purity. Self-discipline was a critical component of a totalitarian Puritanism with an aberrant ideology of chaste sexuality. Any sex before marriage was punishable by death. Militarism was the defining feature of Khmer Rouge rule. All actions, be it the forced evacuation of cities, the implementation of economic programs, or the mass murders, were executed with military discipline and a heavy reliance on the armed forces rather than civilian administrators.

Xenophobia and messianic nationalism, harking back to the Angkor Empire, also played an important role in the Khmer Rouge ideology. The Khmer Rouge perceived the Vietnamese, their eternal enemy, as a deadly threat to their survival. This led to repeated Cambodian incursions into Vietnamese territories in 1977 and 1978. These incursions proved to be their undoing: They sparked the Vietnamese invasion that overthrew the Khmer Rouge regime.

The rise to power of the Khmer Rouge. Many Cambodians, returning in the 1950s from their studies in Paris, flocked to the Indochinese Communist Party, which combined communist movements in Vietnam and Cambodia. Following the Vietnamese victory over the French in 1954, the Vietnamese (as well as the French) withdrew from Cambodia. This split the Cambodian membership of the Party. One thousand of its members transferred to Vietnam, leaving another 1,000 behind in Cambodia, including Pol Pot and the future core leadership of the Khmer Rouge. (Note the small number of Party members at the time.)

In 1966, Sihanouk, the ruler of Cambodia at the time, implemented a campaign of government murder and repression against the communists. As a result, Pol Pot's new Cambodian leadership abandoned political activity in the city for armed struggle in the remote countryside, where the Khmer Rouge could nurture its revolution beyond Sihanouk's reach.

How did Cambodian communists, politically weak and marginalized throughout the 1960s, manage to emerge as the leading party and seize power in 1975? This success can be ascribed to three confluent events: the help and guidance obtained from the Vietnamese communists, the disastrous policies of the United States, and the blunders made by successive Cambodian governments.

After the US invasion of South Vietnam in 1965, conflict spilled into Cambodia. Supplies, from the North Vietnamese government to the guerillas in the South, moved down the Ho Chi Minh Trail, cutting through eastern Cambodia. North Vietnamese forces ultimately controlled significant expanses of border areas. In the early 1970s, the North Vietnamese forces inflicted substantial damage on Cambodian government forces. This provided a powerful boost for the Khmer Rouge. In addition, the Khmer Rouge obtained vital training from the Vietnamese communists.

The North Vietnamese occupation of Cambodian border areas provoked two major responses from the United States, both contributing to the rise of the Khmer Rouge. First, in **1970**, the United States supported a **coup** against Prince Sihanouk by **General Lon Nol**, Sihanouk's former right-hand man and head of the armed forces. Lon Nol duly repaid his benefactors by inviting the United States and South Vietnam to launch an invasion of Cambodia, which lasted for three months. As a result of this move, which was strongly resented by most Cambodians, many joined the antigovernment forces of the Khmer Rouge. In addition, Sihanouk's ouster had a great psychological impact. It prepared Cambodians to replace the authority figure of the king with the new leadership of the Khmer Rouge.

The second US response, which overshadowed the first, was the escalation of the **US bombing of North Vietnamese sanctuaries in Cambodia** in 1969. Between 1969 and 1973, more than half a million tons of munitions (three times as much as the United States had unleashed on Japan during the entire World War II) descended on rural Cambodia. The devastation caused by these saturation bombings was horrendous. Hundreds of thousands of Cambodians were killed, and many more made homeless. Moreover, the assault effectively destroyed the agricultural base of Cambodia. As a consequence, malnutrition and starvation were rampant. Terrified and filled with hatred against the United States and their own government, the Cambodians joined the Khmer Rouge in droves and swelled its ranks, making them a formidable political force.

The genocidal rule of the Khmer Rouge, 1975–1979. By 1975, Pol Pot's forces had grown to over 700,000. They were now ready to confront the government. In April 1975, the Khmer Rouge launched a successful assault on Phnom Penh, the capital and seat of Lon Nol's government of Cambodia. Within hours of arriving at the capital, they were rounding up its 2 million residents for deportation to the countryside. Those who refused to leave were shot on the spot. With such vast number of people leaving at once, congestion was tremendous, and lack of food, water, and medical care, caused many deaths. During the Khmer Rouge regime (1975–1979), Phnom Penh and other cities remained ghost towns. This strategy of annihilating the centers of social and cultural life was pursued throughout history: Whenever a government wanted to destroy a group of people, it annihilated their cities. Classic examples are the Roman obliteration of Carthage, the Nazi assault on Stalingrad in 1943, the Syrian destruction of the rebellious city of Hama in 1982, and the Russian obliteration of Grozny in Chechnya in 1995.

The forced expulsion of the population of the cities marks the beginning of the full expression of Khmer Rouge's genocidal ideology. There were three genocidal institutions: the forced labor system, the mass executions, and the internal purges.[84]

Forced labor imposed an inhuman work regime. People rose before dawn, and were allowed to rest only after dark. Food was distributed exclusively in communal kitchens, and there was never enough. Extra supplies could not be bought, as money and markets were outlawed. Nor could the people supplement rations with produce from their own plots, since all private property was banned. Those who fell sick from disease, overwork, or malnutrition, had little hope of treatment. Medicine was reserved for the Khmer Rouge faithful.

Mass executions were conducted against ethnic minorities, the religious, and "class enemies," such as intellectuals, professionals, teachers, doctors, and the wealthy. People were wantonly murdered. They were shot for knowing a foreign language, wearing glasses, or laughing.

Ethnic minorities, constituting about 15% of the population, were targeted for extermination. Local Vietnamese were persecuted most virulently: Essentially 100% of ethnic Vietnamese perished under the Khmer Rouge. Only half of the Chinese population, which numbered about 400,000 at the outset of Khmer Rouge rule, survived to see its end. The Thai minority of 20,000 was reduced to about 8,000. Of the 1,800 Laotian families only 800 survived. Cambodian Buddhists suffered immensely. Religious sites were emptied and often obliterated. Of the 60,000 Buddhist monks, only 3,000 were found alive after the Khmer Rouge reign.

Violent internal purges became a feature of the Khmer Rouge policy. In 1976 Pol Pot decreed: "A sickness exists inside the party. We need to identify and eliminate the ugly microbes." The language was strikingly similar to that employed by Stalin and his henchmen against party members in the 1930s (see page 190).

Two major regional purges occurred in 1977–1978. Both were carried out by **Ta Mok**, nicknamed The Butcher. The first in the northwestern zone, and the second in the eastern zone bordering Vietnam. Tens of thousands of victims of these purges passed through centers designed for interrogation, torture, and execution. The most notorious center was **Tuol Sleng** in the capital, codenamed S-21, where an estimated 14,000 prisoners died. The commandant of S-21 was **Kaing Guek Eav**, who was the first to be tried by the Courts of Cambodia (see next section). Several leaders of the Khmer Rouge escaped the purges by leaving the country, mostly to Vietnam. Among them was **Hun Sen,** who is heading the present-day government of Cambodia.

The genocide in Cambodia claimed hundreds of thousands of lives. Additionally, diseases and famine swelled the death toll to an estimated 1.7 to 1.9 million out of a population of 8 million (21–24%) at the start of the Khmer Rouge rule.

---

[84] The excesses and atrocities are vividly described by the Chinese Cambodian author Loung Ung in her book "First They Killed My Father: A Daughter of Cambodia Remembers," Mainstream Publishing, 2001; and also in the film "The Killing Fields of Cambodia," directed by Roland Yoffé, 1985.

<u>The end of the Khmer Rouge rule and its aftermath.</u> As in Mao's China and Stalin's USSR, the purges fed on themselves and weakened the Khmer Rouge, and eventually undermined the capacity of the revolution to resist its enemies, the main one being Vietnam. The desire to reclaim Southern Vietnam, which once belonged to Cambodia, fueled the fanatism of the Khmer Rouge. It led, in 1977 and 1978, to repeated Khmer Rouge incursions into Vietnamese territories. These eventually sparked the **Vietnamese invasion** that overthrew the weakened Khmer Rouge regime.

In **December 1978**, 150,000 **Vietnamese** soldiers crossed the Cambodian border, **seized** its capital **Phnom Penh**, and occupied Cambodia for the next decade. Vietnam set up a puppet government composed mainly of recent defectors from the Khmer Rouge. This new socialist government was relatively benign, but it had a hard time organizing a reconstruction program. Pol Pot's policies had ruined the economy; all the competent professionals had been killed.

The Khmer Rouge leadership fled across the border to Thailand, where they formed a coalition with Prince Sihanouk. The coalition functioned as a government in exile. Although Sihanouk served as head of the coalition, he was a mere figurehead, de facto under house arrest:[85] the power lay in the hands of the Khmer Rouge. The coalition fought unsuccessfully for the ensuing decade and a half to return to power.

In a bizarre turn of events—a most depressing episode of diplomacy—the United States moved from branding the Khmer Rouge as communist monsters to embracing them as legitimate Cambodian representatives. The United States led a successful push to grant Cambodia's seat in the United Nations to the anti-Vietnamese coalition dominated by the Khmer Rouge. The old principle was invoked: The enemy of my enemy is my friend. In this case Cambodia, the enemy of the US' enemy North Vietnam, is the US' friend, regardless of its horrible past. Thus, one witnessed the anomalous and sad sight of **Washington backing the genocidal communists**.

In 1989, under international pressure, Vietnam withdrew its army from Cambodia. Cambodia's name was officially restored (under the Khmer Rouge it was called Democratic Kampuchea); the state religion, Buddhism, was restored; and it was once again legal to own land. In **October 1991**, the **Comprehensive Political Settlement** of the Cambodian conflict was signed in Paris. Elections were to be held but were fraught with difficulties and postponed from year to year.

Finally, in **May 1993**, elections took place. Voters gave a plurality to **Prince Ranariddh**, son of Sihanouk. This result displeased Hun Sen, the Khmer Rouge ex-leader and "great survivor of Cambodian politics." He strong-armed Ranariddh to accept a coalition government. **In 1997, Hun Sen launched a coup-d'état**, re-establishing himself as the supreme authority. The absolutist tradition in Cambodian politics was reaffirming itself once again.

<u>A long-delayed quest for justice.</u> Amidst the political turmoil following the overthrow of the Khmer Rouge, the campaign to bring surviving Khmer Rouge leaders to justice proceeded very slowly and haltingly. The project was marginalized through the 1980s by

---

[85] Sihanouk's actions had always been pragmatic and opportunistic. He had initially fought the communists, but when they became powerful, he supported them. His actions were not principled; the aim of his vacillating policies was to maintain or regain an important role in politics.

US and Chinese opposition. The death of Pol Pot in 1998 (of natural causes), and of other leading members of the Khmer Rouge, further blunted the impetus to proceed, as did wrangling between the United Nations and the Cambodian government about the process. In June 2003, the two parties came to an agreement. The Cambodian tribunal was to include international jurists, lawyers and judges who were to play key roles in the proceedings. After further delay, the tribunal, known as the **Extraordinary Chambers in the Courts of Cambodia**, was set up in **May 2006**. It is presided over by 17 Cambodian judges and 13 foreign judges, with the cases presented by two prosecutors, one Cambodian and one foreign. It took an unbelievably long time—30 years!—after the fall of the Khmer Rouge, to establish and convene a special court to try those most responsible for the crimes of that murderous regime.

The judges decided to limit the trial to just five people: the four most senior surviving members of the Khmer Rouge[86] plus a less senior 66-year-old man, named Kaing Guek Eav, also known as comrade Duch (pronounced Doik) who was the commandant of the Tuol Sleng prison in Phnom Penh, also known as S-21.

Duch was the first to be tried because he was the only one of the five accused who was remorseful of his past actions and willing to tell all. He has, in fact, testified in the trials of the other four defendants. As prison commander, Duch supervised the interrogation, torture, and killing of virtually all of the 14,000 inmates of S-21. He was charged with torture, murder, and other inhuman acts.

A few words about comrade Duch.[87] He was born in 1942, and attended the prestigious Lycée Sisowath in Phnom Penh followed by the Institut de Pédagogie, which was directed by Son-Sen, a member of the Cambodian Communist Party's Central Committee, who appointed Duch to be head of S-21.

After the fall of the Khmer Rouge, Duch moved to a village near the Thai border where he was living for years under an assumed name. In 1999, Duch was discovered by the Irish photographer Nick Dunlop. Duch illustrates the often-noted capacity of ordinary even well-meaning men to serve as obedient functionaries of unspeakable atrocities. He had been a devoted revolutionary and a firm believer in the utter goodness of the revolution, and the utter evil of anybody who opposed it. He has since become a born-again Christian, remorseful and ready to atone for his past actions.

Comrade Duch (Kaing Guek Eav) was convicted of war crimes against humanity in July 2010. He is serving a sentence of life imprisonment.

Of the other four ex-leaders of the Khmer Rouge mentioned in footnote 86, two (Ieng Surth and Ieng Thirith) have died. The other two are serving life imprisonment for crimes against humanity and are now being tried for genocide.

---

[86] They were: Nuon Chea, b. 1925 (Pol Pot's right-hand man and deputy secretary of the Central Committee); Khieu Samphan, b. 1931 (Head of State after 1975; he represented the Khmer Rouge in the Paris peace negotiations in 1991); Ieng Sary (Deputy Prime Minister and Minister of Foreign Affairs between 1975 and

Will there be more trials after these? Two more cases have been brought forward: Meas Muth, a high ranking navy commander in the Revolutionary Army of Kampuchea, and Im Chaem, a former district commander. This has resulted in much controversy, with the Cambodian government opposing further prosecutions.

Prime Minister Hun Sen—himself a former Khmer Rouge commander—warned that war and chaos could ensue if the Khmer Rouge Tribunal continued to pursue additional cases. Although this granting of an effective amnesty to a large number of perpetrators of atrocities is being criticized by several human rights groups, an imperfect tribunal, after 30 years of postponements, is far better than no tribunal at all.

Genocides in Bosnia and Kosovo

The dissolution of Yugoslavia in the early 1990s brought genocide back to Europe after nearly half a century. To begin to understand what happened, it is necessary to discuss the creation of Yugoslavia after World War I, and its disintegration 63 years later.

A brief history of Yugoslavia. Yugoslavia, the federation of southern (*yugo*) Slavs, was cobbled together from the disintegrated Austrio-Hungarian and Ottoman Empires after World War I. It was a fragile federation of disparate religions and ethnic entities, prone to violence in time of crisis. A crisis came during World War II when Germany occupied and partitioned Yugoslavia.[88] The Germans were welcomed in Croatia, which was a pro-Nazi state led by **Ante Pavelić** and his **fascist**

Map showing the regions of the former Yugoslavia (now independent states).

Ustasha Party. Serbs and Jews were the targets of widespread massacres; hundreds of thousands of Croatian Serbs were rounded up by the Ustasha and slaughtered. The revenge for this action came decades later.

Muslims in Bosnia also collaborated with the Nazis, earning them the enduring hatred of the Serb people, and sowing the seeds for the genocide committed against Bosnian Muslims five decades later.

The Serbs opposed the German occupation and supported the fierce partisan resistance movement led by Josip Broz, better known as **Tito**. In the later stages of the war, the partisans seized power and captured the capital, Belgrade. After the war, Tito reunited Yugoslavia, merging together Slovenia, Croatia, Bosnia, Serbia, Montenegro, Macedonia, and two autonomous provinces, Kosovo and Volvodina. (See map.)

---

[88] This happened at the time we escaped from Slovakia, in April 1941. Passing through Romania, we saw trainloads of wounded German soldiers, going from Yugoslavia back to Germany.

Tito, a relatively liberal communist, was a strong leader who maintained ties with both the Soviet Union and the United States, playing one superpower against the other, while obtaining financial assistance from both. Tito, a Croatian, worked hard to ensure that no ethnic group dominated the federation. He banned political mobilization along ethnic lines, and was successful in diffusing ethnic tensions and generating a Yugoslav identity—no mean feat.

When strong man **Tito died in May 1980**, his multinational federation began to unravel. A weak collective leadership faltered when confronted by an emergent generation of ethnonationalist politicians, most prominently **Slobodan Milosevic** in Serbia and **Franjo Tudjman** in Croatia. Both started to harass and discriminate against minorities in their territories: Croats in Serbia and Serbs in Croatia.

The disintegration of Yugoslavia; Serbian bid for supremacy. Milosevic sowed the seed of genocide in **April 1987**, on a visit to the restive Albanian-dominated province of **Kosovo**. He was dispatched by the Serb **President Ivan Stambolic** to calm the Serb minority in the region. Instead, he gave an inflammatory, nationalistic speech in which he pledged that the Kosovo Albanians "shall no longer dare to beat you." The enthusiastic reception that Milosevic received from his Serb compatriots propelled his political career. In **September 1987**, he shunted aside his mentor, Stambolic, and **took over the presidency**. In 1989, the Serbs initiated a repressive drive in Kosovo that ended its autonomy. It was the key event that triggered Yugoslavia's disintegration. After the Kosovo crackdown, no ethnic group could feel safe from Serbian aggression.

In 1991–1992 Yugoslavia exploded. In **June 1991, Macedonia, Slovenia and Croatia** declared themselves independent. There was no Serb resistance to Macedonia's independence. But the Serbs tried to resist the secession of Slovenia by sending their troops to fight. They failed to subdue the separatists, and withdrew after only 10 days of fighting.

Croatia was a different matter, as it had (in contrast to Slovenia) a sizable (12%) Serbian population and it was, for the Serbs, worthwhile to fight against Croatian independence. In **December 1991**, after several months of fighting, which included the merciless **bombardment** of the historic Croatian port of **Dubrovnik**, the Serbs in the Krajina region (a narrow strip of land adjacent to the Dalmatian Coast), reinforced by the Yugoslav army, started to cleanse the region of their Croat neighbors.[89] They looted, tortured, raped, and murdered those who remained. Terror reigned; it lay at the heart of ethnic cleansing, both here and, later, in Bosnia and Kosovo. While these Serb atrocities were taking place, the Croat government, led by fascist President Tudjman, was passing discriminatory laws targeting Serbs. The US government, under President George H.W. Bush, recognized independent Croatia, but was unwilling to intervene militarily in the war. As I shall describe later, in 1995 the Croats recaptured Krajina and behaved no less brutally than the Serbs had done before.

Bosnia-Herzegovina (sometimes called just Bosnia) faced the biggest problem, being divided among Bosnian Serbs (Orthodox Catholic Christians), Bosnian Muslims (Sunni), and Bosnian Croats (Roman Catholic Christians). The multiethnic government of Bosnia under the leadership of **Alija Izetbegovic,** also craved independence, but faced a formidable problem. It realized that an attempt to secede from Yugoslavia would surely

---

[89] The expression "ethnic cleansing" was coined in this campaign, and entered the political vocabulary.

mean war with the Bosnian Serbs, while remaining within the federation meant enduring Serbian domination. In **February 1992**, the government of Bosnia-Herzegovina decided to **declare its independence** from Yugoslavia. It was recognized by the United States and the European Union the following month.

The Bosnian Serbs reacted by declaring independence from Bosnia and, under the leadership of **Radovan Karadzic**, set up their own **Serb Republic** (*Republika Srpska*). They were prepared to achieve their goal of dominating Bosnia by isolating ethnic groups, and, if necessary, eliminating them.

War and genocide in Bosnia. Bosnia now became the most brutal battlefield of the Balkan War. The Bosnian Serbs had assembled a formidable army of 80,000 men, which was supported and armed by the Yugoslav government of Milosevic. The head of the Bosnian Serb army was the able and ruthless **General Ratko Mladic**. The Bosnian Muslims were hopelessly outgunned, and the Serbs quickly gained ground. During a mere six weeks in the Spring of 1992, the Serbs, who constituted only a third of the population, managed to dominate and "cleanse" three-quarters of the Bosnian territory.

The Serbian conquests were accompanied by ethnic cleansing and genocide. Local Muslims were rounded up in eerie scenes similar to the ones that had occurred half a century earlier under the Nazis. The terror and fear of a knock on the door, the forced marches, the mass evacuations, the internment in concentration camps, the torture, and the mass killings had returned to Europe in full force. The word "genocide" was first used in this Balkan context.

The atrocities and fighting continued throughout 1993. But, despite media reports of Serb atrocities, the world community remained mostly indifferent. The mandate of the United Nations prohibited its troops from intervening militarily against the Serbs. This gave the Bosnian Serbs a free hand to continue massacring Muslims.

On **February 6, 1994**, the world's attention turned to Bosnia, as a marketplace in **Sarajevo** was struck by a Serb mortar shell, killing 68 civilians. Calls for military intervention were finally heard. US President Bill Clinton issued an ultimatum through NATO demanding that the Serbs withdraw their troops from Sarajevo. The Serbs complied and a ceasefire in Sarajevo was declared. But this did not stop the Serbs from attacking Muslims in other towns of Bosnia, some of which had been declared **Safe Havens** by the United Nations in May 1993.

In one of these Safe Havens, the town of **Srebrenica**, the worst **mass murder** since World War II took place in the **summer of 1995**. On July 6, 1995, General Mladic and his troops swept unopposed into Srebrenica while 400 Dutch UN peacekeepers, looked on without putting forward any opposition. Worse, **Colonel Karremans**, leader of the **Dutch peacekeepers**, praised General Mladic for his military skills, and remarked that the General was after all "a commander and not a gentleman."

The Serb troops seized the 40,000 Muslims of Srebrenica, separating men of fighting age—between the ages of 13 to 60—from the women, children, and old men. Within 30 hours Mladic's men had expelled 23,000 women, children and old men to Muslim territories. Within four days they had **murdered 7,000 men** of fighting age, who were trucked or marched to their places of death (each transport driver was forced to kill one man to deter him from testifying against the Serb troops later). An additional 3,000 men were killed in the act of trying to escape, and 1,500 were locked in a warehouse and machine-gunned. The whole action was carried out with cold-blooded military efficiency reminiscent of past Nazi operations.

And the world stood by.... How could the world have allowed Srebrenica to happen? Why did nobody intervene during the four years of fighting that led to Srebrenica? Many parties are to be blamed: the European countries, the United States, the United Nations—essentially, the whole international community.

Why didn't the United States, at the height of its power after the first Gulf War in 1991, try to avert and halt the violence that had started about that time in Yugoslavia? One reason was that it did not want to endanger the benefit that the victory in the Gulf War had brought to the Bush administration, and thereby jeopardize the chances of Bush's re-election to a second term. In June 1991, Secretary of State **James Baker** made the now famous statement, "**We have got no dog in this fight.**" President H.W. Bush handed the problem to the Europeans, but without American support for action by NATO, the Europeans were powerless and ineffective in their negotiations with the Serb government of Milosevic.

Bill Clinton, as presidential candidate in 1992, uttered bold words threatening the Serbs with bombing and, after being elected in 1992, declared that "ethnic cleansing cannot stand." But behind his eloquent words was—nothing: no policy, planning or intent of military intervention. And so the policy of non-intervention stood for the next three years, till the genocide in Srebrenica.

The behavior of the United Nations was equally deplorable. In 1999, a UN committee concluded that, through its inaction, the United Nations failed to prevent the fall of Srebrenica, and to avert the massacre of the Muslim population. On July 11, 2001, the sixth anniversary of the Srebrenica massacre, **UN Secretary Kofi Annan** stated: **"The tragedy of Srebrenica will forever haunt the history of the United Nations."**

There were a few lonely voices that advocated a more aggressive policy against Milosevic. Among them, one of the most persistent and dogged was that of **Richard Holbrooke**,[90] who had been Assistant Secretary of State for European and Canadian Affairs in the Clinton administration. Holbrooke loudly made known his disgust with the weak western policy as early as 1992 when, as a private citizen, he had made a fact-finding trip to the region.

At the beginning of the Serb siege of Srebrenica in early July 1995, Holbrooke, now US ambassador to the United Nations, vigorously recommended the use of air power against the Bosnian Serbs. But the Dutch government refused to allow air strikes until all its peacekeeping soldiers were out of Bosnia. This failure to defend Srebrenica by air strikes represented the culmination of a long series of tawdry and cowardly decisions by the western nations not to interfere in Bosnia; the consequences of these decisions for the Muslim population were bloody and disastrous.

---

[90] In February 2009, Holbrooke was made special envoy by President Obama to address (and hopefully solve) the problems in Afghanistan and Pakistan. His past performance in the Balkan peace negotiations made him an excellent choice for the task. It was a formidable task to which Holbrooke would bring his considerable diplomatic skills and wisdom until his untimely death in 2010.

The enormous and unopposed crime committed by Mladic left the western nations humiliated and shamed with no choice but to intervene in the Bosnian War. At the end of **August 1995, effective intervention finally began.** Hundreds of NATO warplanes were at last launched against the Bosnian Serbs. Massive bombings destroyed much of the Serbian installations and weakened their forces. It set the groundwork for a peace agreement with Milosevic. Other post-Srebrenica events, that I shall describe next, contributed to the caving in of Milosevic.

Operation Storm. After the ethnic cleansing of Srebrenica, General Mladic turned his attention to the Croats in the western part of Bosnia-Herzegovina and started to harass them. Croatian President Tudjman's reaction was swift. On August 4, 1995, less than a month after the Srebrenica genocide, Croatian forces under the leadership of **General Ante Gotovina** began **Operation Storm**, recapturing in a mere four days the Krajina region that they had lost four years earlier. Two hundred thousand Croatian Serbs, including the entire Croatian Serb army of 40,000 men, fled to Serbia. In the aftermath of the operation, members of the Croatian army and police tortured, murdered, and forcibly expelled the remaining Croatian Serb civilians in a manner similar to that perpetrated by the Serbs against the Croatian four years earlier.

The United States not only gave the green light to Operation Storm: it was actively involved in the preparation, monitoring, and supplying of important intelligence information to the Croatian Army. President Clinton's motivation was to insure a quick and clear victory of the Croatian Army, so that they could transfer their forces into Bosnia-Herzegovina to fight Mladic's Army and retake some of the territory dominated by the Serbs. This, indeed, happened. The Croats entered Bosnia and routed Mladic's army. It was the first time the Serbian wave of conquest had been reversed. Serbian defeats resulted in a more balanced map, dividing the territory of Bosnia-Herzgovina about equally between Serbs and the combined Croat-Muslim population. This became important in facilitating later peace negotiations.

The Dayton Accord. The United States, under the leadership of Richard Holbrooke, US ambassador to the United Nations, tried hard to arrange a peace agreement in Bosnia. However, Milosevic was initially recalcitrant and refused to negotiate. But after three months of heavy NATO bombing, and the successful Croat-Muslim ground assault in Bosnia, Milosevic saw the tide turning against him and was finally ready to talk peace. He had no compunction in abandoning the men he had brought to power, Karadzic and Mladic, in order to make a deal with the western powers and, in the process, garner international prestige as a "peacemaker." The arsonist had turned firefighter.

On **November 1, 1995**, Holbrooke convened the warring factions at the Wright-Patterson Air Force Base in Dayton, Ohio, and, after three weeks of intense negotiations, a peace agreement, the **Dayton Accord**, was signed. It mandated the partition of Bosnia into two parts: the Bosnian Muslim-Croat Federation, and the Bosnian Serb Republic. Each of the three ethnic groups was to be represented equally in most governmental institutions, with the presidency consisting of three members: one Bosnian Muslim and one Croat from the Federation, and one Serb from the Bosnian Serb Republic. The agreement also called for democratic elections, the return of the refugees to their homes, the handing over of war criminals to be prosecuted. To enforce the agreement, a NATO force of 60,000 was to be deployed.

Thus ended the war in Bosnia, in which over 100,000 Muslim civilians had been murdered, and close to two million people had been internally displaced. In the words of Richard Holbrooke, this sordid story represents "the greatest failure of the West since the 1930s."

The Serbian campaign against the Kosovo Albanians—another genocide. After the Dayton Accord, many predicted that Milosevic's political career was at an end, and peace would be restored in the Balkans. They were wrong; Milosevic had not given up his dream of a greater Serbia in spite (or perhaps because) of his plummeting popularity at home. He faced an economy destroyed by sanctions and war, and a political world that seemed to be closing in around him. He had presided over the disintegration of Yugoslavia, losing Slovenia, Croatia, and the Krajina region, and failing to annex the Bosnian Serb territory. Belgrade had become the capital of a shrunken and imploding Yugoslavia. Was it not natural, then, that Milosevic would return to the scene of his greatest past triumph, the Serb land of **Kosovo**?

It was unfortunate that the Dayton Accord of 1995 did not address the question of Kosovo. The American delegates led by Holbrooke were aware of the importance of Kosovo. President H.W. Bush had drawn a red line in December 1992, by declaring that a conflict in Kosovo would so severely threaten American interests as to demand military intervention. However, the Americans were in a hurry to obtain a Bosnia agreement, and Milosevic refused to consider any outside diplomatic meddling in what he considered, unquestionably, "Serb land."

The omission of Kosovo in the Dayton Accord dealt a sever blow to the prestige of **Ibrahim Rugova**, the non-violent leader of the Kosovo Albanians. As a result, Rugova's political primacy was successfully challenged by the leaders of the militant **Kosovo Liberation Army** (**KLA**), a guerilla band that, until recently, had been labeled a terrorist organization by the Americans.

Milosevic responded to the KLA by sending his security forces to storm villages where the guerilla presence was strongest, and to massacre anyone they found. These activities took place throughout 1998. The Americans and Western Allies struggled to negotiate a Kosovo agreement but were confounded by Milosevic's intransigence, and by the Russian support of Milosevic.

Early in 1999, Milosevic began to plan a decisive and brutal resolution of the Kosovo problem. On **March 19, 1999**, the Serbs launched a massive campaign of ethnic cleansing, driving hundreds of thousands of Albanians into neighboring Macedonia and Albania. On **March 24**, the Western Allies reacted by sending **NATO air power** on high altitude bombing missions of Serbian positions in Kosovo, as well as targets in Yugoslavia, including the capital, Belgrade. The Allies were afraid of sustaining casualties, and assumed that their safe tactics of high-altitude bombing would cause the Milosevic regime to quickly crumble. This proved to be a colossal miscalculation.

The Serb campaign against the Kosovo Albanians continued while the bombs were falling, with acts of terror and mass murder similar to those perpetrated in Bosnia four years earlier. This time it was the village of **Meja** where the largest massacre took place, reminiscent of Srebrenica.

On **April 27, 1999**, a large contingent of Serbian troops entered Meja, grabbing villagers from their houses and leading them to the compost heap where they gunned them down and burned the corpses under piles of cornhusks. About 10,000 ethnic Albanians died during the Kosovo War. The killings were accompanied by the largest mass deportation of a civilian population in decades. Some **800,000 Kosovo Albanians were rounded up** and expelled to Albania and Macedonia. Pictures of the exodus horrified the world, and the Allies began to talk about supplementing their bombardment campaign with troops on the ground.

Milosevic, fearing a ground war with the Allies and being pressured by Russia, as well as being chastened by his indictment on war crimes, agreed on May 23, 1999, to a ceasefire. The agreement called for a withdrawal of all Serbian forces, and the introduction of 18,000 NATO troops along with 3,500 UN police. Fearing the revenge of the Albanians, 150,000 Serb civilians fled to the Serbian heartland where they joined the 200,000 still stranded by Operation Storm in 1995.

Kosovo remained until 2008 under Serb sovereignty but international control. Frustrated and disappointed by their status, the Kosovo Albanians declared **independence on February 17, 2008**. They were quickly recognized by the majority of European member states, the United States, and others, but not by Serbia and Russia. Whether Kosovo will become a viable state with its severe economic problems and remaining ethnic strife, is an open question.

The International Criminal Tribunal. And what happened to the perpetrators of the atrocities in the aftermath of the Balkan War? In **May 1993**, even before the main atrocities in Srebrenica and Kosovo were committed, the UN Security Council established the **International Criminal Tribunal for Yugoslavia (ICTY)** in The Hague, to try those responsible for genocide, crimes against humanity, and other violations of international humanitarian law, in the territory of former Yugoslavia. The ICTY does not have its own police force, and relies on the former Yugoslav republics to make arrests. This represents a definite weakness in the courts' ability to bring the indicted people to The Hague, as a large portion of the population and governmental officials consider some of the perpetrators to be national heroes. Tangible results were obtained only after the Europeans made collaboration with the ICTY a condition for membership in the European Union.

The ICTY began its proceedings on May 16, 1996. It indicted 161 individuals. By April 2009, it had tried and convicted 83 Serbs, 19 Croats, 5 Bosnian Muslims, and 4 Kosovo Albanians. These numbers clearly show that the majority of the atrocities were committed by Serbs, although all ethnicities participated in the evil deeds. The verdicts varied from a few months to life in prison. (**Stanislav Galic** was sentenced to life imprisonment for shelling and sniping at Sarajevo.) The main villain, Slobodan **Milosevic**, was **extradited** to The Hague on **June 28, 2001** and charged with genocide. He waged a protracted and spirited defense but **died on March 11, 2006** of a heart attack before a verdict was reached. **Radovan Karadzic**, former President of the Bosnian Serbian Republic, was **arrested** in Belgrade on **July 21, 2008**, after 13 years in hiding. He has been charged with genocide and crimes against humanity. His trial in The Hague ended in 2014; judgment is pending. The last of the notorious trio of Serb leaders, **General Ratko**

Mladic, was captured on May 26, 2011, in his cousin's house in the village of Lazarevo, Serbia, after 16 years on the run. He was extradited to The Hague where he faced the Yugoslav War Crime Tribunal on June 3, 2011. The once burly general, in his late 60s, shuffled into court an old, broken and ill man who had suffered three strokes and two heart attacks. When the charges of genocide and multiple other atrocities were read to him, he dismissed them as "obnoxious" and "monstrous." Judgment is expected in 2017.

Critical questions remain as to why it took so long to capture Mladic, and why it happened when it did. It seems clear that Mladic was protected by high officials in the government, as well as Serbia's orthodox priest. He still enjoys a large following in Serbia; some officials reacted with anger to Mladic's arrest. A spokesman for the ultra-national Serbian Radical Party proclaimed: "Serb traitors have arrested a Serb hero." As for the timing of the arrest, it coincided with the expected release of a report by the war crime tribunal in The Hague, saying that Serbia was not cooperating with the international efforts to arrest Mladic. Such a report would have posed a serious barrier to Serbia's attempt to become a member of the European Union. It is likely that to avoid this situation, the pro-Western president of Serbia, Boris Tadic, decided to finally act.

Epilogue: Two features of the Balkan War stand out. One is the extreme brutality of all parties involved (Serbs, Croats, Muslims, and Kosovo Albanians), and the other is the weak and delayed response of the world to the atrocities committed.

But haven't we witnessed indifference and inaction before? Over half a century ago, when the free world was unwilling to confront Hitler and prevent the Holocaust? And the scenario is being repeated over and over again; in Rwanda, and in Darfur. I dread to think about the future, the ineffective dealing with Iran and other rogue nations that are willing to, and soon may be capable of, destroying the world by acquiring nuclear weapons.

Genocide in Rwanda

In the tiny African country of Rwanda, in just 100 days, from **April to July 1994**, about **a million people were slaughtered**. The daily rate of killing was unprecedented: it was the highest of any recorded genocide—at least five times that in the worst Nazi death camps.

Background: the rift between Hutu and Tutsi. The population of Rwanda (at present about 12 million) is made up of two main groups: the **Hutu**, who are in the majority, and the **Tutsi**, in the minority. The Hutu and Tutsi share the same language, religion, territory, and traditions. The difference between them is not one of ethnicity but rather of social status, as described below.

Before the arrival of the Europeans, there is no history of systematic violence between Hutu and Tutsi. Since the 17ᵗʰ century, Rwanda had a centralized form of political authority that became increasingly authoritarian, reaching its peak during the second half of the 19ᵗʰ century. During this period, traditional obligations of labor came to be imposed on the Hutu alone, thereby polarizing the social difference between Hutu and Tutsi. Further polarization occurred during colonial times.

In **1894**, **Germany** established its **dominance over Rwanda**, taking over its political rule. After the defeat of Germany in **World War I**, Rwanda came under **Belgian colonial**

rule. In the "divide-and-rule" tradition, the Belgians were the first to codify Hutu and Tutsi designations. The Tutsi minority became colonial favorites and protégés. They dominated the political and cultural life during the first two decades of Belgian colonial rule.

Under Belgian rule, the Rwandan population was indoctrinated with the idea that the Hutu were the offspring of Ham, the black son of Noah, cursed by God and destined forever to serve; whereas, the generally taller, and supposedly more refined Tutsi were considered to be the descendants of Egyptians, and were destined to rule.[91] This caste system gradually became a racial distinction that shaped ethnic identity and fueled Hutu resentment. The Belgians further institutionalized the difference by issuing identity cards defining every Rwandan as either Hutu or Tutsi. The identity cards were perpetuated by the post-colonial government, and, in 1994, proved to be a key genocidal facilitator.

After World War II, the Tutsi, who had benefited from their dominant position in education and state bureaucracy under Belgian rule, moved to the forefront of anti-colonial initiatives. The Belgians, perceiving a threat from the Tutsi, made a dramatic switch in policy, transferring their favors to the less educated, less threatening Hutu majority. This unleashed pent-up Hutu frustrations and led to the first massacre of Tutsi, claiming several thousand victims. Tutsi, in the tens of thousands, fled to neighboring Zaire (now the Democratic Republic of Congo), Burundi, Tanzania, and Uganda.

In **1962**, the Belgians relinquished power and **Rwanda became independent**. The new government was dominated by the Hutu, with the Tutsi totally frozen out of formal political power. In a **1973** coup, the **Hutu dictator Juvénal Habyarimana** seized the presidency. Although Habyarimana was a relatively liberal dictator, a tightly knit extremist Hutu group operated an "invisible government" around Habyarimana, and fostered a fierce ethnic hatred against the Tutsi.

In **1987**, Rwandan **Tutsi exiles** formed the **Rwandan Patriotic Front (RPF)**, under the leadership of **Paul Kagame**. Their goal was to overthrow the Hutu government. In 1990, forces of the RPF launched an invasion of Rwanda but were stopped outside the capital by the Hutu army, helped by French commandos. The French supported and assisted the Hutu regime as a bulwark against the British influence in nearby Uganda.

A **peace accord** between the Hutu government and the RPF was signed in **Arusha** (Tanzania) in **August 1993**. It mandated a cease-fire, and guaranteed free elections in less than two years, and the inclusion of the RPF in the government. To monitor the cease-fire and the prelude to elections, the United Nations dispatched 2,500 foreign peacekeepers, to constitute the United Nations Assistant Mission for Rwanda (**UNAMIR**). It was headed by the Canadian **General Romeo Dallaire**.

The Hutu extremists were unhappy with the Arusha Accords, and were chafing to find a pretext to undermine and prevent the Tutsi from sharing power. They launched a vicious propaganda campaign against the Tutsi using the media, in particular the government-controlled radio stations, to fuel hatred and a hysterical fear of the threat posed by the RPF. A typical broadcast declared that "the cruelty of the RPF can only be cured by their total extermination." The Hutu population was being primed for the atrocities to follow.

---

[91] This idea was first propounded by the British explorer John Hanning Speke in his 1863 book "Journal of the Discovery of the Source of the Nile." Speke's hypothesis was widely accepted at the Berlin Conference in 1885, at which the Western powers gathered to carve much of Africa into areas that would be colonized.

<u>The genocide.</u>[92] The trigger for **Hutu action** came on **April 6, 1994**. The plane carrying Rwandan President Habyarimana and Burundi President Ntaryamira, returning from discussions in Tanzania, was shot down as it approached Rwanda's airport at Kigali, killing all passengers aboard.[93] Immediately after the incident, Rwanda plunged into political violence.

The following day, soldiers and militia began murdering thousands of Tutsi and some moderate Hutu. General Dallaire dispatched 10 Belgian peacekeepers to protect the moderate **Hutu Prime Minister Uwilingiyimana**. All 10 were seized, tortured, and **murdered** along with the Prime Minister. This unfortunate incident had far-reaching consequences. It prompted the contingent of Belgian peacekeepers to withdraw from Rwanda. In spite of heated protests from General Dallaire, other countries followed suit. Foreign journalists also departed en bloc.

The withdrawal of foreign troops, the lack of action by the rest of the world, and the French support of the Hutu regime (there were 47 senior French officers embedded in the Rwandan Army), fueled the fury of one of the worst genocides in history.

The Hutu army and militia, joined by civilians, went street to street, block by block, house to house, and dragged Tutsi out of homes and hiding places. They were hacked to death by machetes, often after torture and rape. At roadblocks, those carrying Tutsi identity cards were murdered on the spot. When the perpetrators could not keep up with the killings, they severed the Achilles tendon of their victims to temporarily immobilize them until they could dispose of the backlog.

Tens of thousands of Tutsi sought sanctuary in schools, stadiums and, especially, places of worship. But there was no sanctuary to be had. On the contrary, the flight to hoped-for sanctuaries played into the hands of the killers; it concentrated their victims for easy mass killing. Astonishingly, church figures across Rwanda played a leading role in legitimizing and even inflicting genocidal killing. One such **massacre,** at the **Karama Parish,** stands out as the most concentrated slaughter of the 20th century. In **less than six hours**, 40,000 people were murdered. This was more than were killed in the Nazi's two-day slaughter of the Jews at Babi Yar in 1941, or in the largest single-day extermination spree in the gas chambers of Auschwitz-Birkenau.

A distinctive feature of the Rwandan genocide was the involvement of ordinary Hutu in the slaughter—in fact, they comprised the bulk of the genociders. Machete-wielding civilian mobs, in the hundreds of thousands, eagerly participated in the killing, often of their neighbors, with whom they had lived in harmony for years. Even Hutu women flocked by the tens of thousands to participate in the slaughter of Tutsi and the stripping of corpses. For the first time in modern history, a state succeeded in transforming the mass of its population into murderers. (Note the contrast with Nazi extermination procedures: The

---

[92] For a detailed description, see R. Dallaire, "Shake Hands with the Devil: The Failure of Humanity in Rwanda," Carroll & Graf, 2004; and Samantha Power, "A Problem from Hell: America and the Age of Genocide (P.S.)," Harper Perennial, 2002.

[93] It has never been clearly established who shot down the plane. A French investigation, which many consider biased in favor of the Hutu, concluded that the rocket attack was carried out by the current Rwandan President, Paul Kagame, who, at the time, was the leader of the RPF. Kagame vehemently denies it, and he and many others blame Hutu extremists, who wanted to stop the Hutu president from reaching any compromise with the RPF, and to provide a pretext to exterminate the Tutsi community.

German killers were in uniform, and strict measures were taken to ensure that the civilian population did not witness the mass slaughter.)

The reaction of the international community to the genocide. I turn now to another sad chapter in the annals of the international community which, once again, inactively stood by while a million defenseless victims were murdered.

When the genocide broke out, well-armed foreign forces were flown into Rwanda—but only to evacuate whites. Terrified Tutsi begged the foreign troops for protection, but none was given. No effort was made to evacuate or protect Tutsi civilians, who were left to the mercy of the murderous Hutu. General Dallaire, commander of the UN peacekeeping force, UNAMIR, was ordered by headquarters not to interfere, and to avoid armed conflict. What a terrible and stressful situation for Dallaire and his forces, to stand by while the killings took place before their own eyes!

By April 10, four days after the start of the slaughter, the United Nations and the international community were fully aware that killings on a genocidal scale were occurring in Rwanda. They did nothing, though there were enough UNAMIR troops on hand to stop the killings, at the very least in Kigali, the capital. Worse yet, UN Security Council members, notably France and the United States, cautioned against labeling the killings "genocide," as this would require them to intervene, according to international law. The result of this was disastrous. When the Hutu realized that there would be no outside intervention, the genocide escalated, and murder spread like wildfire.

As the killings escalated, General Dallaire made repeated requests to the United Nations to augment his force to 5,000 men, and to give him a stronger mandate that would allow him to intervene and protect civilians. Instead, the **UN Security Council voted on April 21st to withdraw the UNAMIR contingent**, except for a token force of about 200. Dallaire defied the United Nations, and held on to 450 peacekeepers. Even these few were able to save thousands of lives.[94]

On **May 3, 1994**, President Clinton issued a directive outlining his policy that humanitarian action anywhere in the world has to be in American national interest. He declared: "Whether we get involved in any of the world's ethnic conflicts, in the end, must depend on the cumulative weight of the American interest at stake." [95]

On **May 5**, the Pentagon rejected a proposal by Dallaire to diminish the killings by using Pentagon technology to jam the hate radio messages transmitted by extremists.

On **May 17**, six weeks into the genocide, the United Nations and United States finally agreed to Dallaire's plan to send 5,000 troops to Rwanda. However, the Security

---

[94] Dallaire's frustrations, and the whole conflict in Rwanda, are movingly described in his book "Shake Hands with the Devil: The Failure of Humanity in Rwanda." He describes his sickening defenselessness as he watched the death toll rise, while Washington and the United Nations rejected his requests. As he put it "I arrived in Rwanda a confident warrior, and left a broken man." Indeed, after Rwanda, Dallaire, disillusioned and suicidal, was diagnosed with Post-Traumatic Stress Disorder (PTSD), and in April 2000, at age 53, was discharged from the Canadian Army on medical grounds. After his forced retirement from the military, Dallaire wanted to bring an understanding of PTSD to the public, and pursued research on "conflict resolution and the use of child soldiers." He is the recipient of many awards and honors, and, in 2005, was summoned by the Prime Minister of Canada to serve as a Senator in the Canadian Parliament.

[95] This attitude was, no doubt, influenced by the US tragedy in Somalia just months earlier, when US commandos had their Black Hawk helicopter shot down. Eighteen US soldiers were killed and dragged through the streets, posthumously humiliated. The government was not willing to risk another incident of this kind.

Council failed to establish a timetable, and bureaucracy and bickering delayed the arrival of the troops until after the end of the genocide.

On **June 19**, as the RPF forces were starting to successfully fight the government Hutu army, the UN Security Council approved the French proposal to send their troops to Rwanda. This intervention was a continuation of the long-standing French support of the Hutu government. It permitted the orderly evacuation of nearly 2 million Hutu, including tens of thousands of genociders, to refugee camps in the neighboring Democratic Republic of Congo, where they were under the central control of the same Hutu political structure that had just been responsible for the genocide. The Clinton government, which had spent the period of the mass slaughter placing obstacles in the path of intervention, now leapt into action. US troops arrived within days to begin distribution of water, supplies, and medical aid to the camps. It is ironic that the only effective intervention helped the Hutu genociders rather than the Tutsi victims.

Thus ended a shameful episode of inaction by the international community. And how do the present world leaders, as well as the ones that made policy at the time of the genocide, view Rwanda in retrospect? They all denounce what happened, and are shamed by their failure to intervene and halt the slaughter. To exemplify these sentiments I quote a few leaders:

At the memorial conference at the United Nations in 2004 (10 years after the genocide), UN Secretary Kofi Annan, who, at the time, was head of the UN peacekeeping forces, said: "The international community failed Rwanda, and that must leave us always with a sense of bitter regret and abiding sorrow."

At a candlelight vigil in 2009, marking the 15th anniversary of the genocide, UN Secretary General Ban Ki-moon stated: "To prevent future genocides is a collective responsibility. Only by meeting it, can we truly honor the memory of those who died in Rwanda 15 years ago."

It is interesting and significant that when Bill Clinton was asked in a 2008 interview what event he regretted most during his presidency, he replied that it was the inaction of the United States and the United Nations during the Rwanda genocide.

Was Rwanda too far, too remote, too poor, too little, and perhaps too black, for it to be worthwhile saving from genocide? I don't think so. These may have been contributing factors, but I believe that ultimately the determining factor was the unwillingness of nations to sacrifice their own self-interests for the sake of others. The proof is that inaction in the face of genocide happened also in the heart of Europe. Just a year after Rwanda, the genocide in Srebrenica, Bosnia, took place, unopposed by UN forces (see page 201). And, as I mentioned repeatedly, the inaction during the Holocaust 50 years earlier staggers the mind. In addition, the ineffectiveness of the international community in present-day Darfur shows that a lesson was not learned; in spite of the lofty rhetoric about universal human rights, no effective actions are being taken.

The end of the genocide, and its aftermath. The genocide did not last—in part because the killers were running out of victims, but, more significantly, because the frenzy of the massacres distracted the Hutu regime from effectively confronting the RPF forces, which had organized themselves to combat the Hutu. By mid-June the Rwandan government forces were pushed into a limited zone in the southern part of the country. **By July 17,**

1994, the RPF forces captured the capital, Kigali, and set up a government headed by **Paul Kagame**. The Hutu government fled to the Democratic Republic of Congo, followed by a tide of refugees. The 100 days of hell had come to an end.

Original estimates of the death toll in the Rwanda genocide were around 800,000. A later, more detailed census in July 2000 estimated the dead at over a million, 94% of them Tutsi.

The **new Tutsi government** set up by the victorious RPF showed a façade of pluralism that featured a few Hutu in prominent positions. However, the post-genocidal government was guided by the conviction that Tutsi power was the condition of its survival. The motto "Never Again" was a clear sign of the pledge not to allow Hutu ever again to achieve dominance in Rwanda politics. The French, who had staunchly supported the Hutu government, were shut out of Rwandan politics. French as the second language was officially replaced by English. In a quest for peaceful co-existence, all young Rwandans were obliged to attend "solidarity camps" where they were taught to love one another.

President Paul Kagame was re-elected president in 2010 for 7 years. During his presidency, great progress in economic development has been, and continues to be, made. Tourism has picked up and technological enterprises are flourishing. Some call Rwanda the Silicon Valley of Africa. Unfortunately, this prosperity comes with the curtailment of free expression under Kagame's autocratic rule. Newspapers are state-owned, and voice a pro-Kagame line; the RPF party is the only political game in town. Whether the rule of a small minority can maintain long-term political stability remains to be seen.

Attempts at justice and reconciliation. Progress in meting out justice, and punishing the perpetrators of the genocide has been excruciatingly slow in Rwanda. Many of the perpetrators, including former ministers and leaders of extremist Hutu, took refuge in countries such as the Democratic Republic of Congo, Belgium, France, Canada, and the United States. But the main obstacle to speedy trials is the massive number of people in Rwanda that participated in crimes related to the genocide. The Rwandan government estimates it at 750,000, close to half the adult Hutu population. After the genocide, 120,000 people were arrested.

Just as important as meting out justice and abolishing the culture of impunity that has plagued Rwanda for decades was for the post-1994 government to integrate the innocents, and the repentant survivors into Rwandan society. But how to accomplish these twin goals of **justice** and **reconciliation** posed a formidable—if not impossible—task.

The government's solution, adopted on a pilot scale in 2002, was to utilize a system of justice based on Rwandan customs and tradition: the *Gacaca* **courts** (In the Grass courts). These courts represent a system of participative justice in which the population is given the chance to speak out against the perpetrators of crime and to judge and punish them. Throughout Rwanda's history, neighbors have settled disputes by adjourning to Gacacas, sitting down together to discuss and mediate personal and communal problems. These courts had been very effective in facilitating reconciliation, which enabled people to live in peace and harmony—just what was needed in strife-ridden, post-genocidal Rwanda.

The legal system in Rwanda was in shambles in 1994, and was not up to handling a large number of cases. Between 1996 and 2002, only 6,000 accused (out of 120,000) were tried. At this rate it would take a century to try all detainees. In **November 1994**, the **International Criminal Tribunal for Rwanda (ICTR)** was established in Arusha, Tanzania, under UN auspices. It was organized along lines similar to those of the ICTY that was established a year earlier in The Hague to prosecute perpetrators of genocide in Yugoslavia. It was expected to try mostly high-level suspects and those who played a leading role in the genocide. Although it tried and convicted several prominent figures, it has handled a relatively small number of cases. The ICTR formally closed on December 31, 2015. It remains for the domestic courts of governments around the world to "intensify efforts to bring remaining suspects to justice."

Gacaca courts were implemented on a pilot scale in 2002 and on a nation-wide scale in December 2006: about 12,000 Gacaca courts throughout the country, each with nine elected judges. The judges were respected laypersons selected by the community, and were not paid for their services. About 80% of the population actively participated in the proceedings. During the first nine months of nation-wide trials, about 6,000 trials were conducted. This is approximately the same number as had been processed by the regular courts during the preceding six years.

An important part of the activities of the Gacaca courts was to categorize the accused according to the severity of their crimes. Category 1 comprised the masterminds of genocide—those that planned and organized it. They did not come under the jurisdiction of the Gacaca courts, but of the ICTR in Tanzania. In categories 2 and 3 were perpetrators of murder and lesser crimes. They constituted, by far, the majority of the accused, and were tried mainly by the Gacaca courts.

Although the Gacaca courts seemed like a reasonable solution to Rwanda's judicial dilemma, some severe problems soon became evident. One was corruption. Since the Gacaca courts were more lenient than the ICTR and the regular courts, defendants bribed the judges to classify them as lower than Category 1 offenders so that they would be tried in the Gacaca courts. Of even more concern than corruption was the increase in violence toward genocide survivors who were called as witnesses by the Gacaca courts. In the first half a year of the trials, some 40 witnesses were murdered. Consequently, entire communities refused to testify, afraid of risking their lives. The Gacaca courts officially closed in December 2011, nearly 10 years after they began. According to government figures, close to two million people have been tried, of which about 65% have been found guilty.

As to achieving reconciliation between perpetrators and victims, an obstacle was the refusal of both the Gacaca courts and the ICTR to investigate crimes committed by the Tutsi RPF (whose leader is the current president, Paul Kagame). Understandably, this fuels the resentment of the Hutu toward the government. The cornerstone of the government's policy of reconciliation is the system of education camps, where young people are taught tolerance and non-violence, and that Hutu and Tutsi are artificial categories, imposed by past colonial powers, that need to be abolished.

Twenty-odd years after the genocide, the goals of justice and reconciliation have not yet been reached. At best, we can consider the endeavor to reach these goals as work in progress. It is of utmost importance that this effort succeeds lest the Rwandans face another collective bloodletting.

Genocide in Darfur

The 21st century has barely started but it already has witnessed a horrendous genocide in the Darfur region of Western Sudan.

In **February 2003**, two Darfuri rebel groups, accusing the Sudanese government of oppressing non-Arabs in favor of Arabs and neglecting the Darfur region, attacked government posts. In response, the governments mounted a brutal campaign, escalating into a scorched-earth policy. It sent its forces and proxy militia to bomb, burn villages, loot, rape, and indiscriminately kill civilians. It is estimated that 500,000 civilians have died, and 3 million people have been displaced. And the atrocities continue. It seems that nothing had been learned since the genocide in Rwanda that occurred less than a decade before.

The genocide in Darfur is the most complex to understand, and it has still not run its course. I delve, therefore, into its roots in more detail than I have done in the others.[96]

Background: the geography, population, and early history of Darfur and the Sudan. Darfur, a region the size of Texas, is located in the western part of the Sudan, bordering with Libya, Chad, and the Central African Republic (see map). The population of Darfur is 7.5 million, about a fifth of the population of Sudan. The population of Darfur is ethnically heterogeneous but all of them are Muslims. The main division (and conflict) is between Arabs and non-Arab Africans (also referred to as "Blacks"). The largest non-Arab African ethnic group is the **Fur**, after whom Darfur

Sudan with Darfur crosshatched.

(*Dar-Fur*, the Land of the Fur) was named. They are farmers who live with the other non-Arab groups, the **Mesalit** and **Tunjur,** mostly in central Darfur. The main ethnic group in the north is the **Zaghawa**, non-Arab camel nomads. In the south are the Arab cattle nomads, the **Baggara**, and the most powerful of the Arab tribes of Darfur, the **Rizeigat**.

Darfur was an independent sultanate, dating back to the late **14th century**. Little is known of this early period. The first written chronicles refer to **Sultan Suleiman**, who founded the Keyra Fur Sultanate and reigned from the early part of the **17th century** till the 1640s. He brought Islam to Darfur, putting it on the map of "civilized" Muslim Africa. Darfur was a feudal society with the Sultan appearing almost a divinity to his subjects.

In the late **1780s**, Sultan **Tayrab** invaded and captured the territory of Kordofan (see map) to the east of Darfur, which almost doubled his territory. In **1791**, he founded *El-Fashir*[97] (The Palace), which is still today the regional capital. In **1821, Muhammad Ali**, Viceroy of Egypt, launched his armies upon the conquest of the vast territory south of

---

[96] For a thorough analysis see Gerard Prunier, "Darfur: A 21st Century Genocide," Cornell University Press, 2008. For recent developments in the Sudan see the periodic reports of "Genocide Intervention Network," "International Crisis Group," "Humanitarian Right Watch," and "Save Darfur."

[97] Also spelled Al Fasher (see map).

Egypt. At that time what we now call Sudan had no political existence, in contrast to the Sultanate of Darfur to the west. Darfur was at the height of its power, and tried to resist, but it was no match for the Egyptian troops, who were trained by former officers of Napoleon's army. The Darfuri gave up Kordofan, retreated to their homeland, and Darfur reverted to its original territory. Muhammad Ali's forces did not pursue their conquest in the west, and, instead, advanced to the south and quickly secured control of the Nile Valley down to **Khartoum**, the present capital of Sudan. During the 1840s and 1850s, the Khartoumers, as the Northern Sudanese were called, extended a far-flung network of slave expeditions and other commercial enterprises to the south. The process was extremely brutal, and the memory of it remains today at the heart of Southern Sudanese resentment towards the north.

In **October 1874**, the Governor General of the Sudan, **Ismail Ayub**, was ordered by Cairo to move against Darfur. He captured El-Fashir and overthrew the Keyra Sultanate. The conquest of Darfur by the Egyptians did not last long. In **1881**, a 37-year-old sheikh from the Nile Valley, **Muhammad Ahmad**, proclaimed himself to be the expected **Mahdi**, "the divinely guided one" (roughly equivalent to the Judeo-Christian Messiah). He capitalized on popular resentment throughout Sudan against Egyptian domination. His movement and revolt spread like wildfire, and within four years he defeated the Egyptian forces and its mercenary generals (most famously **Charles Gordon**), captured Khartoum, and founded a new political regime (Mahdist) in the Sudan. Five months after his victory, the Mahdi died and was succeeded by **Khalifa Abdullah**, who had been the deputy of the Mahdi. Abdullah ruled Sudan for 15 years as an efficient despot. But his enforced Mahdism generated strong opposition from many Darfuri, especially the Fur, and others loyal to the old Sultanate.

In **1898,** the Mahdist state collapsed with the defeat of Khalifa Abdullah by the conquering British army led by **Kitchener**. In **January 1899**, the **Anglo-Egyptian Alliance** established Sudan as a **condominium** under the joint authority of Britain and Egypt. As soon as he saw the Mahdist regime collapse, **Ali Dinar** (a relative of the last Keyra Sultan, who had been forced out in **1892**) proceeded to restore the old Keyra Sultanate in Darfur. Cairo and London had little interest in ruling Darfur, and let Ali Dinar rule as a de facto independent sultan for the next 18 years. When World War I broke out, the British became nervous that Ali Dinar would side with the Turco-German forces, and he was denounced as a tyrant and criminal. In **May 1916**, Governor **General Wingate** dispatched an expeditionary force, which defeated the Fur armies near El-Fashir. Ali Dinar and his two sons were killed, and the independence of Darfur passed into history. From then on Darfur had to live within the confines of Sudanese authority, whoever ruled there. It became a neglected appendage of the rulers in Khartoum; this would ultimately lead to its complete collapse into chaos.

<u>Darfur and Khartoum (1916–1985).</u> After Britain took control of the Sudan in **1916**,[98] its only interest in Darfur was keeping order. It administered (or rather under-administered) the region by letting local chiefs administer their tribes on behalf of the government. This benign neglect, parading as the glorification of tribal ways, was a recipe for stagnation, in which the natives were marginalized and isolated from the benefits of the modern world.

---

[98] Actually, it was the Anglo-Egyptian Condominium in which Britain, in effect, wielded the power.

The bulk of the administrative resources was ear-marked for Khartoum and the Nile Province, with only about 5% of the budget left for Darfur. In **1935** there were only four governmental elementary schools in Darfur with an annual budget of 1,200 pounds, and out of 23 intermediate schools operating in the Sudan, only one was in Darfur. And there were no maternity clinics in Darfur, while 18 operated in the rest of Sudan.

A similar situation prevailed in Southern Sudan. These governmental policies, which continued after the **independence of Sudan in 1956**, contained the seeds of the conflicts that would later explode in both regions.

The political landscape in Sudan in the mid-1940s became more and more anti-British. The race for independence from Britain was on. There were two main parties: the powerful neo-Egyptian party *Khatmia* (Unionist Party); and the *Umma*, a neo-Mahdist party led by **Sayid Abd-er-Rahman**, the posthumously born son of the Mahdi. The goal of the Khatmia was the unity of the Nile Valley (i.e., a union with Egypt); the goal of the Umma was an independent fundamentalist Sudan. In the first election of a Sudanese parliament, held in **1953**, the Khatmia, led by **Ismail al-Azhari**, won 50 seats (out of 97), with the Umma taking 22 seats.

Independence of Sudan was achieved on **January 1, 1956**. In the first post-independence elections, held in **1958**, the Mahdist Umma Party won. The Darfuri voted predominantly for Umma and greatly contributed to its victory. But they were, again, not rewarded for their loyalty, and nothing changed in Darfur.

In **November 1958**, the Sudanese army staged a coup d'état, overthrowing the elected civilian government. **General Ibrahim Abboud** took power with the tacit approval of the Parliament. Abboud's dictatorial military regime, and his program of Arabization and Islamization, caused political agitation, and he was forced to resign in favor of a civilian government in **October 1964**.

Sayid Abd-er-Rahman had died during Abboud's military dictatorship and the leadership of the Umma Party went to his grandson, **Sadiq al-Mahdi**, an oriental autocrat, whose complex personality had devastating effects on Darfur and the Sudan. The first post-dictatorial elections held in **May 1965**, were again won by the Umma, who continued to neglect Darfur. This started to rankle some Darfuri and gave impetus to a new party, the **Darfur Development Front (DDF)** led by **Ahmed Ibrahim Diraige**, son of a local Fur. It was open to all tribes, whether African or Arab, who shared a sense of alienation from Khartoum.

In **May 1969**, the parliamentary regime was toppled by a military coup led by Colonel **Jaafar al-Nimeiry**, who ruled for the next 16 years. Sadiq and Diraige were arrested and jailed, but later released. When Sadiq al-Mahdi got out of jail he sought a base from which he could fight Nimeiry. The young revolutionary leader **Muammar Gaddafi**, who had taken power in September 1969 in Libya, and who was at odds with Nimeiry, welcomed Sadiq in Tripoli. Gaddafi, who had an eye on Darfur, was happy to attempt to destabilize the region by using it as a staging ground for fighting the regime of southern Chad, where a brutal civil war was being waged. One of the most anti-Libyan factions of the Chad rebels, led by **Hissan Habre**, was supported by Nimeiry, who allowed them to settle in Darfur, from where they harassed the Chadian army. They were perceived as Arabs, and their presence was not welcomed locally. But Nimeiry was happy to have established an anti-Libyan base in Darfur.

For the Darfuri it meant that once more their own fate was a secondary consideration in Khartoum's geopolitical calculations. Darfuri all across Sudan demonstrated against this neglect, and several students were killed. In **1980**, Nimeiry called in Ahmed Ibrahim Diraige to serve as Governor of Darfur. His Darfur Development Front credentials immediately cooled down the situation. Diraige set out to overhaul completely the provincial government structure. He cut down on the political patronage and corruption, which had proved so disastrous, and formed an ethnically diverse government by filling the ministerial and administrative positions with members of different African and Arab tribes. Alas, all these beneficial changes were overshadowed by the drought and famine that gripped Darfur.

In the **early 1980s**, severe drought and desertification threatened to turn the looming food crisis into a real famine. The Diraige administration was soon engaged in a desperate battle for water resources. They did their best, but they could not make the rain fall and stop the desert from encroaching further south. They needed help from the government in Khartoum, but help was not forthcoming. In **November 1983**, Diraige wrote Nimeiry a letter, to become known as the "famine letter," warning that unless serious food aid from abroad was obtained, a famine in Darfur was unavoidable. Nimeiry did not respond, and on **December 23, 1983**, Diraige went to Khartoum to confront the president personally. Nimeiry flew into a rage, and refused to call for emergency aid for Darfur, as it would compromise his artificial propaganda edifice of a prosperous Sudan. Diraige left the meeting and took a plane to Saudi Arabia, barely escaping arrest. By **August 1984**, the famine could no longer be denied, and Nimeiry finally declared Darfur a "disaster zone," asking the world for food aid. By now the famine was spreading to other parts of Sudan. The US government in Washington, which saw Sudan as a bulwark against Ethiopia's communists and Gaddafi's rogue dictatorship, became concerned and, in **April 1985**, committed itself to 975,000 tons of food aid. But it was too late. A combination of students, trade unionists, and professionals staged an insurrection and, on **April 5, 1985**, overthrew Nimeiry's regime. The clock had been turned back 20 years: In 1964 another civilian insurrection had overthrown another military dictatorship.

The old-guard politicians started to jockey for position, and Darfur, with its largest coherent political vote, was again going to loom large in the electoral landscape. For Sadiq al-Mahdi, still the leader of the Umma Party, winning Darfur was a necessity. But he needed money for his electoral campaign, and turned to Gaddafi for help. He promised Gaddafi to deliver Darfur to Libya in exchange for several million dollars of campaign funds—a promise he undoubtedly never intended to keep. The worst period of Darfur's history was about to begin, and it has not yet ended.

From marginalization to revolt in Darfur (1985–2003). The 1984 famine, which killed 95,000 people out of a total population of 3.1 million in Darfur, had severe political and social consequences for the region. USAID was providing 80% of the food aid, but in a very inefficient and corrupt way. Barely a third of the planned aid arrived at its destination. Libya was taking advantage of the situation, and sent several humanitarian/military convoys to El-Fashir. In effect, it occupied Darfur and began to arm the Arab tribes.

Elections were held in **April 1986**, and Sadiq's Umma Party predictably won with 101 seats. Out of Darfur's 39 seats, 34 went to Umma. The new government under Sadiq al-Mahdi initially supported the Libyan presence in Darfur. This started ethnic tensions between the Arabs and the Africans, who were now at each other's throats. Thus, the new "democratic" government, by admitting Libyan Arabs into Darfur, added incitement to racial hatred. This was worse for Darfur than the neglect shown by previous regimes, including Nimeiry's.

An additional destabilizing factor in Darfur was the frequent incursions of the Chadian army into Darfur, to fight the Libyan forces stationed there, and, in the process, also attack Fur villages. In response, the Fur DDF activists started to create a force of 12,000 fighters to combat the Chadians. The DDF leader, Diraige, in exile in London, was desperately trying to acquire weapons for them. The situation in Darfur became extremely complex with Chadians, Libyans, local African and Arab tribes and Sudan's government troops, fighting each other with nobody knowing precisely who was fighting whom; it reached a point of global unmanageability.

Sadiq's Umma Party presided over a coalition government with two main coalition partners: the relatively moderate **Democratic Unionist Party (DUP)**, which had emerged from the old Khatmia Party, and the **National Islamic Front (NIF)**, a radical Islamist organization that was created by **Hassan al-Turabi** after the fall of Nimeiry in 1985. An important difference between the DUP and the NIF was their approach to the civil war in the south, which has been raging since 1983. On **November 16, 1988**, the DUP signed a peace memorandum with the Southern Sudanese in Addis Ababa (Ethiopia). However, Sadiq, as well as the NIF, refused to ratify it, claiming that it was a party and not a governmental act. On **February 22, 1989**, the Chief of Staff, **General Fathi Ahmed Ali**, gave Sadiq al-Mahdi an ultimatum: accept the peace memorandum or else…. The countdown of a coup had begun.

Meanwhile the fight between the DUP and NIF over the peace process continued and finally came to a head in Khartoum. On **July 1, 1989**, a group of NIF officers led by Colonel **Omar Hassan al-Bashir** overthrew the government of Sadiq al-Mahdi, and formed an Islamist military regime that is still in power.

On **December 12, 1999**, President Omar al-Bashir proclaimed a state of emergency, and forced **Hassan al-Turabi**, the leader of the Sudanese Islamic revolution in 1989, to resign as president of the Parliament, stripping him of his power. To understand this drastic step, we have to look into Turabi's personality and power.

Turabi was a brilliant political tactician, albeit unprincipled and Machiavellian. After the overthrow of Abboud's dictatorship in 1964, he started to reorganize the Islamist party, and, by clever maneuvering, became the undisputed leader of the movement. When the Islamists finally came to power in **June 1989**, the young ambitious radicals of the 60s and 70s had become staid supporters of the establishment (including President Omar al-Bashir), and started to resent Turabi's autocratic ways. They were now in power and in control of the government, eager to start a new course of international respectability, especially as they had recently joined the select club of oil producers. The old man objected to their policies, and had to be gotten rid of before he managed to put their heads on the block. This, then, was the background of the **December 1999** coup against Turabi.

Turabi did not take the loss of power lying down. He launched his own party, the **Popular Patriotic Congress (PPC)**. Most of the members of his new party came from the west, particularly from Darfur, where he cleverly capitalized on the Darfuri feelings of alienation, marginalization and frustration, and their meager representation in the politics of the Khartoum government.

Then, on **February 19, 2001**, the unbelievable happened. Turabi signed, in Geneva, a Memorandum of Understanding with his old southern guerilla opponent, Colonel **John Garang**, leader of the **Sudan People's Liberation Movement/Army (SPLM/A)**, to unite their forces and overthrow the Khartoum government—which owed its existence to the Islamist revolution, led by Turabi himself in 1989.

The SPLM/A together with Turabi's PPC then launched an offensive, trying to move into Darfur from the South, but were defeated by the Sudanese government forces. Khartoum's vengeance was swift and brutal. With thousands of civilians fleeing a murderous combination of aerial attacks and militia raiding, the situation became a small-scale model for what would develop two years later in Darfur.

The Khartoum government used the ouster of the Islamist extremist Turabi to sell itself to the international community as being modern, progressive, and benign. **President W. Bush**, after the al-Qaeda attack on 9/11/01, was eager to find "good Arabs" to collaborate with against terrorism, and found Khartoum a willing partner. At the same time, Washington strongly supported a negotiated settlement of the North-South conflict to pacify the Christian fundamentalist electorate, which was strongly sympathetic to the Christian south.

While the North-South peace negotiations were in progress, the situation in Darfur was rapidly deteriorating. But before describing the escalation of the conflict between Darfur and the government, which ultimately led to genocide, I want to summarize the situation in Darfur, and the attitude of Khartoum towards Darfur at the end of the 20th century.

The regime in Khartoum continued, in the tradition of the British colonial period, to consider Sudan as an Arab country centered along the Nile, with "African appendages" in the West (Darfur) and in the South, where Christian missionaries had "unfortunately been allowed to subvert the people." The non-Arab Muslims were of such an extreme diversity (in language, socio-economic standing, and tradition) that they never formed a cohesive unit. In contrast, the Arabs were cemented by the use of the sacred Arab language—the language of God. This helped to put the Arabs at the center of the landscape of the Sudanese Muslims. Their pre-eminence was bolstered by the fact that 80% of the intellectuals, professionals, and bankers, were Arabs.

The belief of the Khartoum government in the Nile-Arab superiority resulted in complete neglect of any development in Darfur, be it in education, health services, transport, industrialization, or economy. Furthermore, the participation of the Darfuri in the political process in Sudan was severely curtailed.

Despite its general neglect of Darfur, the central government in Khartoum demanded that Darfur supply a disproportionate number of soldiers for the civil war of the North against the South. This led to the irony that the Darfuri were asked to fight for the defense of an ideology that marginalized and discriminated against them at home.

Additional resentment of the Darfuri towards the government was caused by the action of some governors in Darfur,[99] who started to restructure the local tribal administration by filling most positions with their Arab friends from Khartoum, or local Arabs.

These actions and attitudes of the Khartoum government drove the young people of Darfur to take up arms and start a guerilla movement that gradually grew in strength. Thus, in the **late 1990s**, Darfur was a marginalized, frustrated region with sporadic violence taking place. But this distant, troubled West was far from the national conscience of the Khartoum government. Khartoum saw its main problem as being the achievement of peace with the South. Little did the Khartoum government realize that the two conflicts were intertwined, and that peace between the North and South could not be achieved without solving the problems in Darfur.

The start of the insurgency, the counterinsurgency and genocide. Although there were many skirmishes between Darfuri and governmental forces in 2001 and 2002, **February 28, 2003** is generally considered the date the insurgency really took off. On that day, 300 well-organized Darfuri fighters attacked the government garrison in **Golu**, a small town on the border between West and North Darfur. They killed 200 soldiers and forced the garrison to flee. It was an embarrassing defeat of the government forces.

Who were the insurgents, and under what banner did they fight? There were two main insurgent organizations in Darfur. One was the **Sudan Liberation Movement/Army (SLM/A)**, a secular movement led by **Abdel Wahid Mohamed al-Nur**, a Fur lawyer who forged an alliance between the Fur and Zaghawa to form the rebel movement. Although the Zaghawa accounted for only 10% of the population in Darfur, their wealth and influence was large, and disproportionate to their number. Many of the Zaghawa had been officers in the Chadian army, and their military experience played an important role in the successes of the SLM/A. A young Zaghawa named **Minni Minnawi**, a secondary school graduate with no experience in politics or combat, but with great ambitions, became the leader of the Zaghawa faction, which split off to form an independent unit in 2004. In the years that followed, the movement divided and fragmented further until more than half a dozen groups claimed the name SLA.

Darfur's second rebel group was the **Justice and Equality Movement (JEM)**. It was controlled by Islamists from the Kobe tribe, a Zaghawa subgroup more numerous in Chad than in Darfur. JEM was smaller than SLM/A, and never had the military punch the SLM/A initially had. JEM was led by **Khalil Ibrahim**, a highly educated and superb organizer, who had supported the military coup in 1989, and had held a number of posts in the NIF. His political objective was the unity of Sudan, and he strongly opposed the secession of the South. Unlike the SLA, JEM did not advocate separation of religion and state, and adhered to an even more extreme Islamist ideology than the regime in Khartoum. Many of the JEM leaders had served in the Sudan government and had kept important connections in Khartoum that they hoped to use to attack the regime from within. JEM received arms and political backing from Eritrea, and after 2005 from Chad (whose president, Idriss Deby, was a fellow Zaghawa), and from Gaddafi (who was eager to bankroll and arm Khartoum's adversaries).

---

[99] In 1995 Darfur was divided into three regions, West, North and South (see map on page 212), as were the other eight states of the Sudan federation.

The two Darfur rebel groups, SLM/A and JEM, formed an awkward coalition. They were united by deep resentment at the marginalization of Darfur, but with their disparate goals and ideologies, were not natural bedfellows. The regime in Khartoum, with its divide-and-conquer strategy, worked hard, and ultimately successfully, to split up the alliance.

After the February attack at Golu, the rebels continued to attack governmental posts, showing that they meant business. On **April 25, 2003**, they attacked Nyala and El-Fashir, killing many soldiers, capturing weapons, and blowing up airplanes. In May, they killed (in combat) 500 soldiers near **Kutum**, which they managed to take in **August**.

At the beginning of the conflict, the government in Khartoum described the fighting as a local ethnic squabble carried out by "armed bandits." They were unwilling to negotiate with the rebels, opting for a military solution to the crisis, expecting to crush the insurrection easily and fast. But to do that, they had to have the means at their disposal, and the army, made up to a large extent of recruits from Darfur, was not fully trustworthy. To help defeat the insurrection, the Sudanese government decided to support and arm Arab militias, in particular the *Janjaweed* (Devils on Horse), who were a mixture of bandits, highwaymen, criminals released from jail, and members of Arab tribes who had land conflicts with their African neighbors. They were a cruel and brutal bunch, who were now supported and given a clear field of action by the government.

By late **July 2003**, the violence escalated to a new ferocity, culminating in genocide. Government planes bombed villages, killing many civilians, and destroying fixed civilian targets. After the air attacks were over, the Janjaweed on their horses would arrive, loot personal belongings, rape the girls and women, steal their cattle, and kill the donkeys. Then they would burn the houses and shoot all those who could not run away. Utter destruction of the villages was their clear goal. Those who were lucky enough to escape started to congregate in **Internally Displaced Persons (IDP)** camps. The violence targeted not only indigenous residents of Darfur, but also aid workers and peacekeepers, limiting the ability of the international community to conduct relief operations.

Insurgencies are very difficult to suppress when they are supported by the local population, as is the case in Darfur. Examples of such situations abound, in the past and present, e.g., in Algiers, Vietnam, Iraq, Afghanistan, and even the Israeli-Arab conflict. So how can a government that believes in the legitimacy of Arab domination of the Sudan— and has governed Darfur (and to a large extent the South) for decades through varying degrees of neglect, discrimination and violence—win over the local population? No wonder the conflict in Darfur has not been resolved, and continues to this day.

As I mentioned before, the Khartoum government considered the conflict in the South of far greater importance than that in Darfur. As the two conflicts, are, to some extent, intertwined and share some of the same causes, I shall digress and discuss the **origins and developments of the civil war between the North and South:**

Friction and sporadic fighting between the North and South is of long standing; it began after Britain united the two regions in 1917. After Sudan gained independence in **1956**, a civil war broke out that lasted until **1972**. In **1983**, a second civil war, more extensive and brutal than the first, broke out. It lasted for 22 years (till 2005) and claimed the lives of 2 million people (mostly Southerners), and the displacement of 4 million.

Some of the causes of the conflict were similar to those in Darfur: marginalization, neglect, political exclusion of the South by the regime in Khartoum and the unwillingness to share power and wealth, a problem that escalated with the discovery of oil in both regions in the 1980s. An additional, important component was the ethnic and religious (not present in Darfur) divide between the two regions. The North was populated by Muslim Arabs, whereas, the population in the South were Africans who practiced Christianity or traditional African religions.

The fighting force in the South was the **Sudan People's Liberation Movement/Army (SPLM/A)**, organized and led by **John Garang**, an effective, charismatic Southerner, and a colonel in the Sudanese army, with a Ph.D. from Iowa State University. The SPLM/A was supported and armed by Russia (via Eritrea) and developed into a formidable force. By 2003, with both parties exhausted, peace talks between the Khartoum government and Garang's SPLM/A started to show some progress that ultimately led to a peace agreement. Ironically, just at that time the uprising in Darfur took place.

The civil war officially ended with the signing of the **Comprehensive Peace Agreement (CPA)** mediated by a US-led coalition in Nairobi, Kenya, on **January 9, 2005**. It stipulated the formation of a **Government of National Unity (GNU)**, dominated by the **National Congress Party (NCP)**, which is a descendant of he NIF that overthrew Sudan's last democratically elected government in 1989. The head of the NCP was al-Bashir who also served as President of Sudan. The Southern SPLM constituted the minority coalition partner, and was, by and large, sidelined by the NCP, although the leader of the SPLM, Salva Kiir (who succeeded John Garang after his death in July 2005) also served as vice president of Sudan. The SPLM was also the leading party of the semiautonomous **Government of Southern Sudan (GoSS)**. The peace agreement (CPA) required that national elections be held. They were originally scheduled for 2008, but were postponed several times, the latest date being **April 2010**. It also mandated an internationally-monitored referendum to be held no later than **January 9, 2011,** to determine whether the South should secede from the North. On that date, an overwhelming majority of South Sudanese voted to secede from Sudan. But the new independent state plunged into crisis in **December 2013**, with the eruption of existing tensions between President Salva Kiir Mayardit, a Dinka, and the former Vice President **Riek Machar**, a Nuer. The Dinka and the Nuer, the country's two largest ethnic groups, pitched against each other, have been committing horrific attacks on civilians. The fighting between government troops, and opposition factions (led by Riek Machar), has killed thousands and prompted more than 2.2 million people to flee their homes. A tentative, internationally-mediated, peace agreement was signed in **August 2015** by Kiir and Machar. The agreement is potentially very important, and could change the lives of hundreds of thousands of people affected by the civil war. However, dissension within the opposition makes it seem unlikely that the fighting will end anytime soon.

A major flaw of these peace agreements is that the conflict in Darfur is not addressed; it was left out on purpose during all the peace negotiations between the South and North. This seems short-sighted, as peace cannot take root in one part of Sudan while another part remains unstable and prone to extreme violence.

Back to the conflict in Darfur. In **September 2003**, the representatives of the SLM/A and the Sudanese government met in Abéché (Chad) and signed a 45-day truce, which would allow humanitarian aid to arrive in the overflowing IDP camps. However, neither the local guerilla units nor the JEM accepted the truce and the fighting continued, with the Sudanese government perpetrating the most atrocious violations of human rights. The IDP camps were steadily growing, and to add to the misery, the Sudanese government was preventing food aid from abroad to reach them. Worse yet, people who had talked to the USAID representatives who had arrived in Darfur in **mid-February 2004** were immediately arrested after the departure of the USAID representatives. The UN Humanitarian Coordinator, Mukesh Kapila, was advocating an international court to bring to trial the individuals who were masterminding the war crimes in Darfur. But nothing was done, and the Sudanese perpetrators—whose names were known—were still received in international forums. In **March 2004**, Turabi, who had been released from jail in October 2003, held a press conference in which he blamed the government for the situation in Darfur. He was promptly re-arrested on charges of trying to organize a coup.

In **April 2004**, the United Nations was asking for a fact-finding mission to be sent to Darfur, but the Sudan government was dragging its feet in granting permission. When the UN team finally arrived, it was prevented from traveling to regions where the worst atrocities had taken place. Khartoum had one trump card to play against the international community that pressed for more action: If too much pressure were exerted against them, they would call off the peace negotiations between the North and South. It worked, but only partially, and Khartoum slowly submitted to diplomatic pressure to loosen up on the counterinsurgency. Khartoum now began to rely more on the perilous food and medical situation to finish off the job that the militias had started. In effect, people would now die under a different label—**genocide by attrition**. By mid-2004, there were 1.2 million IDPs, 100,000 refugees in Chad, and over a million war-affected persons. The World Food Program (WFP) could supply only a fraction of the requirements for the 2.3 million needy people. Furthermore, as the rainy season commenced, many IDP camps soon became inaccessible and altogether cut off from food supplies.

On **July 11, 2004**, the UN Security Council adopted a resolution that gave Khartoum until August 30 to disarm the Janjaweed. It was the first of similar empty demands that were not heeded. Meanwhile, President Bashir straight-facedly declared that the Darfur crisis was caused by an "international agenda to seek oil and gold from the region."

Peace negotiations about Darfur started in Abuja (Nigeria), but collapsed on **September 15, 2004**, and the European Parliament declared that the situation in Darfur was "tantamount to a genocide." The United Nations demanded that more African Union (AU) troops be deployed in Darfur. But by **October 2004**, the forces of the AU reached a mere 600 soldiers.

By the **end of 2004**, the Sudanese government had mastered the new rules of killing by starvation and disease, and was in no hurry to negotiate with the rebels. The situation was further exacerbated by the growing tensions between the two main guerilla groups: the JEM and the SLM. Ironically, the JEM was more radically Islamist than the government; the JEM refused to discuss the idea of separation of religion and politics, and was jockeying for power in Khartoum. The SLM/A, on the other hand, was resolutely secular, and its main agenda was resolving the situation in Darfur rather than taking power in Khartoum. These disparate goals translated on the ground into squabbles about tactics, and sharing of military supplies and loot, which eventually developed into full-scale fighting between the two movements. Amidst these growing social and economic strains, the guerillas were losing control, and bandit groups and warlords were springing up; Darfur was descending into total anarchy. Further fragmentation of the guerilla groups, which was manipulated and encouraged by Khartoum, made any meaningful peace negotiations very difficult.

After several unsuccessful peace efforts, the international community managed, in **May 2006,** in **Abuja (Nigeria)**, to cobble together a peace agreement, which became known as the **Darfur Peace Agreement (DPA)**. It was not very favorable for the guerillas, and lacked guarantees and enforcement provisions. It called for the disarmament of the guerillas and the Janjaweed, but the government claimed it had no control over the Janjaweed. The DPA also mandated ridiculously low compensation for war victims.

But the main weakness of the DPA was that, besides the Sudanese government, only one rebel splinter group signed it—the Minni Minnawi faction of the SLM/A. The other faction of the SLM/A (led by its founder Abdel Wahid) as well as the JEM, refrained from signing the agreement. The IDPs were also against the DPA, claiming that it would legally enable Khartoum to manipulate them into submission, while the international community would congratulate itself on "having restored peace."

In **late 2010** a larger peace process began in **Doha, Qatar**. But by **May 2011** talks fell apart and JEM, the largest and militarily most sophisticated of the rebel groups in Darfur, removed itself from the process. In a scramble to salvage the Doha talks, international mediators brought together a group of 11 rebel factions for the purpose of negotiations. Called the **Liberty and Justice Movement (LJM)**, it served as the unified voice of the Darfuri rebels. Despite the withdrawal of JEM and the non-participation of many of the other rebel groups, the Doha talks continued, with LJM serving as the main Darfuri negotiator. **On July 14, 2011**, LJM and the Sudanese government finally signed the **Doha Document for Peace in Darfur (DDPD)**.

One big difference between Darfur and South Sudan is that Darfur possesses no natural resources. Consequently, the notion of an independent Darfur is a non-starter, as it could not result in an economically viable state. This had forced some of the rebels, especially JEM, to adopt as their goal a change in the Khartoum government, in the hope of a more equitable distribution of wealth and power. In contrast, the goal of the DDPD is to stop the fighting.

On **November 11, 2011**, JEM joined other rebel groups to create a new political and military alliance, known as the **Sudanese Revolutionary Front (SRF)**. The SRF calls for a change in regime, and the unification of all of Sudan's opposition forces. And the violence continues.

The reaction of the world to the Darfur crisis. At first the Darfur crisis went almost unnoticed, as the international community concentrated on the North-South peace negotiations in Naivasha, Kenya. When it was finally noticed by the world, it was characterized as a quintessential "African crisis": distant, esoteric, violent, rooted in complex ethnic and historical factors which few understood, and devoid of any practical interest for the rich countries—a humanitarian problem that was passed on to the United Nations. The Sudanese press described Darfur as a "tribal conflict carried out by bandits aided by Americans and Zionists."

Slowly the media started to report on Darfur, but it was the interview given by UN Human Rights Coordinator Mukesh Kapila in **March 2004** that galvanized the world. He compared Darfur to Rwanda, which had become the baseline reference for absolute evil and the need to care. It rocked the conscience of the world. Heart-wrenching images of starving children, rapes, evil horsemen, bombing raids, and burning villages, started to appear in the media. It became the horror story of the year.

Why was there such a delay in the media coverage of Darfur? One reason was that it was overshadowed by the Naivasha peace negotiations between the North and South. Another was the puzzlement over the conflict in Darfur. People believed they understood the North-South conflict: it was a religious war in which wicked Muslims killed desperate, struggling Christians. However, in Darfur, Muslims were fighting Muslims—an unexpected and difficult situation to explain. No wonder Darfur was perceived, foremost, as a "humanitarian crisis." It is a "feel-good" designation that needs no explanations: The job of the humanitarians is to alleviate the suffering, and not to analyze the causes of the disaster they are asked to deal with.

Now I want to discuss the specific actions (or inactions) of the various governments and organizations:

1) The **United Nations (UN)** was in a very difficult position regarding the Darfur crisis for a number of reasons. First, it was deeply involved in the Naivasha North-South peace negotiations from which Khartoum threatened to walk away if pressure was put on them concerning their behavior in Darfur. Second, the United Nations was heavily involved in the humanitarian efforts, both in Southern Sudan and in Darfur. Third, the split between Arabs and Black Africans, which was implicit in the Darfur crisis, had many echoes in the United Nations, and needed to be handled with great care and delicacy. Fourth, since China had strong economic interests in the Sudan, the Security Council's resolution had to be watered down and made "toothless," lest China use her veto power. Fifth, if the UN member states called the event a genocide, then, according to the 1948 Geneva Convention, it would be mandatory for UN Secretary General Kofi Annan to act; it was Kofi Annan's nightmare that the member states would fail to give him the necessary financial, military, and political means to do so.

Caught on the horns of so many dilemmas, Kofi Annan had to act with great circumspection, to scold without threatening, and to help without intruding too much. The result was that he appeared weak and irresolute at a time when the United States and the other member states were insisting on more action, even though he knew that those who were applying pressure had no intentions of doing anything. This situation clearly demonstrated the United Nations' practical limitations in crises in which the heavyweight member states do not want to act.

Passing the buck to the African Union (see next section) was the United Nations' face-saving cop-out. "African solution to African problems" was the United Nations' politically correct way of saying, "We really don't want to deal with this problem."

2) The **African Union (AU)** was formed in 2002 from the vestiges of the Organization of African Unity (OAU), which had been heavily criticized for its ineffectiveness. Fifty-four African countries are members of the AU. Its structure is loosely modeled after the European Union (EU). It aims to boost development, eradicate poverty, and bring Africa into the global economy. Its charter allows the deployment of military forces in situation that include genocide and crimes against humanity. It can also authorize the establishment of specific peacekeeping missions. On **July 6, 2004**, the AU decided to get involved in the Darfur crisis, and sent 132 observers and 300 troops to protect Darfur. It was mandated to observe, but not to intervene. By **October 2004**, its force was increased to

6,000 troops. In **July 2004**, the AU authorized the establishment of the **African Union Mission in Sudan (AMIS)**. AMIS started with a force of 150 men, and slowly increased its troop levels in Darfur to 7,700 soldiers over a period of three years (2004–2007). Undermanned, under-equipped, riddled with corruption, hobbled by an inadequate mandate, it was totally ineffective. On **July 21, 2007**, the United Nations voted to replace AMIS by a hybrid UN-AU organization under the name **United Nations African Mission in Darfur (UNAMID)**. A force of 26,000 peacekeepers was authorized, but by the middle of 2009 only 16,000 were in place. Its yearly budget was set at 1.6 billion dollars. On the insistence of the Sudanese government, UNAMID maintains a predominantly African character. UNAMID's mandate is the protection of civilians, security of the humanitarian assistance, and verification of the implementation of agreements. Like its predecessor, AMIS, it is not mandated to intervene by force, and consequently is as ineffective in curbing violence in Darfur as was AMIS.

3) The **US government in Washington**, in 2004, was divided between two camps. The "realists," found mostly in the State Department and the CIA, argued that Khartoum was an important ally in the fight on terrorism, and should not be pressured too much on Darfur. The South Darfur lobby, mostly supported by the US Congress, was strongly anti-Khartoum, advocating strong sanctions and action. President W. Bush tried to accommodate both sides, 2004 being an election year. The results were predictably confusing. For instance, Secretary of State Colin Powell was ordered, during his **September 9, 2004** testimony in Congress, to use the term "genocide," but in the same breath it was recommended that no drastic actions be undertaken. Predictably, the interest level in the Sudan dropped sharply after President George W. Bush's re-election. Interestingly, before her term expired in 2008, Condoleezza Rice said the action (or inaction) she regretted most during her tenure as secretary of state was not having done more to resolve the crisis in Darfur.

Obama, during his presidential campaign, promised to get involved and solve the Darfur crisis, but his administration has not delivered on that promise. On **March 18, 2009**, President Obama appointed Air Force General **Scott Gration** as Special Envoy to Sudan. The son of missionaries, Gration spent his childhood in Africa, speaks Swahili, and has a degree in National Security Studies, all great qualifications for the job. Unfortunately, General Gration was perceived by many as too soft towards the Khartoum government, perhaps a reflection of Obama's conciliatory approach to foreign policy. On **April 13, 2009**, forty non-governmental organizations (NGOs) signed a letter in which they expressed concern about General Gration's conciliatory stance, and reluctance to criticize the government of Sudan.

Friction also developed in **July 2009** between Scott Gration, who told Congress that he thought Sudan was no longer a sponsor of terrorism, and UN Ambassador Susan Rice, who disagreed and continued to call the situation in Darfur genocide. In **October, 2009**, the Obama administration announced its policies toward Sudan. The main points were: 1) end the conflict in Darfur, 2) implement the CPA, 3) ensure that Sudan does not become a haven for terror. These are very laudable goals, but no specific effective measures were proposed to accomplish them. I am afraid that **Obama's mantra of "diplomacy" did not work** on autocratic regimes like al-Bashir's (or, for that matter, on Kim Jong-un in North Korea).

4) The **European Union** (**EU**) presented a complete lack of resolve and coordination over the Darfur-Sudan problem. The French cared only about protecting the regime in neighboring Chad; the British tried to follow Washington, which was a difficult task in view of Washington's ambiguous stance; the Scandinavians and the Netherlands contributed large amounts of money but remained silent; the Germans made anti-Khartoum noises, which they never backed up with any action; and the Italians remained bewildered. Everybody knew that only military intervention could have a drastic effect on the situation, but they were incapable of mustering the will and energy to do, in distant Darfur, what they failed to do at their doorsteps in Bosnia and Kosovo a few years earlier.

5) **China** holds a large share of responsibility in the Darfur horror. The reason is simple: oil. Most of Sudan's oil production (500,000 barrels/day) is exported to China. In exchange, China is investing extensively in the Sudan and is supplying Sudan with fighter bombers and weapons. Most important, it supports Khartoum diplomatically, and with its veto power in the UN Security Council, provides a severe stumbling block to meaningful conflict resolution. For instance, a maritime blockade of Port Sudan would quickly make the Sudanese government comply with the many UN resolutions that were never heeded. However, China would never agree to such an action; and keeping good relations with China is much more important to Washington than the conflict in Darfur.

6) The **International Criminal Court** (**ICC**) in The Hague, remains the lone member of the international community to behave honorably without being hampered by selfish considerations and fears of political fallouts that plagued many of the other actors.

On **June 15, 2006**, the ICC sent a report to the United Nations providing evidence of large-scale massacres and war crimes perpetrated by the Sudanese government. It started to prepare files and summons for the main perpetrators. On **May 2, 2009**, the ICC issued arrest warrants for three leading figures of the Sudanese government: **Ahmed Harun** who held the surrealistic position of Minister of Humanitarian affairs; **Ali Kushaib**, a key leader of the Janjaweed; and **Omar al-Bashir**, President of Sudan, the first sitting president to be charged by the ICC. The arrest warrant for al-Bashir lists five counts of crimes against humanity (murder, extermination, torture, forcible transfer, and rape), and two counts of war crimes (attacks on civilians, pillaging).

A second arrest warrant for President al-Bashir was issued on **July 12, 2010**. This second ICC warrant added three counts of **genocide,** for the ethnic cleansing of the Fur, Masalit, and Zaghawa tribes in Darfur. The new warrant will act as a supplement to the first, whereby the initial charges brought against al-Bashir will all remain in place, but will now include the crime of genocide.

Furthermore, Luis Moreno-Ocampo, the chief prosecutor of the ICC, stated that al-Bashir had siphoned off 9 billion dollars from the Sudanese government, and deposited them in his private account in a London bank. Al-Bashir denied this accusation, and claimed that Sudan is not a party to the ICC treaty, and could, therefore, not be expected to abide by its verdicts. He accused the prosecutor of being a political activist using double standards, because obvious crimes, like those committed in Palestine, Iraq, and Afghanistan, did not find their way to the international criminal court.

On April 26, 2010, the first democratic presidential election in decades was held in Sudan, and al-Bashir emerged the winner. By winning legitimate presidential elections, al-Bashir had hoped to evade the ICC's warrant for his arrest. His hope was fulfilled. He visited several neighboring countries with impunity: Kenya in August 2010, Djibouti in

May 2011, and Libya in January 2012. However, in August 2013, al-Bashir's plane was blocked from Saudi Arabia's airspace when al-Bashir attempted to attend the inauguration of Iranian President Rouhani, whose country is the main supplier of weapons to Sudan.

At present, no one expects to see the accused al-Bashir in court anytime soon.

The United Nations refuses to call the atrocities in Darfur "genocide." The atrocities committed by the Sudanese government in Darfur clearly fall within the definition of genocide, as outlined by the 1948 UN Genocide Convention (see page 179). Indeed, most people, institutions, and governments view it as such.

The first institution to utter the word "genocide" was the Holocaust Memorial Museum in Washington DC, in **May 2004**. Shortly thereafter, in **July 2004**, the US Senate and the House of Representatives declared the crisis in Darfur to be genocide, and on **September 9, 2004**, Secretary of State Colin Powell, in a testimony in the Senate, concurred with this designation.

While the United States and other nations call it genocide, the United Nations stopped short of using such language. On **October 7, 2004**, at the request of the Security Council, a commission of inquiry to investigate the atrocities in Darfur was established. The commission concluded that, while serious crimes against humanity and war crimes had been committed, the Sudanese Government had not pursued a policy of genocide. This conclusion came as a great relief to UN Secretary General Kofi Anan, who feared that calling the event a genocide would make it mandatory for him to act. To what extent the commission's conclusion was influenced by their fear to have to act, remains, in my mind, unresolved. Rhetoric is cheap, especially if it leads to inaction. The general consensus certainly points to the atrocities in Darfur as being genocide.

Comparison of the genocide in Darfur with the Holocaust. I want to conclude this section with an attempt to compare the genocide in Darfur with the Holocaust. The Nazi genocide during the years 1941–1945, is generally ascribed to an aberration by an extremist regime driven by race ideology, and a paranoid hate and fear of Jews. A sophisticated autocratic organization, a highly developed technology, and effective propaganda to imbue the German people with their ideology, enabled the Nazis to kill 6 million Jews, systematically and unopposed.

In contrast, the killing of Black Africans in Darfur is not based on ideology; it is not a systematic policy of the Khartoum regime. It is considered an inconvenient necessity in order to eliminate a group that poses a danger to the Arab regime. In addition, it is fueled by fear of having to share their recently acquired oil revenues. If there is an ideological component, it is the feeling of Arab superiority, which is deeply ingrained in the psyche of the Arab minority. It provided the justification of the regime's domination, and contributed to the violent suppressors of the rebellion that ultimately led to genocide.

Circumstances and conditions that engender violence and genocide

In the previous section I described several genocides in the hope of finding similarities—some common denominator—that would help us to understand the causes that led to their perpetration. But most genocides have their own characteristics and occur under different conditions, as I shall discuss in this section. However, there is one striking commonality to the genocides: they all occurred under **authoritarian rule** in totalitarian regimes. None of the genocides were committed in functioning democracies.

Totalitarian regimes create the situational conditions that can transform people's thinking and actions. The authorities invoke loyalty, duty, and discipline to insure obedience; they assume full responsibility for the actions of the population, which is seduced into abandoning its usual moral values to become "willing executioners"[100] of the feared and admired leader. This was the case in Nazi Germany where people blindly obeyed orders of the government and participated in committing evil acts, or stood passively by. The totalitarian regimes create institutions dealing with education, justice and propaganda, all of which are designed to support and bolster the policies of the regime. Thus, we conclude, the most important difference between states or societies that commit genocide and those that don't is the **system of government**.

I will now discuss, with examples from the previous sections, a variety of circumstances that contribute to the perpetration of genocide: fanatical ideologies, exacerbated traditional hatreds, exploitation of economic motives, waging of wars, the presence of imperialism, and colonial regimes. (See page 180, footnote 71.)

Fanatical ideologies (zealotry). Examples are: the Crusaders who, in the name of God and their religion, tried to kill as many infidels as possible and recapture the Holy Land; the Nazi's biological racism that fueled the Holocaust; the Pan-Turkish extreme nationalism of the Young Turks that brought about the Armenian genocide; the radical Marxism of the Khmer Rouge that envisaged a utopian agrarian society; the genocide in Rwanda, where the "Hamitic hypothesis," artificially created by the Belgian occupiers during the first half of the 20th century, encouraged the Hutus to kill 1.5 million "inferior" Tutsis.

In many of these cases, the ideologies endow the perpetrators with a feeling of superiority, that they are better and more advanced than their victims. In their minds, this justifies expansionist policies that can lead to war and colonization. The ideologies also often provide a smokescreen for the basic instincts of greed, fear, and lust for power.

Traditional hatreds that may have simmered for centuries. The hatred is directed against a particular group that is singled out for being different in some respect. It creates a situation of "us" vs. "them" in which the perpetrators of evil subscribe to a dual set of moral values: Doing harm to members of their own group, "us," is forbidden, but violence and killing "them" is allowed. The differences between the perpetrators and the targeted group may be:

> Ethnic, e.g., the Hutu and Tutsi in Rwanda, the genocide in Bosnia and Kosovo, the genocide in Darfur
>
> Racial, e.g., the Holocaust, white Australians killing Tasmanians and Aborigines
>
> Religious, e.g., the Crusaders, Christian Serbs killing Muslim Bosnians and Albanians

---

[100] D.J. Goldhagen, "Hitler's Willing Executioners," A. Knopf Inc., 1996.

> Nationalistic, e.g., the Armenian genocide, Russians killing fellow Slavs, the massacre of Polish officers in Katyn (1940)
>
> Political, e.g., the Khmer Rouge killing fellow Cambodians

Hatreds, by themselves, seldom precipitate genocides, but they form the proper ambience in which genocides can take place. As Friedländer, referring to the Holocaust, put it aptly in his metaphor: "The anti-Jewish frenzy of the Nazis was not hurled into a void. The flames that Hitler set alight burned as intensely as they did only because a dense underbrush of fanatic anti-Semitism was ready to catch fire. Without Hitler, the arsonist, the fire would not have started; without the underbrush it would not have spread as far and as intensely as it did, and destroy an entire world."[101]

However, a glimmer of hope is brought about by modern technology. The ease of travel, TV, the internet as a social medium, enable us to see other people thousands of miles away as human, like us. It blurs the distinction between "us" and "them" that is the cause of so much deadly violence.

Economic motives. These are, essentially, an expression of the basic human trait of greed. They underlie slavery in America and elsewhere, as well as the aggression against blacks and native peoples. As in the case of ideological differences, economic motives are often cloaked in an ideology of superiority, enhanced by the devaluation and dehumanization of the oppressed. In the Darfur genocide, economic interests, the unwillingness of the Sudanese government to share its oil revenues with Darfur, played a role. Many wars have been fought over economic issues. War has many commonalities with genocide: It can be viewed as an internationally sanctioned form of killing. It is also a great facilitator of genocide, as discussed next.

War. War accustoms society to a pervasive climate of violence. It numbs the senses to reduce the barrier against killing that prevails in normal times. The quest for victory further diminishes the inhibitions toward violence. War engenders obedience to the authority that pledges deliverance from the threat of a mortal enemy. The ease with which people kill one another erodes the boundary between legality and criminality. This point is best illustrated by the leaflet written during World War II by the Soviet author Ilya Ehrenburg, entitled "Kill." He said, among other things: "The Germans are not human beings. If you have not killed at least one German a day, you have wasted the day."

On an operational level, war provides an effective smokescreen for genocide. Traditional sources of information are rigidly controlled, and military constraints prevent investigations and reporting of atrocities. Wartime marshaling of technological resources and infrastructures become accepted facts. For example, the use of rail and freight infrastructures, as well as the construction of concentration camps with efficient ovens to incinerate the victims, was essential to the extermination of millions of Jews. "That's war" becomes an excuse for campaigns of exterminations.

Two great genocides of the 20th century took place during wartimes. The Armenian genocide of 1915 was carried out on the grounds of military "self defense" against an ethnic group accused of collaborating with Russia, the arch-enemy of the Ottoman Empire. The Holocaust took place during World War II; the mass killings started with the German invasion of Poland in September 1939. The large-scale killing under Lenin and epic

---

[101] S. Friedländer, "The Years of Extermination," Harper Collins, 2007.

slaughter under Stalin during the Bolshevik Revolution in Russia is inconceivable without the trauma of World War I.

Imperialism and colonization. Imperialism is a policy undertaken by a state to control foreign economic, physical, and cultural resources. Colonialism is the politico-military form of imperialism that establishes the rule over an alien people geographically separated from the ruling power. It often leads to destruction of native societies, accomplished by massacres, expulsion, forced labor, deprivations (e.g., famines), and the spread of diseases. Examples are: the Herero genocide committed by the Germans in their African colony of Namibia in 1905 (see page 185); the genocide in Darfur perpetrated by the Sudanese government (pages 212–226); slavery and the massacres of indigenous people on the American continent; the India Imperial Famine in 1897–98, during which the British rulers were more concerned about India's balance of payment than about saving lives. (It is estimated that during that period 12–16 million people perished.) Japanese imperialism resulted in massacres, and genocides in the countries they occupied: In the late 19th century, the Japanese occupied Korea and Taiwan; in 1937, they mounted a full-scale invasion of China's eastern seaboard and key internal points; during the Japanese occupation (1937–1945), 2.7 million unarmed Chinese civilians were killed. Another consequence of colonialism was the Congo Rubber Terror, which involved the murderous exploitation of the indigenous Congo population by King Leopold of Belgium, in the second half of the 19th century. Rubber tappers and porters were mercilessly exploited and driven to death. During Leopold's reign, the Congo population dropped from 20 million to 10 million people. In 1960, the Belgians relinquished the territory and handed over the Congo to a pro-western despot, Mobutu Seko. Now, at the beginning of the 21st century, the Congo is again torn apart—in the absence of colonialism—by a destructive military conflict. It shows the multifaceted nature of the causes of destruction and evil. The conflict in Vietnam, a black mark in US foreign policy, also has its roots in colonialism. A bloody attempt by France in 1945–1954 to re-conquer Vietnam, the jewel in the colonial crown, was defeated by a nationalistic, guerilla movement: the Vietcong, headed by Ho Chi Minh. The South Vietnamese opposed the Vietcong and set up their own regime under Ngo Diem; it was supported by the United States In 1961, the United States stepped up military intervention, and, in 1965, invaded South Vietnam to combat the Vietcong. The outcome of this deplorable war was the signing of a peace agreement in 1973, followed by a withdrawal of all US troops. In 1975, the North defeated the South. Fifty-eight thousand US soldiers were killed in Indochina, and 2–5 million Indochinese were killed in the conflict. The atrocities committed by the US forces in Vietnam show the close connection between war and genocide.

In this section, I have discussed the many circumstances that lead to violence and genocide. The multiplicity of paths, usually several of them acting in synergy, keeps us from finding the silver bullet to prevent the commission of evil. But there is one common actor that dominates the scenes. It is Homo sapiens himself (or shouldn't we more appropriately call him Homo calamitus?) We can't change his DNA to reprogram him but perhaps we can try to understand his psyche that leads him to commit such unbelievable, atrocious acts of violence. An attempt in this direction is made in the next chapter.

8. AN ATTEMPT TO UNDERSTAND

Are we "hard-wired" for evil? Is the Holocaust but one manifestation of this? Can we avoid a repetition? Is the human species doomed to self-destruct?

Violence, brutalities, savagery, and slaughters have been with us since recorded history. What seems to be different now from times past is that our technology and destructive power has far outpaced our ability to maintain peace and social order. It is a miracle that the atomic bomb that was developed during World War II has not been used for more than 70 years. But how long can this situation last? It seems to me only a matter of time until a nuclear holocaust raises havoc and destroys us all. In this context, the Holocaust of the Nazi regime will be only a blip in the history of humankind. But perhaps these unfathomable events share a common cause—the inherent evil in us.

What makes the human species annihilate its own kind? Is this aggressiveness and evil hardwired (i.e., genetic), or is it engendered by the environment and upbringing? This is the age-old question of Nature vs. Nurture.

If we want to preserve the human species and, on a smaller scale, avoid a repetition of the Holocaust, we need to understand the forces and dynamics that lead to these horrendously destructive acts. This is a daunting task, and I want to state at the outset that I will not arrive at clear, unique, and definitive conclusions with a final recipe to save humankind. The problem is too complex for that. My goal is to delineate some aspects of the problem: describe factors that lead people to commit evil acts, and discuss how one might resist, oppose, and prevent them. I shall start with a description of two classic experiments that were designed and carried out to elucidate the perpetration of evil. The results of these experiments shock our beliefs in the qualities of human nature.

Two landmark experiments that show our capacity for doing evil

In the 1960s and early 1970s, two social psychologists, Stanley Milgram[102] and Philip Zimbardo,[103, 104] performed two different ground-breaking experiments that showed, with stunning clarity, our capacity for doing evil deeds. I shall discuss the experiments first, and then the conclusions derived from them.

Milgram's Obedience to Authority Experiment

Stanley Milgram was, in the early 1960s, a professor of psychology at Yale University in New Haven, Connecticut. His interest in the problem of obedience to authority came from deep personal concerns about how so many "good" German citizens could have become involved in the murder of millions of Jews.

Milgram set up a conceptually simple experiment. A person comes to a psychological laboratory and is told to carry out a series of acts that come increasingly into conflict with

---

[102] Stanley Milgram, "Obedience to Authority," Harper and Row, 1974.

[103] Philip Zimbardo, "The Lucifer Effect; Understanding How Good People Turn Evil," Random House, 2007.

[104] Milgram and Zimbardo were classmates at James Monroe High School in the Bronx in 1949. As Zimbardo tells it, Milgram was the smartest kid in the class, and Zimbardo the most popular. When they met in 1960 and discussed their past, they found out that Milgram had wanted to be popular, and Zimbardo had wanted to be smart!

his conscience. The question Milgram addressed was how far the participant would comply with the researcher's instructions before refusing to carry them out.

Here is how the experiment was performed: Two people come to a psychology laboratory to take part in a study of memory and learning; they are greeted by the psychologist/researcher, whose serious demeanor and white laboratory coat convey scientific importance; he explains to the participants that they are there to help psychologists find ways to improve people's learning and memory through the use of punishment; one of the participants is designated as a "teacher" and the other as a "learner"; the learner is led to a room, seated in a chair with his arms strapped to prevent excessive movement, and electrodes are attached to his wrist; he is given a set of word pairs to memorize; when the teacher gives a key word, the learner must respond with the correct association; whenever he makes a mistake, he will receive electric shocks in increasing intensity.

The real focus of the experiment is on the teacher. After watching the learner being strapped into place, he is taken into another room and seated in front of an impressive shock generator. Its main feature is 30 switches, ranging from 15 volts to 450 volts in 15-volt increments. There are also verbal designations, ranging from "slight shock" to "danger-severe shock." The teacher is told to administer the test to the learner in the other room. When the learner makes a mistake, the teacher is to give him an electric shock. He is to start at the lowest level (15 volts), and to increase the level by 15 volts each time the learner makes an error.

The "teacher" is a genuinely naïve subject who has come to participate in an important scientific experiment. The learner, or victim, on the other hand, is an actor (an accomplice of the researcher) who actually receives **no shocks at all**. The point of the experiment is to see how far a person proceeds, on a quantitatively measured voltage scale, when ordered by the researcher to inflict increasing pain on a protesting victim. At what point will the subject refuse to obey the researcher?

Initially the learner does well, but soon he begins to make errors, and responds to the electric shocks of increasing intensity, indicating that he is experiencing discomfort: At 75 volts the "learner" grunts; at 120 volts he complains verbally; at 150 volts he demands to be released from the experiment. As the shocks escalate in intensity, the learner's protests grow increasingly vehement. At 285 volts his response becomes an agonized scream. At this point some teachers refuse to continue with the experiment. But the researcher insists on continuing. The researcher reminds the teacher of his agreement to participate fully. Moreover, the researcher reasserts his responsibility for the consequences of administering the shocks. And so the teacher continues. At even more dangerous shock levels (330 volts and higher) there is no sound coming from the learner's room. The implication is that the learner may be unconscious or, worse, dead. Now the teacher really wants to quit, but nothing he says gets him out of this distressing situation: He is sternly told by the researcher to follow the rules and continue to shock—and he obeys.

The result of Milgram's experiment was that two out of every three (65%) of the volunteer teachers went all the way up to the maximum shock level of 450 volts. This was an unexpected and very disturbing result. Remember, after the shock level reached 330 volts, only silence came from the shock chamber, and the teacher could reasonably assume that the learner was unconscious.

Milgram then changed several conditions of his basic experiment to investigate the effect of:

1) <u>Interposing an intermediary.</u> The teacher performed only the testing; an assistant who was assigned to him actually pressed the switch and delivered the shock. In this situation the teacher was further removed from responsibility for administering the shocks, and his obedience to the researcher rose from 65% to 90%.

2) <u>Changing the spatial arrangement between teacher-learner and teacher-researcher.</u> When the victim (learner) was placed in the same room with the teacher, the obedience was reduced from 65% to 40%. When the researcher (the authority) was physically removed from the laboratory, the obedience precipitously declined from 65% to 23%. The teacher was able to resist the researcher far better when he did not have to face him.

3) <u>Reducing the perceived authority of the researcher and the setting.</u> When the experiment was moved to Bridgeport, a less respected and distinguished place than Yale, the obedience dropped from 65% to 48%. When orders were given by an ordinary man with the blessings of the researcher, who excused himself and left, the obedience dropped to a mere 20%. Clearly, the decisive factor is the response to authority.

4) <u>A peer group.</u> Two accomplice teachers joined the "naïve" teacher. When the two accomplices were unwilling at some point to continue to administer shocks, only 10% of the "naïve" teachers obediently continued the experiment. Thus, the effect of peer rebellion is very pronounced.

5) <u>Giving the choice of shock level to the teacher.</u> When the teacher was free to choose any shock level he wished, almost all teachers administered the lowest shock level. Although obedience does not play a role in this experiment, its outcome is relevant in refuting the claim that aggression, rather than obedience, provided the driving force in Milgram's experiments. (See later discussion.)

6) <u>Cultural background.</u> When Milgram's basic experiment was repeated in several countries, essentially the same results as at Yale were found. However, a significant exception was found in Germany, where D.M. Mantell repeated Milgram's experiment in 1970.[105] It is interesting that Mantell's motivation was not to explore whether the result of German upbringing may have played a role in facilitating the Holocaust (as was mine in searching the literature), but rather to compare the results from a nation (the US) "enmeshed in the conflict in Vietnam and disorder at home," with a nation (Germany) "which had been relatively peaceful and quiet for the past 25 years." I find Mantell's motivation almost as interesting as his experimental results! Mantell, repeating Milgram's basic experiment, found 85% obedience, in contrast to 65% found by Milgram. Mantell claims that this difference is statistically not significant. I disagree; to me, it does seem significant. The significance becomes clearer when we look at the results differently, and compare the percent of **defiant** people: In Germany it was 15% (100%–85%), whereas at Yale it was 35%—i.e., more than double.

Zimbardo's Stanford Prison Experiment

In the summer of 1971, Philip Zimbardo, a professor of psychology at Stanford University, extended Milgram's studies beyond the investigation of obedience. He

---

[105] D.M. Mantell, "The Potential for Violence in Germany," *Journal of Social Issues* 27(4), 1971.

designed an experiment to investigate the social forces that elicit evil actions. Zimbardo randomly (by a flip of a coin) assigned 24 experimental subjects to be either "prisoners" or "guards" in a mock prison set up in the basement of Stanford University's psychology building. All of the participants were middle-class, undergraduate students, who had passed a rigorous screening test designed to weed out anyone at risk for mental instability. There were no measurable personality differences between the two groups when the experiment began. Zimbardo himself played the role of warden. The students were paid $15 a day for their participation.

Zimbardo was originally concerned that the participants wouldn't take the experiment seriously enough. To his surprise and eventual horror, the opposite happened: The two groups were consumed by their new roles, and morphed into sadistic guards and emotionally broken inmates. At the beginning of the experiment there were no differences between the two groups; after one week there were no similarities. The guards flexed their power by making the prisoners obey trivial, often inconsistent rules, and forced them to perform tedious, pointless tasks. The inmates were dehumanized by being addressed only by their numbers, which they had to sound off repeatedly in roll calls. They were forced to do endless push-ups, occasionally with a guard's foot on their backs. In short, the guards quickly came to abuse their new-found power by behaving sadistically—demeaning, degrading, and hurting the prisoners.

The prisoners became despondent. In less than 36 hours, one of them had to be released because of extreme depression, disorganized thinking, uncontrollable crying, and fits of rage. Over the next three days, three more prisoners were let go because they exhibited similar symptoms of anxiety. A fifth prisoner was discharged when he developed a psychosomatic rash over his entire body. Even Zimbardo became myopically trapped in his role as warden. He began worrying more about malingering prisoners and the prevention of prison breaks, than about the wave of insanity his experiment had set in motion. It was finally his graduate student, Christina Maslach, who was dating Zimbardo during the Stanford Prison Experiment, who made him realize how far out of hand things had gotten. The study was aborted after just six days and nights, instead of the planned two weeks.

An analysis of the results of the two experiments

The common theme in both experiments is how seemingly normal and good people are made to do evil deeds. Zimbardo calls it The Lucifer Effect, in analogy to the mythological transformation of God's favorite angel Lucifer, the bearer of light, into evil Satan. The social philosopher Hannah Arendt was, perhaps, the first to realize and write about the ease with which normal people commit horrific and cruel acts. She realized during Eichmann's trial in Jerusalem (in 1961) that Eichmann, and many like him, were not brutal, twisted, and sadistic personalities, evil incarnate—but normal, ordinary bureaucrats that felt they were simply doing their job. She found that conclusion terrifying, and advanced the concept of "the banality of evil." Arendt was attacked for trivializing the Holocaust and other genocides, but the results of the two experiments confirm that Arendt came closer to the truth than one dared to imagine.

The details and scope of the two experiments differ sufficiently, and I shall, therefore, address their results and analyses separately.

Milgram's Obedience to Authority Experiment

Obedience to authority is a basic element in the structure of social life, and was long praised as a virtue. However, it takes on a new aspect when it serves a malevolent cause; it is transformed from a virtue into a heinous sin. The moral question of whether one should obey commands that conflict with one's conscience is an age-old dilemma that was already addressed by Plato over 2,000 years ago. Actually, the dilemma of obedience to authority is even more ancient; it goes back to the story of Abraham, who was commanded by God to sacrifice his son Isaac.

Most people would argue for the primacy of individual conscience, insisting that the moral judgment of the individual must override authority when the two are in conflict. But these are abstract discourses and conclusions. What an empirically-grounded scientist really wants to know is not what a person thinks or says, but what he actually does in a concrete situation. This is what Milgram set out to determine in the experiments described earlier.

The chief finding of Milgram's study is the willingness of people to go to any length, on the command of an authority, to perform evil acts of the worst kind—shocking the victim even if he is perceived to be already unconscious. Wouldn't you think that every sensible, normal person would, at that point, quit, drop out, refuse the researcher's demands to go on shocking? Well, the sad fact is that you would be wrong. But so were the "experts" in the field. When Milgram described his experiments to a group of 40 psychiatrists, and then asked them to predict the percentage of people who would go all the way to the end, their consensus was **less than 1%**, in stark contrast to the observed 65%. Where did they go wrong?

Milgram explains the disparity between what the psychiatrists expected and what actually occurred as follows: The predictions were made by focusing on the character of the **autonomous** individual, yet what actually occurred was driven by the **situation** in which the individual found himself. He postulates that the victim, under the influence of the situation, is transformed from an "autonomous" state to an "obedient" state (Milgram calls it an "agentic state"). In this obedient state, the person is transformed into somebody else, different from his former self, with traits not commensurate with his usual, autonomous personality. It is the failure to grasp this transformation, which involves a fundamental reorganization of the person's mental state that caused the inability of the "experts" to predict the outcome of the experiment.

Milgram's results (i.e., 65% obedience in his basic experiment) show that people are tailored neither for complete obedience, nor for complete autonomy. A person can function in either mode, and, depending on the circumstances, will favor one or the other.

Milgram investigated the effect of different conditions on the level of obedience (or, as a physicist would say, the effect on the transition probability from the autonomous state to the obedient state). The results are summarized on page 233. They show the effect of eliminating the direct involvement of the teacher in administering the shocks, the importance of the spatial arrangement of the participants and of the perceived level of authority, the influence of peer support and of the cultural background of the participants.

An additional effect is the repetitiveness of the teacher's action. Were he to break off, he would be acknowledging that what he had done so far was bad. And so he continues on.

Furthermore, there is the gradual increase (in small increments) of the level of punishment. The teacher, no doubt, feels that a small increase in the shock level would not do significant, additional harm (a physicist would call it an adiabatic approach). As we shall discuss later, this played an important role in the escalation of the Holocaust.

In the diagram below, I represent schematically how various external conditions (situational forces) favor either the obedient or the autonomous state of an individual. Conditions that favor the obedient state are indicated by arrows pointing to the right, and those that favor the autonomous state are indicated by arrows pointing to the left.

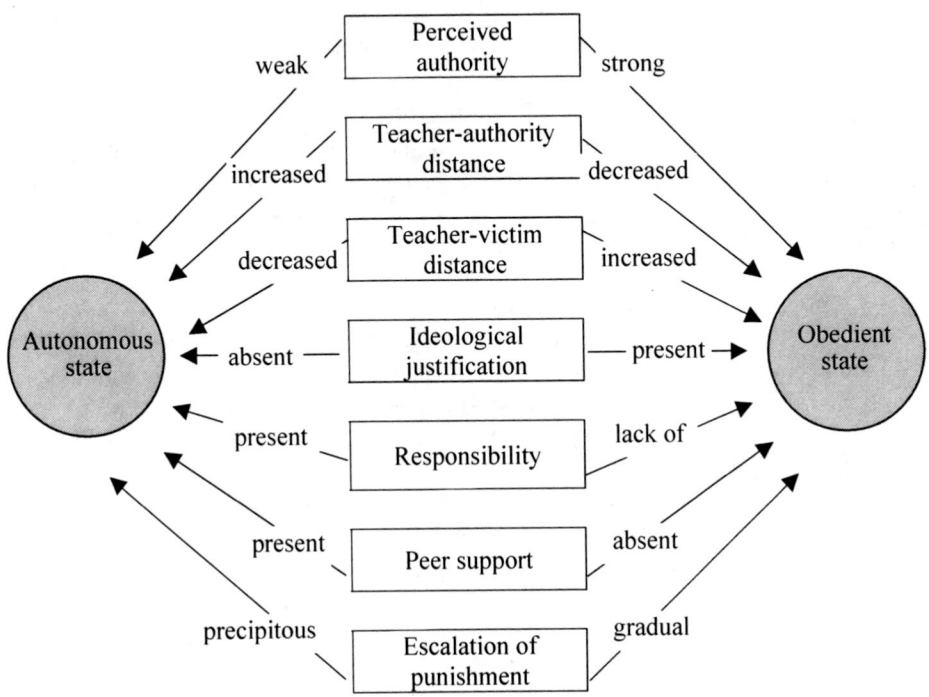

Schematic representation of the effect of external conditions
on the state of an individual.

Before concluding this section we need to address (and refute) an alternate explanation of Milgram's results that postulates aggression, rather than obedience, as the primary driving force. Destructive (aggressive) forces are present in all individuals, but their release, under normal circumstances, is inhibited by conscience. Milgram's experimental setup creates an opportunity to release aggressive tendencies, and for the teacher to harm another person under socially acceptable circumstances. Furthermore, it allows the teacher to do harm under the guise of advancing a socially valued cause (i.e., the advancement of science).

The fact that this explanation is not valid is proven by experiment 5 on page 233 in which the teacher was free to choose any shock level he wished. Practically all teachers administered the lowest shock level. But if destructive, aggressive impulses were really pressing for release, the teachers would have used the higher levels. They did not do that, thereby proving that aggression was not the primary driving force.

In summary, we conclude that in appropriate situations, an individual becomes obedient through a restructuring of internal mental processes that result in an obedient state. The evolutionary pressures that led to the emergence of obedience are discussed in a later section.

Zimbardo's Stanford Prison Experiment

Milgram focused on one aspect of human behavior: obedience. Zimbardo, a decade later, designed a more complex experiment in which several other aspects of human behavior played a role. The one thing that both experiments had in common was the result that people have the capacity to inflict great harm and suffering upon others. In Zimbardo's mock-up prison experiment, the guards underwent, within a few days, a transformation to sadistic torturers, and the prisoners to broken-down victims.

Zimbardo explained the results of his experiment by postulating that individual behavior is largely driven by **situational** forces, which override the beliefs and moral fabric of the individual (the so-called **dispositional** forces). The power of situations to transform thinking, feeling, and action, when one is caught in its grip, is terrifying and awesome. Zimbardo, furthermore, implicates **systems**, the engines that run situations. Systems provide the institutional support, authority, and resources to create situations and allow them to operate. We can then schematically represent the flow of action as:

System Power → Situational Forces → Individual Behavior

System power involves institutionalized permission to behave in prescribed ways, and thereby validates a person's behavior. Such validation usually comes cloaked in the mantle of ideology, which legitimizes whatever measures are necessary to achieve an ultimate goal. Abstract ideology, even if nonsensical and invented, makes people surrender their humanity and compassion. Such was the case in the Third Reich, with its ideology about the superiority of the Aryan race, whose purity needed to be guarded at all costs, and by all means; or about the satanic design of Jews to dominate the world.

What are some of the factors that contribute to the situational forces that make ordinary people engage in evil deeds that are alien to their moral values? Foremost is the obedience to authority that was discussed in connection with Milgram's experiments. In addition, in Zimbardo's experiment, conformity and compliance with the group mentality of the guards made hesitant, potentially recalcitrant members, join the action. The devaluation and dehumanization of the prisoners played an additional and important role in facilitating the perpetration of evil.

It may be instructive to compare the evil perpetrated in the make-believe prison at Stanford with the evil perpetrated in a real prison at Abu Ghraib, Iraq, which occurred about 30 years after the Stanford experiment. There are, of course, significant differences between them. The environment at Abu Ghraib was far more lethal than in the benign prison at Stanford. Furthermore, whereas in the Stanford experiments, guards and prisoners were chosen by the flip of a coin (i.e., they started out as equals), at Abu Ghraib, the status and inequality of guards and prisoners were predetermined. Nevertheless, there are some similarities in the basic situational and systemic forces operating in both cases. Dehumanization of the prisoners at Abu Ghraib was accomplished by stripping them naked. As one guard recounted in a TV interview: "We were told: 'Break them before the interrogation; use your imagination; they are nothing but dogs.'" No wonder that before long, the guards looked at the prisoners as less than human. Boredom operated in both prison settings. It was a potent motivator to take actions that would generate excitement and fun. Most atrocities were performed by night-shift guards, who, in the absence of supervision, felt the safety of anonymity, and therefore, absence of responsibility—which, as we have seen in Milgram's experiments, engenders aggression.

But the biggest failure was that of the system. In the Stanford mock prison, Zimbardo's research team failed to provide top-down constraints to prevent prisoner abuse. Similarly, at Abu Ghraib there was no proper oversight, and no clear guidelines were given to the guards and interrogators to enforce the safeguards of the Geneva Convention.

President George W. Bush ordered an investigation to get to the **bottom** of the Abu Ghraib incident. He should have ordered instead to get to the **top**. Consequently, the root causes of the atrocities committed at Abu Ghraib were not properly analyzed. It was concluded that there were just a few bad apples in a barrel of good ones, when, in actuality, the barrel was bad, as were the barrel-makers (the system). But the judiciary is part of the system, and it is not set up to investigate itself; it is set up to prosecute individuals. And it was less embarrassing for the administration to scapegoat a few individuals at the bottom of the hierarchy, rather than to implicate the command structure and the system.

Conclusions

The conclusions of Milgram and Zimbardo are very similar, although presented somewhat differently, using different nomenclatures. To recapitulate their main point: The evil actions are determined by the situation that the perpetrators find themselves in, rather than their intrinsic character traits, their autonomous selves. Or, as Zimbardo puts it succinctly: situational forces override dispositional forces.

Zimbardo's conclusions go one step further than Milgram's: he points out that it is the prevailing system that drives the situational forces. Thus, in Milgram's experiments it is the scientific infrastructure that endows the researcher with authority, and in the Stanford experiment it is the prison administration (in which Zimbardo played a major part).

Finally, it is noteworthy that neither in Milgram's nor in Zimbardo's experiments did the authority figures use threats or coercion to force the subjects to perform despicable acts. Thus, fear of punishment for defiance did not play a role in the decisions of the participants.

The relevance of the Milgram/Zimbardo experiments to the Holocaust

The main finding of the Milgram and Zimbardo experiments was that ordinary, "normal" people are capable, under appropriate circumstances, of committing violent and evil acts against their fellow human beings. It supports the notion that, during the Holocaust, the German people at large, were not ignorant of the atrocities committed, but compliantly looked on, or participated in them. To what extent were the situations simulated in the Milgram/Zimbardo experiments related to the ones prevailing in the Third Reich during the Holocaust?

Foremost is the **awe of authority**, which engenders obedience and the blind following of orders. Milgram showed that when the authoritarian figure of the researcher in the white coat was replaced by an ordinary person, or when the experiment was moved from prestigious Yale University to Bridgeport (an institution of lesser renown), the level of obedience dropped significantly. In Germany, the authority of the Führer and his henchmen was undisputed. Furthermore, the awe of authority was an ingrained trait of the German people, fostered at home by the authoritarian father, in school by the teachers, and at work by the boss. It is noteworthy that when Milgram's experiment was repeated in Germany, the level of disobedience was less than half of that observed in the US experiments.[105]

The **abdication and diffusion of authority** plays a major role in enabling the perpetrators to commit evil acts. In Milgram's experiments, the researcher (the authority) assured the teacher (the perpetrator) that he takes full responsibility for the teacher's actions. When, in addition, two more assistant teachers participated, who actually administered the shocks following the main teacher's order, the level of obedience increased significantly—the responsibility had been diffused. In Germany, the diffusion of authority was highly developed: Eichmann sat comfortably at a desk, shuffling papers and giving orders for deportations and exterminations of the Jews. (Hitler never issued explicitly-written orders for the "Final Solution," but made his intentions clear to Himmler, Eichmann's superior). The group of SS men putting people on a train, the engineer driving the locomotive transferring people from one location to another, and the SS man dropping pellets of Zyklon B into the gas chambers, were all merely following orders. The individual members of the chain leading to extermination probably guessed the fate of the victims. But the fact that they didn't have to know, and probably didn't want to know, helped suppress their moral judgment and eased their conscience in following orders. The individual members of the chain leading to extermination probably guessed the fate of the victims. But the fact that they didn't have to know and probably didn't want to know helped to suppress their moral judgment, and eased their conscience in following orders.

The **gradual escalation of violence** contributed to the level of obedience in Milgram's experiments. The electric shocks were increased in small steps of 15 volts. At each step, the teacher thought that the small increment would not add significantly to the punishment. The corresponding situation in Germany was the incremental deprivations and the cultural and material destruction that the Jews were subjected to. It started in 1933 with losing their jobs, followed by losing their citizenship and rights, their property, and finally, their identity as human beings. The "Final Solution" was then perceived as the elimination of non-humans.

This attitude was in line with the **ideological justifications**. The German propaganda machine portrayed the Jews as enemies of the state, as inferior people, equating them to parasites and vermin that need to be eliminated lest they contaminate the purity of the superior German (Aryan) race. In Milgram's experiment, the ideological justification was the importance of performing research that would enlarge our knowledge about learning and memory.

In Zimbardo's experiments another social dimension was added: the **dehumanization of the prisoners**. The inmates were addressed only by their numbers, as in the German concentration camps. The guards quickly started to behave sadistically, demeaning and degrading the prisoners. Zimbardo blamed the institutions (the systems) that permit behavior that leads to evil acts. In Zimbardo's experiment it was the prison administration; in Milgram's experiment it was the scientific infrastructure that endows the researcher with authority; and in Germany it was the authoritarian regime with its propaganda machine, ideology, and technical means to commit crimes against humanity.

Are we hardwired for doing evil?

In the previous sections I discussed the capacity of people to abandon their humanity and to commit cruel and evil acts. I also identified the traits (obedience, conformity, aggression) that provide the driving force for these actions. But how did we acquire these traits? Are we hardwired for doing evil?

To answer this question we need to explore whether the traits that lead to evil actions had evolutionary advantages that led them to be incorporated into our DNA by natural selection.

Obedience and conformity are cousins: both of them lead to compliance. They arise from the abdication of our individual initiative to external forces: in the case of obedience, to an authority; and in the case of conformity, to our peers.

Obedience to authority is an outcome of a hierarchical social organization in which the status of each member is clearly defined. It gives stability and harmony to the relations among group members, and ensures an orderly social life in which individuals comply with established rules (laws). Obedience is, therefore, of benefit to the survival of an individual in a community, and thus became a behavior trait selected through evolution.

In addition to being genetically programmed for obedience, human beings are trained throughout their lives to respect authority: parental authority at home, teacher authority in schools and, at the job, the authority of the supervisor. The result is that human beings internalize the hierarchical social structure with its axiom: "Do what the person in charge says." Furthermore, it is an ingenuous system whereby an individual is rewarded for dutiful compliance. This not only carries with it emotional gratification: It ensures the continuity of the hierarchical structure. Thus, the answer to the question "Is it Nature or Nurture?" is that it is both: we are hardwired for obedience, as well as conditioned for it by our environment.

Conformity arises from the fundamental human need to belong: to associate with and be accepted by others. This trait is central to community building and family bonding. Like obedience, it also has an evolutionary advantage and was, therefore, incorporated in our genome.

A series of simple and convincing experiments on conformists was carried out by S.E. Asch in 1941. A group of six subjects was shown a line of a certain length and asked to pick which of three other lines matched it. All but one of the subjects in the group were accomplices who had been secretly instructed beforehand to select one of the obviously "wrong" lines. The naïve subject was placed so that he heard the answers of the other members of the group before he had to announce his own decision. Asch found that under this form of social pressure, the majority of the naïve subjects went along with the group rather than accept the unmistakable evidence of their own eyes.

It is noteworthy that not *all* subjects were conforming in Asch's experiment (as not all teachers in Milgram's experiment were obedient). This seemingly minor detail has important implications in allowing our species to evolve. If conformity were absolute, we would be a static, stagnant society. Individuals have to be left with enough initiative and self-sufficiency to enable them to utilize their innovative potential and flexible response to changing situations. In some individuals this trait is more pronounced, and leads to the small, but important, fraction of non-conformists (and non-obedients). It is from this minority pool that innovators, heroes, and the Righteous Among the Nations are drawn.

That we are programmed for obedience and conformity has clearly been demonstrated in Milgram's and Zimbardo's experiments. But why do these traits have to lead to evil and not to good deeds? Couldn't we just as likely be do-gooders and heroes, rather than criminals-in-waiting? I believe we are not hardwired for evil or goodness, but for plasticity and flexibility to act according to environmental circumstances (i.e., situational forces), which can make us either saints or sinners. The analogy to stem cells comes to mind; they can turn into any kind of specialized cells, depending on the environment they are in. Similarly, we are born with the capacity for good and evil, either of which can be activated by situational forces.

So why does evil predominate? Why are we talking about the banality of evil and not the banality of goodness? Why are we quoting statistics on murders and crimes, and not on heroes and good deeds? I believe the answer lies in the inherent asymmetry of the situation.

This asymmetry has two origins. One is the fact that the potential havoc and devastation that evil can cause has lasting and irreversible effects (e.g., death), in contrast to good deeds, which are more ephemeral and transient. When evil is pitted against goodness, who wins? What chance do hundreds of "good" people have, when pitted against an evil man with a machine gun? The mother Theresas, Gandhis, and Dalai Lamas, don't have a chance against the Hitlers, Stalins, and Pol Pots. What I am saying is that evil has far greater consequences than goodness.

The other source of asymmetry arises from aggressiveness, which is a universal feature of human behavior. This means that, although I have argued that we are hardwired for plasticity, i.e., for doing evil or good, our aggressive nature tilts the actions towards evil. Thus, aggressiveness is an important trait, independent of obedience and conformity. I would like, therefore, to digress, and discuss the evolutionary origins of aggression.

Aggression, according to some people, is an inborn, instinctive (i.e., hardwired) trait (the most prominent advocates of this view were Sigmund Freud[106] and Konrad Lorenz); others believed that aggressive behavior must be learned. However, in recent years, most evolutionary psychologists came to the conclusion that aggression is genetically programmed into humans because it endows them with evolutionary advantages, as discussed below.

Competition between males for potential mates clearly benefits individuals that can intimidate or defeat a competitor through aggressive behavior. The female chooses the strongest, most aggressive male, who can provide the greatest protection for their offspring, thereby propagating the "aggressive gene." This male/male competition for a mate is expected to result in males being more aggressive than females. Indeed, this is borne out by statistics in the United States, where homicides perpetrated by men are 10 times more prevalent than those perpetrated by women. Aggression may also be used to gain territory and access to food supplies, thereby offering improved nutrition for the aggressors and their offspring. Thus, aggressive behavior is a universal strategy for securing reproductive rights or nutritional resources.

In addition, aggression is used by animals (and by our ancestors) to establish a ranking order, i.e., a hierarchical structure in which everybody knows his place. The weaker retreat from the stronger, which limits fighting between the members of the society. A hierarchical structure is a prerequisite for obedience to authority, and establishes a link between aggression and obedience.

In conclusion, obedience, conformity, and aggression are hardwired and reinforced by our social system. These traits have the capacity to make a person abandon his humanity and commit horrendous crimes, or foster his goodness and enable virtues like loyalty and discipline. Unfortunately, evil acts, by their nature, trump goodness, and evil perpetrators, even if in the minority, easily dominate the scene and threaten our survival. How these evil instincts might be curbed is discussed in a later section. (See page 245.)

Can the Holocaust happen again—in the United States?

This question is often asked, but a definitive answer has been difficult to arrive at with certainty. The history of America is replete with violence, human rights abuses, and discrimination: e.g., the massacres of indigenous peoples, slavery, discrimination against Blacks and other minorities, the internment of Americans of Japanese descent in World War II, the McCarthy witch hunt in the 1950s, and the brutalities committed in Vietnam. Although none of these atrocities came close, in scope and magnitude, to the Holocaust perpetrated by the Nazis, they show, as was pointed out in previous chapters, that Americans, Germans, or other groups, do not differ from each other in their genetically predisposed potential to do horrendous harm and evil.

---

[106] An interesting exchange took place between Einstein and Freud in 1932. The League of Nations invited Einstein to arrange an exchange of views with any eminent person of his choice, on an important issue of the day. Einstein took the assignment and chose to explore ways of delivering mankind from the menace of war. How is it, Einstein asked Freud, that propaganda devices succeed so well in rousing men to war? Might it not be that people have within them a "lust for hatred and destruction"? Yes, replied Freud, people are indeed driven to hate and kill. An "active instinct for hatred and destruction" resides in the depth of the human personality.

   To find differences between the behaviors of two people, we need to focus, therefore, on the prevailing situational forces that determine their actions. The elements that shape these forces include the type of government, the system in Zimbardo's works (e.g., autocratic or democratic), the cultural background (e.g., awe of authority, obedience or individualism), the educational system, child rearing practices, deep-seated traditional beliefs, the economic situation, and the state of war or peace. I shall examine some of these as they were during the peak of the Holocaust in Germany (1939–1945).

   Germany had an autocratic regime with a hierarchical structure, led by a man, Hitler, obsessed with a fanatical hatred of Jews, and convinced of the superiority of the German (Aryan) race. Dissent was not tolerated, individuality was suppressed, and absolute obedience to the Nazi Party was demanded. The population was cleverly manipulated, with promises of restoring past glory and prosperity, and seduced to blindly follow the Führer. The authoritarian regime was more in accord with traditional German attitudes than the democracy of the Weimar Republic; the Republic seemed to many Germans alien and weak (see page 6), and violated every authoritarian precept that had been beaten into them in childhood for centuries.

   Although there are many elements that contributed to the Holocaust, blind obedience to authority, which causes the perpetrator of evil to abandon his moral values, is the most important one. I have discussed this topic at length in connection with Milgram's and Zimbardo's experiments (see pages 231–240). Here I want to focus on the history and causes that made obedience an important part of the structure of German society.

   German deference toward authority has ancient roots. It was a medieval pope who called Germany the "terra obediencae." The Württemberg publisher Karl F. Moser wrote in 1758: "Every nation has its principal motives. In Germany, it is obedience; in England, freedom; in Holland, trade; in France, the honor of the King." How did this concept of obedience persist and propagate in German culture for centuries?: through childrearing practices and the educational system.

   The history of childrearing in Germany is a nightmare.[107] [108] deMause vividly describes the mind-boggling childrearing practices at the turn of the 20th century, before World War I. He goes as far as claiming that the practices are the causes of World War I, World War II, and the Holocaust. It led to raising children who were time bombs set to go off in the two world wars and the Holocaust.

   Abuse and neglect started early in life. Breastfeeding of infants was so infrequent that infant mortality in Bavaria at the end of the 19th century was an astonishing 58%, several times higher than in England and France. Upon birth, the practice in Germany was to wrap the newborn in bandages from feet to the neck. The bandages were rarely changed and the infant was left in its own feces and urine. As a result the infants were covered with lice and vermin and smelled so badly that the mothers often put the swaddled infants in a bag and hung them on a tree or put them in an abandoned room. They were never cuddled.

   Obedience formed the cornerstone of the German childhood education. The free will of the infants and children had to be broken, and beating them into obedience was the universal German practice of accomplishing it. For example, Hitler's father frequently

---

[107] Lloyd deMause, "The History of Childhood," New York Psychological Press, 1974.

[108] Aurel Ende, "Battering and Neglect: Children in Germany 1860–1978," *The Journal of Psychohistory* 7, 1979.

battered him into unconsciousness. When the children reached school age, no relief was forthcoming. Schools were veritable beating factories, with other punishment methods supplementing the beating. The resulting fear and trauma of being beaten and abused resulted in childhood suicides. The number of these suicides in Germany was over three times higher than in other European countries.

This, then, was the treatment of children in Germany in the generations responsible for the two great wars and the Holocaust. The trauma of their early childhood experiences was indelibly imprinted on their psyche; the swaddling and beatings must have contributed to their feeling, in adult life, that they were being strangled and encircled by enemies. Much research has been done on this topic in the past decades. The results uniformly show that abusive childhoods are strongly correlated with later preference for military solutions and state violence in resolving social conflicts.[109]

The situation in Germany has slowly but steadily improved over the past 70 years. In 1964, 80% of Germans still admitted to beating their children. Now there are laws that prohibit hitting a child. When, in 1970, Mantell repeated Milgram's obedience experiments in Germany, he found that less than half as many people disobeyed orders than in Milgram's experiments performed in the United States (see page 233). It would be interesting to repeat these experiments in today's Germany to see whether further progress has been made. Contemporary studies, that compare German with US childrearing practices, show that German parents are more controlling, and punish their children more severely than US parents. The emphasis in German homes is still, to a large extent, on obedience; whereas in the United States, independence is encouraged.

In autocratic regimes, such as prevailed in Germany under Hilter, acts that violate the normal moral values of its citizens are more easily committed than in a democratic society, like it exists in the United States, in which dissent and freedom of expression prevails and is guaranteed by the Constitution. Furthermore, societies that promote individuality, like in the United States, are less likely to fall victim to blind obedience.

From the facts and the discussion presented in this chapter, I conclude that the situation in the United States, compared to that in Nazi Germany, makes it highly unlikely that a repetition of the Holocaust can occur here. Unfortunately, however, it cannot be excluded with 100% certainty. In the next section I suggest some guidelines to minimize the probability that acts of violence and genocides are committed.

---

[109] M.A. Milburn and S.D. Conrad, "The Politics of Denial," MIT Press, 1996.

Preventing genocide: guidelines to avoid evil

In 2008, a **Genocide Prevention Task Force,** headed by former Secretary of State Madeleine Albright and past Secretary of Defense William Cohen, was convened. Being seasoned politicians they both knew that moral arguments, by themselves, would not result in meaningful actions. Consequently, they stressed in their report the strategic interest of the United States and the world to prevent and curb genocide.[110] The report points out that genocides fuel instability, usually in weak, undemocratic, and corrupt states, where terrorists can flourish. Furthermore, genocides have long-lasting consequences that go far beyond the states in which they occur. Refugees flow into bordering countries and then across the globe. The need for aid may quickly exceed available resources, and cause a humanitarian crisis. And finally, America's standing in the world is eroded when we are perceived as passive bystanders to genocide.

The committee recommended that the president and his government make the prevention of genocide a national priority. Funds, in the amount of 250 million dollars a year, should be allocated to the prevention of genocide. The National Intelligence Agency should monitor every trouble spot for signs of atrocities that may lead to genocide. Emphasis should be placed on prevention, but when all peaceful means fail, America should send in the Marines as the last resort. Unfortunately, so far no legislation has been passed to effectively implement the recommendations. In December 2010, Senators Feingold and Collins sponsored a resolution in the Senate, based on the Albright/Cohen report, which laid out the framework to prevent genocide and atrocities. The resolution was passed, but again did not lead to a congressional bill.

Logically, it is the United Nations that should be in the forefront of dealing with the prevention of genocide. But as we saw on numerous occasions described earlier, the United Nations proved to be utterly ineffective in this task. The latest example of the failure of the United States and the international community to deal with the prevention of genocide is the slaughter in Syria, which, since 2011, reached the staggering number of 500,000 deaths, most of them civilians. As predicted by the Albright/Cohen report, the Syrian genocide has started to destabilize the neighboring countries (Lebanon, Jordan, Iraq, and Turkey) and has caused a humanitarian crisis among millions of refugees.

While the United Nations and other governments and organizations are debating the issue of the prevention of genocide, I would like to suggest some steps to be undertaken on a societal (state) level to prevent genocides (the first four in the list below), and suggest guidelines for the individual on how to strengthen his/her resolve not to be seduced into performing evil acts.[111]

Assist and support democratic systems

As I have mentioned earlier, none of the genocides discussed have occurred in functioning democracies. It is, therefore, important to encourage and assist states to promote democratic regimes. This is a difficult task that has to be undertaken with great sensitivity and delicacy. No state wants to be told by outsiders how to govern itself. Certainly not by force, as was tried by President Bush in his nation-building attempt in

---

[110] Madeleine Albright and William Cohen, Co-Chairs Genocide Prevention Taskforce, "Preventing Genocide: A Blueprint for US Policymakers," The US Holocaust Memorial Museum, 2008.

[111] Some of these are discussed in Zimbardo's book "The Lucifer Effect."

Iraq, which was a complete failure. What is needed is to provide economic and technical know-how to build up the infrastructure of the country, e.g., the business sector, the educational and judicial system, and other civic institutions. The financial aid should be tied, in a subtle way, to the promotion of human rights, gender equality, freedom of expression, and the other basic values of democracies. The 2011 Arab Spring uprising offered an opportunity to carry out these policies. Unfortunately, they have not been implemented.

Support criminal prosecution of acts of genocide

This establishes a psychological barrier that may inhibit potential perpetrators from committing crimes against humanity. The International Criminal Court in The Hague (ICC) has a mandate to do just that. Unfortunately, the ICC does not have the power to apprehend the indicted perpetrators in their own country. The international community should exert pressure (by sanctions and other means) on the nations, to deliver indicted criminals to the ICC. This is not being done. For example, the indicted Sudanese president Omar al-Bashir is continuing, with impunity, to pursue his genocidal policies in Darfur. (See pages 212–226)

Create and support the appropriate educational system

Education is of utmost importance, not only for imparting knowledge, but also for forming the right attitudes. On a personal level, you can contribute to this process through your participation in PTA meetings, lobbying your congressperson, and through personal discussions with teachers. On an institutional level, the selection of textbooks, curricula, and qualified teachers should be a process open to the scrutiny of the public. Concerning the topic of genocides, the teachers should not shy away from freely discussing the evils that have been, and are being, perpetrated throughout the world, as well as their causes. It is through knowledge of how situational forces operate that we can resist, oppose, and prevent them from leading us into undesired actions. Emphasis should be placed on introducing the students to other cultures, religions, and ethnicities. This will reduce the gap between "us" and "them" that has caused so much evil, suffering, and death in the past. What I am really suggesting is that the topic "Prevention of Genocide" should form part of the curriculum.

Institute laws that prohibit incitement to racial, ethnic, or religious hatred

This includes the banning of racist organizations that advocate violence. It will be a challenge to draft a bill that accomplishes this without violating the 1st Amendment of the US Constitution.

Don't be a passive bystander; oppose unjust systems

Dante's aphorism, "The darkest places in hell are reserved for those who maintain neutrality in times of moral crisis," is as true today as it was seven centuries ago. Since then, it has been rephrased in many different ways. The essence of it is that, in the hierarchy of evils, the evil of inaction is as condemnable as evil actions themselves. It takes, of course, a lot of courage and resolve to go against the flow and to stick to one's moral values in the face of undesirable influences, persuasion, and threats. But there is no question that it is the morally right thing to do.

Solicit others to join your cause. You can make a difference. Two examples of resistance that even the mighty Third Reich yielded to were the opposition to the euthanasia program, and the demonstrations in Berlin against the incarceration of Jews married to Christians (see page 38). The fact that no resistance or demonstrations against the Holocaust took place in Germany, favors the basis of Goldhagen's theme of "Hitler's willing executioners" (see page 30).

Respect just authority, but rebel against an unjust one

Try to critically distinguish between those who, because of their expertise, wisdom, and seniority, deserve respect, and those false prophets, confidence men, and promoters, who should not be respected. Disobey the latter and publicly expose their phoniness: Doing so will eliminate blind obedience—the potential enabler of evil acts.

Keep your identity at all costs

Do not allow others to de-individuate or dehumanize you by turning you into an object, or worse. As the Nazis showed, the gradual dehumanization of their victims made it possible for them to kill 6 million Jews without encountering significant resistance.

Take responsibility for your actions

We become more resistant to undesirable social influences by maintaining a sense of personal responsibility, and by being willing to be held accountable for our actions. By abrogating your responsibility you can easily be led along a path that violates your moral values. Remember that in future trials nobody will accept our pleas: "I only obeyed orders," or "Everybody else was doing it."

Do not sacrifice personal freedom for the illusion of security

The need for security is a powerful determinant of human behavior. We can be manipulated into actions that violate our values when faced with alleged threats to our security. It is the standard play that fascist leaders utilize in perverting society.

Group acceptance is OK, but value your independence

The desire for acceptance into a social group is powerful and will make some people do anything to avoid rejection. However, there are times when conformity to a group norm clashes with your own value system. When pressure to be a "team player," and to sacrifice your personal morality becomes irresistible, step back and leave the group. Try to find another group that will support your values.

Think before acting

Too often we function on automatic pilot, using outdated scripts that have worked for us in the past, not stopping to evaluate whether they are appropriate for the present, new situation. Think before acting and don't enter mindlessly into new situations. Demand evidence to support assertions, separate rhetoric from substance, and try to determine whether the recommended means ever justify the potentially harmful ends.

Be aware of the past and future

Do not abandon your past value system for the expediency of the present moment. Think of the future when you look back, and ask yourself whether you have done the right thing in the face of external pressures.

Guard against slogans, sound bites, and euphemisms

Words are powerful. They can influence us without our being conscious that they shape our orientation toward the ideas they promote. Euphemisms try to hide the true nature of actions. For example, in Germany, nobody talked about extermination; they called it the "Final Solution" (*Endlösung*). Extermination Squads were called "Special Troops" (*Einsatzgruppen*), and the deportations were advertised as "Resettlement" (*Umsiedlung*).

Remember: It is never too late to admit a mistake

To err is human and you don't have to be superhuman to admit it. Don't continue to support bad or immoral actions once you have realized their folly. Not "staying the course" when it is wrong has an immediate cost, but always results in long-term gain. To continue an erroneous path "to save face" can have disastrous effects. Consider how many years the war in Vietnam continued, long after the top officials, like Secretary of Defense Robert McNamara, knew that the war was wrong. Tens of thousands of lives were lost because of his unwillingness to admit his error.

EPILOGUE

I conclude with regret that I have not achieved my goal of truly understanding and thereby exorcising the trauma of the Holocaust. I've succeeded only in asserting that all genocides have at their core the predisposition of man to commit evil acts; that the capacity of a person to abandon his humanity is a fatal flaw that nature has designed into us; and that, ironically, the virtues of loyalty, obedience, conformity, and discipline, that we value so highly in creating an orderly, functioning society, are the very traits which, when not kept in check, create the engines that bind us to malevolent systems of authority.

It is very disappointing to me to conclude 200-plus pages by essentially saying: "I don't understand." Is the Holocaust un-understandable? Or is it a matter of what we mean by "understanding"? I would like to elaborate on this topic. Throughout the discussions on genocides I used psychological/sociological arguments, and concepts that are not part of my background, expertise, or way of thinking as a physicist. I doubt that they could ever lead, for me, to an understanding. I need to understand behavior on a more basic, molecular/physiological level. The traits I have been considering in my discussions, such as fear, greed, hate, the propensity to do evil, and the actions they elicit, need to be explored as neuronal connections within that "master black box" that is the brain. In other words, to truly understand human behavior we need to understand, in detail, how the brain works.

Understanding the brain is a formidable task. A lot of work has, of course, been done in this field, but it seems that we have only scratched the surface. It is heartening that President Obama recognized the importance of research in this area, and launched in April 2013 the Brain Initiative. This is a long-range program; experts estimate that it may take a century to unravel the complex circuitry and dynamics of the functioning brain.

So, will we ever understand the Holocaust on a molecular/physiological level? And if we do, will we be able to prevent another one from happening? Do we have the luxury to wait for a century or more, while the accelerating development and proliferation of weapons of mass destruction are threatening a nuclear holocaust on a global scale that would destroy our civilization, or even cause the demise of the human race? I am skeptical of our chances of survival. It is thus, with sadness and anxiety, that I view the future of our children and grandchildren.

I hope I am wrong in painting such a gloomy picture of the future.

GENERAL INDEX

253

PEOPLE INDEX

Connor, James Jr., 108
Conrad, S.D., 244 fn109
Cretzianu, Alexandre, 121
Cromwell, Dean, 100
Czerniakow, Adam, 25

Dallaire, Romeo, 206–208
Dayan, Shmuel and Moshe, 143
de Gaulle, Charles, 27
de Leon, Moses, 136
Daladier, Edouard, 47
deMause, Lloyd, 243 fn107
Dewey, Thomas, 131
Diraige, Ahmed Ibrahim, 214–216
Dobkin, Eliyahu, 152–154
Dodd, W. E., 96, 99
Dodds, Harold Willis, 116–117
Doenitz, Karl, 52
Dubček, 93
Duch, *see* Kaing Guek Eav
Ďurčanský, Ferdinand, 76, 80, 91

Eden, Anthony, 111, 155, 157, 161
Eichmann, Adolf, 31, 51, 69, 77, 81, 82, 83, 86, 87, 91,
   92, 160, 161, 173, 174, 234, 239
Einstein, Albert, 8, 13, 60, 61, 62, 242 fn106
Eisenhower, Dwight, 43, 44, 56, 172
Eisinger, Terry, 151 fn62
Elkes, Johanan, 24–25
Elon, Amos, 135 fn56
Emerson, Herbert, 161
Ende, Aurel, 243 fn108
Enver, Ismail, 186–187
Erdheim, Stuart G., 113 fn47
Erlander, Tage, 175–176

Fabry, Ula and Andrej, 86
Fathi Ahmed Ali, 216
Feher, Fehér, 17 fn13, 73
Feingold, 245
Feldhendler, Leon, 68
Fellgiebel, Erich, 49
Ferber, Edna, 106
Ferdinand and Isabella of Spain, 4
Fermi, Enrico, 60, 62
Feuchtwanger, Lion, 172
Fiala, Fritz, 82
Fisher, Eugen, 186
Flatow, Alfred and Gustav, 100
Fleischmann, Gisi, 70, 78, 80, 87, 89, 110
Foley, Frank 21
Ford, Henry, 3 fn3
Franco, Francisco, 16
Frank, Hans, 22, 31, 65

Frank, Karl, 171
Freud, Sigmund, 75, 242
Frick, Wilhelm, 98
Frieder, Armin, 80, 85
Friedländer, Saul, 1, 12, 21, 27, 229 fn101
Fritz, Gejza, 83
Fromm, 49, 50
Fry, Varian, 166, 171–172
Füredi, Robert K., 78
Furrer, Jonas, 97
Fürst, Viliam, 80

Gaddafi, Muammar, 214–215, 218
Galewski, Marceli, 41
Galic, Stanislav, 204
Garang, John, 217, 220
Gemeaha, Muhammad, 6
Gerö, Trude and Tomy, 88, 90
Gershen, Kurt, 32
Ghazni, Mahmud, 191
Ghengis Khan, 181
Gilbert, Martin, 12 fn9, 24
Gillette, Guy, 132
Gisevins, Bernd, 45
Givoni, Shmuel, 88
Glick, David, 20
Glickman, Marty, 100
Globočnik, Odilo, 31
Goebbels, Joseph, 10, 12, 14, 17, 30, 38, 44, 49–50, 53,
   105, 167, 171, 191
Goerdeler, Karl F., 45, 47
Goetz, Amos, 34
Goldberg, Herman, 100
Goldhagen, D.J., 30, 38, 228 fn100, 247
Goldmann, Nahum, 149
Golomb, Eliyahu, 149
Gordon, Aaron David, 143
Gordon, Charles, 213
Gordon, George, 96
Göring, Hermann, 10, 12, 52, 53, 54, 55, 66, 76, 95,
   167, 186
Gotovina, Ante, 202
Goudsmit, Samuel, 61
Gration, Scott, 224
Graves, Philip, 3 fn3
Green, Milton, 99
Green, William, 101, 130
Griese, Irma, 34
Gromyko, Andrei, 176
Groves, L.R., 63
Gruenbaum, Yitzhak, 151, 153–155, 157
Grynszpan, Zyndel and Hirsch, 17
Gunther, John, 106

264

265

ACRONYMS

AAU	Amateur Athletic Union
AJC	American Jewish Committee
AK	Armia Krajova (Home Army)
AL	Armia Ludowa (People's Army)
AMIS	African Union Mission in Sudan
AOC	American Olympic Committee
AU	African Union
BBC	British Broadcasting Corporation
BILU	Bet Ya'akov L'chu V'Nelcha
BKB	Bar Kochba Bratislava
CIA	Central Intelligence Agency
CPA	Comprehensive Peace Agreement
DDF	Darfur Development Front
DDPD	Doha Document for Peace in Darfur
DP	Dislaced Persons
DPA	Darfur Peace Agreement
DUP	Democratic Unionist Party
ERC	Emergency Rescue Committee
EU	European Union
FPO	United Partisan Organization
GNU	Government of National Unity
GoSS	Governmentof Southern Sudan
HSLS	Hlinka Slovak Nationalistic People's Party
ICC	International Criminal Court
ICTR	International Criminal Tribunal for Rwanda
ICTY	International Criminal Court for Yugoslavia
IDP	Internally Displaced Persons
IGC	Intergovernmental Committee on Refugees
IOC	International Olympic Committee
IZL	Irgun Zvai Leumi
JA	Jewish Agency
JCA	Jewish Colonization Agency
JDC	Joint Distribution Committee
JEM	Justice and Equality Movement
KbP	Carpathian-Ruthenian German Party
KGB	Komitet Gosudarstvennoy Bezopasnosti
KLA	Kosovo Liberation Army
LJM	Liberty and Justice Movement
MRF	Mobilillzation and Rescue Fund
NATO	North Atlantic Treaty Organization
NCP	National Congress Party
NGO	non-governmental organization
NIF	National Islamic Front
NKVD	Narodny Komissariat Vnutrennikh Del
NSDAP	Nazi Party (National Socialistic Workers Party)
OAU	Organization of African Unity
OSS	US Office of Strategic Services
POW	Prisoner of War
PPC	Popular Patriotic Congress
RAF	Royal Air Force
RPF	Rwandan Patriotic Front
SA	Sturmabteilung (Brownshirts)
SDP	Sudetendeutsche Partei
SS	Schutzstaffel
SLM/A	Sudan Liberation Movement/Army
SPLM/A	Sudan People's Liberation Movement/Army
SLS	Slovenska Ludova Strana (Slovak People's Party)
SRF	Sudanese Revolutionary Front
UN	United Nations (Elsa see pg 201, and more)
UNAMID	United Nations African Mission in Darfur
UNAMIR	United Nations Assistant Mission for Rwanda
UNRRA	United Nations Relief & Rehabilitation Administration
USSR	United of Soviet Socialist Republics
WJC	World Jewish Congress
WRB	War Refugee Board
WZO	World Zionist Organization
ZAC	Zionist Action Committee
ZO	Zionist Organization
ZUV	Jewish Central Office for the Land of Slovakia

CPSIA information can be obtained
at www.ICGtesting.com
Printed in the USA
FSOW01n0710301217
42534FS